Handbook of Short-Term Dynamic Psychotherapy

Handbook of
Short-Term Dynamic
Psychotherapy

PAUL CRITS-CHRISTOPH

AND

JACQUES P. BARBER

EDITORS

BasicBooks
A Division of HarperCollins*Publishers*

Library of Congress Cataloging-in-Publication Data

Handbook of short-term dynamic psychotherapy/ Paul Crits-
Christoph and Jacques P. Barber, editors.
    p. cm.
    Includes bibliographical references and index.
    ISBN 0–465–02875–6
    1. Brief psychotherapy. 2. Brief psychotherapy—Case
studies. I. Crits-Cristoph, Paul, 1954– II. Barber, Jaques
P., 1954– .
    [DNLM: 1. Psychotherapy, Brief. WM 420 H2365]
RC480.55.H35 1991
616.89'14—dc20&

DNLM/DLC   91–21997
for Library of Congress   CIP

To Kathy and
To Smadar, Natalie, and Adam

Contents

Contributors

Jacques P. Barber, Ph.D.,
Assistant Professor, Center for Psychotherapy Research, Department of Psychiatry, University of Pennsylvania

Howard S. Baker, M.D.,
Clinical Associate Professor, University of Pennsylvania; Attending Psychiatrist, Institute of Pennsylvania Hospital

Karin Barth, M.D.,
Director of Clinical Education, The University Psychiatric Hospital, Bergen, Norway

Lorna Smith Benjamin, Ph.D.,
Professor of Psychology, University of Utah

Jeffrey L. Binder, Ph.D.,
Psychologist, Adult Programs, Cumberland Hall Psychiatric Hospital, Nashville, Tennessee

Paul Crits-Christoph, Ph.D.,
Associate Professor, Director, Center for Psychotherapy Research, Department of Psychiatry, University of Pennsylvania

Walter Flegenheimer, M.D.,
Research Associate, Brief Psychotherapy Program, Beth Israel Medical Center, New York

Mardi J. Horowitz, M.D.,
Professor, Langley Porter Psychiatric Institute, University of California at San Francisco; Director, Program on Conscious and Unconscious Mental Processes, John D. and Catherine T. MacArthur Foundation

Julie S. Kurcias, B.A.,
> Research Assistant, Center for Psychotherapy Research, Department of Psychiatry, University of Pennsylvania

Michael Laikin, M.D.,
> Coordinator, Short-Term Dynamic Psychotherapy, Brief Psychotherapy Program, Department of Psychiatry, Beth Israel Medical Center, New York

Lester Luborsky, Ph.D.,
> Professor, Center for Psychotherapy Research, Department of Psychiatry, University of Pennsylvania

James Mann, M.D.,
> Professor, Training and Supervising Analyst, Boston University School of Medicine, Boston Psychoanalytic Institute

David Mark, Ph.D.,
> Instructor in Psychiatry, Department of Psychiatry, University of Pennsylvania

Leigh McCullough, Ph.D.,
> Assistant Professor, Center for Psychotherapy Research, Department of Psychiatry, University of Pennsylvania

Geir Nielsen, M.D.,
> Cand. Psychology, Chief Psychologist, Department of Clinical Psychology, University of Bergen, Norway

Henry Pinsker, M.D.,
> Associate Director, Department of Psychiatry; Coordinator, Supportive Psychotherapy Program, Beth Israel Medical Center, New York

Jerome Pollack, M.D.,
> Physician in Charge, Child Psychiatry Division; Coordinator for Brief Adaptive Psychotherapy Program, Beth Israel Medical Center, New York

Richard Rosenthal, M.D.,
> Physician in Charge, Psychiatric Substance Abuse Division, Beth Israel Medical Center, New York

Hans H. Strupp, Ph.D.,
> Professor, Department of Psychology, Vanderbilt University

Arnold Winston, M.D.,
> Director, Psychiatry Department; Director, Brief Psychotherapy Program, Beth Israel Medical Center, New York

CHAPTER 1

Introduction and Historical Background

Paul Crits-Christoph, Jacques P. Barber,
and Julie S. Kurcias

In recent years much has been written on the topic of brief psychotherapy (Budman & Gurman, 1988). Clinicians of varying orientations as well as therapy researchers have been shifting toward the brief therapy model as the standard, and long-term therapy is becoming the exception. Many observers (such as Koss & Butcher, 1986) note that brief psychotherapy can now be considered the treatment of choice for most patients seeking help.

A number of factors explain this trend toward briefer therapies (Garfield & Bergin, 1986; Koss & Butcher, 1986). These include (1) the development of crisis-oriented therapies arising out of the community mental health movement; (2) the advent of the cognitive and behavioral treatments, which were originally defined as brief treatments; (3) the focus on brief therapy in research studies because of the practical difficulties of studying long-term treatments; (4) the increasing awareness among clinicians that most patients desire a treatment of short duration; and (5) the pressures from insurance companies to lower costs.

Cost is more important than ever as HMOs and managed care approaches have come to dominate the health care environment. Many of the large HMOs have set a firm limit of twenty outpatient visits for mental health treatment, and, in fact, encourage therapists to treat patients in as few sessions as possible. It is not surprising that clinicians, especially those connected to such HMOs, are increasingly drawn to theoretical models

1

that specify a priori a time-limited brief therapy. The alternative for these therapists is to consider their cases to be interrupted long-term treatments, a rather unsatisfying view. Nevertheless, few training programs in clinical psychology or psychiatry teach short-term methods, therefore not preparing their trainees for the real world and increasing the gap between theoretical courses and actual treatment.

Although psychoanalysis per se has often been looked upon as the quintessential long-term, expensive treatment modality, psychodynamically oriented writers have been at the forefront of the movement toward short-term treatments. The purpose of this book is to summarize the short-term dynamic treatments that have evolved over the past few decades.

Several of the approaches represented are traditionally associated with the field of short-term dynamic therapy, including the approaches of James Mann, Peter Sifneos, Habib Davanloo, and David Malan. As psychotherapy researchers, we became aware of a number of other brief dynamic therapy approaches that were evolving out of a research context and were less well known to clinicians. In addition, we knew of clinicians who were interested in applying some of the newer clinical perspectives within the psychodynamic approach to a short-term format. Thus, we realized that a large number of separate brief dynamic therapy approaches existed. We hope not only to acquaint readers with this larger array of treatments but also to compare the approaches. Later in this chapter we will describe how we attempted to facilitate comparison by requesting the same information from each chapter's contributors.

One consequence of the expanding array of brief dynamic psychotherapies is confusion about which psychotherapies meet the definition of brief dynamic psychotherapy. In an attempt to sort out this confusion, we suggest the following criteria for describing a psychotherapy as short-term dynamic.

1. The theory about the origin of maladaptive behavior is psychoanalytically inspired. This includes the theories of psychotherapy schools such as Freudian, neo-Freudian, interpersonal, object relations, and self psychology. The scope of many of these approaches is broad, but, in our view, it is not necessary to incorporate all aspects of these elaborate theories for a treatment to be defined as brief dynamic. Instead, it is sufficient that some of the central concepts—such as the role of conflicts, developmental history, unconscious motivations, and repetitive interpersonal behavior—are used as the foundation for a brief treatment.

2. The techniques of treatment, for the most part, are psychoanalytically inspired. That is, the therapist makes use of clarifications and interpreta-

tions, pays attention to the transference and countertransference, and addresses other repetitive, often maladaptive, patterns of behavior, especially in the interpersonal domain. In general, no direct advice is given. Unlike formal psychoanalysis, brief dynamic psychotherapies use free association for specific issues and not as a general rule of treatment.

3. Treatment is time limited. Patients are seen at regular intervals for a limited number of sessions, but in general not less than once every week during the active phase of treatment. Depending on the goals of treatment and the patient's pathology, treatment is in most cases shorter than a year and may be as short as twelve sessions.

4. Patients are selected for treatment. That is, not every patient is considered appropriate for brief dynamic therapy.

5. A focus for treatment is developed. In most cases, patients and their therapists define one or more major problems around which treatment will focus. In order to maintain a focus, therapists tend to be more active. In contrast, psychoanalysts let their patients' thoughts wander and allow them to discuss various unconnected issues.

Although we are tempted to view all the aforementioned criteria as necessary and sufficient for defining a specific form of psychotherapy—brief dynamic psychotherapy—we anticipate that at times only four of the five criteria may fit. Therefore, we suggest that these five criteria fit a prototypic view of definition: the more a form of therapy meets the criteria, the more it is likely to be defined as brief dynamic psychotherapy. Furthermore, each criterion in turn is likely to follow a prototypic definition. That is, the degrees to which the techniques follow psychodynamic principles are disparate; thus, up to a certain point, the more the treatment techniques follow these principles, the more likely the treatment will be defined as brief dynamic psychotherapy.

THE FIRST GENERATION: FREUD AND THE ROOTS OF BRIEF DYNAMIC THERAPY

In the early years of psychoanalysis, Freud practiced what would now be considered brief psychotherapy. He successfully treated many patients in limited periods of time. The cases of Katharina (Breuer & Freud, 1895/1955) and Gustave Mahler (Jones, 1955) are examples of successful analyses performed by Freud in just a single session spanning several hours.

As Freud's career progressed, his psychodynamic theories became more numerous and intricate and his objectives for psychoanalysis became more ambitious. One very striking change in psychoanalysis was that treatment became progressively longer as the years went by. At the time "Studies on Hysteria" (Breuer & Freud, 1895/1955) was written, Freud's approach to analysis was to begin with the symptoms and to work on eradicating them one by one. By 1905 Freud had developed a more complex formulation of the structure of neuroses and abandoned this rather straightforward technique for a lengthier process (Freud, 1905/1956a).

During this period Freud still viewed shorter treatments favorably as long as the end result was positive. He explained that he required six months to three years for successful treatment but that his patients were severely ill, and he speculated that with healthier patients the course of treatment would be shorter (Freud, 1904/1953a).

Later on, in "Further Recommendations in the Technique of Psychoanalysis," Freud became skeptical about the efficacy of short-term treatment. He wrote that although shortening the analytic process was still a "reasonable wish," it was impeded by the length of time required for profound changes in the mind to come about (Freud, 1913/1963b, p. 142). In describing a case history of infantile neurosis, Freud (1918/1956b) emphasized the importance of gaining scientific knowledge through each analysis and said that short-term analyses were insignificant in this regard. Later, other psychoanalytic theorists would challenge Freud's giving scientific knowledge priority over therapeutic gain. Finally, in 1937 Freud wrote "If we wish to fulfill the more exacting demands which are now made upon therapeutic analysis, we shall not shorten its duration whether as a means or an end" (Freud, 1937/1963a, pp. 241–242).

Thus, it is clear that throughout Freud's psychoanalytic career there was a trend away from short-term treatment until eventually he renounced it altogether. Some of Freud's contemporaries became distressed with the steady shift toward longer treatment periods and worked toward reversing this trend. Among them were Sandor Ferenczi, Otto Rank, Franz Alexander, and Thomas French.

Ferenczi was the first psychoanalyst to experiment with methods aimed at shortening the length of psychoanalysis. In 1920, at the Sixth International Congress of Psycho-Analysis, he presented his ideas on how the psychoanalytic process might be shortened. He suggested increased activity from both the patient and the doctor as a means "to enable the patient . . . to comply more successfully with the rule of free association and thereby to assist or hasten the exploring of the unconscious material" (Ferenczi, 1926/1950, p. 198). The doctor's "activity" was to prescribe either the performance of certain behaviors or the cessation of certain behaviors, thus making the patient an active participant in the treatment. Ferenczi argued that his method of active therapy did not alter Freud's method in any essential way. He said that interpretations themselves are active interventions because they change the direction of the patient's thoughts and help uncover repressed ideas.

Ferenczi emphasized that increased activity was to be used sparingly and was only a supplement to analysis, "whose place it must never pretend to take" (1926/1950, p. 208). Active techniques were often employed by Ferenczi in the analysis of phobic patients. In such cases he directed his patients to carry out the avoided activity. These interventions, although occurring within a generally psychoanalytically informed treatment, have obvious similarity to the later brief behavioral treatments for phobias.

Another active technique that Ferenczi used was to tell the patient to cease previously unnoticed pleasurable activities (such as masturbation and tic-like twitches). As a result, new memories would become conscious and treatment would be accelerated. Ferenczi explained that active techniques are effective because they create new intrapsychic tension and conflict, which in turn bring repressed thoughts and memories into consciousness. A more subtle technique of Ferenczi's was to demand that patients finish their sentences when they broke off in the middle of a thought. In this way he uncovered heretofore repressed material.

Ferenczi and Rank collaborated in their mutual desire to reduce the growing confusion among psychoanalysts. This collaboration resulted in the publication of *The Development of Psycho-Analysis* (Ferenczi & Rank, 1925/ 1956) and the introduction of several concepts that are central to brief psychodynamic therapy as it is practiced today. In that book they wrote that the emphasis placed on gaining theoretical knowledge through analysis was hindering the efficacy of therapy. Ferenczi and Rank wanted to see the psychoanalytic method turn more to the treatment itself and away from theory, which they felt was largely unnecessary. They believed it would then be easier for doctors to acquire psychoanalytic knowledge and to shorten and simplify treatment. When a longer treatment period was necessary for a better outcome, Ferenczi and Rank did not object, but they strove to eliminate unnecessary prolongations.

Ferenczi and Rank asserted that present life events deserved more attention than details of childhood. They saw the very purpose of psychoanalysis as being to replace "affective factors of experience for intellectual processes" (Ferenczi & Rank, 1925/1956, p. 62). This concept became the focus of Franz Alexander's work some twenty years later.

Rank, in his own right, developed key ideas that have become an integral part of contemporary brief psychodynamic therapy. Although his theory of the trauma of birth (Rank, 1929/1973) did not gain acceptance, an important component of therapy emerged from it. It was through this theory that Rank recognized the importance of the separation issue in therapy. By setting a termination date he created a therapeutic atmosphere in which working on the issue of separation from the analyst became central. This approach was a forerunner of Mann's (1973) therapy, which also set a firm termination date (twelve sessions) and emphasized separation and loss (see chapter 2).

Rank (1929/1936) emphasized the role of the patient's "will" in the therapeutic process, asserting that once the patient's will was motivated toward change, the analysis could be shortened. Thus, Rank became the first to recognize formally that the patient's level of motivation to change affects the therapeutic outcome. Contemporary short-term psychodynamic theorists continue to emphasize this motivational factor.

Perhaps the most important work concerning brief psychodynamic therapy was done by Franz Alexander and Thomas French in the 1940s. In *Psychoanalytic Therapy* (1946) they challenged many facets of classical psychoanalysis. The ideas proposed by Ferenczi and Rank were the starting point for Alexander and French, particularly the emphasis on emotional experience over intellectual understanding in analysis. This emphasis guided their conception of how analysis should be conducted.

One very important concept that stemmed from the belief in the primacy of emotional experience in the therapeutic process is that of the corrective emotional experience. Alexander and French believed that patients must have a corrective emotional experience in therapy if any progress is to be made. A corrective emotional experience occurs when the therapist helps the patient overcome past traumatic experiences. The therapist facilitates the corrective emotional experience by recreating previously intolerable emotional situations under the more favorable circumstances of the therapeutic relationship. The phenomenon can occur in daily life experiences as well as in therapy. However, the transference relationship has particular characteristics that help the patient resolve old conflicts. The patient experiences the conflict with the therapist much less intensely than the original one. Also, in order to encourage the corrective emotional experience, the therapist intentionally assumes a very different attitude toward the patient than did the person in the original conflict. When the patient's behavior continues in the old patterns, the therapist reacts only as the actual situation dictates. In this way the therapist can help the patient understand intellectually and, more important, feel the irrationality of the inappropriate emotional reactions.

Classical psychoanalytic theory professes that the therapeutic process occurs mainly during sessions. Alexander and French believed that the therapeutic process extends to the patient's everyday life and argued against the classical orientation for several reasons. They said that many treatments were unnecessarily prolonged and that weekly sessions would often be sufficient or even preferable to the traditional daily sessions. In some cases daily sessions might actually become detrimental, allowing the patient to avoid real-life experiences. Daily sessions also reduced the intensity of the patient's emotional experience in therapy by masking his or her dependence on the therapist, thus slowing the therapeutic process. By decreasing the frequency of sessions the patient could become aware of these dependent needs and analyze them with the therapist.

The classical orientation made analysts afraid to interrupt treatment even when a break would be helpful. Alexander and French found that planned interruptions in treatment can be a useful technique. Interruptions lasting one to eighteen months can be used as a means to determine which of the patient's difficulties still need work, to increase the patient's confidence in his or her ability to function without the therapist, and to help the therapist decide when the patient is ready for termination. Interruptions should also enable patients to see whether they can apply what they have learned in therapy to real-life situations.

THE SECOND GENERATION: THE EMERGENCE OF MODERN DYNAMIC THERAPIES

With the writings of Malan (1963, 1976, 1979), Mann (1973), Sifneos (1972, 1979), and Davanloo (1978, 1980), brief dynamic therapy arrived as an important treatment option. These four authors are often seen as the main contributors to the field of brief dynamic psychotherapy. Their contributions have been reviewed in detail by many others (Bauer & Kobos, 1987; Burke, White, & Havens, 1979; Gustafson, 1986; Horowitz et al., 1984; Marmor, 1979). Three of the approaches are represented in this book: chapter 2, by Mann; chapter 3, by Nielson and Barth, on Sifneos's approach; and chapter 4, by Laikin, Winston, and McCullough, giving their adaptation of the Davanloo approach. Each of these chapters presents an account of the development of the approach.

Although his method is not directly represented in this book, Malan made a number of contributions that influenced many of the subsequent brief dynamic therapy models. Malan (1976) placed a strong emphasis on the careful selection of patients for brief dynamic therapy. This selection is done both through screening out inappropriate referrals (such as substance abusers, suicidal patients, and grossly self-destructive or acting-out patients) and through a psychodynamic evaluation. Malan not only attended to historical details during the evaluation but also introduced trial interpretations as a way to assess the patient's suitability for treatment. This aspect of brief dynamic therapy was later expanded by Davanloo (1980).

Another contribution by Malan (1976), building upon the work of Balint, his teacher (see Balint, Ornstein, & Balint, 1972), was the delineation of a circumscribed focus for treatment. Determination of a focus becomes a core aspect of the evaluation process; if a clear focus cannot be separated from the general presenting psychopathology, then the patient is deemed to be inappropriate for short-term dynamic therapy. Patient and therapist must agree on a focus for treatment to proceed. The focus then serves to structure the therapist's work and to single out the most important issues; interpretations are made relative to the circumscribed problem area, with other issues having lower priority or not being dealt with at all. The concept of therapeutic focus has become perhaps the sine qua non of brief dynamic therapy methods.

THE THIRD GENERATION: RESEARCH AND THE NEW BRIEF DYNAMIC THERAPIES

As the popularity of brief dynamic therapy grew during the 1980s, a number of additions to the "traditional" four approaches began to appear. These new approaches often arose out of research environments. Psychotherapy research in the early 1980s had advanced to a level of methodological rigor that, among other improvements, required researchers studying treatment outcome to standardize the psychotherapies they were investigating. This standardization was in the form of treatment guides or manuals for the training and supervision of therapists. In the words of Lester Luborsky and Robert DeRubeis (1984), the implementation of treatment manuals could be regarded as a "small revolution" in the nature of psychotherapy research. Treatment manuals, as opposed to earlier books on psychotherapy, specified in detail how therapy should actually be conducted. They often included information on how to select patients for treatment, the goals of treatment, a theory of psychopathology, the techniques to be used, and, in some cases, a scale to assess the extent to which therapists adhered to the techniques recommended in the manual.

Treatment manuals were first developed for the cognitive-behavioral treatments (for example, Beck, Rush, Shaw, & Emery, 1979). Within the psychodynamic camp, Luborsky (1984) and Hans H. Strupp and Jeffrey L.

Binder (1984) were the first to put forth treatment manuals. Luborsky's (1984) supportive-expressive treatment, offered in both time-limited and time-unlimited formats, was actually a codification of the main principles of psychoanalytic therapy given in a variety of other writings (including Freud, 1912/1958a, 1913/1958b, 1914/1958c; Bibring, 1954; Fenichel, 1941). The Strupp and Binder (1984) time-limited dynamic therapy approach was the first to represent an interpersonal (that is, Sullivanian) perspective on short-term dynamic therapy. Although he did not produce a formal treatment manual, Mardi J. Horowitz (1976), working specifically with patients evidencing a stress response syndrome, developed his own version of short-term dynamic therapy in a twelve-session format similar to Mann's (1973) treatment. All three of these additions from psychotherapy researchers are represented in this book (chapters 5, 6, and 7).

Over roughly the past decade, researchers at Beth Israel Hospital in New York City have been active in conducting studies of the efficacy of short-term approaches (Winston et al., in press). One of their studies compares the more confrontational, affect-oriented Davanloo-type approach with a less confrontational, more cognitively oriented dynamic therapy—treatments that are described here in chapters 4 and 8. Another ongoing study by the Beth Israel group includes a purely supportive (but dynamically informed) treatment modality. Supportive psychodynamic therapy has received increasing attention (see Rockland, 1989) and has always been widely practiced in clinical settings. By including a chapter on supportive therapy (chapter 9), we hope to capture the full range of treatment options available to the dynamic researcher and clinician alike.

In addition to having been connected with ongoing research in brief dynamic therapy, we were aware of the elegant efforts of Lorna Smith Benjamin in developing a conceptual system (Structural Analysis of Social Behavior, SASB) for coding interpersonal behavior (Benjamin, 1974; McLemore & Benjamin, 1979); the system has been applied to psychotherapy data (Benjamin, 1977, 1979, 1986; Henry, Schacht, & Strupp, 1986). Chapter 10, by Benjamin, represents the first complete description of a brief dynamic therapy guided by the SASB model. Because the therapy is developed directly out of a coherent taxonomy of interpersonal behavior, Benjamin's chapter is somewhat different from the other clinical approaches presented here, which tend to emphasize psychotherapy technique.

Concurrent with the emerging literature on brief dynamic therapy and the advent of treatment manuals, the self psychology (Kohut, 1971, 1984) orientation was becoming a major new perspective within psychoanalysis. It seems likely that self psychologists were being confronted with the same pressures to provide treatment in a brief format that had affected other clinicians. A few applications of self psychology to briefer therapy have appeared (for example, Ornstein & Ornstein, 1972; Deitz, 1988). In chapter 11, Howard J. Baker extends the previous writings on this topic.

Several approaches to brief dynamic therapy do not appear in this book. We have not included Malan's treatment model because Malan has (or had at the time this book was planned) abandoned his own perspective in favor of Davanloo's (Malan, 1980). The unique psychoanalytic model of the Mount Zion psychotherapy research group (Weiss & Sampson, 1986) has also been applied to brief therapy; the theory and research relating to this approach have been well described elsewhere (Silbershatz & Curtis, 1986). Also not included here are a number of approaches that are primarily integrations of existing models (such as Gustafson, 1986; Bauer & Kobos, 1987).

The last chapter of this book compares the various approaches to short-term dynamic therapy. Similarities and differences between the methods are presented in regard to selection criteria, length of treatment, stages of the therapeutic process, theories of change, and techniques. The chapter concludes with some guidelines for sorting out the potentially confusing array of treatment methods that now exist in the domain of brief dynamic therapy.

OUTLINE OF THE CHAPTERS

Because this handbook is designed to facilitate comparisons of methods, we asked that contributors cover the following topics: (1) origins and development of the method, (2) the selection of patients for treatment, (3) application to specific populations, (4) goals of treatment, (5) theory of change, (6) techniques, (7) case examples, and (8) empirical support. Within our guidelines, however, we allowed contributors flexibility to cover whichever topics were most developed or essential to their specific approach.

The sections are elaborated as follows.

Origins and Development

This section describes the origins of the approach, previous writings that were most influential in shaping the treatment model, and major changes over time.

Selection of Patients

This section indicates which types of patients are most suitable for the treatment and which types should not be treated with the approach. If appropriate, there is a discussion of how patients are selected.

Applications to Specific Populations

Within the range of patients that meet the inclusion criteria, we asked whether the authors have had experiences with certain subgroups (e.g., in terms of diagnosis, personality types, or age). The authors also address any special issues or modifications of the approach that are relevant to these different subgroups.

Goals of Treatment

Here are set down the goals of treatment from the patient's point of view and how these goals are elicited and set at the beginning of treatment.

Theory of Change

The purpose of this section is to describe what changes during treatment and which clinical factors are responsible for change. If the approach is unique with regard to how psychodynamic conflicts, defenses, and so on, lead to changes in symptoms, those theoretical constructs may be elaborated. The relative importance of psychodynamic, patient, and therapist variables in their contribution to the process of change is discussed.

Techniques

In this, the main section of the chapter, the techniques used in the approach and the principles that guide the selection and implementation of interventions are described in detail. How should the success of interventions be evaluated? Does the technique change over different phases of treatment?

Case Examples

The essence of each method is illustrated using a case example and discussion. This section includes actual transcript material or several brief illustrations, with discussion of key elements of the patient–therapist interchange.

Empirical Support

This section includes a summary of the results of research on the approach, particularly efficacy research. The authors may also describe other relevant research, such as process studies, predictive studies, or single case studies. A delineation of how the research bears on the validity of the treatment or its theory of change is also included when available.

We hope that this handbook will educate clinicians and researchers about the range of treatment options within the dynamic umbrella and will help clarify the similarities and differences among them. Although this book brings together a wide variety of treatment models, we by no means consider it the definitive summary of the field. The field is in a period of expansion and flux, with a number of clinician-researchers in Europe and North America currently collecting data on the process and outcome of brief dynamic therapy. This book captures a slice of this evolutionary process, and it is our hope that it will help organize thinking and efforts to progress beyond the current theories. We anticipate, for example, that the next generation of short-term dynamic therapies will be designed for specific patient types, along the lines of Horowitz's work (chapter 7). Whether these patient groups are best defined by *DSM IV* categories, psychodynamic formulations, or some other way of classifying patients' problems remains an agenda for research.

References

Alexander, F., & French, T. M. (1946). *Psychoanalytic therapy*. New York: Ronald Press.

Balint, M., Ornstein, P. H., & Balint, E. (1972). *Focal psychotherapy: An example of applied psychoanalysis*. London: Tavistock.

Bauer, G. P., & Kobos, J. C. (1987). *Brief therapy: Short-term psychodynamic intervention*. Northvale, NJ: Jason Aronson.

Beck, A. T., Rush, A. J., Shaw, B., & Emery, G. (1979). *Cognitive therapy of depression*. New York: Guilford Press.

Benjamin, L. S. (1974). Structural Analysis of Social Behavior. *Psychological Review, 81*, 392–425.

Benjamin, L. S. (1977). Structural analysis of a family in therapy. *Journal of Consulting and Clinical Psychology, 45*, 391–406.

Benjamin, L. S. (1979). Use of Structural Analysis of Social Behavior (SASB) and Markov chains to study dyadic interactions. *Journal of Abnormal Psychology, 88*, 303–319.

Benjamin, L. S. (1986). Operational definition and measurement of dynamics shown in the stream of free association. *Psychiatry, 49*, 104–129.

Bibring, E. (1954). Psychoanalysis and the dynamic psychotherapies. *Journal of the American Psychoanalytic Association, 2*, 745–770.

Breuer, J., & Freud, S. (1955). Studies on hysteria. In J. Strachey (Ed. & Trans.), *The standard edition of the complete works of Sigmund Freud* (Vol. 2, pp. 125–134). London: Hogarth Press. (Original work published 1895.)

Budman, S. H., & Gurman, A. S. (1988). *Theory and practice of brief therapy.* New York: Guilford Press.

Burke, J. D., Jr., White, H. S., & Havens, L. L. (1979). Which short-term psychotherapy? *Archives of General Psychiatry, 36,* 177–186.

Davanloo, H. (Ed.). (1978). *Basic principles and techniques in short-term dynamic psychotherapy.* New York: Spectrum.

Davanloo, H. (Ed.). (1980). *Short-term dynamic psychotherapy.* New York: Jason Aronson.

Deitz, J. (1988). Self-psychological interventions for major depression: Technique and theory. *American Journal of Psychotherapy, 42,* 597–609.

Fenichel, O. (1941). *Problems of psychoanalytic technique.* Albany, NY: Psychoanalytic Quarterly.

Ferenczi, S. (1950). The further development of an active therapy in psychoanalysis. In E. Jones (Ed.) & J. I. Suttie (Trans.), *Further contributions to the theory and technique of psycho-analysis* (pp. 198–217). London: Hogarth Press. (Original work published 1926.)

Ferenczi, S., & Rank, O. (1956). *The development of psycho-analysis* (C. Newton, Trans.). New York: Dover. (Original work published 1925.)

Freud, S. (1953a). Freud's psycho-analytic method. In E. Jones (Ed.) & J. Riviere (Trans.), *Collected papers: Early papers* (Vol. 1, pp. 264–271). London: Hogarth Press. (Original work published 1904.)

Freud, S. (1953b). On psychotherapy. In E. Jones (Ed.) & J. Riviere (Trans.), *Collected papers: Early papers* (Vol. 1, pp. 249–263). London: Hogarth Press. (Original work published 1904.)

Freud, S. (1956a). Fragment of an analysis of a case of hysteria. In E. Jones (Ed.), A. Strachey (Trans.), & J. Strachey (Trans.), *Collected papers: Case histories* (Vol. 3, pp. 13–21). London: Hogarth Press. (Original work published 1905.)

Freud, S. (1956b). From the history of an infantile neurosis. In E. Jones (Ed.), A. Strachey (Trans.), & J. Strachey (Trans.), *Collected papers: Case histories* (Vol. 3, pp. 473–479). London: Hogarth Press. (Original work published 1918.)

Freud, S. (1958a). The dynamics of transference. In J. Strachey (Ed. & Trans.), *The standard edition of the complete psychological works of Sigmund Freud* (Vol. 12, pp. 97–108). London: Hogarth Press. (Original work published 1912.)

Freud, S. (1958b). On beginning the treatment: Further recommendations on the technique of psychoanalysis. In J. Strachey (Ed. & Trans.), *The standard edition of the complete psychological works of Sigmund Freud* (Vol. 12, pp. 212–244). London: Hogarth Press. (Original work published 1913.)

Freud, S. (1958c). Remembering, repeating, and working through: Further recommendations on the technique of psychoanalysis. In J. Strachey (Ed. & Trans.), *The standard edition of the complete psychological works of Sigmund Freud* (Vol. 12, pp. 145–156). London: Hogarth Press. (Original work published 1914.)

Freud, S. (1963a). Analysis terminable and interminable. In P. Rieff (Ed.), *The collected papers of Sigmund Freud: Therapy and technique* (Vol. 3, pp. 233–271). New York: Collier Books. (Original work published 1937.)

Freud, S. (1963b). Further recommendations in the technique of psychoanalysis. In P. Rieff (Ed.), *The collected papers of Sigmund Freud: Therapy and technique* (Vol. 3, pp. 135–156). New York: Collier Books. (Original work published 1913.)

Garfield, S. L., & Bergin, A. E. (1986). Introduction and historical overview. In S. L. Garfield & A. E. Bergin (Eds.), *Handbook of psychotherapy and behavior change* (pp. 3–22). New York: Wiley.

Gustafson, J. P. (1986). *The complex secret of brief psychotherapy.* New York: Norton.

Henry, W. P., Schacht, T. E., & Strupp, H. H. (1986). Structural Analysis of Social Behavior: Application to a study of interpersonal process in differential therapeutic outcome. *Journal of Consulting and Clinical Psychology, 54,* 27–31.

Horowitz, M. J. (1976). *Stress response syndromes.* New York: Jason Aronson.

Horowitz, M. J., Marmar, C., Krupnick, J., Wilner, N., Kaltreider, N., & Wallerstein, R. (1984). *Personality styles and brief psychotherapy.* New York: Basic Books.

Jones, E. (1955). *The life and work of Sigmund Freud* (Vol. 2). New York: Basic Books.

Kohut, H. (1971). *The analysis of the self.* New York: International Universities Press.

Kohut, H. (1984). *How does analysis cure?* Chicago: University of Chicago Press.

Koss, M. P., & Butcher, J. N. (1986). Research on brief psychotherapy. In S. L. Garfield & A. E. Bergin (Eds.), *Handbook of psychotherapy and behavior change* (pp. 627–670). New York: Wiley.

Luborsky, L. (1984). *Principles of psychoanalytic psychotherapy: A manual for supportive-expressive treatment.* New York: Basic Books.

Luborsky, L., & DeRubeis, R. (1984). The use of psychotherapy treatment manuals: A small revolution in psychotherapy research style. *Clinical Psychology Review, 4,* 5–14.

Malan, D. H. (1963). *A study of brief psychotherapy.* New York: Plenum.

Malan, D. H. (1976). *The frontier of brief psychotherapy.* New York: Plenum.

Malan, D. H. (1979). *Individual psychotherapy and the science of psychodynamics.* London: Butterworth.

Malan, D. H. (1980). The most important development in psychotherapy since the discovery of the unconscious. In H. Davanloo (Ed.), *Short-term dynamic psychotherapy* (Vol. 1). New York: Jason Aronson.

Mann, J. (1973). *Time-limited psychotherapy.* Cambridge, MA: Harvard University Press.

Marmor, J. (1979). Historical aspects of short-term dynamic psychotherapy. *Psychiatric Clinics of North America, 2,* 3–9.

McLemore, C. W., & Benjamin, L. S. (1979). Whatever happened to interpersonal diagnosis? A psychosocial alternative to DSM-III. *American Psychologist, 34,* 17–34.

Ornstein, P., & Ornstein, A. (1972). Focal psychotherapy: Its potential impact on psychotherapeutic practice in medicine. *Journal of Psychiatry in Medicine, 3,* 311–325.

Rank, O. (1936). *Will therapy* (J. Taft, Trans.). New York: Alfred A. Knopf. (Original work published 1929.)

Rank, O. (1973). *The trauma of birth.* New York: Harper & Row. (Original work published 1929.)

Rockland, L. H. (1989). *Supportive therapy: A psychodynamic approach.* New York: Basic Books.

Sifneos, P. E. (1972). *Short-term psychotherapy and emotional crisis.* Cambridge, MA: Harvard University Press.

Sifneos, P. E. (1979). *Short-term dynamic psychotherapy: Evaluation and technique.* New York: Plenum.

Silbershatz, G., & Curtis, J. (1986). Clinical implications of research on brief dynamic psychotherapy: II. How the therapist helps or hinders therapeutic progress. *Psychoanalytic Psychology, 3,* 27–37.

Strupp, H. H., & Binder, J. L. (1984). *Psychotherapy in a new key: A guide to time-limited dynamic psychotherapy.* New York: Basic Books.

Weiss, J., Sampson, H., & the Mount Zion Psychotherapy Research Group. (1986). *The psychoanalytic process: Theory, clinical observations, and empirical research.* New York: Guilford Press.

Winston, A., Pollack, J., McCullough, L., Flegenheimer, W., Kestenbaum, R., & Trujillo, M. (in press). Brief psychotherapy of personality disorders. *Journal of Nervous and Mental Disease.*

CHAPTER 2

Time Limited Psychotherapy

James Mann

ORIGINS AND DEVELOPMENT

In 1962 the outpatient department of the division of psychiatry at the Boston University School of Medicine had too few professional therapists to provide for a growing list of patients awaiting assignment. Because the outpatient department was staffed by psychiatry residents at the time, the problem became mine as director of psychiatric education.

Not unexpectedly, a review disclosed that a significant number of patients were being seen regularly over long periods of time, even for years. Since they were being treated by residents who rotated from one psychiatric service to another every six months their treatment was interrupted twice a year. An examination of the records of some of these long-term patients revealed that, although they apparently related well to their new therapists, they tended to reexamine with each therapist much of what had already been discussed. Further, we noted that these patients did not appear to react strongly to the loss of the previous therapist; thus, we wondered whether transference to the institution and to the outpatient department had become more significant than transference to the therapist. It would seem that patients could go on forever, having their dependent needs well gratified—although their best interests would not be served. Patients awaiting treatment remained at a disadvantage.

In 1950 I had been director of the first outpatient department at Boston

State Hospital, where I experimented briefly with time limited group psychotherapy, also under the duress of having a small staff and many patients. Since 1947 I had been working very closely with Elvin Semrad and had come to appreciate not only his unique, intensely penetrating, empathic interview style but also that the resonant chords he always struck in the hearts and minds of his patients played out the invariable theme of separation and loss with the psychotic patients he interviewed. He made apparent their need for a nurturant object of constancy.

Having long believed that the line from so-called normality through neurosis through various mental disorders into psychosis is a continuum along which, given the right toxic circumstances, any of us could descend at almost any time, I came to understand that the repetitive series of separations and losses that every human being endures forms the outline of the self-image that each person constructs.

The significance of time became clear to me in long-term work with psychotic patients, with psychotherapy patients, and with patients in psychoanalysis. No matter how long the treatment lasted, and no matter which therapeutic model, the prospect of the end of treatment was always an unstabilizing experience for the patient and had repercussions in the therapist. The reality of time, with its multiple meanings of separation, loss, and ultimately death, became of overriding importance in every instance.

Confronted years later with the personnel–patient problem at Boston University, I felt it appropriate to apply my fifteen years of work and thought. I decided to implement a plan in which selected outpatients would be offered twelve sessions of treatment by second- and third-year residents. I thought twelve sessions following an evaluation should be enough in which to pinpoint a significant issue, elaborate it, and work it through to termination. Extant brief therapies did not specify length, although any therapy labeled brief would be expected to have some kind of time limit.

I wrote a fairly detailed description of the model and sent it to each of the residents, along with a memorandum proposing that each try it. I soon realized that I was asking for a drastic change from accepted methods and was not surprised that passive resistance prevailed. I decided that I would begin a seminar in Time Limited Psychotherapy (TLP) and asked the residents to select a patient for me to treat in twelve fifty-minute sessions following the evaluation. I knew that the residents would never choose an "easy" patient for me. Furthermore, as their experienced psychoanalyst mentor, I felt it would be instructive for the residents to see me make mistakes.

At the start the seminar was limited to residents, who observed my work through a one-way mirror. As we progressed, social workers, psychologists, and psychiatric nurses were invited and we instituted closed-circuit television. In a brief meeting before each session we discussed what had gone on in preceding sessions and speculated on what responses we might anticipate in the upcoming session. After each session we met again for further discussion of the dynamic flow and reactions.

My private practice was primarily psychoanalytic, but as I found that my ideas about separations, losses, and time and their influence on the image of the self were being verified in my seminar and in my supervision of residents engaged in TLP, I began to treat a number of private patients in this mode. I still do. Over a period of some twenty-five years of seminars, supervision, and private practice the elaboration of details, substance, and subtleties substantiated the importance of what I have called the *central issue* as a means of entering immediately into the core of the patient's need for help. The combination of time and the central issue (Mann & Goldman, 1982) is very different from the usual concept of focus in brief psychotherapy. The concept of the central issue incorporating time, affects, and self-image also enables the therapist to glean a remarkable amount of information very quickly from the patient.

SELECTION OF PATIENTS

With the accumulation of experience our early caution about the suitability of patients for TLP has given way to the recognition that a wide variety of patients can be treated by this model. In this connection, the process in TLP is productive of so much information in the first three or four sessions that if a serious diagnostic error has been made and the patient is deemed unsuitable for this treatment, a change to some other kind of treatment may be easily made.

Two generalizations about selection can be made. First, TLP is indicated following a positive assessment of ego strength and its capacity to allow for rapid affective involvement and equally rapid disengagement—a measure of the capacity to tolerate loss. The capacity to tolerate loss is assessed in the evaluative interviews, during which the therapist learns from the patient how the inevitable multiple losses of life have been managed.

Second, in spite of significant defects in mothering and the absence of an early predictable environment, there are many patients who, for reasons not well understood, enjoy a resilience that allows them to emerge with relatively intact egos capable of rapid affective involvement and of tolerating loss. Each patient, regardless of the presenting complaint or early history, should be evaluated on his or her own terms with regard to ego strength, without preconceived theoretical biases. The assessment must be in terms of the relative success revealed in the life history with respect to work and in relations to others.

These two generalizations aside, there are many neurotic patients with strong dependent longings who may refuse to become involved on any short-term basis, who will attempt to prolong treatment, or who may leave early in anticipation of termination. However, those who are aware of their dependency and have tried to come to grips with prior loss are often eager for help. The time limitation may be a very positive challenge for entry into successful treatment. There are also patients whose dependency may have been fostered by too much treatment with too many therapists. This kind of patient may do very well in TLP.

Patients with narcissistic disorders may tend to consider TLP as far too brief for their important problems and refuse treatment. But those with relatively mild narcissistic difficulties may experience the twelve sessions as a challenge and work effectively. They often require approval and positive feedback from the therapist. They can tolerate loss provided they feel that they have done a good job.

Into the categories of anxiety, hysterical, depressive, and obsessional disorders fall a host of dynamic issues that are amenable to TLP. Patients may present with a variety of symptoms, ranging from anxiety and depression to conversion reactions or obsessions. Under these headings characterological problems may predominate, such as repetitive unsatisfactory love relationships, problems in work or school adaptation, or difficulty with peers.

Maturational issues arise when an important psychological equilibrium has been broken, for example, when a person suffers a real or symbolic loss or leaves one phase of life and enters a new one. All significant life changes are experienced as losses and will become manifest in the vulnerable person in symptoms or in maladaptive behavior. For example, entering college, leaving home, graduating, choosing a career, changing jobs, getting married, becoming a parent, seeing children leave home, retiring, and growing old are all states of transition and change, and there are many more. All states of transition and change entail giving up something familiar for something that invariably is uncertain—no matter how much preparation is made—and the response is always a reaction to loss.

The contraindications for TLP are quite clear and are most likely those of any kind of brief psychotherapy. Certain diagnostic categories a priori demand indefinite long-term involvement with the patient. Schizophrenia in any of its subtypes, bipolar affective disorder, and schizoid characters are examples. Obsessional characters with major and almost exclusive defenses of isolation and intellectualization have a limited capacity for affective experience, although they may appear otherwise. They may seem to engage rapidly and disengage equally rapidly without any affective concomitants. Working with them is like writing on water.

My experience with borderline patients has been somewhat different when the patients possess some effective neurotic defenses and are not likely to fall into a transference psychosis. It has been possible to treat them with referral for long-term treatment on completion of TLP. The initial work clears away much of the defensive manipulation that often consumes one or two years of therapeutic groundwork before the patient begins to engage the therapist constructively.

Finally, the psychological elements involved in such conditions as rheumatoid arthritis, ulcerative colitis, regional enteritis, and severe asthma also demand long-term affiliation with the therapist.

THE GOAL OF TREATMENT

The single goal of TLP is to diminish as much as possible the patient's negative self-image. Symptoms that may have brought the patient in for help and that have served to defend against and to obscure the central issue are resolved as a byproduct of the process. Resolution of the central issue leads to the following changes.

1. The patient experiences an expansion of the ego and consequently a greater sense of independence and of self.
2. The always present harsh superego, which had constantly served to reinforce the negative self-image, is softened. The patient comes to regard himself or herself more charitably.
3. The healing process in TLP, as in all psychotherapy, includes the introjection and incorporation by the patient of the good object found in the therapist. A new internal positive reference source becomes available to the patient.
4. The automatic defense mechanisms, which had been used to cope, albeit ineffectively, are replaced by the awareness of choices. The patient learns not to respond in automatically determined, maladaptive ways.
5. Better feelings about the self allow for a broader vision of the pa-

tient's relationships with others and facilitate different and better ways of responding.

The experience of TLP is highly emotional, experiential, insightful, and cognitive in its effects. The theoretical underpinnings of TLP, an understanding of the process, and the goals and aims of TLP are all based on traditional psychoanalytic principles. Yet, as in any brief psychotherapy, engagement with the patient is imperative. TLP is not by any stretch of imagination a miniature psychoanalysis, nor does the therapist aim to make conscious what was unconscious. A psychoanalytic understanding of theory, process, aims, and goals makes it possible for the therapist to translate underlying mental processes in terms of the defect the person feels as a chronically painful part of his or her being and daily existence. TLP requires neither a charismatic therapist nor one with unique skills for certain patients. It requires only the good training that every therapist should have and the empathic sensitivity reinforced by personal psychotherapy or analysis.

THEORY OF CHANGE

TLP exercises its unique influence through the two major points of the treatment proposal, the therapist's statement of the central issue and the setting of the termination date at the start of treatment. The process these points set in motion illuminates the relationship between persistent negative feelings about the self over the lifetime of the patient and the origins of these feelings in the inability to effect separations without suffering undue damage.

It is fair to say that in any form of brief psychotherapy it is not feasible to work slowly through the patient's layers of defense. The central issue as posed by the therapist will, among other things, bypass defenses temporarily, control the patient's anxiety, and stimulate the rapid appearance of a therapeutic or working alliance as well as a positive transference. The result is the rapid evolution of the therapeutic process. For brief psychotherapy, time becomes a major factor in itself.

Time and our concept of time are the means we employ to integrate in our minds and in our feelings what was, what is, and what will be. What was, often consists of events of significance to us, which we recall as memories. Memories are intimately related in most instances to important people in our lives. It follows that memories cannot be separated from time. As we recall memories, knowledge about ourselves increases little by little because memory and knowledge are the same thing. A good initial psychiatric interview and the work of continuing therapeutic sessions serve to link and to expand time. As we review and pick up threads of the patient's past, present, and future we are also expanding the patient's awareness of what was, what is, and what will be. In all psychological treatment the patient works toward facing up to the past in order to gain some mastery over the present and to be freer in shaping the future.

We are all familiar with the constrictions of time in our daily lives and with the means we employ to escape from its bonds. Relaxation by any method induces a sense of decreased time pressure. Alcohol, marijuana, meditation, and anti-anxiety medications, for example, all induce the feeling that time is moving more slowly—as does simply taking time off from work. In mystic states and in ecstatic states connections between past, present, and future are broken so that time is experienced as unending. By contrast, in fragmented states such as depersonalization, derealization, and acute psychotic decompensation time is without meaning, empty and exquisitely painful. I have written earlier (Mann, 1973) of my experience with "golden memories" in patients in analysis, who derived a sense of great warmth and familiarity from them but were unable to place them in time or in space. Further analysis revealed early recollections and fantasies about the mother and the wish to be comforted, warmed, and nurtured endlessly.

In states of health one does not feel the passage of time; there is no sense of growing older. On pleasurable occasions time seems to move swiftly and in painful circumstances time moves very slowly. For the therapist, for instance, it is common experience for a session to pass very quickly with a motivated, psychologically minded, hard-working patient but very slowly with a plodding, circumstantial patient who never seems to get to the point.

We think of time in categorical and in existential terms. The categorical is time as noted on clocks and calendars, whereas existential time is lived in and experienced. The development of time sense goes hand in hand with the development of reality sense. Prisoners or hostages in isolation, for example, can maintain reality by keeping an accurate record of the day and date.

With any kind of treatment the patient will have unconscious expectations of some kind of magical cure, of fulfillment, of becoming transformed into what he or she always wished to be. There is an expectation that the therapist will turn back time and will repair what was, to make a new present and ensure a different and better future. I believe this to be true in all treatment, whether it be medical, surgical, psychopharmacological, behavioral, psychotherapeutic, or psychoanalytic. The greater the ambiguity in regard to the duration of treatment is, the more what I call child time, with its endless expectations of total fulfillment, predominates. Thus we see the regression that invariably occurs in long-term psychotherapy and in psychoanalysis. The structure of these approaches facilitates planned regression so that over the long term there will occur the slow but steady analysis of layers of defense, of varied transference manifestations, and of powerful dependent wishes and demands. The more specific the duration of treatment is, the more rapidly is child time confronted with real time and the work to be done. In this sense, TLP presents a deadline for the patient to meet from the start.

The way a person assesses ongoing lived time is determined by how he or she perceives personal adequacy in the face of some challenging reality. The reality may be outside the person or entirely intrapsychic. In the latter, the ego perceives a situation that it deems important to its well-being, to its needs and aspirations. As a result, an internal question arises of whether and how the person can cope. In other words, intrapsychic reality becomes a challenge to the self. The assessment of our capacity to cope can be made only on the basis of past experience. If we doubt our adequacy or believe that we are in fact inadequate, then tension arises within the ego and is felt as anxiety or depression or both. Anxiety speaks to uncertainties about the future while guilt speaks to the past ("I should have") and to the future ("I should"). The perception of a potential threat to our adequacy leads to anxiety ("I am in danger and I must mobilize myself to act"). The belief that inadequacy is actual leads to depression and in severe instances means a person is hopeless and helpless and will always be so. In most cases, both anxiety and depression are present and the patient is covertly transmitting doubts about the existence of a future.

TECHNIQUES

The Central Issue

In any form of brief psychotherapy it is essential to get as quickly as possible into the core of a significant problem, perhaps one of a number of problems that the patient presents. It is the entrance into and the establishment of the patient's core problem that I call the central issue; the central issue is very different from the more usual concept of focus of treatment.

The first step in arriving at the central issue is to engage in a way of listening that we may find too unfamiliar. As we take a history we listen attentively to the facts of the case; as the patient relates painful events we discover how the patient reacted to and felt about each of them. But there is a further dimension to listening. As the patient relates many painful incidents we must ask ourselves this question: *How must this person have felt about himself or herself as he or she was experiencing, living, and enduring the particular incident?* It is not a question that the patient can answer at the time since the complaints or symptoms have served to defend against awareness. Rather it is for the therapist silently to ask and to answer the question, for this question and the answer to it measure the therapist's empathic capacity. It is in the answers to this question, repeated many times, that the therapist will arrive at the central issue. What I look for in the patient's history are recurrent painful events, especially those that, although they may be very different, are experienced and reacted to symbolically as if they were the same. I am looking for the patient's chronic and presently endured pain; this is pain that the patient feels he or she has always had, has now, and expects to have in the future. In the absence of change there is no sense of past, present, or future in the patient's rigidly held conceptions of the self; the patient holds the parallel conviction that nothing about the self can change.

The patient's chronic and presently endured pain can be further defined as being a privately held, affective statement by the patient about how he or she feels and has always felt about himself or herself. The central issue is linked with the patient's time line or history and the various affects associated with it. This affective statement about the self to the self has never been revealed to others and has been allowed to enter consciousness only in fleeting moments, when it has been promptly warded off by automatic adaptive, coping devices. A simplified but common example is the person who has a profound need for acceptance to verify her own worth but who repeatedly finds rejection and automatically responds with a smile, which effectively keeps the pain out of sight. Although the chronic pain, the negative feeling about the self, is obscured defensively, it remains preconscious and when posed to the patient is experienced as a clarification and not as an interpretation of an unconscious construct never before in consciousness.

The recurrent painful events that feed the sense of a chronic and presently endured pain are also the affective component of the patient's belief that he or she has been victimized. It is difficult to discern any neurotic or emotional conflict in which the patient does not feel unjustly victimized. As children all of us were "victims" inasmuch as all experienced helplessness in the face of parental demands ranging from mild to abusive. The childhood victimization tends to become perpetuated as a guiding fiction in the life of the adult. That is to say, the adult continues to find and to respond to certain events in the same affective way he or she experienced and reacted to them as a child. What was once real in the life of the child continues into adult life as a fiction about the self. The misrepresentation of the self is enhanced by the addition of unconscious fantasies surrounding the painful events from early childhood and from adolescence. A child may feel that he or she is bad when faced with the question why parents no longer live together. The adolescent in the same situation may not only feel that he or she is bad but may also suffer "bad" sexual fantasies about one parent or the other.

A clinical vignette will illustrate the selection of the central issue. A man in his late forties complains of depression, feeling blocked in his work, and being preoccupied with uncertainty about his future. He is fully aware that he has been successful in his work and equally aware that his work has been recognized by others whose opinions he has valued. Recently he was expecting an appointment to a position offering even greater recognition, but he failed to win it. His history revealed that he was the son of successful and manipulative parents who had impressed him with the need to carry himself in appearance, style, and behavior as though he were not of the immigrant group from which his parents had come. He yielded to the demands, always successfully until the recent failure. Many additional details in the history made clear that as long as he could remember he had carried within him the profound sense of being a phony; at every step of his career he suffered anxiety, which he never understood, in the form of constant terror that he would be found out. The symptoms that brought him for help served to conceal and defend against the awareness and conviction about himself as a phony. He had never pondered or spoken about the sense of being a phony. Rather, there had been only flashes of awareness with immediate defense to remove the discomfort. As he recounted the many painful events of his life and as I asked myself how he must have felt about himself as he endured each particular event, it became possible to tell him that I recognized the nature of his problem and could express it in terms of his negative image of the self, an image he had carried all his years, carries now, and will carry into the expectable future, along with a sense of despair about ever being able to change the image.

All patients have a conscious and unconscious wish for redress of their grievances. It is conscious in that the patient wishes for appropriate recognition of his or her need in his or her own world. The person's contemporaries have no way of recognizing that need since they are regularly confronted with the person's adaptive devices, which effectively disguise the pain. Unconsciously the patient wishes for reunion with early important persons because the patient believes that those who are held directly responsible for the pain would be the most desirable healers. In this connection the time limit of TLP with its induction of magical expectations facilitates hope that reunion with the original figures will be effected.

Because recurrent painful events and responses are what is significant in this context, it follows that not everything a patient may tell us is important. Time is often wasted in brief psychotherapy listening to circumstances or events that do not have an existence over time; that is, there is no affective connecting link from event to event. Therapists are familiar with the rigid obsessional patient who may wander through a whole session of unrelated minutiae. In TLP the therapist's attention is directed throughout the twelve sessions to information that is directly or indirectly related to the central issue. Information felt to be unrelated to it should be understood as resistance to further progress. The most fruitful approach to removing the obstacle is to turn it aside by interrupting (many therapists hesitate to interrupt a patient) and suggesting that the patient go back to some specific item from earlier in the session or from the previous week. There are times when an unusually enlightening and difficult session may be followed in the next meeting by the patient's apparent need to take a breather and speak of unimportant details. There will be no objection by the patient if the therapist appreciates the need, allows it for some ten or fifteen minutes, and then helps the patient to resume the important work.

The statement of the central issue in terms of the chronic pain arising out of the negative self-image reverberates from the deepest levels of the unconscious, through the layers of ego defense, and into the patient's conscious experience of self. It spans the patient's experience of time from the remote past through the immediate present into the expectable future. It speaks to the exquisite poignancy with which each person privately endures his or her being.

Components of the Central Issue

The central issue includes time, affects, and the negative image of the self. A statement is made at the very beginning of treatment that links a profound notion about the self to factors of time (as duration) and intense affect. The ability to tag traumatic events as occurring at a particular moment is less important than the fact that each patient remarks on the "always"—that he has always felt that way about himself. Powerful traumata deeply influence unconscious guilt or narcissistic equilibria or both. They affect relationships back to the primary internal objects, the parents. Since the feelings have their origin in childhood, when the earliest introjections occur, objective time is obliterated as far as the affective experience is concerned, and the felt myth about the self is experienced as always having been there.

The affective result of trauma blurs a person's perception of time, which in turn increases negative affect, which increases the sense of hopelessness. Our patients speak therefore of an impossible past, an unhappy present, and a forbidding future in which the pain of the past and present must be continued. It is the inclusion of these factors that makes the central issue so effective. The formulation is invariably experienced as a powerful empathic statement in which the therapist is experienced as standing both within and alongside the patient. The usefulness of the central issue is further enhanced by the fact that it never includes conflict with important others in the life of the patient. These will emerge soon enough in a setting of trust and positive transference as these are encouraged and stimulated by the central issue.

Since the awareness of this kind of central issue is warded off by the automatic adaptive devices of the patient, it follows that the complaints brought by the patient as the reasons for seeking help will never include the central issue. Rather, we hear the familiar ones—anxiety, depression, symptoms that substitute for depression, difficulties with others, and the like. Conversely, the patient's complaints will never be the central issue in TLP.

Consider the following case. A woman in her late forties consulted with me about her rebellious teenage daughter, who, she said, was driving her crazy. This might appear to be an instance that called for counseling the patient about alternative ways of managing a teenager. Never assuming anything without first taking a careful history, I soon learned that this woman was in fact caring and sensitively attuned to the needs of her daughter and that she had tried a variety of acceptable means to bring reason into their relationship. Her history further revealed that at the ages of three and four the patient, in response to her mother's aspirations, had performed publicly on the stage. She recalled being directed in one scene to enter a frightening dungeon. She was terrified but did it and never forgot the terror. Later she was pressed into ballet and music, always submitting to her mother's ambitions, which also included superior school performance. This remained the story of her developmental years, including the college years, during which she lived at home. She escaped only when she married and moved to another city.

I have highlighted some of the recurrent painful events early in her life; there were many more later. In all of these experiences her automatic response had been obedience. The central issue that was formulated and proposed to be our work for the twelve sessions was as follows: "You are a woman of recognized ability and talent but what troubles you now and always has is your readiness to feel controlled and helpless." The statement elicited an immediate affirmative response; the work of therapy was to learn with her what had happened in the course of her life to lead her to feel this way about herself. We concluded that the rebellious daughter had exercised control over her as only a teenager can, a circumstance that rekindled her own experience of helplessness and consequently distorted her relationship with the girl. Once the mother was relieved of the myth that she was still readily made to feel helpless, she and her daughter became better able to get along with each other.

The varieties of chronic pain out of which arise negative feelings about the self are limited by the finite range of feelings available to all human beings. The limited range may be summarized as glad, sad, mad, frightened, or guilty:

Glad: loving, happy, contented, euphoric, peaceful, feeling wanted

Sad: unhappy, discontented, depressed, feeling unwanted

Mad: irritated, annoyed, irked, angry, raging, furious, feeling like a bad person

Frightened: anxious, nervous, afraid, feeling helpless

Guilty: troubled, uneasy, ashamed, feeling humiliated

Any other feeling is derivative of or within the range of these five. Because the feelings are universal, a negative statement about the self can be identified in everyone regardless of social class, education, cultural background, or economic status, and when identified reinforces the patient's motivation for help. Each life story is unique in the kinds of people involved and in the events that have transpired but each is the same insofar as one or another of the feelings has been experienced by all. There is no person or group who possesses some unique, never previously recorded feeling. Cultural differences may make the expression of complaints different—for example, one person may wail and shriek with minimal pain, another may be spartan; one person may refer all complaints to the body, another to various hexes or spirits—but the painful feelings disguised by the complaints are the ones we all share.

The central issue directly links the past, present, and future that constitute the patient's time line with the affects that accompany memories, regressions, fantasies, developmental arrests, and spurts. All of these emerge as the unspoken, painful, negative self-image. A person evaluates

29

ongoing lived time in accord with his or her assessment of adequacy; the affective assessment of the self links present circumstances with future outcomes in light of past outcomes in similar (real or symbolic) situations.

Consider another case. A woman in her thirties was depressed, anxious, and sleeping poorly. She had been in psychotherapy for ten years and had developed an intense erotic transference which almost assumed the character of a delusion. When at one point she learned that her therapist had separated from his wife she was certain that he would reach out to her; when he divorced she felt that at last her chance had come. Yet he had never made overt physical moves or suggestions to her. Further, since she had terminated treatment herself some six months earlier she had tried to effect relationships with other men and found herself choosing the wrong kind of person and being frightened by any overtures. Her history disclosed that early on she had been in sharp competition with an older sister for the affection of their father and felt she had succeeded until adolescence, when her father seemed to withdraw from her completely. She recalled being admired by a highly desirable high school classmate and feeling that something must be wrong with the boy because he admired her. She told of other experiences with men who seemed interested in her and then withdrew without warning. The central issue proposed to her was this: "You are a woman who is successful in your work and you also have a number of creative interests. Nevertheless you are troubled now and always have been troubled with the deep sense that there is something about you that makes you unworthy."

The therapeutic process that followed is familiar to anyone practiced in psychoanalytic psychotherapy—it is similar in content but very different in process. In TLP the process is so accelerated, the dynamic events so telescoped that a major task for the therapist is to keep up, to understand and be prepared to respond to the flow of past and present events within the purview of the central issue. Positive and negative transference, resistance, countertransference, and the ready and evident appearance of all the ego defenses occur as in any psychotherapy. In this particular case, our work around the central issue served to undo the erotic transference and lead her to seek acceptable men. She had been struggling all her life with the feeling of her unworthiness; she had employed various means to cope with it, but the unrelenting pain continued despite her best efforts. She had fought the good fight for her father's attention and admiration and to the degree that she felt she had been successful in competition with her sister, she had felt herself to be worthy. When her father withdrew from her in her adolescence she was correct in her perception but could understand it only in terms of her lack of worth. It never occurred to her, for example, that his withdrawal might have had to do his own discomfort at being confronted by her blooming womanhood.

A degree of helplessness is the lot of every child insofar as control by adults is inevitable. The pain of separation, with its accompanying feeling of abandonment, is also inevitable because even in the best of circumstances separation is never achieved without pain. Multiple repetitions of separation throughout life are simply a given for everyone. Each separation means a loss, giving up something. Unconsciously separation means giving up nurturance in all its meanings and has ambivalence as a consequence. Each separation brings into the preconscious the sense of leaving and of being left. At the conscious level each separation is experienced in the person's accustomed automatic adaptive mode. Depending on the nature and meaning of the particular person or circumstance the conscious experience may range from ego syntonic sadness to total denial of the separation's significance to counterphobic behavior to overt depression to degrees of psychological disintegration. Further, with each separation and its accompanying sense of loss there is always the possibility of another decrement in the image of the self—of feeling more helpless, more controlled, more unworthy, more unlovable, more inferior, more undeserving, or the like.

Summary

The messages in the central issue are quite clear. First, and very important, there is recognition of the patient's efforts to master the chronic pain. Second, the therapist's statement reveals awareness of how the patient feels and has always felt about the self despite his or her best coping efforts. In each instance the work of treatment confines itself to learning what events in the life of the patient have led to this kind of conclusion about the self. It is well to note that the central issue as formulated and presented to the patient becomes the paradigm of the transference to follow. Thus, it is to be expected in the termination phase of treatment that the man who feels unwanted, even irrelevant, will feel that treatment comes to an end because the therapist, too, does not want him around. Or the woman who feels stupid and a phony is certain that the therapist finds her so and is pleased to send her away. Or another patient comes to feel that the therapist finds him to be second-rate and unacceptable.

Note again that the central issue includes time, affects, and the negative image of the self; it is formulated by the therapist after having gained sufficient information in the evaluation. It is then presented to the patient as the therapist's view of the problem that brought the patient for help.

The next step is to gain the patient's reaction to the central issue. In my experience, instances in which patients have rejected the statement of the central issue are very rare. An occasional patient has remarked that the stated problem was not why he or she came for help. I ask if there is something more important to examine about himself or herself. The answer has always been no. Some patients respond with such enthusiasm that I am signaled to watch for an adaptive mode; the patient may try too hard to please. Such a mode is significant in the course of treatment. The patient may need to please so that his or her desirability may be confirmed through the therapist's agreeing to continue treatment indefinitely. There are some patients who hesitantly accept the central issue and express doubt about it but are willing to consider it. Occasionally patients will ask how I found out about them so soon. In any case, each patient is given the opportunity to object and to reject or to accept the formulation.

The question may be asked whether the formulation of the central issue poses difficulties for the learner. I believe that it is fair to say that anyone who chooses to be a psychiatrist or clinical social worker or clinical psychologist possesses a long-cultivated, even if out of consciousness, empathic capacity. I have remarked earlier that the formulation of the central issue is a measure of that capacity. For some therapists the ability to appreciate how this or that patient has always felt about the self comes readily and may need only the confidence that comes with experience. Others are not so ready to allow themselves to feel what the patient feels without becoming lost in identification with the patient. To meet that problem I have used group formulation of the central issue followed by weekly group supervision in the instance of one patient. It is essential that the group be experienced in long-term psychotherapy and enjoy mutual relationships that will allow for constructive supervisory sessions. In group formulation, one member volunteers to present a new case and the group then works together to formulate out of the data presented the central issue. Slowly there emerges out of the contributions of the members a growing consensus and then agreement on the final formulation as each ponders how the patient must feel about the self in relation to the information available.

It may be helpful to have further illustrations of the central issue as derived from the patient's history.

- To a thirty-six-year-old member of a minority who found himself in a conflictual situation in his field of work and became physically sick followed by depression: "You are a man of ability in your particular field and have done very well in it. Yet you feel and have always felt that there is something about you that makes you feel that you are unwanted, even irrelevant."

- To a forty-two-year-old woman who suffered an acute disorganizing experience which led her to consider divorce: "You have tried hard all your life to be and to do the acceptable things. What hurts you now and always has is the feeling that you are stupid and a phony."
- To a twenty-two-year-old man, a graduate student struggling with the question of staying in or leaving school: "You are a man of high intelligence and you know it. You also know that you can succeed in the work you have begun. However, what bugs you now and always has is the feeling that you are second-rate, unacceptable."
- To a thirty-five-year-old professional man with an acute phobia: "You are a big man [physically and in his field of work] who has achieved successfully and yet when you are alone you feel helpless."

A brief consideration of the evaluative interviews out of which the central issue is formulated is in order. A proper evaluation depends on the experience and skill of the interviewer in promoting the willingness of the patient to speak freely about him or herself. Generally, a one-hour history-taking interview should suffice to warrant a tentative formulation by the therapist of the central issue. A second interview is conducted to clarify or to obtain details about aspects of the patient's history to illuminate still further the central issue. Most often during the third meeting between patient and therapist the therapist offers the central issue as his or her definitive view of the patient's problem. A third preliminary interview may be necessary since some life histories are much more complicated than others. I have found that if a central issue remains elusive after three or four interviews, a severe kind of pathology may be present that in itself warrants as prolonged an evaluation as necessary to establish a clear diagnosis. The claim that evaluative interviews are already part of the treatment process is true to the extent that patient and therapist are sizing each other up and that for the patient the first meeting may well be the ending as well as the beginning of a relationship. Because the central issue as set forth here is so different from what the patient expected to be the therapist's diagnosis and because the complaints that bring the patient for help are never the central issue, the designated first of the twelve sessions to be offered the patient is the beginning of a novel experience for the patient.

Once the patient has accepted the central issue, the next step is for the therapist to inform the patient of the treatment schedule, the duration of each session, and the date of the final, twelfth session. I have found it most useful to see each patient once each week for forty-five or fifty minutes rather than more often, on the grounds that each session becomes quite stressful for the patient as much painful, affect-laden material pours out. The patient can use the weekly interval to react and to respond alone before the next meeting. Invariably there is much for the patient to digest.

Upon being told of the schedule, the patient is asked to react and respond. The most common question is how I know that twelve meetings will be enough to make progress on the particular issue. I regard this question as real and as an unconscious resistance to the idea of a known date of separation and loss. My usual response is to turn the question back by asking what makes the patient feel that twelve sessions will not be enough. The patient realizes that he or she truly does not know and will have to await the turn of events. Agreement to the twelve sessions follows. There are also unconscious reasons for the acceptance of the treatment proposal. These have to do both with magical expectations of change over a short period of time and with the unconscious expectation of repair and reunion and the end of loss.

Phases of Treatment

Most cases proceed in a predictable pattern. TLP is unique in that the patient knows exactly when treatment has begun, the precise midpoint of treatment, and the end date of treatment. These become guideposts for the therapist, although they are farther from the patient's awareness. Almost without exception, patients tend to suppress and often repress the end date. As a result they may be consciously unaware, for example, of arriving at the midpoint of treatment at session six. Unconsciously, however, many patients respond to the midpoint with certain behaviors. The same applies as the end of treatment approaches and the patient seems oblivious to the end at hand.

The statement of the central issue invariably stimulates an outpouring of information. Frequently the information consists of associations that corroborate the central issue. During the first three or four sessions the patient brings forth a mass of information about himself or herself, the family, and others, with recollections of painful events that the patient may not have thought about consciously for many years. With the flood of information there is also palpable evidence of the patient's positive transference.

As the sixth session comes or is passed patients often say nothing about the time left. Instead, what was a positive attitude may become ambivalent. Nothing magical has occurred and the patient is still the same person. There may be complaints that a symptom has become worse or that nothing has changed in any way even though the patient may have spoken gladly about feeling better by the fourth or fifth session. The ambivalence is unconsciously determined by the shadow of the impending separation. The ambivalence that marked earlier separations arises once more within the transference. The patient may remark with evident annoyance that everything that could be said has already been said and that there's nowhere to go. Rather than reacting with anxiety based on uncertainty, the therapist recognizes the meaning of the patient's behavior and encourages further elaboration of the patient's ambivalence so that significant associations to many other separations and the feelings that were experienced are seen as importantly connected with the central issue.

If by the ninth or tenth session the patient has made no reference, direct or indirect, to the approaching end of treatment, the therapist must bring up the subject. One simple method is to ask the patient if he or she knows how many meetings are left. In any case, the end of treatment must be made the subject of discussion for the last three (or four, if the patient brings it up) sessions. The termination phase is invariably painful for the patient and often for the therapist as well.

The central issue is experienced in vivo within the transference and must be resolved as much as possible. I have remarked earlier that there are reasons for the patient's ready acceptance of the limit of twelve sessions. When patients are offered only twelve sessions they may conclude that perhaps they are not doing as poorly as they had thought. As I have mentioned, they unconsciously expect some kind of magical cure. Within the transference the brief treatment means also that relief will come in relation to the important early significant sources of the pain. Further, at the beginning, three months of treatment seem to the patients to be forever. We may think about but not affectively comprehend what we will feel about an event three months hence. Also, the limited duration of treatment suggests that patients will not become tied to the therapist; their independence, however muted, will be preserved. This last factor is of special import to adolescent patients (including patients of college age) who are fearful of the challenge arising out of the conflict between their wish to be fully independent and their desire to remain dependent. The structure of TLP offers from the start a measured dependence with an assured end.

The termination phase is a crucial aspect of the process, as it is in any kind of psychotherapy. The major work of this phase lies in the interpretation of the transference in terms of the patient's feelings about the therapist. By this time, a great deal of evidence has been obtained confirming the patient's repetitive feelings about the therapist in the same terms as experienced with earlier significant persons. These feelings are also direct affirmations of the origin of the patient's negative self-regard. Interpretations are best made in the familiar triangular configuration—that is, in terms of the therapist, important people in the patient's present situation, and the origins of affects in relation to important persons in the patient's past. If we understand that the central issue is the consequence of a host of unconscious, preconscious, and conscious elements that eventuate in everyone a sense of what one is, it follows that the interpretations made are not about aggressive or libidinal needs and intentions but rather are about derivatives of these expressed in living, existential terms. For example, in any kind of brief treatment, for the therapist to recognize the patient's unconscious fantasy of castration and then to express it in those terms is nonsense. It is meaningless even for the sophisticated patient to speak in such a way. Genuine affective meaning is reflected when the same fantasy is conveyed to the patient through the central issue and therefore in terms of the patient's feeling unmanly or defective or lacking.

A satisfactory termination is one in which the patient leaves treatment feeling sad. Ambivalence, which previously had always led to feelings of anger or depression with concomitant self-derogation, has changed into awareness of positive feelings even in the face of separation and loss. Sadness in place of depression allows for separation without self-injury. The goal of TLP is explicit and single-minded in every case. It is to help patients diminish, to reduce as much as possible, the negative feelings about the self. Symptoms that patients may have brought among their complaints are addressed, if at all, in terms of the central issue. In most instances, the symptoms are not addressed at all and diminish or disappear as a byproduct of the process. Relief of symptoms is not the goal of treatment.

The Therapist and TLP

Inexperienced therapists may be immediately enthusiastic about doing TLP. The promise of relatively rapid therapeutic returns is enticing. But resistance to TLP among experienced therapists is common and must be understood.

First, most therapists gradually take on a therapeutic stance and process with which they become familiar and comfortable. To be asked to engage in a very different process immediately creates anxiety. Therapists who have established their competence to their own satisfaction may experience the new stance as a threat to their ability as well as to their adaptability.

Second, the time limit raises the hackles of some therapists. We therapists are used to having as much time with our patients as both deem necessary. It is not at all unusual for a patient's dependence to be fortified by the therapist's practice and by a need by both participants to maintain the dependence.

Third, the argument is often made that the duration of treatment should be negotiated by patient and therapist. In fact, not much surrounding psychotherapy is negotiated these days. Fees are now set at all outpatient departments with little or no leverage for the patient; therapists rarely set fees that are best for the patient. Nor do therapists set the dates and duration of treatment against their own best interest. A colleague once told me that TLP was "money-limited therapy." Perhaps objecting to the time limit can be seen as a rationalization to protect against an even greater resistance.

Setting a termination date at the start of treatment is very difficult for therapists since it is easier to work slowly toward an indeterminate end. Terminations are difficult for both patients and therapists since patients and therapists alike suffer the scars and sometimes the open wounds of separations and losses. To announce what seems like a goodbye at the start resonates in the same way in both patients and therapists. Patients' most ready defense is to suppress or repress the end date as if bargaining to feel better soon. Therapists' defense may be too great a readiness to find patients to be unsuitable for TLP.

Finally, there may arise the very interesting situation in which the central issue proposed to the patient as the work of therapy is a similar issue for the therapist. Surely few, if any, therapists of any persuasion do not live with some degree of negative self-image. In the best instances negative self-image has been modified in personal therapy. In a few others the therapist's negative feelings may not contaminate the therapeutic process. Certain safeguards can be taken to avoid interference from the therapist's problems. First, TLP is for experienced therapists. Second, a background of sound training and experience in the dynamics of the unconscious, transference, resistance, defense, and countertransference is essential, which means having sufficient exposure to and work with long-term psychotherapy to have learned to bear and to understand patients' anxiety without reacting against them. Finally, a most desirable addition to therapist's training would be personal psychotherapy—or, better, a personal psychoanalysis.

CASE EXAMPLE

A sample case presented in detail will show some aspects of the process from start to finish. The patient was a forty-two-year-old married woman whose family consisted of her husband, one son in high school, and another in the fifth grade. Total obsession with her older son's school grades brought her for help. She would follow every test that he took and would look into his book bag to see what he should be studying. She was aware of nagging him about schoolwork but could not stop herself. Unless he achieved a top grade in any test she could feel herself grow cold toward him, even physically cold. She dreamed about his grades and was adamant that he get into a prestigious college. She concluded that she was crazy and had better do something about it before her son had to apply to college.

She had been in therapy for about two years as a graduate student. It was "the thing to do," but she really went to find out if she was crazy. Years later she was treated briefly about a problem with her husband. She presented herself as a slender, attractive, neat, and articulate woman. She was physically well and slept well, but in her waking hours she was almost constantly tense and seemed desperate for help.

She was the only child of immigrant parents. Her father held a menial job and both parents could barely speak English, even after years in the United States. She stated that father was "irascible, primitive, always hollering." He had died some years before and the patient was proud that her interventions had resulted in an additional year of life for him. She recalled being embraced by him in his happiness when she was admitted to a competitive high school. Her mother was alive and resided in a distant city. The patient had never gotten along with her, feeling that her mother was snobbish, that she put on airs and felt that everyone she knew was a bad person. The parents continually fought and her father would tend to blame the patient for their battles. She wished her father were still alive because she had come to feel much wiser about him.

She had gone to a state university and then on to graduate school to prepare for a profession. At graduate school she felt her teachers to be poor; she failed in part and left with a master's degree. Three years later she decided to complete her studies and graduated at another university. Married about twenty years, she experienced her husband as more attached emotionally to the children than to her. She described her older son as healthy and a good kid despite her nagging. At one point he had said he hated both his parents and closed himself in his room for almost two days.

She impressed me as an obsessional woman with a need for perfection not realized within herself which she projected onto her son with the unspoken demand that he make her whole by being accomplished intellectually, socially, and in his chosen career. She could then borrow his status as her own and thereby become what she felt she never had been, was not, and never could be by herself. There were other details that clarified the central issue. For example, her graduate school teachers were not in reality poor. In fact, the small class was a select group drawn only from the best universities. It was in that class that she found herself asking, "What am I doing here?" After all, she had come from the family of an uneducated father with his menial work, a pathologically suspicious mother, and very cramped and unattractive living quarters. How must this very intelligent and alert young woman have felt about herself as she observed her father as a model, and how must she have felt about herself having a snobbish mother whose "superiority" was soon evident as craziness?

The central issue presented to her as our work in the twelve meetings was as follows: "You are a woman of ability and talent. You are aware that you have not capitalized professionally on your ability and talent because what troubles you now and always has is the feeling that you are unworthy, even defective." She agreed that this was so and yet was surprised that I had come up with this statement in the light of the problem that brought her to me. She could readily acknowledge the accuracy of the central issue but wondered whether working on this about herself could be of help to her son. I suggested that we would find out in the course of our work together.

She corroborated the central issue with a number of associations: how she had never had a room of her own, how she had had to be a parent to her parents since she would read and translate letters in English and make out checks and other forms for them. She always behaved well but would be struck with terror when her father glared at her in anger. Sometimes she thought of herself as a witch; sometimes she felt that her parents never understood her needs. I emphasized her feelings of victimization both in her past and then by her son. How much nicer her world could be if he just got good grades and thereby made her feel better about herself, even if only for the moment. Early in treatment she brought a picture of her with her parents taken when she was six or seven. She was surprised to find that they looked so nice as a family.

As we moved along in the treatment process, she referred to herself as "killer Sue" in recollection of incidents with her mother in which she felt responsible for various of her mother's illnesses, each of which led, in her mind, to the brink of death for her mother. She became aware of the fantasy that her anger could kill and the enormous guilt that followed, with its destructive effects on her image of herself. She saw that nagging her son carried with it clear tones of anger and was followed by guilt and self-denigration. Further along she spoke of the kiss of death when her first therapist said that she was intuitively gifted. She felt that people who wished to know her must have something wrong with them and that I was defective if I was interested in seeing her and in dealing respectfully with her. Positive transference was manifest very early not only in her wondering if I was defective for my interest in her but also in her early questioning whether she could continue to see me at least once a month when the twelve sessions ended. Driving to see me was "like a dream" in that she could hardly believe that I could accept her as not crazy. On the other hand she wanted me not to care too much for her because she thought I would throw her out if she got angry with me.

In the presence of a solid alliance and transference we could now move directly into the problem with her son. I was able to tell her that she made demands on him in order to repair her own sense of defectiveness but that her expectations could never be fulfilled outside of herself. She said that she had begun to feel less pressure to nag him. At the treatment midpoint, she felt like a "waif," an orphan, and that such thoughts made her tearful. She and her husband meshed well, she said: she gave and he didn't. She told of a recurrent dream in which she is in her parents' bedroom with them. Suddenly she goes out the window into the street. She is not hurt although the room is high above the ground. Actually, during her childhood she had long slept in the same room with her parents; although unconscious sexual aspects of such an arrangement are present in a young girl, I choose to interpret the dream in terms of the central issue. In those terms the dream revealed her feeling that no one cared about what happened to her. The interpretation was followed by a review of her feelings about herself as a little girl who found ways of dealing with her abusive parents by being good but who could not escape her private feelings as one who was bad, a witch, a killer, and crazy.

The shadow of termination was on her mind as she told me that she was almost late for her appointment, although, she added, she was never late for anything. She had met with an old schoolmate who, to the patient's chagrin, was well established professionally and whose son was absolutely destined for Harvard. The patient felt jealous and angry. On her return home she quickly set upon her son with her demands. I remarked on how much the visit with an old friend had activated her own past with feelings about herself as primitive and unacceptable. Further into the end phase, she related a dream in which she is bleeding to death. She runs to her internist but he is not available and there is no one to help her. In her associations she revealed that the internist was a high school classmate. Again there emerged the feeling that there was never anyone around who would understand her needs. The desire to remain with me was implicit. She made another attempt at continuation by telling me that she was aware of a deep love for her mother but that the idea of closeness was frightening lest she also become crazy.

Her struggle to remain with me became explicit in a repeat of her dream of going out of the parents' bedroom window except that this time the house is mine. In another dream I am lying beside her and she feels I should not be doing that. As she had with her father, she felt that I did not wish to see her, that I would be glad to be rid of her because she was "intractable." It was easy for me to speak to her of her obvious affection for me, like that I had seen in her for her father, from whom she felt she had never gained validation for her womanhood or for her acceptability as a woman. I added that this perceived failure on her part had seriously interfered with her relations with men as well as contributed heavily to the sense of herself as unworthy and defective.

In the last, the twelfth session, she said that she felt that I liked her and she could accept that as well as the idea that she was not crazy. She finally knew that she expected her son to save her, and she felt ready to let him grow up and away. She felt better about herself and thought she might be ready to become much more active in her profession, even perhaps venturing to publish some of her work. She was sad about leaving me and cried. She asked again if she could call me, and I told her that she should give herself at least six months to digest the work we had done and to experiment further in making changes, that if she felt the need at that point she should feel free to call me.

One year later she asked to see me. She reported feeling so much better about herself that she could hardly believe it. For the first time she had gone away with her husband only and had thoroughly enjoyed it. Her son had done very well on the SATs and life felt very good. Before leaving she asked if she could see me the following April, when college acceptances would be announced. I said yes. At that visit she said she had hoped that her son would have chosen a university in the area; instead he had been waitlisted at several very good universities but had chosen one that was patently not up to the others, not very far from home. She knew very well what her choice would have been but was able to let him make his own and to feel comfortable about it.

One year later she called again. Her son was happy at college, active in sports but not very interested in getting good grades. She chose to see him

41

as a fine boy despite that. She was now enthusiastic about her increased professional activities, which were providing enormous satisfaction. With considerable pride she announced that she had submitted papers for publication and had already received approval on one of them. I spoke to our mutual appreciation of her wish for her son to do well in whatever he was engaged in but that now she no longer needed his performance as a means of gaining respect for herself. She could do that on her own.

EMPIRICAL SUPPORT

The effectiveness of TLP is known to me and to my colleagues through our experience and through the follow-up interviews that we have done. The preset limit of twelve sessions has become increasingly popular, although the theory and technique of TLP have not been adopted. Unfortunately, there have been no large-scale, carefully organized research projects on the efficacy of TLP. A very large project proposed by the psychology department of a major American university was denied federal funds. At the time TLP may have been regarded as too radical. There is an ongoing, carefully structured research project in TLP being done in Jerusalem. Haim Dasberg and Gaby Shefler of the Ezrat Nashim Mental Health Community Center reported in a presentation (1989): "Our results suggested that Mann's TLP has clear positive outcomes. The outcomes are consistent with the therapy rationale. That is, the changes occur in self esteem, social functioning and target symptoms."

CONCLUSION

TLP provides a model of psychoanalytically based psychotherapy of brief duration that is teachable. The structure is clearly outlined; with some experience the process becomes almost predictably visible. TLP does not require a charismatic therapist; rather it requires being part of or a graduate of a good general training program in psychoanalytic psychotherapy. It requires also a willingness to step out of the traditional mode and a readiness to engage patients actively within the framework of a reasoned approach. It is not a short-term psychoanalysis, but it touches very quickly on what is most important to all people: the self-description that makes our existence either quite bearable or ridden with pain. With its specific time limit and the concept of the central issue, TLP brings to the forefront of the treatment process the major psychological plague all human beings suffer, namely the wish to be close, to be as one with another, to be intimate, the fulfillment of which demands learning how to tolerate separation and loss without undue damage to our feelings about the self.

References

Dasberg, H., & Shefler, G. (1989, June). *A randomized controlled outcome and follow-up study of James Mann's time limited psychotherapy in a Jerusalem community mental health center.* Paper presented at the meeting of the Society for Psychotherapy Research, Toronto.

Mann, J. (1973). *Time limited psychotherapy.* Cambridge, MA: Harvard University Press.

Mann, J., & Goldman, R. (1982). *A casebook in time limited psychotherapy.* New York: McGraw-Hill.

CHAPTER 3

Short-Term Anxiety-Provoking Psychotherapy

Geir Nielsen and Karin Barth

INTRODUCTION

Short-Term Anxiety-Provoking Psychotherapy (STAPP) is a focal, goal-oriented, psychodynamic psychotherapy. It was first developed by Peter Sifneos in the late 1950s and has been systematically presented in two of his books: *Short-Term Psychotherapy and Emotional Crisis* (1972) and *Short-Term Dynamic Psychotherapy: Evaluation and Technique* (1979, 1987).

Based on psychoanalytic principles, STAPP aims to resolve pathological psychic conflicts and help those suffering from them to learn new ways of being in their interpersonal relationships. The criteria for undergoing STAPP have been developed for more than three decades and tested extensively. Combined with systematically described technical principles of intervention, this makes STAPP one of the best defined approaches to brief dynamic psychotherapy hitherto presented. Although introduced long before the concept of manualized therapies (Luborsky, 1984) arrived on the psychotherapeutic scene, the principles of STAPP can easily be transformed into manualized forms (Svartberg, 1989).

STAPP is offered only to individuals who have considerable amounts of ego strength but, while facing new life situations and as a result of being unable to overcome their emotional sufferings, have developed circumscribed psychiatric symptoms or difficulties in their interpersonal relations (Sifneos, 1972).

The main features of the STAPP approach are brevity, emotional reeducation, problem solving, and limited goals. It is presupposed that the patient is able to cooperate in a therapeutic alliance, and that he or she is able to benefit from an essentially interpretive, insight-oriented technique. Therapy is conducted as weekly, face-to-face interviews. The number of interviews is not specified in advance, nor is there a termination date set. Typically, the number of sessions is tailored according to each individual's needs and treatment progress, although the total number of sessions ideally should not exceed twenty.

The outcome of STAPP is evaluated according to symptomatic, adaptational, and psychodynamic criteria. Positive outcome findings have been reported from several follow-up studies, with deep and enduring changes still observed many years after therapy had ended (Sifneos, 1987).

In this chapter we outline the main characteristics of STAPP, its historical background, criteria for selection of patients, the underlying theoretical assumptions, principles of technique, and some outcome findings.

Unlike the majority of approaches described in this handbook, STAPP is not here described by its developer. Therefore, in order to be as fair as possible to the essence of STAPP, we have chosen to stay as close as possible to Peter Sifneos's own formulations. This notwithstanding, some inaccuracies and distortions of the genuine STAPP approach may come through; any such errors should be considered entirely our responsibility.

ORIGINS AND DEVELOPMENT: A CLINICAL ANECDOTE

Sifneos (1972) has dated the beginning of STAPP to the year 1956, when he met a twenty-seven-year-old man, a student, who came to Massachusetts General Hospital in Boston requesting treatment for severe anxiety, mainly phobic symptoms, and a variety of somatic complaints. The symptoms, some of which the patient had suffered from since childhood, intensified and became acute shortly after the young man had decided to get married. The wedding day was already agreed upon, and would come three months later. However, barely the thought of being a center of attention during the wedding ceremony would make the patient extremely tense and uncomfortable. These feelings had rapidly generalized to other situations wherein he was exposed to enclosures of some sort or to crowds of people, such as riding public transportation or even in private cars. The patient's discomfort had become so intense that he had to walk to school.

His somatic complaints, for which no organic basis had been found, included stomach pains, trembling sensations, transient impotence, breathing difficulties, perspiration attacks, and occasional diarrhea.

The patient saw his symptoms as interfering severely with his wedding plans, and he arrived at Massachusetts General Hospital with the hope of finding someone who could help him get rid of his symptoms within the time that remained before the wedding.

The psychiatric admission team concluded that it was unrealistic to attain the patient's goals within the time available. One of the evaluating psychiatrists stipulated a treatment length of at least three years.

Stopping the narrative here for a moment, we have to remember that the dominating attitude among psychoanalytically oriented therapists at that time was that long-term psychotherapy was the treatment of choice for all patients suffering from neurotic difficulties. As Bruce Sloane and Fred Staples ironically comment, "For if little psychotherapy was good, more was better, and most was best" (1979, pp. 1–2). It was also strongly believed that attempts at deeper changes should be avoided and that interpretations should be kept at a relatively superficial level—that is, avoiding dreams, transference, and childhood origins of neurosis (Malan, 1963).

Hence, when Sifneos, contrary to the conclusion reached by the admission team, decided to accept the patient for short-term psychotherapy, he challenged the clinical wisdom of the day. The actual therapy was offered on a once-a-week basis, with the first session scheduled exactly seven weeks before the patient was going to marry.

Sifneos's psychodynamic formulation of his patient's difficulties pointed to unresolved oedipal conflicts. Choosing these as the targets for therapeutic exploration, active confrontations, and early transference interpretations (within the context of a rapidly established working alliance), Sifneos was able to treat his patient successfully in six interviews before the wedding. During the course of this short treatment period, it was possible to have a dynamically rich therapy. The patient gained a substantial amount of insight into the relationship between his current symptoms and his sexual wishes for his mother during childhood, the feelings caused by his father's death (when he was four), and later wishes for his stepfather's death.

By the end of therapy, the symptoms had diminished significantly. Although he felt a little apprehensive, all went according to schedule at his wedding. He became once again able to use public transportation and had overcome most of his somatic complaints. In a follow-up interview several years later, he was judged clinically as completely recovered from his neurotic problems and exhibited no symptoms.

Encouraged by the remarkable results obtained with this patient, Sifneos decided to identify the curative mechanisms and to explore the limits of this kind of therapy. In his retrospective analysis of the case he came to the conclusion that a main change factor had been his helping the young man to face unpleasant emotional conflicts underlying his symptoms. Thus, therapy had certainly been more anxiety provoking than anxiety suppressing. Under the special conditions of having a patient highly motivated for self-understanding, a rapidly established working alliance, and the transference, Sifneos had been able to use anxiety-provoking questions and confrontations to induce a (benign) emotional crisis in his patient. The crisis in turn mobilized the man's problem-solving capacities and contributed to a new defense mechanism configuration. Following this focal dynamic change, the patient was able to abandon his phobias as well as his physical symptoms.

Having completed this first successful case, Sifneos and his co-workers eagerly sought patients with problems amenable to the same kind of anxiety-provoking technique. Over a period of four years they treated fifty new patients, many of whom were seen in follow-up interviews one to two years after therapy had ended. Systematic follow-up evaluations of twenty-one patients, using specified criteria for improvement and adequate research methodology, indicated that all had benefited considerably from their treatment.

Since then, Sifneos has been continually attempting to further develop, evaluate, and refine his treatment model. Most of his work has been done at the Beth Israel Hospital in Boston, with which Sifneos has been associated since 1968. The STAPP model has also been clinically tested and researched in several other settings throughout North America and Western Europe (Sifneos, 1987). Thus, current applications of the model can be said to rest on a firm clinical base.

SELECTION OF PATIENTS

The successful application of STAPP requires a careful preselection of patients. Therefore, all prospective candidates should undergo a thorough clinical evaluation, particularly with regard to ego functioning and motivation for change.

Sifneos (1987) has recently summarized the most common types of presenting complaints of patients accepted for STAPP: anxiety, or anxiety in conjunction with other symptoms (for example, physical symptoms without an organic basis), phobias with obsessive thoughts, grief reactions, mild depression, and interpersonal difficulties.

Looking closer at the list, we see that the items are all complaints frequently encountered in typical neurotic patients. This underscores the fact that STAPP is a therapy that should be offered only to patients within the neurotic range of the psychiatric spectrum. Excluded from the beginning are patients with psychotic symptoms, major affective disorders, alcoholism or heavy drug abuse, suicidal tendencies and acting out, and severe (pregenital) character pathology (such as severe schizoid, borderline, or narcissistic personality disorders).

However, no patient should be selected for STAPP (or probably for any form of brief dynamic psychotherapy) on the basis of a presenting complaint or psychiatric diagnosis only. These are rough criteria that can serve no more than preliminary screening purposes. The final selection has to be made on the basis of identifiable ego resources and specified personality assets. For a good STAPP patient, this would mean that the evaluating clinician will give an affirmative answer to the following main questions:

1. Can the patient circumscribe his or her chief complaint or assign top priority to one out of several difficulties?
2. Did the patient have at least one meaningful relationship with another person during his or her childhood?
3. Can the patient interact flexibly with the evaluator, that is, experience and freely express feelings during the interview?
4. Does the patient give evidence of psychological sophistication?
5. Does the patient show adequate motivation for change and not only for symptom relief?

Lack of space allows us to give only a rough operationalization of the criteria. The interested reader should therefore consult the more thorough definitions available in Sifneos's recent works (such as Sifneos, 1987). However, for the present readers to be able to grasp the criteria and their theoretical rationale, a few elaborating comments have to be made.

All five questions should be answered from clinical information obtained through the evaluation interview, and the answers should be yes or no. Of course, there are cases for which neither alternative seems to fit very well. However, the evaluator should still stick to the dichotomized (forced-choice) response format.

For question 1 to be answered in the affirmative, the patient must, first, be able to specify a chief symptom or difficulty and, second, assign that symptom priority over a period of time. If the patient voices more than one complaint, the evaluator should ask which one problem he or she wants to solve. A patient who is experiencing a variety of difficulties obviously faces a dilemma. Solving this dilemma, that is, being able to choose, is indicative of ego strength. It is evidence of the patient's being able to face the reality that not all difficulties can be solved in a limited period of time. Thus, this criterion also indicates tolerance for frustration and demonstrates the ego's capacity for delay. All things considered, this criterion is one of the quickest ways to differentiate patients who will do well with this sort of therapy from those who will require longer-term assistance (Flegenheimer, 1982).

Identifying a chief complaint is only part of the game. It is also implied in this criterion that the complaint can be meaningfully understood as a manifestation of an underlying circumscribed problem. *Complaint* denotes the patient's subjective distress and discomfort. A circumscribed *problem* is formulated by the evaluator, based on the patient's life history; it is a psychodynamic hypothesis that can explain the patient's main difficulty on the basis of underlying psychological conflicts. These conflicts ("specific internal predispositions," or SIP), of which the patient is at most vaguely aware, must be clarified, since they will become the basis of the therapeutic focus—the main targets of the therapist's technical maneuvers (Sifneos, 1979). In a "pure" STAPP the ideal focus is on an underlying problem most often rooted in oedipal/triangular conflicts. Patients with core problems at a preoedipal level are not considered appropriate candidates for STAPP.

A meaningful relationship, as elicited in question 2, is a relationship described in terms of trust, mutuality, and sharing. For a yes score on this question, the patient must be able to recall and to give examples from childhood of personally meaningful and stable give-and-take interactions with a key person. Vague, general statements of friendships, positive attention, or admiration should never pass as sufficient evidence. On the other hand, examples of the patient's having been willing to sacrifice for the benefit of someone else, that is, examples of altruism, should be considered particularly good measures.

Patients who fail according to the second criterion are usually seen as socially and emotionally immature individuals, often suffering from bad object representations. Most of them have little ability to withstand anxiety, and they often seek therapy primarily as a source of emotional gratification.

The third criterion is partly related to the second, as they both address the patient's ability to relate to and interact with others. Needless to say, for this criterion to be of any value, it is presupposed that the evaluator possesses sufficient relational capacity and interpersonal skills. A patient who is unable to express feelings such as fear, sadness, or anger during the interview in most cases suffers from strong emotional blockades that preclude being helped by a strongly transference utilizing and interpretive short-term therapy like STAPP.

Not only must the patient demonstrate a capacity for emotional expressiveness; he or she must also be able to show some emotional flexibility—being able to express different kinds of feelings as the topics and the nature of the interaction change. The patient's emotional interaction with the evaluator often predicts later transference patterns.

Psychological sophistication (question 4) is a somewhat difficult item to assess, and its definition has undergone many changes over the years. Originally, this criterion was a simple equivalent to above average intelligence. Efforts were made to assess sophistication not by psychological tests but by obtaining evidence of superior academic achievement or work performance (Sifneos, 1969). It soon turned out, however, that the original construct was too cognitive a conception of intelligent adaptation. In our own work, we therefore prefer the term *problem-solving capacity* (Barth, Nielsen, Havik, et al., 1988).

As this criterion is now used, it also requires that the patient give some evidence of psychological mindedness, being open to understanding phenomena in psychological terms and willing to investigate the possibility that his or her symptoms may be related to intrapsychic conditions. A certain readiness for such understanding is, of course, necessary when the therapy purports to provide insight in a short period of time. Most often excluded by this criterion are patients who habitually externalize their problems.

The final criterion, as represented by question 5 (motivation for change), was originally formulated as motivation for psychotherapy. As data accumulated, it became more and more clear, however, that the critical factor was not motivation for psychotherapy as such, but rather an intent, or willingness, on the part of the patient to make concentrated efforts toward fundamental psychological change. Thus, motivation for change should not be confused with simple wishes for symptom relief.

Since motivation for change is probably the single most important selection criterion, it is divided into seven subcategories by which motivation is assessed:

1. Can the patient recognize that the symptoms are psychological in origin?
2. Is the patient honest in reporting about himself or herself?
3. Is the patient willing to participate actively in the evaluation?

4. Does the patient demonstrate interest in and curiosity about himself or herself?

5. Does the patient show openness to new ideas introduced by the evaluator?

6. Are the patient's expectations of the results of the treatment realistic?

7. Is the patient willing to make reasonable and tangible sacrifices (such as paying a reasonable fee and seeing the therapist at a mutually convenient time)?

All these subquestions refer to what may be observed in the interview situation, and again the scores are simply yes or no. To score a positive answer to the main question 5, at least five of the subcriteria must have been fulfilled.

Clinical judgment, by definition, always implies some uncertainty, and the assessment of selection criteria is both difficult and impressionistic. This notwithstanding, there is growing evidence from controlled studies that experienced clinicians achieve acceptable interscorer reliability and agreement with the selection criteria for STAPP (Heiberg, 1976–1977; Husby, 1983; Barth, Nielsen, Havik, et al., 1988). Yet since none of the reliability coefficients is perfect (in the Bergen studies varying between $r = .88$ and $r = .68$), it must be realized that important as these criteria may be, "they should not be looked upon too rigidly but used only as guidelines" (Sifneos, 1969, p. 293).

GOALS OF TREATMENT

Virtually all brief therapies stress the need to select among issues and to concentrate upon a chief one (Small, 1979). Focalization, which David Malan defines as "the ability of therapist and patient together to find a focus quickly which is acceptable to both of them" (1963, p. 213), is therefore considered a cardinal feature of psychotherapies that are short by design.

With a limited amount of time, it is unproductive to have the therapeutic issues float freely, changing from session to session, all according to the patient's momentary preoccupations. Although free associating can be a very useful approach in long-term treatment, in short-term cases it hinders optimal progress.

However, focalization as such does not guarantee that the therapy will turn out successfully. It is equally important that one select an *appropriate* focus. Although some authors (for example, Wolberg, 1965) suggest that specific symptoms can be identified as targets for concentrated therapeutic intervention, most dynamically oriented therapists question the value of that approach.

In STAPP, the focus should always be a psychodynamic one. Furthermore, experienced therapists agree that the focuses that respond best to STAPP are unresolved oedipal conflicts; but loss, separation issues, and grief may also be acceptable ones. The prototype STAPP candidate is a patient struggling with conflicts of a triangular, more than dyadic, nature.

For the therapist, identifying a focus implies two somewhat different tasks. First, the therapist must arrive at a psychodynamic formulation that crystallizes the specific conflicts to be resolved. Second, the therapist must be able to translate these theoretically based formulations into words that the patient will understand and accept as a meaningful focus for collaborative work. To proceed with other anxiety-provoking strategies before a mutually agreed upon focus has been established diminishes the probability of success drastically. Or, put in a more positive way: "Mutual agreement about the focus constitutes the therapeutic contract, which establishes limits to therapeutic work and lays the foundation for the therapeutic alliance. In addition, the contract serves the purpose of making the patient take an active responsibility in treatment" (Bauer & Kobos, 1987, p. 58).

In focalization, STAPP differs from most other forms of short-term dynamic therapies, including the Intensive Brief Psychotherapy of Malan (1963) and the Intensive Short-Term Dynamic Psychotherapy developed by Habib Davanloo (1986). While Malan and Davanloo introduce the focus gradually through interpretation, the STAPP therapist makes it part of the therapeutic contract by specific evaluation procedures in the first session. Through this highly anxiety-provoking maneuver the emotional tone is set from the first hour of treatment. In several other respects, the models of Sifneos, Malan, and Davanloo share important features.

It is clearly an exaggeration for John Garske and Andrew Molteni (1985) to write that prospective STAPP candidates are "forced" to admit and agree that their symptoms are really manifestations of more central processes. But it is considered an absolute requirement for the patient at least to indicate a willingness to explore such possibilities.

For the patient to agree upon a focus is also to agree upon a fundamental treatment goal: to resolve psychic conflicts by the means of exposing oneself to, and with the therapist's help examine, the areas of emotional difficulty that one tends to avoid. With gradually hightening awareness of conflictual feelings and their historical roots in childhood, and with the aid of the corrective emotional experiences (Alexander & French, 1946) of the therapeutic relationship, the patient will also be able to enjoy more satisfying interpersonal relationships in his or her "real" life.

THEORY OF CHANGE

Thus far, no one has elaborated a comprehensive theory of change for STAPP in particular. From what has been said in previous sections, however, the reader will probably have concluded that STAPP is basically anchored in classical (not orthodox!) psychoanalysis and psychoanalytic ego psychology. Assumptions about the causes of psychopathology and interpersonal conflicts are closely connected with assumptions about their resolution. Together the two sets of assumptions constitute the rationale behind the therapist's activity.

In principle, the STAPP theory of change is rather simple and parsimonious. The main operating mechanism is supposed to be the patient's learning to solve an emotional core problem, as it is being evoked in the transference by the therapist's anxiety-provoking technique. Learning to solve an emotional conflict gives rise to self-understanding and a feeling of well-being. Further, it leads to the development of new attitudes, which in turn facilitate improved personal and interpersonal functioning (Sifneos, 1969).

Basically, it is supposed that every symptom holds a psychodynamic meaning, hidden from the patient's conscious awareness, and that anxiety may be used as a motivating force for the patient to explore that meaning. In turn, the new cognitive and intellectual insights that emerge will help the patient to change his or her maladaptive behavior. Or, to put it in slightly different terms: by learning to recognize maladaptive reaction patterns, unmasking their historical source and meaning, and having corrective emotional experiences with the therapist, the patient achieves more inner freedom and ego autonomy. Being freed from longstanding parataxic distortions, the patient is enabled to adopt more flexible, self-directive, and mature ways of relating to other people. Thus, according to STAPP theory, lasting behavioral and symptomatic improvement is thought always to arise from the patient's having attained significant psychodynamic change and a new "internalized dialogue," which makes him or her more resistant to specific internal and external stressors.

Looking at therapy as a particular form of experiential learning and problem solving, Sifneos (1972) compares the role of the STAPP therapist to that of "an unemotionally involved teacher" or mentor, an analogy neither original nor unique among psychoanalytically oriented therapists. Even Freud in his early writings (for example, Freud, 1905/1953) described his approach to treatment as a special form of "after-education," and later Franz Alexander and Thomas French (1946) alluded to learning concepts in their pioneering efforts to shorten psychotherapy.

Interesting, but rarely attended to, is the fact that the learning concept of STAPP may serve as a bridge to recent developments in behavioral psychotherapy, especially with regard to so-called exposure treatment (Marks, 1981). The essence of that approach, which is considered a particularly efficient therapy for phobias, has been cogently outlined this way:

> In order to help this type of individual, it is necessary to change the avoidance behavior into some type of approach behavior. . . . [If] the client can be encouraged and supported to actually approach the situations he or she has avoided, there is an opportunity to secure positive change. If the client enters the previously anxiety-avoiding situation and the expected negative consequences are not forthcoming, a reduction in anxiety may ensue. (Garfield, 1989, p. 33)

Compare this with the following two brief statements by Sifneos as they pertain to STAPP: "[The therapist uses] anxiety-provoking questions to stimulate the patient to look into the areas of conflict which he tended to avoid" (Sifneos, 1969, p. 393), and "Past emotional conflicts and difficulties become reactivated and the patient reexperiences, as one may say 'alive' during the psychotherapeutic interview, the painful aspect of his past emotional difficulties" (Sifneos, 1965, pp. 128–129). As the reader will easily see, the exposure component is here no less present than in the behavioral approach. Probably the main difference between the two approaches is that in the latter, exposure is ensured in relation to external fears or situations, while in STAPP the feared "situation" is an intrapsychic one, such as forbidden wishes, fantasies, or feelings. However, an effective agent of change in both forms of therapy is the patient's encounter with experiences usually avoided. In our opinion, such similarities in operating mechanisms should motivate therapists toward exploring the possible gains of integrative therapeutic efforts (see Nielsen & Havik, 1989).

TECHNIQUES AND CASE EXAMPLE

Formulating the Therapeutic Contract

The therapeutic contract formulation represents a transition from assessment to therapy proper. The contract constitutes a mutual agreement about the thematic focus of treatment and also about the limitations of the therapeutic venture. Sifneos maintains that "the therapeutic contract serves the purpose of making the patient take an active responsibility in the development of his psychotherapeutic work and sharing the difficulty which will be encountered as an equal partner, not as one dependent on the evaluator" (1979, p. 55). Preferably the contract should be formulated toward the end of the evaluation interview, in connection with the therapist's summary of his or her impression of the patient's problems. At the latest the contract should be completed at the beginning of the first regular session.

Here is an example from an interview with a thirty-four-year-old female school counselor:

THERAPIST: If I understand you right, . . . you say that the pain in your muscles and joints of your hand and your tendonitis in your elbow have something to do with your tendency to force yourself beyond your own limits. You suggested that your pain might have something to do with your being too nice a person, too easy to get along with. It is very easy for you to say yes, and you take too big a share of what should have been joint liabilities. This happens more often between you and your female friends and between you and your mother. (*The patient is listening attentively and nods her head.*)

For the last couple of months you have managed to diminish this tendency somewhat in relation to your mother. But that makes you feel guilty and also mobilizes some anxiety. (*The patient sighs in confirmation.*)

You mentioned particularly that you used to have more difficulties with women than with men in this respect, which corresponds with your feeling that it is generally easier for you to get along with men than with women. Remember your own words: "There is something delicate here." (*The patient nods.*) You also said that you hope that therapy will help you to discover new connections in your life which may help you to say yes and no more according to *your* limits and *your* wishes. And I do agree. Let us therefore concentrate on finding out together what it is you call delicate in your relation with men on the one hand, and between you and women on the other, and maybe especially between you and your mother and father.

PATIENT: Yes, fine. When can I see you again?

The therapist has given a summary at the end of the evaluation interview. Using the patient's own words and formulations, she outlined the essence of the dynamic hypothesis that would guide her work. The patient obviously accepts the therapist's formulations and seems to be eager to get started on their joint venture.

Sifneos claims that in presenting his dynamic hypothesis and the contract, the evaluator must "be able to substantiate his impression by solid evidence in the form of specific examples of events, fantasies, and memories given to him by the patient and amassed during the course of the whole evaluation" (1979, p. 50).

Establishing a Good Working Alliance

The example above strongly indicates that a fairly good *working alliance* between therapist and patient is already emerging. The patient herself has already done some of the "work" of putting her complaints into an interpersonal framework. But she has not yet managed to grasp the full dynamic meaning of what she is telling.

Building a good working alliance is a fundamental technical challenge for every STAPP therapist. The therapist tries to nourish the alliance both directly and indirectly, through verbal and nonverbal means. In the case just mentioned, the evaluator echoes the patient's formulations, thus enabling her to feel herself recognized and understood. Most probably the patient perceives the evaluator as an attentive and interested other, who acknowledges and confirms her own thinking. In short, the patient is being approached as an equal partner, expected to contribute actively to the joint therapeutic work.

The working alliance is also strengthened by the therapist's active support whenever the patient is working hard within the therapeutic (oedipal) focus. Here is another example from the same patient's evaluation interview:

THERAPIST: What about your father?

PATIENT: He was such an extravert, an easygoing kind of person. He was an attorney, working for the county administration. He loved to talk to people. . . . Yes, very extravert. When he was mad at something or someone, he got it out of his system immediately, then he could go on again. Mostly he was very good tempered and very cheerful. . . . Yes— *(tears well up)*.

THERAPIST: What did you especially appreciate with him?

PATIENT: Well, I guess— yes, it was that he always found the time— *(silently crying)*.

THERAPIST: That meant a lot to you?

PATIENT: Yes *(crying hard, searching for her handkerchief)*.

THERAPIST: This is difficult for you, thinking of your father.

PATIENT: *(Sobbing)* I am thinking of when I used to visit him at his office. He used to close the office and go with me for a walk in the shopping areas downtown.

THERAPIST: That sounds nice. When you visited him, he seems to have treated you as a very important person, and he gave you all his attention. What more did the two of you like to do together?

PATIENT: He liked to boss me around *(smiles through her tears)*. He liked to go fishing, and I had to be his assistant, or if he was to do some practical work at our country place, you know . . . I used to protest, to make him stop bossing me around, but it was nice that he wanted to have *me* around and not my brothers.

THERAPIST: I understand that your father is now dead. When did he die?

PATIENT: Ten years ago *(still crying)*.

THERAPIST: I see, ten years ago, but it is still hard for you to talk about him, knowing that he is not around you any longer.

PATIENT: Yes *(sobs)*, it is very painful, grievous. But I am astounded that I should cry like this now.

THERAPIST: I see. It sounds as if you were very close to your father, and that you do have some very nice memories.

PATIENT: Oh, yes *(smiles and goes on telling about some nice, sunny memories from childhood)*.

Transference Issues

Another technical consideration to be made early is the use of the transference. Usually, positive transference feelings predominate in the early phases of STAPP, and it is recommended that the therapist deal with them immediately, not waiting for the transference to appear as a resistance to be interpreted later (Sifneos, 1979, p. 78).

In the following passage the evaluator is summing up, preparing for the contract formulation:

THERAPIST: So, here we are. You agreed to come and talk to me at a most inconvenient hour of the day for you and despite my being a woman, when you wanted to see a male therapist. Could this have anything to do with your problem—that is, saying yes and being nice, though you didn't really want to do just that, but something else?

PATIENT: Yes, yes, I guess you are right.

THERAPIST: So we are right in the middle of it?

PATIENT: Yes *(tears in her eyes)*. You might say I thought that if I did this, I mean, came down for this interview, I could get accepted for therapy now, without having to wait for another half a year.

THERAPIST: Perhaps that was exactly the way it used to happen between you and your father? You did something for him, were a nice girl, so that you could have his attention, and then make an arrangement with him and come before your brothers?

PATIENT: Um, it sounds awful the way you put it! I haven't thought of it that way, but yes, I guess so, it was important for me to get his attention, as it has been to get yours.

In this example the patient recognizes the therapist's early transference interpretation, thus starting on her therapeutic work immediately. This is often the case with properly selected STAPP patients. However, a patient may also choose to test the therapist, like our school counselor did in her first regular session:

PATIENT: I have been thinking about my situation. Somehow I feel that I have done it again—been too compliant. I mean, in spite of right now having too many duties, I mean, I knew that those weeks coming up would demand too much of me. They always do, when my husband goes away on his business trips. I should have postponed the start of my therapy . . . I feel I haven't got the time right now . . . All the same . . . Well, then I started to think of a friend of mine who went psychotic during her therapy with Dr. X [a woman], so—

THERAPIST: In a sense I think you are saying that you do not trust me as a woman, and therefore not as your therapist either? Perhaps you are afraid that I will mess it all up and leave you confused, or withdraw, like your mother used to do?

PATIENT: Well, we all got very frightened, you know. My friend almost managed to kill herself.

THERAPIST: Oh, yes, I understand that, it certainly must have made a strong impression on you. But I also hear you say that you *do not trust me.* I am just like all the other women, your mother and the rest, not to be trusted with important stuff. Your mind is so replete with important stuff that you are ready to withdraw and give it all up. It is too dangerous to look into, or to be trusted to a woman.

PATIENT: Um . . . Well, it is somewhat confusing, but I see your point. And, well, I recall my first thoughts about going to a female therapist, as I told you when we first met . . . But, but, when I think of our last session . . . You were very warm and understanding . . . helping me, but also very direct and strong. You kept your track, didn't give up or withdraw. It is all quite confusing.

THERAPIST: So in one way you recall me behaving more like your father, giving you time, listening, and so forth, and not allowing you to muddle about, talk me out of the track of what *you* really meant was important. On the other hand, I am also a woman, whom you don't know if you dare to trust, and who makes your life more complicated.

PATIENT: Um, yes, I am afraid you are right again. *(The patient then talks about a memory that had come to her mind shortly after the evaluation interview.)*

Sifneos (1979) maintains that early transference moves like these can be difficult to handle, since the working alliance has not as yet become consolidated. Our patient showed a reaction common to many STAPP patients. She came in touch with emotionally significant material, which provoked so much anxiety that she even considered dropping out of therapy. But the material obviously also stimulated the patient's curiosity, thus serving as an important driving force for further explorative work.

Like Malan (1976), Sifneos claims that the therapist's interpretations should focus particularly on therapist–parent connections, the so-called past–transference links. This provides the patient with significant insight. It also contributes to the *corrective emotional experience.* Together, these two important treatment factors facilitate the resolution of the patient's past and present interpersonal conflicts (Sifneos, 1979, p. 80).

Sifneos (1979, 1987) also discusses countertransference issues. In his opinion there are few countertransference problems in a typical STAPP. Of course, there may be episodes of, for example, dislike of the patient. But "the therapeutic alliance and the common problem-solving goals have an overriding influence on these difficulties and become instrumental in producing a positive result," he argues (Sifneos, 1979, p. 92). Looking over our own clinical experience, we agree that the countertransference feelings that come up are most often positive, and that they can be relatively easily resolved or handled.

Didactic Interventions, Anxiety-Provoking Questions, and Patient Responsibility

A successfully conducted STAPP may often contain a didactic component. For example, the therapist takes an active, didactic role when telling the patient what to expect from treatment, when outlining the rules to be followed, and when summarizing examples of new learning and better problem solving evidenced by the patient's behavior during treatment.

Sometimes didactic and interpretive interventions can be combined, as in the following sequence (from the sixth interview). The patient opens the dialogue:

PATIENT: This is very hard. I feel reluctant. I let all thoughts just come. It is kind of new and unfamiliar. I become insecure. . . . I am wondering if I am saying what you expect of me. You are kind of anonymous. You are receiving without saying yes or no. I want a response from you.

THERAPIST: Now try listening to your own words. What does it remind you of?

PATIENT: Well, you know at home we always got a reaction, from either mum or dad. Yes, and my oldest brother especially. He was even more closely supervised. I managed to get permission to stay out later than my brothers had managed at the same age. I don't think I ever took correction from my mother, though. But I do remember that she once tried to correct me, but I didn't listen, though I knew she was right. It was always my father's opinion that was of most significance to me.

THERAPIST: You seem to carry the idea that I expect something special from you, that I should guide and correct you like you were guided back home. Remember that you are just as good a judge of what is important to talk about as I am. What is going on between us is of course important, so if you have more thoughts about why I should guide you, you can continue on that subject. However, if you find it more important to talk about why your father's opinion was of greater importance to you than your mother's, you can choose that.

The patient returns to the same topic in a later session, demonstrating that she has been working on it and that she wants to cooperate. Although it costs her quite a lot, she is providing much meaningful material.

PATIENT: Now I can understand my own clients' frustration when they expect to be guided on what to do. With you, I have had to learn what it is like to have to find out for myself what I want to do, or think, or feel. It all has to come from myself, from my inside, so to speak. I also have to sense how it is when I am trying to resist when it is uncomfortable . . . And that is uncomfortable, too.

You know, last time you asked for an example of me rebelling against my mother. I could feel my frustration toward her, but I couldn't remember any concrete situation. But as soon as I got outside your door, I remembered one: I went out to our country place with some friends, though my mother had forbidden me. Instead of arguing with her, I deceived her. They [the parents] found out, of course. Well, nothing really happened, but it was not that—it was that on remembering this incident, I found that I still avoid direct confrontations with her. I evade conflicts. That was humiliating to discover, so I continue to beat about the bush (*sighs*), I—

THERAPIST: Can you give me an example of you going around and not standing up for yourself in relation to your mother?

PATIENT: Well, it was a couple of days ago. She asked me to give her a hug. She complained that it was so long since she had one. I felt so bad . . . it felt so artificial. I should have managed it better. . . . I do wish I could have said, "I don't feel like giving you a hug right now."

THERAPIST: How do you understand that?

PATIENT: Um, it is somewhat complicated. . . . I remember how nice it was to lie between mum and dad in their bed, mother holding my hand and playing with my foot, and father fondling my hair, which I loved him to do. Somehow I decided very early that I should never be like my mother. She couldn't even cope with her children. She started to cry when things became difficult for her. Somehow I consciously decided to become better than her.

THERAPIST: Better than your mother? How?

PATIENT: Well, I remember our skiing trips high up in the mountains. We had to climb the hillsides. They were steep, you know. The girls started to cry and refused to go any further. I felt contempt for them: Why couldn't they pull themselves together and go on?

THERAPIST: You felt contempt for your mother, too?

PATIENT: It was somehow important to be the best. You know, I picked up sports, sports my father was interested in. But I never was interested in the stuff my mother was good at, cooking and sewing, for example.

THERAPIST: You were afraid of not being able to knock your mother out in that area, too?

PATIENT: Um (*blushing*), I haven't thought of it that way . . . I got the thought the other night that my nice, pleasing behavior has something to do with my competition with the other girls. When I compete I can even exceed the limits of what I can cope with. I am using my brothers' measures.

THERAPIST: What do you mean? Please give an example.

PATIENT: Well, one week after I had given birth to my first child, I still had stitches and couldn't sit, but I started immediately to see my clients again. Well, it was completely crazy when I think of it today.

THERAPIST: How do you explain your behavior? Why did you do such a thing, and why was it so terribly important to reach that mountain peak? Why was it important to be the best, better than your mother?

PATIENT: I don't know.

THERAPIST: Oh, come on, now you are beating about the bush again.

PATIENT: I think I wanted recognition from my father. . . . Yes, that was very important, that he acknowledged me, that he showed his love for me. (*She goes on giving examples of what she used to do to please her father.*)

The therapist actively urges the patient to be specific and to avoid vagueness. She is continuously asking for examples and encouraging her to verbalize her own understanding of the situation. Thus, the therapist is also making anxiety-provoking clarifications and confrontations, relying on the working alliance and on the patient's motivation for change. These therapeutic efforts are immediately rewarded. Significant information keeps flowing. All along the way, the patient is encouraged to take responsibility for her actions and feelings.

Therapist Activity

As the examples show, the STAPP therapist is actively challenging the patient by questions, confrontations, clarifications, or transference interpretations. Activity is also exemplified by the therapist's forcing the patient to stay within the chosen treatment (oedipal) focus, by avoiding complex pregenital characterological issues, and by supporting the patient's attempts at more adaptive problem solving.

Sifneos strongly maintains that for the therapist to be able to handle the transference issues and the anxiety-provoking confrontations and clarifications, he or she has to be sensitive and convey that "instead of being a threat with his challenges, competitive postures, and strong resistances, he is eager to help the patient deal with the anxieties which he experiences" (1979, p. 94).

Furthermore, the therapist must actively help the patient to take full responsibility for himself or herself and to learn to choose the best way out of a variety of tempting neurotic maladaptive options. By continuously reformulating the material presented by the patient into interpretations, particularly of past–transference links, the therapist uncovers new connections, thus providing the patient with new insights and better possibilities for effective problem solving.

Dealing with Defenses

Traditional psychoanalytic technique calls for always dealing with the defenses first; in contrast, the STAPP approach permits the therapist to confront and interpret the underlying impulse or wish rather directly. Such head-on maneuvers are possible because the STAPP therapist, having provided a trusting environment by using the therapeutic alliance and positive transference, can afford to be selective and to concentrate on the specific areas wherein most of the patient's dynamic conflicts exist. Sensitively paying attention to verbal and nonverbal clues, the therapist proceeds to elicit and, if necessary, to push hard for painful associations, fantasies, or wishes. Having succeeded in reducing resistances through questions, anxiety-provoking confrontations, and clarifications, the therapist is usually rewarded with the sudden emergence of a fantasy, dream, or memory, "which pops, so to speak, out of the patient's unconscious and which confirms in a relevant and triumphant way the truth of his interpretations" (Sifneos, 1979, p. 95).

Here is an example of how our patient's defenses and resistance were challenged in the tenth session:

PATIENT: There is something I have found somewhat problematic for some time. . . . I have decided to talk about it today. I feel as if I am holding myself back when I am having sex with my husband.
THERAPIST: Yes? Go on.
PATIENT: I feel as if my mother is listening . . . I think she can hear us.

You see, she has her own bedroom just above ours. I know I should say "so what," but it doesn't help me. I am still feeling uncomfortable.

THERAPIST: Uncomfortable? Please try to explain.

PATIENT: Um . . . I am thinking of my Danish boyfriend. With him it was quite different. I was much more free, much more alive. I did live more freely in Denmark. There I was not so regular and noble, not daddy's little girl!

THERAPIST: How did you feel, living like that?

PATIENT: (*Giggles*) Oh, it was great! (*Becoming serious again*) But I remember I started to get some anxiety from time to time.

THERAPIST: Anxiety? In what connections?

PATIENT: Um, I don't know, just anxiety.

THERAPIST: Oh, come on, don't hide yourself!

PATIENT: Well, somehow I rebelled against being my father's nice little girl . . . or was it during those periods I had those dreams. I dreamt very often that I was dead and everyone was standing around the coffin talking about me. I still have many dreams like that. . . . I dreamt the other night that my husband died. But this time I got so furious—how could he leave me alone, to sort everything out?

THERAPIST: What are you trying to tell me?

PATIENT: Trying to tell you? I don't know. You asked me . . . what was it again?

THERAPIST: Yes, what was it? What are you trying to tell me?

PATIENT: (*With tears in her eyes*) I had the impression that I had to be obedient toward daddy all the time. Conform to his rules, or else he should turn away from me. He wouldn't be fond of me any more (*silently crying*) . . . wouldn't love me any more.

THERAPIST: Do you say that your anxiety has something to do with rebelling against your father, on the one hand, and with challenging your mother on the other? How do you explain that?

PATIENT: Strange to think that I dared to invite my Danish boyfriend home! Somehow I should show my father—show him that I wasn't that little girl of his any longer. On the other hand, they weren't there any more, my feelings for my boyfriend. He had become more indifferent to me. But those weeks at home . . . I was quite . . . enticing. But it was always mum who was most openly critical toward my boyfriends. (*A long silence, tears in her eyes.*)

THERAPIST: Well, go on . . . what bothers you?

PATIENT: I am thinking of my father. . . . He got his first heart attack just a few weeks after my boyfriend had left. I . . . I have been . . . I haven't been able to drop the thought that it was my fault—that I had provoked him, so that he got the heart attack (*crying hard*).

THERAPIST: Are you telling me that you were deliberately making your father jealous?

PATIENT: (*Mumbles.*)

THERAPIST: What do you say? Yes or no? Were you deliberately making your father jealous?

PATIENT: Well, I am afraid that was just what it was (*still crying*).

THERAPIST: But how do you want me to understand why you should make your father jealous? And how do you explain the immensely strong feelings between the two of you, feelings that you believe could have killed your father?

PATIENT: I don't know. But it was terrible thinking that he could have died. It got me stuck in the old groove again. I became the nice girl again. I didn't go back to Denmark where I had planned to continue my studies. Instead I stayed with my parents and got myself a job (*crying*).

THERAPIST: I understand that you are fond of your father and that thinking of having hurt him is difficult. (*Patient sobs.*) But how do you explain that your feelings . . . his feelings . . . almost killed him? Why did you have to make him jealous?

PATIENT: I don't know . . .

THERAPIST: Oh, come on, of course you know! Just tell me!

PATIENT: I don't know what you are hinting at. *You* tell me! (*Somewhat irritated.*)

THERAPIST: It is not my business to tell you. You are the one who knows how it was, how you were feeling. A minute ago, you told me that you had a wonderful time not being daddy's little girl in Denmark. In spite of that you had some periods of anxiety. You felt free and brought your boyfriend home so that your father should see, you said. And you also said that you were astounded at yourself daring to bring your boyfriend with you. You said that although your feelings for your boyfriend had vanished, you were behaving in an enticing way. You were the one who said that you were afraid that you had provoked your father so that he got a heart attack. The very first time that we talked about you and your father, you used the word *delicate* to describe your relationship, do you remember?

PATIENT: Um . . . yes, I was very proud of him, I loved to walk beside him in town, letting the others see what an elegant, smart man he was.

THERAPIST: Well, go on.

PATIENT: I remember another dream I had after he had died. In the dream he was dead, but I could very clearly and vividly feel the smell of his clothes. I could feel that smell very strongly. . . . It was very nice. I stood there remembering how he used to smell when I hugged him . . . and then suddenly he was alive again, standing there close to me. You know, smells have always meant a lot to me when I am in love (*blushing*). Yes, um, it is almost like a love story. . . . After his illness he was very much changed. He became more dependent and helpless. He wanted me to nurse him. My mother didn't do it well enough. It had to be me. He was often sitting at the window waiting for me for hours. I remember I used to have rather mixed feelings about that. I was proud that he preferred me to my mother, but somehow it was too much, too, and that made me feel awkward. I felt that I had been naughty. I had to be his very nice little girl again to make it up. It was a difficult time, with mother's jealousy and all that. . . . I was happy when I could leave for another job two years later. My husband-to-be persuaded me to come to his place and work. Thinking of it now, I might say that I ran off. I couldn't handle it any longer. His feelings toward me, my feelings . . . it was a mess.

THERAPIST: Do you see any connection between this and your present difficulties, that is, to feel free and uninhibited when you and your husband make love?

PATIENT: What do you mean? Oh, yes, that I feel my mother can hear us . . . Well, yes, that . . . I don't know (*cries*).

THERAPIST: Come on, don't be evasive.

PATIENT: Well, um, I guess I feel somehow I shouldn't make love . . . mother is somehow against it, I imagine. . . . I mean, it is all screwy.

THERAPIST: Go on.

PATIENT: Um, you want me to say that I think I make love with my father, when I am with my husband?

THERAPIST: I do not want you to say anything in particular. But you have agreed to talk about what *you* remember, what *you* feel, what *you* are thinking of. Don't talk it away. Well, do you think that your sensitivity for your mother's opinion and for her disapproval is because you think that you are making love with your father? Yes or no?

PATIENT: (*Cries*) I . . . well, there are something there . . . but not quite . . . well, yes, it must be . . . it is crazy. . . .

(*The hour ends here.*)

The therapist was pressing the patient incessantly, but at the same time she was carefully listening for the immediate effects of her confrontations and interpretations. All along she relied on the positive transference and the rapidly established working alliance. The therapist actively summarized the evidence that had accumulated and fed it back to the patient. The patient came up with two memories: in the first she is proudly walking at her father's side, and in the second (the dream) her father is called back to life by her strong memory of his smell. She even uses the phrase "like a love story" to characterize their relationship.

In preparing for the next (eleventh) session, the therapist was wondering whether the patient would fall back into her habit of receding from confrontations, "juggling." To arrest such tendencies, Sifneos (1979, 1987) claims that it is a good measure, if not an imperative one, to take notes during the sessions, so that the therapist can confront the patient with his or her own words when necessary.

But let us now meet our patient in the eleventh session. She starts out by telling that it has been a difficult week, with a lot of tension, and so on. She continues as follows:

PATIENT: Once again I have been thinking of my father, and came to think about his funeral. My husband couldn't come to the funeral, but came a few days later. We went out to the cemetery together and sat down. There we had our first real conversation. I remember quite vividly that after that I wanted to become pregnant. We made love together, as we never had done before. I felt so open and receptive towards him and very much alive.

THERAPIST: It sounds as if you are telling me that your father used to be between you and your husband.

PATIENT: Um, yes. I am afraid you are right. . . . But still the period after my father's death was a very difficult one for me. I often felt so lonely. . . . You know, even after I was married, I went to my father with my problems.

THERAPIST: What kind of problems?

PATIENT: Well, ordinary, everyday practical ones, like asking for help with the lighting in the yard, which I couldn't get to work, and so forth. I never talked to my husband about such problems. I was the organizer of all these things in the house . . . well, with my father's help. I also recall that father and mother competed to write most often to me, just as they had done when I was living abroad. I had to be careful, being equally attentive to both of them! (*She goes on talking about her love and affection for her father. She smiles and compares her situation with her own daughters' feelings for their father.*)

68

They, my father and mother, had talked about mother coming to live with me. I should take care of her when he died. Well, that I didn't know until she actually moved in with us. I felt it an unpleasant duty, and also felt terribly guilty for not being happy to help my mother, taking on the daughterly duty, you know. Why me? Why not my brothers? Just the thought that I am so negative towards her makes me feel guilty. But the other night I got the idea that this negative feeling, the feeling of an unpleasant duty, that I always have to do something for my mother . . . to be nice to her . . . to do all sorts of things for her, has something to do with my feeling that I have to make up for what I felt for my father, loving him more than her. . . . Strange, you know, the other night . . . my mother has a cold and had to be in bed. Earlier I would have felt that I should stay at home and nurse her, be with her all the time, and be frustrated. This time, however, I could *choose* to go to see her or not. I didn't have to do it. I felt free to go or not to go, so I saw her in the morning and went to my job as usual, without a bad conscience. I served her dinner, all right, and later in the evening I popped in because I wanted to—I didn't have to. In spite of her cold we did have such a nice time together. I can't remember having had it so nice with her, just the two of us.

(*The patient goes on to talk about her former relationship with her mother, and about her balancing between mother and father.*)

The patient confirmed that she understood the dynamics and that she had taken responsibility for her feelings and actions. She had begun to work continuously with memories and fantasies that emerged; she also had new experiences with her mother. It turned out that the tenth session was the height of this therapy. Quite often after a STAPP treatment, the patient points to one particular hour as a peak experience or as a turning point.

During the next five hours our patient worked with her grief over her father's death, which she had not been able to do properly in the past. She also came up with additional memories connected to her oedipal problem—for example, a memory from her puberty, when she proudly showed her first bra to her father and he rejected her and ridiculed her. She also recalled an early memory when she was expelled from her parents' bedroom, because her older brother came home with a baby that her parents had to take care of, and the baby had to sleep in the parents' bedroom, where she used to lie.

Termination

In most STAPP cases termination is initiated quite naturally and logically when the patient has solved his or her focal (oedipal) problem. It is the patient just as often as the therapist who raises the termination issue. The therapist should look for concrete evidence of change, according to criteria specified for each individual patient at the beginning of treatment. For example, for the patient we have been following in this chapter, the solid evidence of change was her becoming able to perceive her father in a more realistic way—that is, not overidealizing him; to have greater acceptance for her mother and for herself as a woman; to be less competitive toward women in general; and to achieve a better sexual relationship with her husband—that is, a relationship with more reciprocity. She was also expected to feel less jealous of her own children and to have less pain in her hands and arms. Finally, it seemed realistic to expect some anxiety reduction.

For the last couple of sessions the patient worked hard on her relationship with her parents. On the one hand she struggled to keep the nice, smooth picture of her handsome and gallant father. But at the same time she forced herself to see other dimensions of him, for example, his tendency to boss and dominate the rest of his family. The patient more and more allowed herself to see how she had let him control her life, making both small and large decisions for her, even including her occupation and husband. Such discoveries aroused her anger, but she eventually managed to handle her ambivalent feelings.

As for her mother, she stated:

PATIENT: I have noticed lately that my mother is trying to understand me and my life situation. For example, she can understand that I am often coming tired from work. The other day she had made some stuffed cabbage for me and my family. . . . She knows I love that, but I rarely have time to prepare it. Somehow I can see now that she has a lot of consideration for me, not just demanding things from me, as I felt before. She is well meaning, but can't manage all the things she wants to do. It is as if I finally hear her saying that even if we disagree about a lot of things, she does love me all the same!

In the sixteenth session she talked about herself, her marriage, and her relations with others in her life.

PATIENT: I am now enjoying more positive feelings about being a woman. Sex is more joyful nowadays. I haven't got mother with me in bed any longer (*laughs*). I can allow sexual thoughts to come through to my mind and enjoy my fantasies. I haven't had any of my anxiety dreams for a long time. . . .

I do have it much better with myself nowadays, but it gives me a sour taste thinking of how I exploited the fact that I was the only girl and the youngest one at home. Think of my jealousy towards my brothers, and even, as a grown-up, towards my own children . . . and, of course, my mother! Every minute I was working hard to be at the center of attention, to get proof of being loved, of being the preferred one. . . .

In relation to my husband I have been shifting my position from at times being a little girl demanding him to be my father, and at times being an adult, competing with him. I did the digging in the garden and the painting, etc., in the house, while he had to do the laundry. Although he had to be the best of men, I had to be better than him. At times, I have put him on a pedestal, as I did with my father. But not any longer! . . .

I had to confront my daughter's teacher. I mean she didn't perform her job properly. But this time I managed to talk to her in a grown-up way. Not like last year, when I was scolding her for her incompetence. This time I could listen to her version, too, and we came to an understanding. That was quite satisfying. She took my point, and we could sort it all out to be best for my girl. . . .

I am going to take a year off from my job and start studying again, just for pleasure.

The patient's physical symptoms had vanished, as had her anxiety. There were many indications that her oedipal problem had been resolved, so in spite of her general wish to continue therapy, before the nineteenth session she decided the time had come for her to stand on her own feet.

Sifneos claims that STAPP patients recognize clearly when their problem has been solved. But they might delay the ending for a while. However, "soon (they) realize that it is useless to prolong a situation which seems to be rapidly coming to an end" (1979, p. 156). Sifneos also maintains that this tendency has to do with the positive transference feelings for their therapists and with the strength of the therapeutic alliance, the two basic pillars of the STAPP technique.

To recapitulate, there are ten main technical ingredients of STAPP (Svartberg, 1989).

1. The therapist is generally active and somewhat directive.
2. Transference manifestations are handled early. It is particularly important to identify and interpret "parent–therapist" connections, that is, the past–transference links.
3. The therapist tries actively to keep the patient within the therapeutic focus—in most cases, the oedipal triangle. Pregenital issues and characterological disturbances are systematically avoided.
4. The therapist encourages, and even presses, the patient to specify and to exemplify as concretely as possible his or her statements and verbalizations.
5. The therapist puts effort into having the patient take responsibility for his or her own wishes, feelings, fantasies, and actions.
6. The therapist frequently uses questions and statements such as Why? Why do you think so? How do you explain that? What do *you* think? What are *you* trying to tell me now? Don't run away from *your* problem! It is not my business to answer your questions! What are *your* feelings about this?
7. The therapist continuously applies pressure to the patient's focal defenses (the infantile triangle).
8. The therapist actively supports the patient when she or he is working hard within the focus.
9. The therapist and patient work hard to get a chronological overview of important events in the patient's life. The patterns observed are redundantly recapitulated for the patient.
10. The therapist recapitulates the information the patient is producing, particularly in periods of strong resistance.

APPLICATION AND MODIFICATIONS

Although some therapists attempt to discover an infallible technique applicable to most, if not all, patients, the "pure" STAPP approach should be seen (at least at this point) as having utility for a relatively small and carefully specified population. Having its roots in classical psychoanalysis with regard to assumptions about the cause of psychopathology and related interpersonal conflict, the STAPP model suggests that the primary curative factor will be insight into this conflict. For a treatment that is straightforward and intentionally anxiety-provoking, it is essential that the therapist stick to clear cut and conservative selection criteria. For this reason, some observers have characterized prototypic STAPP candidates as ripe plums (Peake, Bordin, & Archer, 1988). Fairly often candidates are well-educated young adults struggling with problems in the developmental phase of intimacy versus isolation, that is, conflicts usually expressed in difficulty with heterosexual or peer relationships (Burke, White, & Havens, 1979). Working on such problems within the transference relationship often reactivates more basic (oedipal) conflicts that can be effectively resolved through interpretations of the past–transference link.

In an outpatient sample in Boston 26 percent (47 out of 182 patients) were found to fulfill the criteria for STAPP (Sifneos, 1973). Similarly, for the patients in the Bergen Project on Brief Dynamic Psychotherapy (Barth, Nielsen, Havik, et al., 1988), STAPP could be recommended in 10 out of 44 cases (23 percent). However, with a typical inpatient sample at the University Psychiatric Clinic in Oslo, Astrid Heiberg (1975) reported that less than 10 percent fulfilled the STAPP criteria.

For us, as for our colleagues in Oslo (see Husby, 1985), it has been a challenge to investigate the possibility of offering some form of short-term dynamic psychotherapy also to patients who fall short of satisfying the selection criteria for STAPP. If it is possible to document any substantial therapeutic gain in such cases, the potential utility of shorter forms of treatment within the mental health service system will increase significantly.

In order to reach more patients, we decided to free ourselves from the strictly dichotomous response format of Sifneos's evaluation form. This was done by adding a number of subquestions, thus contributing to a more differentiated picture of ego resources than yielded by the original form (see Dahl et al., 1978; Husby, 1983; Barth, Nielsen, Havik, et al., 1988). For example, we expanded questions 1 and 3 as follows:

1. Is the chief complaint well circumscribed? *Subquestion:* If not, reasonably circumscribed?
3. Can the patient interact flexibly with the evaluator? *Subquestion:* If not, is there any evidence of trust and contact?

Using the modified evaluation form we were able to differentiate three groups of patients. The first group had a yes score on all main questions; these were excellent STAPP candidates. The second group had, as a minimum, a positive score on all five subquestions, in addition to showing motivation for change. Such patients, who often had some dependency problems or more maladaptive defenses, were assumed to benefit from a less anxiety-provoking approach, like Malan's (1963) Brief Intensive Psychotherapy (BIP). Finally, patients with a no score on one or more of the resource items and/or insufficient motivation for change were offered treatment according to a brief integrative psychodynamic approach (Nielsen et al., 1984; Nielsen & Havik, 1989).

While both STAPP and Malan's BIP are essentially interpretive forms of therapy, our integrative model uses a wider scope of strategies and procedures—such as supportive, behavioral, and cognitive coping techniques (Marmor & Woods, 1980; Wachtel, 1985). Such active interventions, which may even include hypnosis, are used as adjuncts to the usual psychodynamic techniques. In the integrative model, transference still represents a key consideration. However, there is less concern than in STAPP and BIP with internal conflict per se, and greater emphasis on actual events that may have affected the patient's self-esteem, interaction with others, and anticipation of the quality of his or her personal environment (Chrzanowski, 1977). Insight is slightly deemphasized as a critical change factor, while the mechanisms of corrective emotional experience, gradual exposure to fear-arousing fantasies and situations, and the provision of coping experiences and mastery experiences hold more central positions.

Theoretically, the integrative model is rooted in interpersonal psychoanalysis and represents a way of thinking that some authors prefer to call cyclical psychodynamics (see Goldfried & Wachtel, 1987).

With the modifications described above, we have found Sifneos's evaluation form to be a clinically reliable instrument, which may assist the therapist in the selection of the right form of treatment for patients of varying ego resources and motivation for change (Barth, Nielsen, Havik, et al., 1988). Systematic outcome studies (Barth, Nielsen, Haver, et al., 1988) have taught us that the modifications here described allow us to make short-term dynamic psychotherapy a treatment of choice for a large number of patients encountered in our everyday clinical practice.

EMPIRICAL SUPPORT

With well-defined inclusion criteria, relatively homogeneous groups of patients, narrow treatment focuses, specified technical operations, and clearly defined parameters for measuring change (Sifneos, Apfel, Bassuk, Fishman, & Gill, 1980), the STAPP approach provides favorable conditions for pursuing good outcome research. Over the years, a number of well-designed follow-up studies have been carried out in various centers in North America and Europe. In most of these studies, outcome has been evaluated according to both symptomatic and dynamic criteria for improvement, as well as criteria for improved adaptive functioning (such as interpersonal relations with key persons in the patient's environment, problem solving, and work or academic performance).

With his group at Beth Israel Hospital in Boston, Sifneos has pursued a large number of systematic case studies of outcome and two controlled group studies. The most recent study (Sifneos, 1987) included fifty patients (thirty-six experimental and fourteen waiting list controls). All patients had been clinically judged as suffering from unresolved oedipal conflicts, and all fulfilled the inclusion criteria for STAPP. At the end of their waiting period, the data showed, eleven out of fourteen control patients were rated as "unchanged," while three had some symptomatic improvement and were rated as "little better." In contrast, at the end of therapy thirty out of the thirty-six experimental patients were rated as either "recovered" or much better," according to criteria that included both symptomatic and dynamic change. Only three patients were rated as "unchanged." By the time the control patients had also finished their therapies, thus increasing the total number of treated patients, the ratings of either "recovered" or "much better" applied to eighty-six percent of the sample.

In Norway, three recent outcome studies (Husby et al., 1985a, 1985b; Høglend et al., 1988; Barth, Nielsen, Haver, et al., 1988) have yielded results very similar to those reported by Sifneos. Two of the studies (by the Husby and Barth teams) included long-term follow-up interviews. The follow-up findings contained strong evidence that improvement observed at the end of therapy was being maintained several years after therapy had ended. For most of the patients, therapeutic gain had even increased during the follow-up period. Worth mentioning is also the fact that clinically rated improvement in the patients was cross-validated through findings with psychological tests (MMPI and SCL-90), administered before therapy started and at three follow-ups (Nielsen et al., 1988; Barth, Nielsen, Haver, et al., 1988).

Finally, in their follow-up interviews many of those patients who continued to improve after therapy had ended referred to some kind of "internalized therapeutic dialogue" as the most important change factor. Thus, it seemed that these patients during therapy had been particularly well "educated" in asking themselves good questions and then answering them in a therapeutically useful way.

To our knowledge, no studies have been reported comparing STAPP to

75

any alternative psychotherapy or to a placebo kind of control condition. Thus, nonspecific effects have not been ruled out, and there is no published evidence that STAPP is uniquely effective. However, a preliminary comparative analysis of our own data revealed that patients treated by the STAPP method improved at a faster rate than patients treated with either Malan's (1963) brief intensive approach or the brief integrative psychodynamic approach described in a previous section. We may take this as an indicator that STAPP is not only an effective but also a cost-effective form of treatment.

References

Alexander, F., & French, T. M. (1946). *Psychoanalytic therapy.* New York: Ronald Press.

Barth, K., Nielsen, G., Haver, B., Havik, O. E., Mølstad, E., Rogge, H., & Skåtun, M. (1988). Comprehensive assessment of change in patients treated with short-term dynamic psychotherapy: An overview. A 2-year follow-up study of 34 cases. *Psychotherapy and Psychosomatics, 50,* 141–150.

Barth, K., Nielsen, G., Havik, O. E., Haver, B., Mølstad, E., Rogge, H., Skåtun, M., Heiberg, A., & Ursin, H. (1988). Assessment for three different forms of short-term dynamic psychotherapy. *Psychotherapy and Psychosomatics, 49,* 153–159.

Bauer, G. P., & Kobos, J. C. (1987). *Brief therapy: Short-term psychodynamic intervention.* Northvale, NJ: Jason Aronson.

Burke, J. D., Jr., White, H. S., & Havens, L. L. (1979). Which short-term psychotherapy? *Archives of General Psychiatry, 36,* 177–186.

Chrzanowski, G. (1977). *Interpersonal approach to psychoanalysis: Contemporary view of Harry Stack Sullivan.* New York: Gardner Press.

Dahl, A. A., Dahl, C. I., Heiberg, A., Husby, R., Olafsen, O. M., Sørensen, T., & Weiseth, L. (1978). A presentation of a short-term psychotherapy project at the Oslo University Psychiatric Clinic. *Psychotherapy and Psychosomatics, 29,* 299–304.

Davanloo, H. (1986). Intensive short-term dynamic psychotherapy with highly resistant patients: 1. Handling resistance. *International Journal of Short-Term Psychotherapy, 1,* 107–131.

Flegenheimer, W. V. (1982). *Techniques of brief psychotherapy.* New York: Jason Aronson.

Freud, S. (1953). Fragment of an analysis of a case of hysteria. In J. Strachey (Ed. & Trans.), *The standard edition of the complete psychological works of Sigmund Freud* (Vol. 7, pp. 7–122). London: Hogarth Press. (Original work published 1905.)

Garfield, S. L. (1989). *The practice of brief psychotherapy.* New York: Pergamon Press.

Garske, J. P., & Molteni, A. L. (1985). Brief dynamic psychotherapy: An integrative approach. In S. J. Lynn & J. P. Garske (Eds.), *Contemporary psychotherapies: Models and methods* (pp. 69–115). London: Merrill.

Goldfried, M. R., & Wachtel, P. L. (1987). Clinical and conceptual issues in psychotherapy integration: A dialogue. *Journal of Integrative and Eclectic Psychotherapy, 6,* 131–144.

Heiberg, A. (1975). Indications for psychotherapy in a psychiatric clinic population: A survey. *Psychotherapy and Psychosomatics, 26,* 156–166.

Heiberg, A. (1976–1977). Indications for psychotherapy in a psychiatric clinic population: Reliability and validity of evaluations. *Psychotherapy and Psychosomatics, 27,* 18–25.

Høglend, P., Fossum, A., Amlo, S., Engelstad, V., Heyerdal, O., Hultman, K., Sørbye, Ø., & Sørlie, T. (1988). Dynamisk korttids psykoterapi: Langtidsoppfølgingsstudie av 54 pasienter [Dynamic short-term psychotherapy: A longterm follow-up of 54 cases]. *Tidsskrift for Den Norske Lægeforening, 108,* 295–297.

Husby, R. (1983). *Measured effects of short-term dynamic psychotherapy.* Unpublished doctoral dissertation, University of Oslo, Faculty of Medicine.

Husby, R. (1985). Short-term dynamic psychotherapy: 3. A 5-year follow-up of 36 neurotic patients. *Psychotherapy and Psychosomatics, 43,* 17–22.

Husby, R., Dahl, A. A., Dahl, C. I., Heiberg, N. A., Olafsen, O. M., & Weisaeth, L. (1985a). Short-term dynamic psychotherapy: 1. The Oslo group's form to score outcome, the reliability testing of this form and observer characteristics. *Psychotherapy and Psychosomatics, 43,* 1–7.

Husby, R., Dahl, A. A., Dahl, C. I., Heiberg, N. A., Olafsen, O. M., & Weisaeth, L. (1985b). Short-term dynamic psychotherapy: 2. Prognostic value of characteristics of patients studied by a 2-year follow-up of 39 neurotic patients. *Psychotherapy and Psychosomatics, 43,* 8–16.

Luborsky, L. (1984). *Principles of psychoanalytic psychotherapy: A manual for supportiveexpressive treatment.* New York: Basic Books.

Malan, D. H. (1963). *A study of brief psychotherapy.* London: Tavistock.

Malan, D. H. (1976). *The frontier of brief psychotherapy.* New York: Plenum.

Marks, I. (1981). *Cure and care of neurosis: The theory and practice of behavioral psychotherapy.* New York: Wiley.

Marmor, J., & Woods, S. M. (Eds.). (1980). *The interface between the psychodynamic and behavioral therapies.* New York: Plenum.

Nielsen, G., Barth, K., Haver, B., Havik, O. E., Mølstad, E., Rogge, H., & Skåtun, M. (1988). Follow-up assessments in psychotherapy: Methodological considerations and some experiences from the Bergen Project on Brief Dynamic Psychotherapy. *Journal of the Norwegian Psychological Association, 25,* 75–84.

Nielsen, G., & Havik, O. E. (1989). Brief dynamic psychotherapy: 2. Principles for a pragmatic integrative model. *Journal of the Norwegian Psychological Association, 26,* 1–16.

Nielsen, G., Havik, O. E., Barth, K., Haver, B., Mølstad, E., Rogge, H., & Skåtun, M. (1984). Evaluering av pasienter i korttidspsykoterapi: En prosjektillustrasjon [Evaluating patients in brief psychotherapy: A project illustration]. *Nordisk Psykologi, 36,* 65–74.

Peake, T. H., Bordin, C. M., & Archer, R. P. (1988). *Brief psychotherapies: Changing frames of mind.* Newbury Park, CA: Sage.

Sifneos, P. E. (1965). Seven years' experience with short-term dynamic psychotherapy. In M. Pines, & T. Spoerri (Eds.), *Psychotherapy and psychosomatics: Selected lectures* (pp. 127–135). Basel: Karger.

Sifneos, P. E. (1969). Short-term, anxiety-provoking psychotherapy: An emotional problem-solving technique. *Seminars in Psychiatry, 1,* 389–398.

Sifneos, P. E. (1972). *Short-term psychotherapy and emotional crisis.* Cambridge MA: Harvard University Press.

Sifneos, P. E. (1973). An overview of a psychiatric clinic population. *American Journal of Psychiatry, 130,* 1032–1036.

Sifneos, P. E. (1979). *Short-term dynamic psychotherapy: Evaluation and technique.* New York: Plenum.

Sifneos, P. E. (1987). *Short-term dynamic psychotherapy: Evaluation and technique (2nd ed.).* New York: Plenum.

Sifneos, P. E., Apfel, R. J., Bassuk, E., Fishman, G., & Gill, A. (1980). Ongoing research on short-term dynamic psychotherapy. *Psychotherapy and Psychosomatics, 33,* 233–241.

Sloane, R. B., & Staples, F. R. (1979). Foreword. *The Psychiatric Clinics of North America, 2,* 1–2.

Small, L. (1979). *The briefer psychotherapies.* New York: Brunner/Mazel.

Svartberg, O. M. (1989). Manualization and competence monitoring of Short-Term Anxiety-Provoking Psychotherapy. *Psychotherapy, 26,* 564–571.

Wachtel, P. L. (1985). Integrative psychodynamic therapy. In S. J. Lynn, & J. P. Garske (Eds.), *Contemporary psychotherapies: Models and methods* (pp. 287–329). Toronto: Merril.

Wolberg, L. (1965). *Short-term psychotherapy.* New York: Grune & Stratton.

CHAPTER 4

Intensive Short-Term Dynamic Psychotherapy

Michael Laikin, Arnold Winston,
and Leigh McCullough

ORIGINS AND DEVELOPMENT

Intensive Short-Term Dynamic Psychotherapy (ISTDP) was developed by
Habib Davanloo (1980) as a technique to break through the patient's
defensive barrier. The technique facilitates the examination of repressed
memories and ideas in a fully experienced and integrated affective and
cognitive framework. Davanloo based his ideas on the work of a number
of psychoanalytic therapists. In this section we will examine the influence
of some of the more important figures in the development of Intensive
Short-Term Dynamic Psychotherapy.

Freud (1905/1953) in his early work used many of the techniques of
brief psychotherapy. He was extremely active in attempting to confront
and overcome the patient's resistance. He maintained a focus by concentrating on connections to a specific symptom. When Freud shifted from the
cathartic method to free association, psychoanalysis became a long-term
treatment, since maintenance of a focus is directly opposed to free association.

Sandor Ferenczi and Otto Rank (1925) in *The Development of Psychoanalysis,*
commented on a number of ideas that became central to ISTDP. They
believed that intellectual knowledge without affect serves as a resistance.

Therefore, they stressed that the therapist must be active to evoke the affect that was achieved with the cathartic method. Ferenczi and Rank took the position that change comes about through a combination of affect and intellectual understanding of the original conflict in the transference.

Franz Alexander and Thomas French continued the work of Ferenczi and Rank with their concept of the corrective emotional experience. They believed that the reliving of early conflicts within the transference allows the patient to experience "those emotional situations which are primarily unbearable and to deal with them in a manner different from the old" (1946, p. 67).

It is clear that these writers realized that an active transference approach, bringing together affective and cognitive elements, was critical in producing positive outcome.

In 1944, Lindemann reported on his work with survivors of the Coconut Grove fire and focused on acute and delayed grief, as well as pathological and normal mourning. Davanloo, building on the work of Lindemann, recognized the importance of pathological mourning and the necessity of dealing with it early in treatment if short-term dynamic psychotherapy was to be effective.

David Malan (1976) and Peter Sifneos (1979) were instrumental in developing highly focused brief psychotherapies using substantial work in the transference. Sifneos emphasized the use of confrontation and anxiety-provoking questions to keep the level of tension relatively high in order to shorten therapy. Malan introduced the use of the triangles of conflict and person, which help define the field of inquiry so that a clear focus can be maintained. He also developed the idea of trial therapy to help establish a patient's suitability for brief dynamic psychotherapy.

Davanloo (1980), building on the work of these authors, developed Intensive Short-Term Dynamic Psychotherapy, which is highly confrontational and emphasizes affect. Davanloo pays special attention to the defensive layering of highly resistant patients using Wilhelm Reich's (1949) ideas about character resistance. During the evaluation interview he actively employs trial therapy techniques and attempts to achieve an affective breakthrough either in the patient–therapist relationship or in some other important relationship in the life of the patient. Davanloo believes that the breakthrough sets the stage for access to the patient's core conflicts and allows repressed memories to enter consciousness.

In the early 1980s our group at Beth Israel Medical Center in New York City became interested in pursuing Davanloo's approach and subjecting it to systematic research (Winston et al., 1989). Since we began the technique has evolved so that affect is not so heavily emphasized. Instead, the focus is both affective and cognitive, and an attempt is made to integrate the two (Laikin and Winston, 1990). In addition, with more resistant patients a cognitive restructuring is often done in the initial phase of treatment so that patients with many ego syntonic symptoms can recognize their defenses and increase their capacity to experience affect. Then the initial phase of treatment is much less confrontational, enabling the therapist to build a therapeutic alliance that can withstand the defensive and characterological analysis that must take place.

SELECTION OF PATIENTS

Intensive Short-Term Dynamic Psychotherapy can be applied to a wide variety of outpatients. It is suitable for patients with personality disorders primarily of the *DSM III-R* Cluster C group, such as avoidant, dependent, obsessive-compulsive, and passive-aggressive, as well as the histrionic personality disorder from Cluster B. Davanloo suggests that this therapy can produce good results in patients suffering from longstanding neurosis or maladaptive personality patterns with either an oedipal or a loss focus or both.

Because cognitive restructuring techniques are emphasized some patients with more severe psychopathology and less integrated ego structure, such as those with borderline and narcissistic personality disorders, can benefit. Patients with this level of psychopathology will require substantially longer treatment.

Exclusion criteria for this therapy are the following: severe Axis I diagnosis, such as schizophrenia, bipolar disorder or severe major depression, organic mental disorder, significant suicidal impulses, and marked acting out behavior, as well as drug and alcohol abuse.

Evaluation of patients is performed during the initial interview and should include trial therapy (Malan, 1976; Davanloo, 1980). A significant portion of the evaluation interview should consist of an application of the techniques of ISTDP. If the patient can respond with increased motivation based on an affective experience accompanied by understanding or insight, suitability is established. However, if the patient develops overwhelming anxiety, fragmentation, identity confusion, paranoid ideas, or other signs of a fragile structure, the interviewer should stop challenging the patient and begin a more supportive approach.

THEORY OF CHANGE

The experience of feelings is central to change in Intensive Short-Term Dynamic Psychotherapy. Alexander and French wrote: "In the course of one interview the patient may react with violent anxiety, weeping, rage attacks, and all sorts of emotional upheavals together with an acute exacerbation of his symptoms—only to achieve a feeling of tremendous relief before the end of the interview. Such experiences, although curative in effect, are painful; they might be described as benign traumata. . ." (1946, p. 66). Alexander spoke of the corrective emotional experience, which is a positive reenactment in therapy of past conflictual relationships. Employing differential therapeutics is essential, as there are two broad categories of patients (Okin, 1986): the less resistant group, patients who manifest little character pathology and readily experience their feelings, and the more highly resistant group, patients who possess rigid character structures. In the less resistant group, change is believed to occur as the therapist facilitates affective and cognitive experiencing of repressed conflictual feelings and urges, while clarifying the associated defenses, symptoms, and anxiety. Whenever resistance to experiencing feelings and impulses is manifested, it is clarified and confronted through a steady defense analysis (to be described later) until resolved. This constant pressure to experience feelings and urges with frequent challenge to resistance produces an intrapsychic crisis by exposing the self-destructiveness of longstanding ego syntonic character patterns. This crisis produces intense affects, which tap into a reservoir of unconscious thoughts, memories, and feelings and activate the unconscious therapeutic alliance. This dynamic flow speeds and compresses the psychoanalytic process.

Fostering change in the highly resistant group of patients with characterological rigidity requires an additional preliminary stage: restructuring of the defenses. In this group, it is believed, there is always some—and usually extensive—inhibition, deflection, or regression from the appropriate experience and expression of feelings and impulses (in fact, the difficulty is seen as pathognomonic of character pathology). Change is initiated by systematically helping such individuals to identify and experience their feelings and impulses and differentiate defenses and anxiety. When this restructuring phase is accomplished, as indicated by the patient's access to feelings and impulses, more previously unconscious material will become available. For example, a woman who is chronically depressed recognizes the link between her depression and anger and then recounts previous incidents when she became depressed and now realizes that she was angry.

Once the therapeutic alliance is established, work centers on linking the points of the triangle of person—composed of transference, current people, and past people—with regard to impulses/feelings, defenses, and anxiety, the triangle of conflict (illustrated in figure 1, found in the following section). This constant experiencing and linking of conflicts is believed to rapidly resolve neurotic symptoms and interpersonal patterns. Another major agent of change is the frequent analysis of the transference relationship, especially for highly resistant patients, with whom the analysis of transference resistance leads to the restructuring of the triangle of conflict, and the subsequent recognition and experience of feelings and impulses. This central role of the transference reflects the position of psychoanalytic theorists such as Merton Gill (1982).

TECHNIQUE

Introduction

Intensive Short-Term Dynamic Psychotherapy (ISTDP) is a treatment that follows the principles of psychoanalytic therapy. The best test for suitability is the evaluation, or trial therapy, in which the techniques of ISTDP are applied and carefully monitored. The major innovations which speed and intensify treatment are the following:

1. High therapist activity level
2. Maintenance of focus
3. Early and extensive analysis of the transference
4. Analysis of character defenses to achieve a high level of affective and cognitive involvement at all times
5. Extensive linkage of the therapist–patient relationship (transference) with other significant relationships in the patient's life.

Sessions are weekly, face to face, fifty minutes long, with a maximum of forty sessions. Traditional psychoanalytic abstinence and neutrality are observed (Greenson, 1967). The therapist does not give direction, advice, or praise and does not gratify but rather explores personal inquiries by the patient.

Evaluation

The evaluation or trial therapy plays a special role in ISTDP. As the term trial therapy implies, there is a testing of the specific innovative techniques of this therapy to determine whether a patient can respond favorably and benefit from ISTDP. The evaluation covers several phases. First is the survey, which is a superficial assessment of the current difficulties via the two triangles without getting prematurely entangled in challenging resistance. Next is the challenge, which has two parts: step 1, a low-pressure cognitive phase in which defenses are clarified, then step 2, a more intense phase of challenge and pressure to exhaust the patient's resistance. The result is clearer access to previously unconscious conflicts. This is followed by the interpretive phase, in which current and transference problems are clarified and then linked to their core genetic antecedents. These phases vary and depend on the patient's level of resistance.

The central dynamic sequence is Davanloo's schema for the evaluation of moderately to highly resistant patients. Davanloo points out, "Of course not all trial therapies consist exactly of this simple sequence. The phases tend to overlap . . . [with] a good deal of repetition . . . [and tend to] proceed in a spiral rather than a straight line. . . . [It is called] the central dynamic sequence . . . [and should be] seen as a framework which the therapist can use as a guide" (1988, p. 100). The following list summarizes Davanloo's eight phases of the trial therapy.

1. Inquiry into current difficulties and initial identification of defenses.
2. Pressure leading to more resistance.
3. Clarification and confrontation of defenses and appeal to the patient to make defenses ego alien.
4. Challenge the transference resistance, which intensifies due to steps 1 through 3. Special attention is paid to self-defeating and self-torturing aspects of defense.
5. Emergence of mixed feelings in the transference, which signals the beginning of clearer access to the unconscious.
6. Analysis of transference around the triangle of conflict and linkage to other significant figures.
7. Completion of the diagnostic inquiry.
8. Connecting the core neurosis to current symptoms and character.

It is a mistake to rigidly apply this paradigm, since it varies from patient to patient. If the basic principles are applied in a heuristic manner to tracking and challenging resistance, a sequence will evolve that is appropriate to the patient. This model is a good first approximation or initial guide. In our experience, there is a natural path that unfolds with each patient–therapist pair that cannot be anticipated. That is why we prefer our simpler, more flexible model, which covers the same issues.

Survey.

The evaluation opens with a survey. Current problems are elicited with minimal challenge. In this phase diagnosis, character structure, and defenses are assessed. This information is filtered through the triangle of conflict (Freud 1925–1926/1959) and the triangle of person (figure 1).

For example, a man complaining about being overlooked for a promotion by his boss declares he felt depressed (D):

THERAPIST: How did you feel (I/F) toward your boss (C)?
PATIENT: I was a little (D) annoyed (I/F).
THERAPIST: So, in the face of your annoyance (I/F) with your boss (C) you became depressed (D).

No challenge is made at this time to have the patient fully experience the impulse/feeling. The questioning is aimed at a clear, specific, psychodynamically informative account.

There are some circumstances in which the current problem survey is briefly deferred. If a patient presents a great deal of initial transference feeling, or is depressed, anxious, or in a crisis, these areas should be clinically reviewed before moving to the general survey. These precautions avoid stressing a fragile patient. If there are no contraindications, all the

Figure 1

The Two Working Triangles

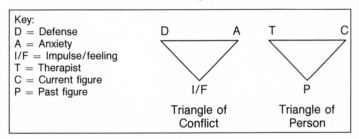

Key:
D = Defense
A = Anxiety
I/F = Impulse/feeling
T = Therapist
C = Current figure
P = Past figure

current areas of disturbance are delineated in the course of the survey. The current sexual life is explored, whether or not that is a source of complaint for the patient. The patient is challenged only if there is so much resistance that numerous efforts to get the current history fail. There is acknowledgment of resistance, such as, "You're smiling as we discuss your anger," but the resistance is not pursued at this time.

Challenge Step 1.

After the survey is completed, the challenge phase begins with the most troublesome current problem. This is the defense or character analysis, which is a continuous process that occurs in two phases (McCullough, in press).

The first step is a cognitive familiarization of patients with their defenses in relation to feelings and anxiety (the triangle of conflict). The therapist applies steady low pressure to enable the patient to be specific, clear, emotionally involved, and able to declare and experience feelings. This first phase is managed in one of two ways, depending on the level of resistance of the patient. Patient resistance covers a continuous range, but for didactic purposes we delineate two groups—high resistance versus low resistance (see table 1). Patients with low resistance can differentiate the points of the triangle of conflict, have ego dystonic defenses and symptoms, show high motivation, present relatively simple focal problems, and relate well to the therapist. The predominant resistance is repression, often accompanied by guilt feelings, which also serve resistance. Because resistance in this group is low, the evaluative phase of therapy is generally brief.

TABLE 1

Patients' Resistance Characteristics

Low Resistance	Characteristic	High Resistance
Good	State of differentiation of triangle of conflict	Poor
High	Motivation	Low
Simple	Complexity of psychopathologic foci	Complex
Ego alien; fewer	Character defenses	Ego syntonic; more
Good	Interpersonal relatedness	Fair to poor

Note: In actuality, patients' resistance falls along a continuum.

In the moderately to highly resistant group, the first step is generally longer and plays a crucial part in preparing the groundwork for future interventions (Fosha, 1988). These types of patients are characterized by an inability to clearly describe and differentiate impulse/feeling, defense, and anxiety, and instead report vague depressive or anxietylike symptoms, migraine headaches, or gastrointestinal and other psychosomatic disorders. Many of their defenses and symptoms are ego syntonic; their motivation is poor and they have many infantile conflicts. They frequently present in a vague and poorly related manner. The bulk of their resistance is manifested as self-defeating interpersonal patterns that signify a harsh, punitive superego. Resistant patients frequently exhibit a lack of emotional involvement, which often signals early life deprivation, loss, and a sense of not being valued. They have erected emotional barriers to ward off closeness in order to avoid experiencing painful yearnings, losses, anxiety, and other dysphoric affects.

In contrast to the first group, which comprises excellent psychotherapy candidates, patients in this second group have frequently failed at several previous treatments and are the most difficult patients to treat. They need a longer first phase, known as cognitive restructuring of the triangle of conflict. This is the preinterpretive phase in which the triangle of conflict is delineated but interpretations of underlying dynamics are deferred. The marker that heralds the end of the cognitive pressure phase is the initial emergence and experience of feelings, frequently starting with annoyance toward the therapist for the relentless pressure directed at warded off affect and content. This annoyance is accompanied by sadness, pain, guilt, and longing. If step 2, consisting of challenge and pressure for intense affect, is applied prematurely to this group, misalliance often results. Too much anxiety is mobilized; or the patient, lacking the recognition of ego syntonic defenses or character armor, may feel attacked by the therapist.

Consider step 1 with such a patient.

THERAPIST: So you became depressed (D) in the face of your annoyance (I/F) with the boss (C), but how did you experience the annoyance (I/F)? Depression (D) is not annoyance (I/F).

In this example the patient does not consciously experience annoyance. Instead depression is used defensively, which may be a characterological way of dealing with anger. The goal in ISTDP is to obtain fully experienced feeling based on three parameters: (a) physiological arousal, (b) motoric manifestations of activation such as raised voice and body movement, and (c) cognitive acknowledgment of the inner urges in fantasy.

PATIENT: Well, I walked out of there (D).
THERAPIST: Walking out is avoidance (D) and distancing (D); that still doesn't tell us your inner experience of annoyance (I/F).

A less resistant patient soon starts to tell about the impulse/feeling. "I felt my blood rushing with adrenaline in my chest and arms." With this group, we move rapidly to step 2, since there is a clear understanding of the triangle of conflict. In the more resistant group, further work is necessary to restructure the ego's capacity to experience affects.

PATIENT: I don't know how I experienced annoyance.
THERAPIST: When you say "I don't know (D)" it is a declaration of helplessness (D) as we try to investigate your annoyance (I/F).
PATIENT: I am helpless (D) a lot of the time.

This is an ego syntonic character defense with which the patient is identified. The therapist must continue steady low pressure, attempting to dissect out and undermine ego syntonic defenses.

THERAPIST: So you remain helpless (D), and we still don't know how you experience annoyance (I/F).
PATIENT: I feel my throat tighten (A) and butterflies (A) in my stomach.
THERAPIST: So you become anxious, your throat tightens and butterflies in your stomach. So we see that in the face of your annoyance (I/F) you become anxious (A), but that still doesn't describe how you experience your annoyance.

The therapist steadily differentiates the triangle of conflict and helps the patient distinguish defenses and anxiety from the impulses/feelings. Again, in step 1 the pressure is relatively low. After some work on the first focus (feelings toward the therapist) the same affective focus will be investigated toward another person with the focus maintained on the original impulse/feeling in relation to this new person. Through a series of such analyses of the triangle of conflict with different figures, a progressively higher level of affective experience is achieved, with maladaptive defenses becoming ego alien. When the patient is no longer using regressive defenses such as depression, helplessness, somatization, detachment, uninvolvement, and so on, step 2 is commenced and heavier pressure is brought to bear on the remaining resistance.

A special technique of ISTDP called portraiting or imagery is often employed. The patient is asked to visualize a scene in great detail, such as the actual or fantasied death bed scene of a parent or, as in the preceding example, a conflict with the boss, with appropriate affective involvement. This technique begins in step 1 and is used in all phases of ISTDP when a specific incident or fantasy is being focused on. Resistance to specificity, clarity, and emotional involvement is challenged. This visualization technique facilitates full cognitive involvement along with physiological and motoric expression. The technique helps intensify emerging feelings such as anger, sadness, grief, closeness, and sexuality.

A comparison of ISTDP with learning theory–based therapies (McCullough, in press) is warranted. ISTDP uses techniques such as flooding (Boudewyns & Shipley, 1983) and Implosion Therapy (Stamfl & Levis, 1967). In ISTDP patients are prevented from avoiding painful stimuli (flooding) and are asked to let their feelings go and essentially construct an image or fantasy around the particular feeling (Implosion Therapy or exposure treatment). The flooding model applies more to less resistant patients who can immediately experience affect, whereas a systematic desensitization model parallels the restructuring process with highly resistant patients.

Challenge Step 2.

The intensive challenge to transference resistance is believed to be the key to therapeutic success with highly resistant patients in ISTDP (Been & Sklar, 1985). Step 2 is a more intense challenge and pressuring of the resistance. In this phase the therapist is highly active, rapidly challenging and exhausting successive layers of defense. This constant pressure helps crystallize the resistance.

The pressure comes through a series of steps, including challenge and pressure to the defenses and finally the "head-on collision" (Worchel, 1986), an appeal for the patient to give up the defenses. This appeal points out the self-destructive and self-defeating nature of the defensive barrier, the need to fail and suffer as well as to defeat the therapist by defeating oneself (highlighting superego resistance). These motivational statements are made when the resistance is nearly exhausted, as evidenced by a high level of physiological and motoric arousal. Resistance such as the avoidance of pain and the instinctual attachment to early objects must frequently be challenged as well.

The constant pressure builds up a mixture of feelings toward the therapist and includes anger at having defenses immobilized, a wish for closeness, and a painful sense of what has been lost in other intimate relationships. Davanloo (1980) believes the experience of this complex of mixed feelings toward the therapist with a high level of intensity unlocks access to unconscious material toward current and past significant others. These feelings surge to the surface, and additional defenses are mobilized to prevent the affective outpouring. As the affect emerges, the unconscious therapeutic alliance (Langs, 1978) surfaces. These are the forces in the patient battling the resistance and craving intimacy and satisfaction in life. These forces assist the patient in discarding previously ego syntonic defenses as their self-defeating nature becomes obvious. At this juncture, the therapist is challenging in two ways. One is pressing for the experience of feelings (I/F) and the second is challenging the massive barrier of defenses the patient has erected, a barrier that blocks his or her ability to be intimate with people, the "wall" (Davanloo, 1986).

Resistance is conceptualized on two levels. First is the already mentioned micro level, composed of various defenses: obsessional, regressive, tactical, nonverbal, and transference resistance (see table 2).

These defenses combine to form a barrier or wall against emotional closeness, the macro level. After these individual defenses have been identified, they are reframed as elements of the barrier against intimacy. This is a powerful intervention that heightens the intrapsychic conflict and helps make the defenses dystonic.

TABLE 2

Types of Defenses and Resistance

Obsessive	Regressive	Tactical	Nonverbal	Transference
Intellectualization	Compliance/Defiance	"I suppose"	Body posture	Resistance against closeness
Undoing Reaction formation	Weepiness Passive-Aggressive	"Perhaps"	Eye contact	
Sarcasm	Projection	Verbal maneuvers to distance patients from their feelings	Vocal quality	Resistance against rage
Isolation of affect	Somatization		Fidgeting	
	Dissociation /denial		Tics	
	Acting out		Clenching of fists, jaws Sighing	

The concept of unlocking the unconscious applies to the moderately to highly resistant group of patients whose rigid defenses and character style allow extremely limited fluidity for their affects, feelings, and fantasies. This unlocking occurs on two levels. First is the increased ability to experience and tolerate affects, known as restructuring the triangle of conflict. Feelings are no longer reflexively channeled to symptoms (depression, anxiety, psychosomatic symptoms) or defenses. Instead the patient consciously acknowledges and tolerates the affect. A good analogy is comparing a lightning rod and a capacitor. As soon as the charge hits a lightning rod (here, defenses and symptoms) it is discharged. On the other hand, a capacitor accumulates and stores charge, introducing a time delay. The reflexive cycle of symptoms and defenses is broken and a measured (delayed) response is made. The charge or urge is brought under the auspices of conscious awareness and control. This is the highest state of maturation and integration. Simultaneously with this enlarged capacity comes a new awareness that past symptoms and defenses were used in early life to ward off strong feelings and impulses toward ambivalently experienced relationships. It now becomes clear that past behaviors such as obsequiousness or helplessness were defenses against rage and pain (T-C-P linkage). Affectively intense memories can now emerge and will reveal the genetic core conflicts through the process of clarifying and experiencing the points of the triangle of conflict in relation to the three points of the triangle of person. This emergence of painful, conflicted early memories is the second part of the unlocking. A complete past history is not obtained at this time, only a past history that spontaneously emerges in regard to the current difficulty. A complete systematic past history is obtained after the current areas of disturbance are completely surveyed. However, it must be understood that whenever significant resistance emerges the therapist should return to resistance/defense analysis.

Interpretation.

After the triangle of conflict is understood and experienced, the interpretive phase of the evaluation begins: the linkage between I/F, D, and A is repeatedly made in regard to T, C, and P. Next the inventory of the current areas of difficulty is returned to and completed, including current sexual functioning. A medical history to rule out significant contributing illness is obtained. Then a systematic survey of early life is undertaken, including relationships with parents, siblings, and other significant early figures; sexual development; and academic and social functioning. This is again a dynamic inquiry based upon the two triangles. When a significant relationship is examined, triangular involvement is explored. Particular attention is paid to identify and link early dynamic constellations that resonate with current conflicts. Depending on the time available and complexity, a partial understanding, consisting of some of the early relationships, or a complete understanding, based on working with and experiencing conflicts with all early figures, is obtained. The best evidence that a patient's problems are appropriate for and will respond to ISTDP is a successful trial therapy. There are three indications of success in trial therapy:

1. Obtaining at least one T-C-P linkage during the evaluation in a fully experienced affective and cognitive framework.
2. Seeing a change in the patient's functioning or the use of more adaptive defenses in the next sessions.
3. Observing the appearance of memories or dreams related to the patient's core conflicts.

To summarize, the evaluation is the true test for treatability with ISTDP and the period during which the techniques are initially tested. The proper fine tuning of technique to the individual patient is empirically discovered by progressively increasing the level of pressure in the preinterpretive phase and monitoring the patient's ability to respond, anxiety level, and defensive style. The therapist should always be ready to moderate the pressure if the patient manifests too much anxiety or fragility in response to the challenge. In a successful evaluation, a patient reports immediate symptom attenuation or relief and shows an alteration in his or her character defense pattern.

In Beth Israel's research protocol, the evaluation is limited to two two-hour sessions. In nonresearch settings the evaluation may run as long as three to four hours, over one session or more as needed.

Therapeutic Contract.

The therapeutic contract grows out of the findings of the evaluation. In a successful evaluation, an affective/cognitive breakthrough occurs, with T-C-P linkages subsequently established for some or all of the patient's current and core issues. This usually leads to emotional relief and an increased motivation to work on the problems. The therapist asks whether the patient wishes to explore current and early life conflicts and their linkage, as was done in the evaluation. If the patient agrees, a summary is made of the findings, again focused on the two triangles, as well as on dyadic and triadic dynamic and characterological issues highlighted in the evaluation. The therapist states that these are the problems to be faced and sets the meeting time and financial arrangements. The patient is told that the maximum number of sessions is forty. There may be fewer, depending on the patient's characterological complexity and level of resistance.

Treatment

The techniques used in the treatment phase are similar to those of the evaluation. Treatment continues to be organized around the two triangles, with high therapist activity, ongoing challenge of significant resistance, and maintenance of focus with special attention to the analysis of transference resistance.

The patient is told at the start of the first postevaluation session that treatment proceeds best if each session is started with whatever comes to mind. This opening is called the adaptive context (Langs, 1978) and is composed of elements of the two triangles in a psychodynamic matrix. This context is thought to reflect the aspect of the core conflict that is emerging from repression into consciousness, with its associated resistances. When the therapist understands the adaptive context, including the interpersonal and the dynamic (triangular, dyadic), the understanding is summarized and feelings are inquired into. Resistance is then challenged as previously, but with the added knowledge obtained in the evaluation of the patient's character structure, defensive operations, and underlying conflicts. Again, the goal is full affective/cognitive involvement. Once this is obtained in the C or T, a linkage is sought in the P. This is the process of elucidating the core conflicts and working them through. In a treatment that is progressing well, the amount and intensity of resistance and challenge tend to decrease as the sessions progress. The use of the transference analysis also diminishes as therapy progresses. There are upsurges of resistance, which require more challenge when particular conflicts are reached. The principle, as in other psychoanalytic treatments, is that the transference is a tool to handle resistance and is addressed when necessary toward this end. Triangulation is also introduced and explored. For example, if work is done in regard to the mother, the father's role should be inquired into; if a patient describes an intimate scene, feelings toward the intruding therapist should subsequently be explored.

Certain issues must be addressed early in treatment. One of these issues is pathological mourning; this must be handled early on because the repressed ambivalent feelings and resistances put a massive drain on the patient's energy to work in treatment, much as a severe depression does.

Pathological mourning must be activated and worked through before more intensive dynamic exploration can be successfully undertaken. In moving to activate the pathological mourning into acute grief (Winston & Goldin, 1985), the typical defense analysis is necessary to facilitate the experiencing of ambivalent feelings. Pathological mourning should be briefly activated in the evaluation, but a broad survey is still the goal. The pathological mourning is then more systematically addressed in the early sessions.

From the evaluation's elucidation of the current problems stated by the patient, together with the characterological difficulties identified and linked to the clarified core conflicts, it becomes clear what issues need to be addressed in the treatment phase. If the evaluation is incomplete, elucidating only part of the core dynamics, the first few sessions should be used to complete the survey of core genetic conflicts. It is believed that a more thorough evaluation leads to a significantly shorter treatment. The treatment plan is focused on these early life issues, which should correspond to current symptoms and character patterns.

Termination

The end of treatment can be natural and simple in cases in which the original problems were uncomplicated oedipal issues. In such cases a patient will appear for a session and report many areas of change and improvement. Subsequent review shows no residual problems. Termination is set for the next session and feelings toward the therapist and about saying goodbye are investigated, with associated feelings and memories explored.

In more complicated treatments, especially where loss has been a major focus, termination will continue the working through of feelings about other losses. In these patients, three to five sessions are allotted at the end to focus on a thorough experience of the "death" of the therapy and other unresolved grief. Frequently, losses not discussed earlier in treatment will now emerge—for example, a grandparent who had a special relationship with the patient. In this group, it is the therapist's job to be sure the mourning process is not avoided, or the gains from treatment may be significantly diminished to defend against painful feelings.

TRAINING OF THERAPISTS

Intensive Short-Term Dynamic Psychotherapy calls for rigorous individual and group training of at least two years for therapists experienced in psychoanalytic psychotherapy. This training consists of one hour of individual videotaped supervision for each hour of treatment, as well as a weekly one-and-a-half-hour group supervision to follow various types of patients through the course of treatment. We have extended this training to psychiatry residents and psychology interns. All training is based on a manual. There is a concomitant didactic course on theory and technique.

CASE EXAMPLE

The following case demonstrates some phases of ISTDP treatment. The evaluation phase is emphasized due to its central importance in ISTDP. The dialogue comes from transcribed videotaped sessions.

The patient was a fifty-year-old divorced woman who was unemployed but had supported herself and her son, who was then nine, for many years. She sought treatment because she wanted more pleasure out of life, was lonely, overworked, and chronically depressed and weepy. She had a sporadic relationship with an older man, who was impotent and gambled. He was unreliable, sarcastic, and insensitive to her needs. She had an antagonistic relationship with her ex-husband, her son's father, who was also unreliable and self-centered, and who contributed little financially to the rearing of their child. There were few women and no men in her life whom she considered as friends or supports. Her relationship with her older sister, who lived a comfortable, financially secure married life, was poor.

Her relationship with her son was loving, but she feared she might die and abandon him. Her father died suddenly when she was nine years old, which was a devastating loss for her. Recently, she did have a benign tumor removed from her neck, and she suffered from hypertension, as well as overwork, but her health was generally good.

The evaluation was the second of two evaluations by different interviewers. We use this format as a training experience in interviewing, as well as to obtain a more complete picture of the patient. The patient reacted to being asked to repeat what her problems were by rolling her eyes and laughing. The therapist chose to ignore her immediate reaction and to attempt to get the current problems mapped out first. This effort failed, as the patient remained vague and circumstantial for the first few minutes and then mentioned again, "Last week I said exactly the same thing." At this point, the therapist decided the warded off feelings and thoughts toward the interviewer for having to repeat her story were blocking the process and decided to defer the survey of current difficulties until this resistance was addressed.

After a few minutes of vague complaints the session continued.

THERAPIST: I noticed that you smiled (D) when I mentioned that we'd start from scratch. . . . What is your reaction (I/F) to that?

PATIENT: Well, obviously it's a repetition . . .

THERAPIST: Right, you mentioned that, a repetition, let's see how you feel (I/F) about having to go through it again because I notice you're smiling (D) a lot when you start to mention repetition. Do you notice that? (*The therapist is starting to work in the triangle of conflict, linking I/F to D.*)

PATIENT: Yeah, I'm aware of that. I understand the manner in which the program works (D). I guess I'm kind of interested in going beyond that, however, I recognize that . . .

THERAPIST: So, intellectually (D) you know how the program works, but let's see what you're *feeling* (I/F) about having to go through it again.

PATIENT: O K, I'm bored (D) but I'll repeat it . . .

THERAPIST: Well, bored is not really feeling, it's detachment (D), isn't it? But what's your feeling (I/F) about having to repeat . . . ?

PATIENT: My feeling, um . . .

THERAPIST: . . . you like it?

PATIENT: Not particularly, no, well somewhere around September of last year I was told that I'd have to have surgery for a growth in my neck (D) . . . (*The patient attempts to change the focus.*)

THERAPIST: The surgery in your neck is obviously important, but before we move to that you were mentioning the boredom and having to repeat, and I was trying to look at what your feeling is about that.

The therapist asked for the patient's feelings toward him about having to repeat the story. The patient rapidly resorted to a variety of defensive maneuvers—rationalizing, smiling, boredom, changing the topic, and compliance, rather than declaring her feelings. The therapist began differentiating the triangle of conflict by pointing out these defenses and labeling them "not feelings." The therapist's first task was to determine the patient's ability to declare and experience her feelings, and from this determine whether restructuring would be necessary (placing her in the less resistant or more resistant group). The interview continues:

PATIENT: My feeling is I guess that I've been living with a lot of history for a long time, very close up front and, um . . .

THERAPIST: I notice you're having a lot of trouble looking at me (D) as you start to talk about this and again you smile (D).

PATIENT: I don't consider myself an evasive person (D), I really don't . . .

THERAPIST: . . . but you bring up the word *evasive* now.

PATIENT: Well, one who does not or isn't capable of eye contact is usually removing themselves from something. I don't think I'm particularly . . . (*The patient's defense of breaking eye contact, a form of distancing, is not ego syntonic since she identifies it herself.*)

THERAPIST: But isn't that how you are right now with me?

PATIENT: O K.

THERAPIST: You notice that about yourself, right now?

PATIENT: O K, I accept that. I just think that, you know, for two hours . . . (*The use of rationalization is ego syntonic and needs more low pressure work as described in step 1.*)

THERAPIST: The issue is that you have some reaction about repeating. You say you're bored (D), but that's a detached state, not a feeling, you see? What do you feel (I/F) about having to go through it again here with me?

PATIENT: I don't know, maybe you're touching on something. I thought about that a lot, after last week's meeting, I'm not sure, other than real feelings of sadness at times. I'm not sure that I have a lot of handles on feelings and I think maybe that's because—how can I phrase it?—Right, because the feelings came up about, you know, what was I feeling and I said to myself, in thinking about it, what are my feelings? I'm not sure I can identify them.

THERAPIST: O K, so they're all very vague (D). Isn't that what you're . . .

PATIENT: I don't know (D) that it's all very vague or . . .

THERAPIST: But you say you don't know (D).

PATIENT: . . . or an unconscious effort on my part to detach myself from feelings.

THERAPIST: Well, for whatever reason, right now as we try to look at your feelings you are very vague (D), whether the reasons are conscious or unconscious, you see that here with me you're vague?

PATIENT: Yes.

THERAPIST: Because there is a lot of talking about feelings, intellectualizing (D), but you don't declare how you feel (I/F) about having to repeat yourself. You mention that you thought about it after last week's session and I asked you if you liked that.

PATIENT: O K, I'm thinking, I'm thinking what can be gleaned (D) . . .

THERAPIST: Yes, but you see you go on to rationalize (D) a lot.

PATIENT: O K.

THERAPIST: You see what I'm saying about rationalizing (D).

PATIENT: O K, so I guess that's what I'm doing, I really don't want to address feelings and maybe that's true.

THERAPIST: O K, so let's look at that because this is a major obstacle that we have to address, because what is our job here? You see, what's your goal? It's to get some understanding about your feeling life.

PATIENT: That's true, and that's probably one of the main motivations of being here.

THERAPIST: Right, and then right from the start you don't want to look at your feelings, you see that? That's going to be very self-defeating if that's the direction you go in, you see, if part of you doesn't want to look at your feelings.

(The therapist believes the defenses are now less ego syntonic and increases the pressure by a motivational statement addressed to the patient's self-defeating tendency [superego resistance].)

PATIENT: I'm . . . probably aware of that and maybe that's why I'm sitting here in . . .

THERAPIST: O K, so let's look at this because you're saying there's part of you that doesn't want to look at feelings, that wants to rationalize?

PATIENT: I don't know that I don't want to look at feelings, or I really don't know (D) . . .

THERAPIST: You see, you begin rationalizing again (D).

PATIENT: Why?

THERAPIST: You give excuses—"I don't know if I want to look at feelings or I don't"—but I'm saying do you see this is a problem, right now for us, that as soon as we try to look at your feelings . . .

PATIENT: Yeah . . .

THERAPIST: . . . you start to rationalize (D) and you avoid (D) the issue. You're being an evasive person, in your own words, and again you're smiling (D) when I point out your evasiveness.

PATIENT: Smiling as opposed to crying.

THERAPIST: Do you feel like crying (I/F) right now?

PATIENT: No.

THERAPIST: But, you see, the issue is that you don't like having to repeat. Is that right?

PATIENT: That's true.

THERAPIST: So, how do you feel (I/F) toward me for having to repeat?

PATIENT: I don't know, I guess there would be (D) a degree of annoyance (I/F).

THERAPIST: "there would be"—you make it questionable, "there would be" (D), you see?

PATIENT: Yes.

THERAPIST: Because again you're smiling (D). Isn't that striking to you, the smile when you say you're annoyed (I/F)? I mean, isn't that the opposite of annoyance, a smile?

PATIENT: I would say that I have a difficult time expressing anger (I/F) or . . .

THERAPIST: Well, I see that now.

PATIENT: . . . or dealing with anger (I/F) . . . um . . .

THERAPIST: So, this is a major issue that we have to look at, because what we see right away is you're being an evasive person, as you put it, that you put on a facade of a smile when you're feeling angry with me, do you see that? (*The therapist is starting to address the patient's characterological style of distancing, the wall, which is composed of all the defenses.*)

PATIENT: With you or probably with most people . . .

THERAPIST: Uh-huh, so, then, it's not just a problem here between us; this is how you are on the outside, too.

PATIENT: I would have to . . . I think so, I think so.

THERAPIST: So, then, this is a major problem that we need to look into, right, if you're going to put on a facade when we're trying to take a look at the emotional difficulties in your life.

PATIENT: I don't think . . . I can tell you right off the bat that I don't think I'm going to walk through that door and suddenly be a different person than I am . . . um . . .

THERAPIST: You mean, in other words, there's going to be a part of you that's going to hang on to the facade.

PATIENT: There's no doubt in my mind that I . . .

THERAPIST: O K, let's look at that. Would you say you have a tendency to be a stubborn (D) person?

(*As one defense is given up, a new one comes more clearly into view. In this case it is stubbornness. Notice too that the therapist maintains the pace by interrupting the patient when she starts to rationalize.*)

PATIENT: I would say probably (D).

THERAPIST: Probably (D), I mean is it . . .

PATIENT: Yeah, I would think so . . .

THERAPIST: So, in other words, the stubborn (D) side of you can hang on to this facade and procrastinate (D)?

PATIENT: The stubborn (D) side of me has been cultivated, I think, as a tool for me to live . . . um . . . and be able to survive.

THERAPIST: O K, so then this is another critical issue that we have to look at, you see, because I'm saying to you that it's important for us to look at your honest thoughts and feelings.

PATIENT: I absolutely agree with you. (*This statement indicates that the therapeutic alliance is improving.*)

THERAPIST: You see, but right away the idea is that you're not going to be able to let that down, that you're not going to be able to let that facade down for a long time. You know, you're looking sad (I/F) right now, you're looking really sad.

PATIENT: You're right. (*The patient turns down her head as she starts crying.*)

THERAPIST: But you don't want me to see that either. You see how you need to keep distance (D), right here with me now? That you don't want me near your feelings.

PATIENT: It's true.

THERAPIST: Let's see what it is that brought the sadness (I/F) to you.

PATIENT: I'm amazed that I'm crying.

THERAPIST: What's in your thoughts along with the sadness? (*These tears are the first breakthrough of feelings.*)

PATIENT: I guess I have always tried very hard to put a lid on feelings, on my feelings, because I was never . . . um . . . or rarely able to express them without being blown away.

THERAPIST: How do you mean?

PATIENT: From very early on . . .

THERAPIST: Right now are you fighting it, if you're honest with yourself. I mean, is part of you trying to keep a distance even as you experience a lot of pain?

PATIENT: No, I'm just trying very hard to maintain my composure.

THERAPIST: This is what I mean. Part of you wants to keep the lid on, even now, isn't that the case?

PATIENT: Um . . .

THERAPIST: Because I see you struggling. I mean, obviously there's tremendous feeling (I/F) in you right now and you're starting to talk about a lot of painful issues from the past but even as we, together, try to understand your difficulties part of you wants to keep the distance (D), keep the barriers and not let me into your intimate thoughts and feelings.

(*As feelings emerge, there is an effort to suppress them; the therapist must clear this residual resistance.*)

PATIENT: I would guess that's probably true, it's conflict of being frightened of revealing what I'm really feeling because my experience has not been a terrific one when I've done that.

THERAPIST: So, there's a lot of fear about closeness and openness.

PATIENT: Absolutely true, there's no question in my mind that I . . . and not only is that true but I think I've chosen people who have been important . . . have played important roles in my life . . . um . . . who are incapable of hearing or dealing with feelings, and I don't think that's an accident, I think that I definitely made a conscious effort, whatever the design was I just filled in the tapestry.

THERAPIST: So, then the question is how that's going to be here with me, you see, because I'm the one now who wants to get to know your intimate thoughts and your intimate feelings.

PATIENT: I don't think it's going to be easy, I really don't, but then I say to myself I really want to do it, and generally when I am determined to do something I do it! . . .

Am . . . I am ready to make changes. I don't think those changes are going to be easy or painless, but I've come to a stage in my life where I really believe it's time that, um . . . (*The patient is declaring a high level of motivation.*)

THERAPIST: O K, well, then, let's look. You started to tell me about your surgery, a lump in your neck that you mentioned earlier.

This transcript reflects the first fifteen to twenty minutes of the evaluation session. The patient displayed both ego alien defenses such as breaking eye contact, a form of distancing that she immediately acknowledged as a problem, and ego syntonic defenses such as rationalization. Her rationalizing required repeated highlighting by the therapist so that her feelings toward him about repeating her story could be clarified. This combination of ego syntonic and alien defenses places the patient in the moderate resistance range. She also had psychosomatic symptoms, which indicate higher resistance. Other defenses became clear as well, especially stubbornness. As evidence of a good therapeutic alliance appeared, indicated by the patient's linking her avoiding eye contact and evasiveness, and her agreeing that one goal in therapy would be to understand her feelings, a challenge to her self-defeating behavior (superego resistance) was initiated. It became clear that part of the patient's problems were her characterological difficulties, especially various forms of distancing. She agreed that she used her facade with everyone (T-C linkage). Then a wave of sadness and crying emerged, which the patient attempted to control. This was the first breakthrough of more intense feelings. Although anger was the initial topic, sadness about her loneliness and lifelong struggle surfaced. This is typical in moderately to highly resistant patients. The breakthrough of sad feelings results in a high level of motivation. The patient declared: "I really want to do it, and generally when I am determined to do something I do it!"

This part of the interview lasted twenty minutes. The evaluation then continued to survey her current problems. It became clear that she was angry with her ex-husband. As an effort was made to look at this anger, resistance increased. Finally, the patient recalled an incident when she actually attacked him. This attack was determined to be an isolated event, indicating that the patient did not have an impulse control problem. She described her rage as a "bolt of lightning" exploding in her chest, accompanied by the urge to lash out at him. Her voice was raised and her upper body was animated. She was asked, "What if you did let it all out in fantasy?" She struggled against this idea, again resorting to stubbornness. Finally, she admitted really wanting to hurt him by punching his face. In actuality, she had sat on his chest and punched his arms, avoiding more vulnerable targets. As the therapist pressed for more fantasy, the patient spontaneously declared her hatred of her mother and how she would have liked to lash out at her. As she described her violent feelings toward her mother, she was shaken by a wave of nausea. This was followed by tears of depression and hopelessness. More restructuring work was done around the triangle of conflict in regard to these violent feelings and the accompanying depression and anxiety.

Throughout the evaluation, the three parameters of feeling (motoric, physiological, and fantasy) were being assessed. As this was done, the therapist indicated that lashing out verbally or physically is not recommended and actually may be a form of defense.

Over the first several sessions, more work was done on restructuring the patient's ability to tolerate rage and intimacy. Many violent memories and dreams surfaced. Her violent fantasies toward her ex-husband and her mother were linked. She remembered that after her father's death, she had to share her mother's bed. Every night she would fall out of bed trying to remain far from her mother, who was very critical and jealous of her close relationship with her dead father. The mother blamed her for her father's death ("you loved him to death") and constantly repeated how she wanted to abort the patient, but the father had stopped her. During the fourth session, the patient had an urge to dismember and chop up her ex-husband, which she related to cutting up chickens as a young girl and finally linked to violent feelings toward her mother. Around the seventh session, her mother actually died. Although she had been estranged from her mother for years, she was able to attend the funeral. To her surprise, she cried at the funeral.

After the tenth session, the patient stopped complaining of being depressed and was no longer weepy. As the treatment progressed she obtained a suitable job and reported feeling much lighter and more alive. In a moving session in the midphase of treatment, she described a date with an abusive man. Once she heard how sarcastic and abusive he was, she informed him she would not tolerate abuse and ended the date. Later that session, she described new empathy for her mother, who slaved to raise her, and anger at her father for being self-centered and abusive toward her mother. With great pain and tears, she acknowledged how painful it must have been for her mother to receive the father's abuse and then see him cuddle his little princess. No wonder her mother hated her. This was a major shift, since her father had always been idolized. She now linked the abusive men in her life with her father.

As the treatment moved toward termination, the patient was ambivalent, feeling she was not ready. Nearing the end mobilized anger and sadness toward the therapist. These feelings were linked to mixed feelings about other prematurely lost people, her father and mother.

At the six-month follow-up, the patient reported maintaining all her previous gains. She no longer suffered from depression and had an appropriate job. She was much closer to her son, her sister, and several friends. The patient achieved significant characterological improvement and symptom resolution.

EMPIRICAL SUPPORT

Davanloo (1978, 1979, 1980) has performed three clinical studies on ISTDP. His patients were seen for an average of twenty sessions. They included patients with neurosis and longstanding personality disorders. Baseline and outcome assessments were performed by independent evaluators. Forty percent of patients had follow-ups of five to seven years. Davanloo reported substantial clinical gains, which were maintained at termination and long-term follow-up.

The efficacy of ISTDP has been examined in a more systematic study (Winston et al., 1991). ISTDP was compared with Brief Adaptive Psychotherapy (BAP) and a waiting list control group. Patients with longstanding personality disorders, including avoidant, dependent, histrionic, obsessive-compulsive, passive-aggressive, and mixed personality disorders, were treated by experienced therapists. Both therapies (ISTDP and BAP) showed significant improvement on target complaints, SCL-90, and the Social Adjustment Scale, compared with waiting list control subjects (see table 3). Effect sizes for ISTDP ranged from .80 to 1.35. The two therapy groups were similar in overall outcome but showed differences on the anxiety and depression subscales of the SCL-90. ISTDP was significantly better on the depression subscale, while BAP patients were more improved on the anxiety subscales. In addition, findings at midphase (Trujillo & McCullough, 1985) indicated that ISTDP patients had more symptoms, including anxiety, than on admission. These findings may indicate that ISTDP is effective at mobilizing affects (particularly anxiety) that may take some time to work through.

We examined a number of therapist and process variables in ISTDP and BAP using a coding system developed for videotaped psychotherapy sessions (McCullough et al., 1985). ISTDP therapists are very active, intervening at the rate of approximately 2 interventions a minute. In a session there are an average of 12.7 patient-therapist interventions and 27.3 interventions related to current and past figures (see table 4). Since ISTDP is twice as active as BAP, many therapist interventions occur more frequently in ISTDP than in BAP. However, it is clear that ISTDP uses more affective and verbal probes (22.9 [11.1 percent] versus 5.9 [5.7 percent]) while BAP has relatively more questions and cognitive probes (22.8 [21.9 percent]

TABLE 3

*Admission and Termination Means and Effect Sizes
for Global Outcomes across Groups*

	BAP (N = 17)	STDP (N = 15)	Controls (N = 17)	Analysis of Convarience	
Target Complaint I[a]					
Admission	10.47	10.08	11.69	F =	12.46
Termination	6.67	5.91	10.25	P =	.0001
Effect size	1.23	1.35	.46	SD =	3.10
SCL-90 Global Score[a]					
Admission	44.55	43.77	47.38	F =	4.84
Termination	36.27	36.62	44.06	P =	.01
Effect size	1.11	.96	.45	SD =	7.45
Social Adjustment Scale[a]					
Admission	2.06	2.13	2.15	F =	6.68
Termination	1.74	1.76	2.18	P =	.003
Effect size	.70	.80	−.07	SD =	.45

Note: Effect size was computed by subtracting the termination mean from the admission mean and dividing by the standard deviation of the combined control and experimental groups.
[a]The scores of the two groups given therapy were significantly different at termination from those of the control group (p < 0.05, Duncan Multiple Range Test).

versus 27.6 [13.4 percent]). These process results indicate that ISTDP has more of an affective focus than does BAP, while both therapies actively use the transference and have an interpersonal focus.

In another process study using patients treated with either ISTDP or BAP, we were unable to find single therapist or patient variables that correlated with outcome (McCullough et al., in press). However, when variables were examined in context (patient response to a therapist intervention) we found a significant contribution of transference interpretation followed by patient affect to improvement at outcome. Furthermore, Taurke, Flegenheimer, McCullough, Winston, & Pollack (1990) demonstrated that two patient variables (the ratio of patient affect to patient defense) were significantly correlated with outcome in our pooled sample of ISTDP and BAP patients.

CONCLUSION

ISTDP appears to be an effective treatment. It has a significant range of application, which is being broadened as modifications are added. There are unique technical aspects, which require extensive and systematic training. ISTDP is believed to be a sound training model as well (Laikin, 1990). We are committed to ongoing research to further define elements of technique and patient selection.

TABLE 4

Average Frequencies of Occurrence per Session of Therapist Behaviors in the Two Treatment Groups

Behavior	BAP	STDP	t	p
Questions and cognitive probes	22.8	27.6	1.31	ns
Affective and nonverbal probes	5.9	22.9	5.95	.0002
Clarification	16.5	27.0	1.33	.0012
Confrontation	13.8	30.8	5.19	.0002
Addressing defensive behavior	15.0	34.5	1.19	.0005
Addressing anxiety	3.3	3.8	.76	ns
Addressing warded off impulses	4.8	12.6	3.4	.004
Patient–Therapist interventions	8.3	12.7	1.69	.11 (ns)
Intervention related to current and past figures	11.5	27.3	3.67	.004
Advice/support	3.1	3.6	.50	ns
Total therapist activity	104.0	206.0		

References

Alexander, F., & French, T. M. (1946). *Psychoanalytic therapy*. New York: Ronald Press.

Been, H., & Sklar, I. (1985). Transference in short-term dynamic psychotherapy. In A. Winston (Ed.), *Clinical and research issues in short-term dynamic psychotherapy*. Washington, D C: American Psychiatric Press.

Boudewyns, P. A., & Shipley, R. H. (1983). *Flooding and implosive therapy: Direct therapeutic exposure in clinical practice*. New York: Plenum.

Davanloo, H. (Ed.). (1978). *Basic principles and techniques in short-term dynamic psychotherapy*. New York: S. P. Medical and Scientific Books.

Davanloo, H. (1979). Techniques of short-term dynamic psychotherapy. *Psychiatric Clinics of North America, 2*, 11–22.

Davanloo, H. (Ed.). (1980). *Short-term dynamic psychotherapy*. New York: Jason Aronson.

Davanloo, H. (1986). Intensive short-term dynamic psychotherapy with highly resistant patients: 1. Handling resistance. *International Journal of Short-Term Psychotherapy, 1*, 107–133.

Davanloo, H. (1988). The technique of unlocking the unconscious, pt. 1. *International Journal of Short-term Psychotherapy, 2*, 99–121.

Ferenczi, S., & Rank, O. (1925). *The development of psychoanalysis* (C. Newton, Trans.). New York: Nervous and Mental Disease Publishing.

Fosha, D. (1988). Restructuring in the treatment of depressive disorders with Davanloo's intensive short-term dynamic psychotherapy. *International Journal of Short-Term Psychotherapy, 3*, 189–202.

Freud, S. (1953). Fragment of an analysis of a case of hysteria. In J. Strachey (Ed. & Trans.), *The standard edition of the complete psychological works of Sigmund Freud* (Vol. 7, pp. 7–122). London: Hogarth Press. (Original work published in 1905.)

Freud, S. (1959). Inhibitions, symptoms and anxiety. J. Strachey (Ed. & Trans.), *The complete psychological works of Sigmund Freud* (Vol. 20, pp. 87–156). London: Hogarth Press. (Original works published 1925–1926.)

Gill, M. M. (1982). *Analysis of the transference: Vol. 1. Theory and technique.* New York: International Universities Press.

Greenson, R. R. (1967). *The technique and practice of psychoanalysis* (Vol. 1). New York: International Universities Press.

Laikin, M. (1990, May). *ISTDP as a resident training model.* Paper presented at the meeting of the American Psychiatric Association, New York.

Laikin, M., & Winston, A. (1990). *Manual for intensive short-term dynamic psychotherapy.* Unpublished manuscript, Department of Psychiatry, Beth Israel Medical Center, New York, NY.

Langs, R. (1978). *The listening process.* New York: Jason Aronson.

Lindemann, E. (1944). Symptomatology and management of acute grief. *American Journal of Psychiatry 101,* 141–148.

Malan, D. H. (1976). *The frontier of brief psychotherapy.* New York: Plenum.

McCullough, L. (in press). Intensive short-term dynamic psychotherapy: Change mechanisms from a cross-theoretical perspective. In R. Curtis & G. Stricker (Eds.), *How people change: Inside and outside of therapy.* New York: Plenum.

McCullough, L., Trujillo, M., & Winston, A. (1985). *A videocoding manual of psychotherapy process.* Unpublished manuscript, Department of Psychiatry, Beth Israel Medical Center, New York, NY.

McCullough, L., Winston, A., Farber, B. A., Porter, F., Pollack, J., Laikin, M., Vingiano, W., & Trujillo, M. (in press). The relationship of patient–therapist interaction to outcome in brief psychotherapy. *Psychotherapy.*

Okin, R. (1986). Interpretation in short-term dynamic psychotherapy. *International Journal of Short-Term Psychotherapy, 4,* 271–279.

Reich, W. (1949). *Character analysis.* New York: Farrar, Strauss and Cudahy.

Sifneos, P. E. (1979). *Short-term dynamic psychotherapy: Evaluation and technique.* New York: Plenum.

Stampfl, T., & Levis, D. (1967). The essentials of implosive therapy: A learning-theory-based psychodynamic behavioral therapy. *Journal of Abnormal Psychology, 72,* 496–503.

Taurke, E., Flegenheimer, W., McCullough, L., Winston, A., & Pollack, J. (1990). Change in patient affect defense ratio from early to late sessions in brief psychotherapy. *Journal of Clinical Psychology, 46,* 657–668.

Trujillo, M., & McCullough, L. (1985). Research issues in short-term dynamic psychotherapies: An overview. In A. Winston (Ed.), *Clinical and research issues in intensive short-term dynamic psychotherapy.* Washington, DC: American Psychiatric Press.

Winston, A., & Goldin, V. (1985). Pathological mourning in Intensive Short-Term

Dynamic Psychotherapy. In A. Winston (Ed.), *Clinical and research issues in Intensive Short-Term Dynamic Psychotherapy.* Washington, DC: American Psychiatric Press.

Winston, A., McCullough, L., Pollack, J., Laikin, M., Pinsker, H., Nezu, A., Flegenheimer, W., & Sadow, J. (1989). The Beth Israel psychotherapy research program: Toward an integration of theory and discovery. *Journal of Integrative and Eclectic Psychotherapy, 8,* 344–356.

Winston, A., Pollack, J., McCullough, L., Flegenheimer, W., Kestenbaum, R., & Trujillo, M. (1991). Brief psychotherapy of personality disorders. *Journal of Nervous and Mental Disease, 179,* 188–193.

Worchel, J. (1986). Transference in Intensive Short-Term Dynamic Psychotherapy: Techniques of handling initial transference. *International Journal of Short-Term Psychotherapy, 2,* 135–146.

CHAPTER 5

Short-Term Supportive-Expressive Psychoanalytic Psychotherapy

Lester Luborsky and David Mark

ORIGINS AND DEVELOPMENT

Dynamic psychotherapy is the oldest, the best known, and the most widely practiced of the many forms of psychotherapy. Its techniques gradually evolved into the two treatment forms used today: classical psychoanalysis and psychoanalytic psychotherapy. Dynamic psychotherapy, which is our simpler term for psychoanalytic psychotherapy, has itself developed two formats: open-ended and time-limited.

This chapter is specifically devoted to a review of the techniques of the time-limited, manual-guided, dynamic supportive-expressive (SE) psychotherapy described in Luborsky (1984). The chapter does even more: it offers a set of principles and techniques that are ordered in their importance for this therapy.

A brief note is needed at this point to explain the terms *supportive* and *expressive*, even though they will be more fully explained later in the chapter. *Supportive* refers to the techniques aimed at directly maintaining the patient's level of functioning; *expressive* refers to the techniques aimed at facilitating the patient's expressions about problems and conflicts and their understanding.

The ideas about how to conduct this form of psychotherapy found their way into the manual from conventional psychodynamic sources. It should be obvious already that the manual was never intended to offer a new psychotherapeutic system, but rather to capture the essence of the technical system inherent in the writings of those who were among the accepted propounders of the method. By far the most influential source was Freud's six papers on technique: 1911/1958b, 1912/1958a, 1912/1958e, 1913/1958d, 1914/1958f, and 1915/1958c. But some of the other writers who based themselves on Freud also had an impact on the manual: Bibring (1954), Fenichel (1941), Luborsky and Schimek (1964), Menninger and Holzman (1973), and Stone (1951).

The essential substance of the system is derived from the above writers as summarized by Lester Luborsky and David Mark. Lester Luborsky's clinical experiences came from the apprentice training at the Menninger Foundation; much of the training there was in supportive-expressive psychotherapy, which was the main form of psychotherapy in addition to classical psychoanalysis. In his thirteen years there, he changed supervisors annually, gaining the benefit of a range of points of view. He also learned about dynamic psychotherapies from his nine years of psychoanalytic training and from his six years as head of the termination evaluation team in the Menninger Foundation Psychotherapy Research Project (Kernberg et al., 1972; Wallerstein, 1986). David Mark's experience has also been with training, practice, and research in dynamic SE psychotherapy; some of it has been in collaborative projects with Lester Luborsky.

The ideas for the format of the manual also evolved over time. The evolution was helped along because the manual was used daily in the teaching of dynamic psychotherapy in the Department of Psychiatry at the University of Pennsylvania. Beginning around 1970, the manual was only in the form of a Socratic conversation—questions and answers of the kind that were typical in the supervision for dynamic psychotherapy. The current manual format for dynamic SE psychotherapy took shape in 1976 and was eventually further formalized in Luborsky (1984). This format had the three essential components of a clinical manual that would be suitable for research (Luborsky & DeRubeis, 1984): a set of the most accepted principles of the technique, examples of each of the principles that make unmistakable what is intended, and a set of scales for each of the main techniques so that independent judges can estimate the degree to which any sample of therapy conforms to the manual. This manual format for dynamic SE psychotherapy obviously has filled a widespread need in both practice and research. In the years since its publication, it has been translated into German, Italian, Japanese, Portuguese, and French.

In 1978, a more continuous immersion in a time-limited (twenty-four-session) version of the manual began through experiences in the orchestration of a supervision group of therapists who were treating heroin-addicted patients for the Woody et al. (1983) project. Starting in 1987, an even briefer (sixteen-session) version was constructed for the treatment of patients with *DSM III-R* diagnosis of major depression. The experiences in these studies have contributed to the creation of two special adaptations of the SE manual for time-limited psychotherapy: one for drug dependence (Luborsky, Woody, Hole, & Velleco, 1977) and another for major depression (Luborsky et al., 1987).

SELECTION OF PATIENTS

Because research has not yet provided tested conclusions about which patients are most suitable for any of the psychotherapies, including short-term supportive-expressive psychotherapy, we must rely on the considerable clinical experience from its applications and especially from the ongoing supervision groups using time-limited dynamic SE therapy. The experience has shown that this form of psychotherapy is suitable for many kinds of patients. The breadth of usefulness of dynamic SE psychotherapy for patients with different degrees of psychiatric severity is largely based on the individually determined mix of its supportive and expressive components for each patient. For instance, more supportiveness is to be given to the sicker patients along with only sparing and cautious use of expressive techniques. But we also recommend screening out most patients who are psychotic or borderline, as well as patients who find it extremely difficult to tolerate becoming dependent and then separating, when this difficulty is shown in an inclination to suicide.

There is one research-based recommendation about patients who should be excluded: those diagnosed as antisocial personality (Woody, McLellan, Luborsky, & O'Brien, 1985). This finding was based on the time-limited treatment of *DSM III-*diagnosed, drug-dependent patients. The patients in this *DSM III* category appear to be the only ones who are almost completely unresponsive to psychotherapy. Yet even for this group there are mitigating conditions derived from the presence of dual diagnoses: for example, when the antisocial personality diagnosis is accompanied by depression (Woody, McLellan, Luborsky, & O'Brien, 1985), or when there are signs that a helping alliance can be formed and therefore that the prognosis with psychotherapy is somewhat improved (Gerstley et al., 1990).

Clinical experience also shows that some kinds of patients require much longer therapy. Patients with personality disorders, for instance, may require longer treatment, especially when the personality disorder is added to an Axis I diagnosis (Reich & Green, in press). Instead of the usual short therapy in the range of sixteen to twenty-five sessions, they may require a year to two years. Because it is difficult to predict which patients will do well with which treatment length, a trial of short-term therapy can be given at times. Such trials typically do no harm. If a brief trial is not sufficient, the longer term treatment can then be given.

The general manual applied in its time-limited version is suitable to guide the therapist in the treatment of a broad range of patients. But manuals tailored for specific diagnoses and personality types have been written. The oldest of these is the adaptation of the general manual for drug-dependent patients, mainly methadone-treated heroin addicts (Luborsky, Woody, Hole, & Velleco, 1977), which has had several editions. The manual is for time-limited treatment (twenty-four sessions in twenty-four weeks) and has these special emphases: (1) introducing the patient to psychotherapy and engaging the patient in it; (2) specifying the goals; (3) developing a therapeutic alliance and providing sufficient support; and (4) keeping the therapist abreast of the patient's illicit drug use and of the current level of methadone. An adaptation of this manual for cocaine abuse disorders is being developed (Mark, Crits-Christoph, & Luborsky, 1990).

Another version of the general manual was developed in 1987 for the time-limited (sixteen sessions in sixteen weeks) dynamic psychotherapy of *DSM III* major depression (Luborsky et al., 1987). The special adaptations of the general manual for time-limited therapy of major depression include: (1) selecting and maintaining an interpretative focus; (2) dealing with the special themes of depressed patients, especially suicidal ideation; and (3) dealing with the time limit and the termination.

SELECTION OF GOALS OF TREATMENT

Starting within the very first sessions, goal setting is helpful in open-ended SE psychotherapy; it is crucial in time-limited SE psychotherapy.

The focus on goals tends to speed the therapeutic work by strengthening the impetus to change. The goals specify the patient's desired changes, so they help the patient to keep in sight the motive for continuing to come to treatment and for trying to change. As a further benefit the setting of goals, along with the time limit, may halt the patient's regressive tendencies, such as the propensity to feel unmanageably dependent.

The therapist may have learned about the patient's goals from the pretreatment evaluation, but certainly in the beginning sessions the therapist should "listen in order to establish what the patient's problems are and then let the patient try to cast these in terms of goals ordered in importance" (Luborsky, 1984, p. 61). The goals that are selected early in treatment usually remain the goals throughout the course of treatment, especially in time-limited psychotherapy.

If the patient does not state any problems in the form of goals in the first session, the therapist may say: "Tell me about the problems you wish to work on." The discussions that follow result in an agreement with the patient about what the goals will be for the time-limited treatment. Although the therapist may contribute to the decision, the goals have to be ones that the patient experiences as his or her own. It helps the patient to feel understood and self-directed when the goals are expressed in the patient's own words. The therapist may help in clarifying the relative importance of each goal. The therapist may guide the choice even further only in those few instances when a decision is to be made about goals that are clearly beyond achieving within the limited period of the therapy.

In addition to the patient's direct statements about goals, the goals are often implicitly expressed in the patient's wishes in the narratives they tell about interactions with other people. The goals in these narratives can also be about a desired change in the expected responses from other people or in the responses of the self. The therapist may be assisted, therefore, by listening to the patient's narratives, by following the basic Core Conflictual Relationship Theme (CCRT) method (to be described) as it is applied clinically during the sessions, and by identifying the relationship themes that are most pervasive across the narratives.

In the case of Ms. A, the therapist offered a not uncommon kind of help in framing a patient's goals. In the first sessions the patient responded to the therapist's question about her goals by saying: "My problem is that I'm unhappy." She explained: "I wish to work on finding a more suitable boyfriend than the ones I've had." The therapist continued to try to reframe the patient's goal more broadly. By the end of the second session, the therapist understood the patient's central relationship pattern in terms of her wishes to be taken care of by a man whom she saw as older and wiser. Ms. A had gone through a series of such relationships, and in each one she had become infuriated and eventually depressed. The therapist therefore said:

THERAPIST: It sounds to me that you've been drawn to men who are older and who seem to be wiser and at first you are awed by them, then the relationship begins to wear on you and you feel suffocated and then depressed, seeing yourself as the eternal student. We've seen this with R, your boss, and with B and D, your two boyfriends. Working on this pattern would fit in with your goal to become less unhappy and less vulnerable to depression by dealing with these kinds of relationships that you have gotten into. Perhaps understanding this pattern and dealing with it would fit with your goals for our work.

THEORY OF CHANGE

What is presented here is an integration of the main curative factors as offered by representative authorities (as reviewed in Luborsky, 1984). These factors fall into two main classes of questions about the therapy: What changes? and How do the changes come about? Each of these classes of questions requires assessment of the three main curative factors: (1) the helping relationship established; (2) the self-understanding gained; and (3) the degree of internalization of the gains achieved.

Our summary of what changes specifies these factors: (1) the patient's increased sense of having a supportive ally in the struggle to overcome the repetitive self-defeating patterns of behaviors and thoughts; (2) the patient's increased understanding of the symptoms and the related Core Conflictual Relationship Theme (CCRT) problems containing major components of which the patient had been unaware. The understanding allows changes in the symptoms and greater mastery over the conflicts that lead to the symptoms (as these are expressed in the CCRT); (3) a more internalized control-mastery system in relation to the conflicts, so that the gains are maintained after the treatment ends.

How do the changes in each of the three areas come about, according to the theory? Each area has both a patient and a therapist curative component.

1. For achieving a helping relationship, the patient component is the patient's ability to experience the relationship with the therapist as helpful. The therapist's contribution in this area is complementary: it is the therapist's ability to facilitate the patient's experience of a helping relationship with the therapist. The therapist is assisted by certain structural components in dynamic SE psychotherapy, including the regularity of the sessions; the pretreatment agreement on number of sessions; the therapist's role in helping the patient achieve the goals; and the therapist's attitude of sympathetic understanding.

2. For improving self-understanding, a patient component is the patient's motivation for the expressive aspect of dynamic SE psychotherapy. The

patient has an opportunity to reexperience with the therapist and with others the conflictual relationship problems in the here and now and so to gain more meaningful insight that can lead to greater freedom to change. Self-understanding is facilitated as the patient sees new editions of the old relationship problems repeatedly appearing in the relationship with the therapist and with others. As Freud (1914/1958f) noted, a patient will either remember or repeat the conflictual relationship problems in the relationship with the therapist. Remembering or repetition may serve as ways to find increased mastery of the problems (Mayman, 1978). The repetition may also serve as an opportunity to test the relationship with the therapist in relation to the patient's expectations (Weiss & Sampson, 1986).

The therapist's contribution toward achieving understanding is aided by the ability to engage the patient in the process of achieving understanding. This is done by involving the patient in working through the successive editions of the relationship problems as these are expressed in the relationship with the therapist and with others. The transference relationship is the locus of much of the resistance to change.

3. For the third facet of the theory of change, incorporating the gains, the patient component is the patient's ability to hold on to the gains of treatment after its completion by internalization. Most patients are able to maintain the gains, although with some erosion over time (Atthowe, 1973). Internalization is a gradual process by which external interactions between the person and others are taken in and replaced by internal representations of these interactions. But retention takes more than internalization capacity; the gains have a surer chance of being retained when separations, especially termination, are worked through in terms of their meanings (Luborsky, 1984, pp. 172ff.). A common meaning of termination, for example, is that the absence of the therapist will mean the disappearance of the gains because the gains are dependent on the presence of the therapist.

Taking all of the curative factors together, it is difficult to decide on the relative power of the supportive versus expressive components in the patient's acquiring and retaining benefits from psychotherapy. So far, there appears to be more evidence for the power of the helping relationship factor than for the power of the expressive factor aimed at achieving understanding (Luborsky, Crits-Christoph, Mintz, & Auerbach, 1988).

TECHNIQUES AND EXAMPLES

The techniques are aimed at helping the patient achieve his or her goals. The choice of these techniques always begins with the therapist's understanding of the patient. Although we describe the techniques in less detail than is found in the original manual (Luborsky, 1984), we order them here in their relative importance in the time-limited mode, from most essential to helpful but not crucial. The techniques are listed under headings phrased as recommendations and are followed by explanations and examples.

Most of the examples were selected from the psychotherapies of patients treated at the Center for Dynamic Psychotherapy of the Department of Psychiatry at the University of Pennsylvania. The center specializes in treating patients with a *DSM III-R* diagnosis of major depression with a time-limited psychotherapy as guided by the general manual (Luborsky, 1984) and supplemented by a dedicated depression manual for dynamic supportive-expressive psychotherapy (Luborsky et al., 1987). As is typical in our center, three evaluations are made: initial, termination, and follow-up. An evaluation of one patient, Ms. Smyth, will be summarized briefly. We will then illustrate from Ms. Smyth's therapy the essentials of the Core Conflictual Relationship Theme method (Luborsky & Crits-Christoph, 1990), because many of the recommended techniques depend on the therapist's understanding of the transference by the use of this transference-related measure.

Initial Evaluation of Ms. Smyth

The pretreatment diagnostic evaluation by a SADS (Schedule for Affective Disorders and Schizophrenia) reference interview yielded a *DSM III* diagnosis of major depression plus dysthymia. At that time, Ms. Smyth was a thirty-two-year-old single woman. She was a recovering alcoholic who had been abstinent for three years. She came for treatment for depression (with a moderately high Beck Depression Inventory score of 25), after having failed a job training program. The therapy began inauspiciously when she showed up half an hour late and said that she was unable to schedule a next appointment. The therapist's reaction was one of anger, which the therapist did not express but used to recognize what the patient was setting up in her. When the patient said she was afraid of "sabotaging" herself, the therapist did say she thought the patient was correct to be concerned. In the course of the early sessions, the patient and therapist agreed to work on the goal of learning to be able to turn away from negative relationships so as to avoid being sabotaged by them.

Termination Evaluation of Ms. Smyth

Ms. Smyth continued to have difficulty in keeping appointments. Nevertheless, she benefited remarkably well from therapy and surprised the therapist by how well she did: at termination, she was recovered (her Beck Depression Inventory score was 6). The therapist concluded in her termination evaluation: "I would not have thought someone with such severe depression and who already was making full use of self-help therapeutic groups [such as Alcoholics Anonymous] could have resolved her depression without the use of psychopharmacotherapy."

In the termination interview, Ms. Smyth stated that she was generally feeling "good," and "everything's a lot better." Shortly after beginning therapy, she had begun seeing a man with whom she was pleased. She had set up a stable living arrangement with a female roommate and was working regularly in a clerical job with which she was not pleased. She still complained of premenstrual symptoms—tension and headachy feeling. Recently her period was late; she was concerned about being pregnant, and believed she may have had a miscarriage. She generally seemed in dramatically less turmoil and was less pessimistic and much more confident and hopeful. She gave the impression that she could take care of herself; at the time of the initial evaluation she had had a desperate, disorganized quality.

Six-Month Follow-up of Ms. Smyth

Ms. Smyth remained free of depression; her Beck Depression Inventory score was 9. She had been working full time, although still at the same kind of work. Ms. Smyth found out she was pregnant by the man with whom she had been involved. She planned to be married, but the man was waffling on commitment. The patient was angry, anxious, and worried about the situation, but felt she could handle whatever happened; she planned to have the baby. At the first news of pregnancy, she had developed a probable generalized anxiety disorder and had missed some work. She and her boyfriend had entered weekly couples' therapy at that time, and they continued in it. She had also maintained involvement with Alcoholics Anonymous. She continued to live with the roommate and maintained contact with her own family and a few close friends. Although this had been a difficult time due to the pregnancy and the ambivalent boyfriend, she expressed a resolve that she would get by, whatever it might take. Even with these stressors, although initially frantic for a short while, she was now basically OK and was not on medication for depression or anxiety.

CCRT Evaluation of Ms. Smyth

To briefly explain the CCRT method, Ms. Smyth's narratives about relationship episodes from session 3 (in highly condensed form) are presented in figure 1. The method requires that the clinician find the components that are most common across the narratives. In each narrative the clinician attends especially to three components: the patient's wishes from the other person, the other person's actual or expected response, and how the patient responds. The CCRT reflects a sequence of the most frequent types of each of these three components; that is, the CCRT is the pattern that is most pervasive across the self–other relationship narratives. The CCRT is a general relationship pattern that recurrently becomes activated, although with variations, throughout the therapy and perhaps throughout life. In figure 1, Ms. Smyth's narratives about relationship episodes with each other person are presented in the small peripheral circles. The CCRT that is extracted from the five narratives is summarized in the core circle. The CCRT contains two versions of the same most pervasive wish, "to get care and help" and "to reject and oppose unhelpful relationships" (in all five narratives). The expected response from others is "are rejecting" (in four narratives) and the response from self is "to be angry" (three narratives) and "To feel bad, sad, or ashamed" (three narratives). The response of self includes the main presenting symptom, that is, depression.

A detailed explanation of the CCRT procedure is in Luborsky and Crits-Christoph (1990) along with evidence that Freud's twenty-two observations about the nature of his transference concept and the corresponding data from the CCRT are largely congruent. In everyday use, the CCRT method helps to guide the therapist in making transference formulations. One of the major advantages over unaided transference formulations is that clinicians can agree with each other through following its guidelines (Crits-Christoph et al., 1988).

The rest of this section lists the main techniques in dynamic SE psychotherapy. Each one is introduced as a recommendation, and each one is followed by an account of how to do it, with examples. Each recommendation ends with asterisks to show its order of importance from crucially important, *** to important, ** to helpful *.

Figure 1

Ms. Smyth, Session 3: Relationship Episodes and Core
Conflictual Relationship Theme

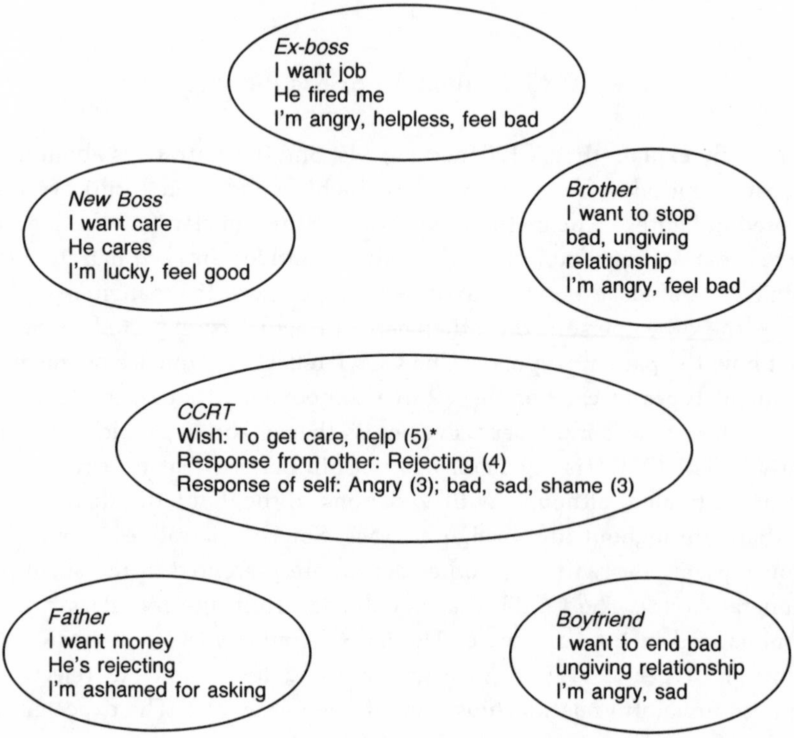

Ex-boss
I want job
He fired me
I'm angry, helpless, feel bad

New Boss
I want care
He cares
I'm lucky, feel good

Brother
I want to stop
bad, ungiving
relationship
I'm angry, feel bad

CCRT
Wish: To get care, help (5)*
Response from other: Rejecting (4)
Response of self: Angry (3); bad, sad, shame (3)

Father
I want money
He's rejecting
I'm ashamed for asking

Boyfriend
I want to end bad
ungiving relationship
I'm angry, sad

*These parentheses give the number of relationship episodes in the five shown in which the component appears.

Helping Alliance

Be sensitive to allowing the patient to form a helping alliance. (***) This is the most central supportive technique. It usually requires, as Freud (1913/1958d) advised, that the therapist merely refrain from doing anything to interfere with the development of rapport with the patient. Especially in the early part of the treatment, nothing more is needed than to listen sympathetically in order for an attachment and a positive component to the relationship to begin to form. Only with some patients, particularly those with high psychiatric severity, is anything more required in the form of fostering a helping relationship by the techniques of supportive psychotherapy (Luborsky, 1984).

Here is an example from Ms. Smyth's third session:

PATIENT: Yeah, I mean, that's a big deal [to not drink for three years]. In alcoholics' eyes it is an anniversary.

THERAPIST: You have been successful. It sounds to me that you have already been taking important steps for yourself.

Through this comment, the therapist is letting the patient know that she recognizes that the patient has been trying successfully to improve herself. The effect of such responses is to convey sympathetic understanding and in that way to allow the further growth of a helping alliance.

The CCRT for another patient, Ms. Waterman, included (1) a wish to be taken care of, (2) an expected response from others of not being taken care of, and indeed, of being condemned for having such a wish, and (3) a response from self of guilt, feeling she is bad for having such a wish.

In session 3, after the therapist gave an interpretation about this main theme as she understood it, the following exchange ensued:

PATIENT: I know I do that [feel guilty and then get depressed]. I don't know. I'm just so stupid.

THERAPIST: It seems to me that you experienced this theme here again, condemning yourself with "I'm so stupid."

This therapist's response is a clear illustration that interpretations can have, and typically do have, both a supportive and an expressive impact. The therapist is conveying the view that it is possible for the patient to take an attitude of acceptance rather than of condemnation toward her feelings.

Central Relationship Patterns

Formulate and respond about the central relationship patterns. (***) This is clearly the most vital expressive technique. It begins early in the treatment, often with the therapist's formulation of the central relationship pattern by the Core Conflictual Relationship Theme method. The therapist should consider which aspects of the pattern are most conflictual and problematic for the patient and where the patient might be able to make changes. On the basis of this understanding, the therapist should recurrently respond with aspects of the CCRT as the focus of the therapy. Maintaining this focus aids the working-through process and facilitates the development of the helping alliance. As we have noted earlier, an interpretative technique can not only convey understanding but also solidify the alliance.

Ms. Johnson, for example, is ambivalent about getting help. She has a strong need to present herself as having no difficulties. Her father looks up to her for needing no help. But her mother infantilizes her—for example, buying her nightgowns that would be suitable for a child. In fact, she was at the time attending law school. In the third session she managed to tell the therapist what she had not been able to before: that she failed an exam for the second time and "it is a hidden hell in my life."

The patient's CCRT reflected this ambivalence; it was expressed in her conflict between wishes. One wish was to achieve spectacularly and without revealing any difficulty, while the other wish was to receive nurturance. It was of course difficult to receive nurturance when she did not indicate the need for it.

> THERAPIST: You want desperately to succeed in quite a big way. This would be difficult for anyone and anyone would want to be reassured in times of doubt. But you are unable to get this because you do not want to give any indication that you're having any difficulties.

At this point a comparison with other short-term psychotherapies is in order. The reliance on a focus and its maintenance happens to be generic to short-term psychotherapies (Koss & Butcher, 1986). But the major locus of the differences among short-term therapies is in how the focus is chosen. In dynamic SE psychotherapy the focus relates to the patient's goals as these are expressed in the CCRT. This reliance on the CCRT means that the focus will differ from patient to patient because CCRTs differ from patient to patient. The evidence of such differences among patients is a benefit of the empirical grounding of the CCRT method. The patient-specific appropriateness of the focus is also likely to be experienced by patients as a sign that they have been understood. In contrast, some other types of short-term psychotherapies have a more uniform focus across different patients; this greater uniformity may be a product of overreliance on a uniformly applied theoretical basis and bias for choosing the focus. One example is Habib Davanloo's (1980) form of psychotherapy, in which the focus is likely to be on the patient's passivity as a way to deal with anger. That focus may well fit some patients but certainly is not likely to be uniformly appropriate for all patients.

Relationship Spheres

Attend and respond to each sphere of the relationship triad, including the one with the therapist. (***) This technique has much in common with the earlier one.

The focus in the earlier one is on responding to the central relationship pattern; in this technique it is on responding to it in each relationship sphere (Luborsky, 1984). There is a special reason for responding in each sphere—it improves the patient's learning about the existence of a general pattern to see it reappear in each sphere of this triad: current in-treatment relationships, current out-of-treatment relationships, and past relationships. The therapist should understand and then use the redundancy of the theme across the three spheres. Of the three spheres, attention to the in-treatment relationship with the therapist has the likelihood for the greatest potential for beneficial impact when carried out with tactful moderation. Particularly when the patient is unusually upset, the therapist should consider whether or not the stress is generated by the current in-treatment relationship and whether the source of the stress parallels out-of-treatment relationships and, possibly, past ones as well. With regard to past relationships, an important test of relevance is the appearance of the same patterns in both current in-treatment and current out-of-treatment relationships. The function of the therapist's pointing to such triads or dyads is to help the patient in recognizing the omnipresence of the central relationship pattern.

Take an example from Mr. Dean's treatment. At the end of the session he summed up by saying, "I'm getting a lot from you . . . but how can I be sure?" In the next session he described his relationship with his wife and her typical statement to him, "You can never say things that are positive about me or about things I've given you." The patient was reminded of what had happened in relation to his mother in the past and concluded that "she would not or could not give enough of what I needed and I must have felt deprived by her." In this example of relationship triads, it is the behavior in the present both in the treatment and out of the treatment that was most in need of interpretation because it had been hardest to see. The relationship pattern in the past by itself did not have the convincing power of the relationship patterns in the present, and the convincing power derived mainly from the parallels evident with the here and now. Through this process, the patient went on to recognize the parallels in the three spheres, and seeing the triad gave him a convincing view of the importance of the pattern.

Consider another therapist statement from the treatment of Ms. Johnson:

THERAPIST: You wanted your father's love but you felt that he believed you to be a child who could do anything without any problems. He would not want to hear any problems. It's hard with telling such things now. And its hard telling *me* such things.

It is worth noting how difficult it is generally for the patient to express feelings about the relationship with the therapist. This observation is an old one. Freud (1914/1958e) noted how hard it is to express one's feelings to someone present as contrasted with someone not present. The same difficulty is often evident in the therapist's responses as well. Despite the obvious importance of paying attention to and using the experiences of the patient in relation to the therapist, therapists tend to be reluctant to use the current in-treatment relationship with the patient as much as it deserves to be used.

The Symptom in the Conflictual Pattern

Understand and respond about where the symptom fits into the pattern. (∗∗∗) The symptom can be understood in the context of the CCRT as one of the responses of the self. The therapist's responses, therefore, should make clear from time to time the wishes and responses from others that are most conflictual and that are associated with the symptom, as Ms. Johnson's therapist did:

> THERAPIST: When you get so upset with trying to get caring responses and feeling you can't get them, you used to begin to lose hope, blame yourself, and end up depressed.

This therapist's response referred to the patient's wishes for care that were associated with frustrating and rejecting responses from others, in which she felt sabotaged, sad, and then symptomatic—depressed. The response in this example reflects the patient's CCRT derived from her narratives; it shows that this sequence is a pervasive one.

Separation

Attend to and respond to concerns about getting involved in the therapy and then separating. (∗∗∗) Attention to attachment and separation is vital to the success of the treatment enterprise, in terms of both the gains achieved at termination and the long-term maintenance of the gains.

One helpful procedure is to give appropriate reminders about the treatment length. In time-limited therapy, the therapist must begin the therapy by reviewing its agreed-upon length; then, from time to time during the therapy, that expected length needs to be reaffirmed.

In the last half of the therapy, and even more in the last few sessions, the therapist needs to attend to the meanings of the termination. As we have noted previously, a frequent meaning involves a worry about whether the gains can be maintained without the continued presence of the therapist. At this time it is common to see a revival of the symptoms as a way of dealing with this meaning of termination. The paraphrased thoughts typically are the following: "If I don't see you the gains are lost because they depend on your presence; they are not part of me. They are part of you and what you do for me." When these thoughts are reviewed with the patient, the symptoms usually subside again and the gains are evident once more.

At the end of therapy, there is always some discussion of what kind of contact the patient could or should have with the therapist after termination. These contacts range from a telephone call or a letter telling the therapist how the patient is doing, to consideration of further treatment. If the symptoms remain, a reevaluation for further treatment may be necessary. A procedure that is helpful to many patients in the maintenance of the gains is to plan from the outset on a few follow-up sessions that involve a review and reevaluation of the patient's status.

The Patient's Awareness

Responses should be timed in relation to the patient's awareness. (∗∗) This is a standard technical principle. It is not difficult to apply because the therapist usually has an idea of what the patient knows and does not know. Although it is not useful to make interpretations that are too far out of the range of the patient's awareness, such interpretations do not usually do much damage. The therapist can just go on and try responses with less of a gap between the interpretation and the patient's awareness. To do this merely requires that the therapist relisten and get recentered on what the patient is again presenting.

Poor timing might also occur if the therapist feels an urgency to show understanding even before the therapist's understanding is sufficiently formed. The best advice the therapist can give to herself or himself is to be patient and listen; sufficient understanding will come. It is inevitable that there will be times in which understanding is lacking, but it is also to be expected that at unpredictable moments the understanding will come.

Testing the Therapist

Recognize the patient's need to test the relationship in transference terms (**) The therapist should recognize that revivals of the transference relationship in the current relationship may be viewed as a test of the relationship with the therapist. Weiss, Sampson, and the Mount Zion Research Group (1986) point out the value of considering whether each expression of transference is the patient's need to determine the safety of bringing out an issue in the relationship, to test the therapist's response, to test whether the therapist will respond in the old expected terms. At these times, the therapist can be most helpful by (1) remaining neutral and not acting in the negative ways that the patient expects or is afraid of from other people and by (2) interpreting the testing aspect of the patient's behavior. Consider the following exchange from Mr. Quinn's therapy:

PATIENT: I heard about the way you solved the staff problem. It was just common sense. But I get anxious saying that to you.

THERAPIST: It may make you anxious because you are not sure *this* relationship can stand your expressing critical thoughts.

Framing Symptoms as Ways of Coping

Frame the symptoms as problem-solving or coping attempts. (**) The patient and therapist have something to gain from recognizing that the patient's symptoms are an attempt, although often a painful one, to cope with the patient's wishes and expected responses from others. For example, the patient is not just an anxious person. The anxiety may be a signal of feeling incapable of succeeding (as in the example from Ms. Johnson). One of the values of thinking in terms of the patient's wishes and their consequences is that the patient can become less frightened of or less condemnatory of her or his symptoms. The symptoms can then be seen constructively, as signs of underlying conflicts (for example, Ms. Johnson, who, in spite of her pose of having no difficulties, could use recognition of her symptoms as a warning that she was getting into deep water). The patient can then think of new ways of managing and the conflicts may appear more controllable.

Countertransference

Reflect on your usual types of countertransference responses. (**) Even the most expert and experienced therapists are sometimes susceptible to countertransference responses. But in fact some therapists probably become less susceptible to expressing them, after repeated experiences, because they develop ways of reflecting on such responses. Also, they may recognize some of the countertransference responses sooner and therefore become able to overcome them sooner. One concrete way to recognize an incipient countertransference response is to notice the inclination to respond countertherapeutically to the patient. Such inclinations provide a good basis for understanding the patient because they can give the therapist an informative experience about what the patient is conveying and even how other people may often respond to the patient.

Mr. Patrick's therapist felt bored and inclined to reject the patient. After noticing this state, the therapist realized what the patient was doing to set up the state in him. The patient was presenting him with an impasse. The patient was testing him to see whether the therapist would accept him, but the condition for acceptance was that the therapist would do nothing that fit the category of acting like a therapist. The realization not only lessened the therapist's boredom, but also led to effective interpretations.

A common kind of countertransference is the inclination for the therapist to behave in ways that fit into the patient's expectations and fears about the ways others will respond—a kind of negative fit (Singer & Luborsky, 1977). A patient may, for example, communicate a fear that people will dominate; then the therapist may in fact become dominating. The therapist *may* then realize that, in fact, he or she has become dominating. The implication of this observation about such negative fit is that patients not only expect certain responses, but they may also stimulate those responses in others. The wise therapist knows that this may occur and is able to recognize it and use the stimulated enactment therapeutically. The prior knowledge of the patient's CCRT may serve to alert the therapist to what the patient expects and fears, which may make it easier for the therapist to anticipate how he or she might be inclined to react.

Timing Interventions

Interventions should be timed to suit the length of a session. (*) In a fifty-minute session, the first five or ten minutes are usually best for mostly listening in order to get a sense of the unfolding of the main issues that the patient is beginning to present. It is a good practice to keep the last five or ten minutes as a period for the patient to assimilate what has just been worked on rather than to present entirely new topics. If major new interventions are made in that period, there may not be enough time available for the patient and therapist to deal with their repercussions.

Limiting Interventions

Interventions should be limited in complexity and length. (*) In the service of the patient's ease of learning and understanding, it is good to avoid overcomplex and long-winded responses. When the patient is presented with too much all at once, he or she can become confused. Ordinarily, it is more effective to present complex material piece by piece so that it can be assimilated and the therapist can hear the patient's response to each piece.

Shifts in State

The patient's shifts in mental state can be an opportunity for responses. (*) Marked shifts in the patient's state can provide an entree to an expanded understanding of the patient's dynamics. Many of these shifts are associated with the development of a symptom. Studies of the immediate contexts in which symptoms appear have shown the special opportunities when such shifts occur. Two examples are sudden shifts in depth of depression (Luborsky, Singer, Hartke, Crits-Christoph, & Cohen, 1984) and shifts in terms of memory, such as momentary forgetting (Luborsky, Sackeim, & Christoph, 1979; Luborsky, 1988).

Mr. Quinn illustrates the point.

> PATIENT: I had a dream—I don't remember what it was. It wasn't anything remarkable, there was no sex involved in it. We were just talking or something like that so that just made me a little tight, I don't know why *(voice drops)*. *(This is a shift point.)*
> THERAPIST: What made you tight?

PATIENT: Talking about her.

THERAPIST: Can you catch what it was?

PATIENT: Just the thought of her, I guess. Oh, I know, I got it, it was that I said, well, a guy like me could be with her but you know a million times stronger. If it is me, then I'm not strong enough, that's what bothered me.

THERAPIST: So it bothered you that you felt you were not strong enough and had lost a sense of control. Then it upset you and made you feel less worthwhile and then depressed.

PATIENT: Yes.

The interpretation fits in with what was known about the CCRT for this patient, which was the following: "I want to feel in control and competent and to show it. I can't; the other person has control. I don't; I blame myself; I get depressed."

Even communication sequences with only small shifts are worthy of being tracked. For example, for Mr. Dean, a frequent sequence was (in paraphrase): "What my wife did was good. . . . but if I tell her that, she'll spend too much." The sequence begins with an expression of positive feeling and appreciation which is quickly followed by the fearful state of feeling that he will be drained by her spending. When the therapist understands this sequence, the information may be useful for interventions.

Therapist's Accuracy

The match of patient's with therapist's messages is a measure of the adequacy of the therapist's responses. (*) A good test of the adequacy of the therapist's responses in a session is the degree of match between the essences of both the patient's and the therapist's messages. The patient's message can be found by reviewing the session to see to what extent the interpretations correspond with the patient's main communications (Auerbach & Luborsky, 1968). It has been shown (Crits-Christoph, Cooper, & Luborsky, 1988) that accuracy of the interpretations, in terms of their congruence with the CCRT, is significantly correlated with the outcome of the patient's therapy.

In concluding this section, we will comment briefly on the degree to which dynamic SE psychotherapy fits the usual characteristics of the short-term or brief psychotherapies listed by Mary Koss and James Butcher (1986). The characteristics dynamic SE psychotherapy shares with the other brief therapies include the following: it takes fewer than twenty-five sessions; the attempt is made to establish the therapeutic alliance quickly; its goals are limited to those within the main focus of the therapy; and the maintenance of the focus means that the therapist is a highly active participant.

Finally, a caveat is in order for the use of these *or any* technical recommendations: do not overdo any of them just for the sake of adherence to the manual. These are general recommendations; they are to be applied to fit each patient. For example, do not make more interpretations of the current relationship with the therapist than are appropriate for the particular patient. The basis for the special caveat about this recommendation to interpret the relationship with the therapist has been that, *when it is used correctly,* it can be a good learning experience for the patient.

EMPIRICAL SUPPORT

There is a long history of research on dynamic SE psychotherapy, although only a modest amount is on its time-limited form (Miller, Luborsky, Barber, & Docherty, in press). One of the earliest investigations of dynamic psychotherapy was the Penn Psychotherapy Study (1968–1973). The sample size was seventy-three, and the average length of the treatment was about forty-three sessions (Luborsky, Crits-Christoph, Mintz, & Auerbach, 1988). The results showed that more than two-thirds of the patients benefited moderately or much. Although this study was done before the era of manuals, a small sample was reexamined and found to have used the central components of the later dynamic SE manual.

The VA-Penn Study, which began in 1978 (Woody et al., 1983) was the earliest major manual-guided comparative study of time-limited dynamic SE psychotherapy. The comparisons were among dynamic SE psychotherapy, cognitive-behavioral psychotherapy, and drug counseling for heroin-addicted patients on methadone. Both psychotherapies outperformed the drug counseling, but the two psychotherapies were not significantly different from each other in efficacy. In 1986, a larger cross-validation, now nearing completion (Woody et al., 1991), was begun in three different drug treatment centers where the comparison was between dynamic SE psychotherapy and drug counseling.

In a study by A. R. Childress (personal communication, May 1990) with cocaine-dependent patients, assignment was to one of four groups: (1) supportive-expressive (SE) plus a cue exposure component; (2) SE plus a control activity; (3) drug counseling plus cue exposure; (4) drug counseling plus a control activity. The SE was provided three times a week during a two-week inpatient phase, followed by weekly sessions during an eight-week outpatient phase. Preliminary results indicate that patients in the first three groups have better retention and treatment outcome (using several measures of clinical status, including drug use) than does the fourth group. Even more interesting is the retention rate observed in group 1: at last analysis, this group attended almost 7 weeks (6.8) out of 8 possible outpatient weeks. Furthermore, the retention rate at 4 weeks after discharge from the inpatient phase was similar to the retention rate in the more intensive (thirty hours per week) day hospital (thirty-day) program. These results suggest that cocaine addicts can be engaged in SE psychotherapy, and that even weekly sessions (when preceded by a more intensive inpatient phase) can retain the majority of patients in the psychotherapy.

The most recent study of dynamic SE psychotherapy is still in progress; it uses the adaptation of the manual for major depression, and is aiming for a sample size of thirty-five (Luborsky et al., 1991). Preliminary inspection of the results shows that patients have benefited.

As part of the study of drug-dependent patients, we examined the adherence to the manual of each of the therapists (Luborsky, McLellan, Woody, O'Brien, & Auerbach, 1985). We noticed that there were large differences in adherence; we then found that these differences in adherence correlated with outcome of the treatment—the greater the adherence, the greater the benefit to the patient. We even found that there were differences in degree of adherence within each therapist's caseload, and that these differences also were related to outcome. That first observation about the relation of adherence and outcome was based on only a four-item adherence scale. Now Barber, Crits-Christoph, and Luborsky (1989) have made a new forty-five-item scale and have launched studies of its reliability and predictive validity. The new scale also makes the potentially valuable distinction between adherence and quality of the treatment.

Much more research is needed on the efficacy of dynamic SE psychotherapy and of dynamic psychotherapies in general (Miller, Luborsky, Barber, & Docherty, in press). The result of nonsignificant differences in Woody, McLellan, Luborsky, & O'Brien (1983) is typical of comparative psychotherapy studies of all kinds (Smith, Glass, & Miller, 1980); it is also typical for comparisons of dynamic versus other psychotherapies (Luborsky, in press). Of twenty comparisons, sixteen showed nonsignificant differences. This strong trend may be a reflection of the difficulty of any form of psychotherapy in showing superior performance to other psychotherapies or of limitations in designing assessment measures in outcome studies (Luborsky & Fiske, in press). Future work on dynamic SE therapy

131

will focus more on specific manuals for applying the therapy to specific psychiatric disorders. Manuals have been started for personality disorders, generalized anxiety disorder, chronic depression disorder, and cocaine abuse, so that we hope, in time, to come closer to the hoped-for knowledge of which treatment is best for which disorder.

It is not just efficacy of the dynamic psychotherapies that has been investigated: a progressively larger research investment has been devoted to studies of the theoretically relevant factors that influence efficacy. It may well be that the differences in performance of a therapy from one study to another has much to do with variations in their curative factors. Most of the main propositions of dynamic therapy, especially dynamic SE therapy, have already been examined by at least a few studies, as reviewed in Luborsky, Barber, and Crits-Christoph (1990) and in the two most recent books from the Penn Psychotherapy Project: Luborsky, Crits-Christoph, Mintz, & Auerbach (1988) and Luborsky and Crits-Christoph (1990). Significant predictive results have been found for these factors: psychiatric severity, the positive therapeutic alliance, and the accuracy of interpretation (Crits-Christoph, Cooper, & Luborsky, 1988). The predictive potential of two other factors is at the forefront of the current research agenda: self-understanding has achieved mixed results so far (Crits-Christoph & Luborsky, 1990), while internalization is already off to a good start and guided by promising instruments in a program by David Orlinsky and Jesse Geller (in press). We can look forward in a few years to a significant increase in our tested knowledge of how and how much these factors influence outcomes of dynamic SE psychotherapy.

References

Atthowe, J. (1973). Behavior innovation and persistence. *American Psychologist, 28,* 34–44.

Auerbach, A. H., & Luborsky, L. (1968). Accuracy of judgments of psychotherapy and the nature of the "good hour." In J. Shlien, H. F. Hunt, J. P. Matarazzo, & C. Savage (Eds.), *Research in psychotherapy* (Vol. 3, pp. 155–168). Washington, DC: American Psychological Association.

Barber, J. P., Crits-Christoph, P., & Luborsky, L. (1989). *The Penn Scale of adherence for supportive-expressive psychotherapy.* Unpublished manuscript, University of Pennsylvania, School of Medicine.

Bibring, E. (1954). Psychoanalysis and the dynamic psychotherapies. *Journal of the American Psychoanalytic Association, 2,* 745–770.

Crits-Christoph, P., Cooper, A., & Luborsky, L. (1988). The accuracy of therapists' interpretations and the outcome of dynamic psychotherapy. *Journal of Consulting and Clinical Psychology, 56,* 490–495.

Crits-Christoph, P., & Luborsky, L. (1990). The measurement of self-understanding. In L. Luborsky & P. Crits-Christoph (Eds.), *Understanding transference: The CCRT method* (pp. 189–196). New York: Basic Books.

Crits-Christoph, P., Luborsky, L., Dahl, L., Popp, C., Mellon, J., & Mark, D. (1988). Clinicians can agree in assessing relationship patterns in psychotherapy: The core conflictual relationship theme method. *Archives of General Psychiatry, 45,* 1001–1004.

Davanloo, H. (Ed.) (1980). *Short-term dynamic psychotherapy.* New York: Jason Aronson.

Fenichel, O. (1941). Problems of psychoanalytic technique. Albany, NY: Psychoanalytic Quarterly.

Freud, S. (1958a). The dynamics of transference. In J. Strachey (Ed. & Trans.), *The standard edition of the complete psychological works of Sigmund Freud* (Vol. 12, pp. 97–108). London: Hogarth Press. (Original work published 1912.)

Freud, S. (1958b). The handling of dream interpretation in psychoanalysis. In J. Strachey (Ed. & Trans.), *The standard edition of the complete psychological works of Sigmund Freud* (Vol. 12, pp. 89–96). London: Hogarth Press. (Original work published 1911.)

Freud, S. (1958c). Observations on transference-love: Further recommendations on the technique of psychoanalysis. In J. Strachey (Ed. & Trans.), *The standard edition of the complete psychological works of Sigmund Freud* (Vol. 12, pp. 157–171). London: Hogarth Press. (Original work published 1915.)

Freud, S. (1958d). On beginning the treatment: Further recommendations on the technique of psychoanalysis. In J. Strachey (Ed. & Trans.), *The standard edition of the complete psychological works of Sigmund Freud* (Vol. 12, pp. 212–244). London: Hogarth Press. (Original work published 1913.)

Freud, S. (1958e). Recommendations to physicians practicing psychoanalysis. In J. Strachey (Ed. & Trans.), *The standard edition of the complete psychological works of Sigmund Freud* (Vol. 12, pp. 109–120). London: Hogarth Press. (Original work published 1912.)

Freud, S. (1958f). Remembering, repeating and working through: Further recommendations on the technique of psychoanalysis. In J. Strachey (Ed. & Trans.), *The standard edition of the complete psychological works of Sigmund Freud* (Vol. 12, pp. 145–156). London: Hogarth Press. (Original work published 1914.)

Gerstley, L., Alterman, A., McLellan, A. T., & Woody, G. (1990). Antisocial personality disorders in patients with substance abuse disorders. *American Journal of Psychiatry, 147,* 173–178.

Kernberg, O., Burstein, E., Coyne, L., Applebaum, A., Horowitz, L., & Voth, H. (1972). Psychotherapy and psychoanalysis: Final report of the Menninger Foundation's Psychotherapy Research Project. *Bulletin of the Menninger Clinic, 36,* 1–275.

Koss, M. P., & Butcher, J. N. (1986). Research on brief psychotherapy. In S. L. Garfield & A. E. Bergin (Eds.), *Handbook of psychotherapy and behavior change* (pp. 627–670). New York: Wiley.

Luborsky, L. (1984). *Principles of psychoanalytic psychotherapy: A manual for supportive-expressive treatment.* New York: Basic Books.

Luborsky, L. (1988). Recurrent momentary forgetting: Its content and context. In M. Horowitz (Ed.), *Psychodynamics and cognition* (pp. 223–251). Chicago: University of Chicago Press.

Luborsky, L. (in press). The efficacy of dynamic psychotherapy. In N. Miller, L. Luborsky, J. P. Barber, & J. Docherty (Eds.), *Handbook of dynamic psychotherapy research and practice.* New York: Basic Books.

Luborsky, L., Barber, J. P., & Crits-Christoph, P. (1990). Theory-based research for understanding the process of psychotherapy. *Journal of Consulting and Clinical Psychology, 58,* 281–287.

Luborsky, L., & Crits-Christoph, P. (1990). *Understanding transference: The CCRT method.* New York: Basic Books.

Luborsky, L., Crits-Christoph, P., & Barber, J. P. (1991). *Outcome and factors influencing outcome of psychotherapy for depression.* Unpublished manuscript, University of Pennsylvania.

Luborsky, L., Crits-Christoph, P., Mintz, J., & Auerbach, A. (1988). *Who will benefit from psychotherapy? Predicting therapeutic outcomes.* New York: Basic Books.

Luborsky, L., & DeRubeis, R. (1984). The use of psychotherapy treatment manuals: A small revolution in psychotherapy research style. *Clinical Psychology Review, 4,* 5–14.

Luborsky, L., & Fiske, D. (in press). Design principles for evaluating dynamic psychotherapies. In N. Miller, L. Luborsky, J. P. Barber, & J. Docherty (Eds.), *Handbook of dynamic psychotherapy research and practice.* New York: Basic Books.

Luborsky, L., Mark, D., Hole, A. V., Popp, C., Goldsmith, B., & Cacciola, J. (1987). *Time-limited supportive-expressive dynamic psychotherapy of major depression.* Unpublished manuscript, University of Pennsylvania.

Luborsky, L., McLellan, A. T., Woody, G. E., O'Brien, C. P., & Auerbach, A. (1985). Therapist success and its determinants. *Archives of General Psychiatry, 42,* 602–611.

Luborsky, L., Sackeim, H., & Crits-Christoph, P. (1979). The state conductive to momentary forgetting. In J. Kihlstrom & F. Evans (Eds.), *Functional disorders of memory* (pp. 325–353). Hillsdale, NJ: Lawrence Erlbaum.

Luborsky, L., & Schimek, J. (1964). Psychoanalytic theories of therapeutic and developmental change: Implications for assessment. In P. Worchel & D. Byrne (Eds.), *Personality change* (pp. 73–99). New York: Wiley.

Luborsky, L., Singer, B., Hartke, J., Crits-Christoph, P., & Cohen, M. (1984). Shifts in depressive state during psychotherapy: Which concepts of depression fit the context of Mr. Q's shifts? In L. N. Rice & L. S. Greenberg (Eds.), *Patterns of change* (pp. 157–193). New York: Guilford Press.

Luborsky, L., Woody, G., Hole, A. V., & Velleco, A. (1977). *Manual for supportive-expressive dynamic psychotherapy: a special version for drug dependence* (rev. ed. 1/31/89). Unpublished manuscript, University of Pennsylvania.

Mark, D., Crits-Christoph, P., & Luborsky, L. (1990). *Supportive-expressive psychotherapy for cocaine abuse.* Unpublished manuscript, University of Pennsylvania.

Mayman, M. (1978). Trauma, stimulus barrier, ego boundaries and self-preservation: Ego psychology in Beyond the pleasure principle. In S. Smith (Ed.), *The human mind revisited: Essays in honor of Karl A. Menninger* (pp. 141–158). New York: International Universities Press.

Menninger, K., & Holzman, P. (1973). *The theory of psychoanalytic techniques* (2nd ed.). New York: Basic Books.

Miller, N., Luborsky, L., Barber, J., & Docherty, J. (Eds.). (in press). *Handbook of dynamic psychotherapy research and practice.* New York: Basic Books.

Orlinsky, D., & Geller, J. (in press). Patients' representations of their therapists and therapy: A new focus of research. In N. Miller, L. Luborsky, J. P. Barber, & J. Docherty (Eds.), *Handbook of dynamic psychotherapy research and practice.* New York: Basic Books.

Reich, J., & Green, A. (in press). Personality and outcome of Axis I disorders. *Journal of Nervous and Mental Disease.*

Singer, B., & Luborsky, L. (1977). Countertransference: The status of clinical vs. quantitative research. In A. Gurman & A. Razin (Eds.), *The therapist's handbook for effective psychotherapy: An empirical assessment* (pp. 431–448). New York: Pergamon Press.

Smith, M., Glass, G., & Miller, T. (1980). *The benefits of psychotherapy.* Baltimore: Johns Hopkins University Press.

Stone, L. (1951). Psychoanalysis and brief psychotherapy. *Psychoanalytic Quarterly, 20,* 215–236.

Wallerstein, R. S. (1986). *Forty-two lives in treatment: A study of psychoanalysis and psychotherapy.* New York: Guilford Press.

Weiss, J., Sampson, H., & the Mount Zion Psychotherapy Research Group. (1986). *The psychoanalytic process: Theory, clinical observations, and empirical research.* New York: Guilford Press.

Woody, G., Luborsky, L., McLellan, A. T., O'Brien, C., Beck, A. T., Blaine, J., Herman, I., & Hole, A. V. (1983). Psychotherapy for opiate addicts: Does it help? *Archives of General Psychiatry, 40,* 639–645.

Woody, G., McLellan, A. T., Luborsky, L., & O'Brien, C. (1985). Sociopathy and psychotherapy outcome. *Archives of General Psychiatry, 42,* 1081–1086.

Woody, G., McLellan, A. T., Luborsky, L., O'Brien, C., Blaine, J., Fox, S., Herman, I., & Beck, A. T. (1984). Psychiatric severity as a predictor of benefits from psychotherapy. *American Journal of Psychiatry, 141,* 1172–1177.

Woody, G., McLellan, A. T., Luborsky, L., & O'Brien, C. (1991). Psychotherapy for methadone maintained opiate addicts: Results of a validation and cross-validation. Paper presented at the annual meeting of the Society for Psychotherapy Research, Lyon, France.

CHAPTER 6

The Vanderbilt Approach to Time-Limited Dynamic Psychotherapy

Jeffrey L. Binder and Hans H. Strupp

ORIGINS AND DEVELOPMENT

Several important developments have influenced our approach to Time-Limited Dynamic Psychotherapy (TLDP) and have in turn contributed to advances in research and practice. The first, and most important, relates to the growing role of research, that is, the recognized need for disciplined scientific study of the phenomena and processes in our domain (Strupp & Bergin, 1969; Bergin & Strupp, 1972). The Vanderbilt Psychotherapy Research Team has been committed to this objective since the early seventies; the research efforts of one of us (Hans Strupp) date back to the early 1950s. As in all scientific endeavor, the key to our research is specificity: to study psychotherapeutic phenomena and processes, one must define and, if possible, quantify them; global descriptions will not suffice.

The second impetus for the development of TLDP derived from the Vanderbilt I study (see the section on empirical support), which highlighted the neglected (or underestimated) issue of the management of hostility in the therapeutic relationship. This finding constituted a major reason for focusing TLDP on the patient–therapist relationship and the study of countertransference reactions, both of which may be regarded as the *Leitmotif* of the Vanderbilt research group.

We wish to note the influence of societal pressures, exemplified by demands from insurance companies and governmental agencies for specification of the treatments they are being asked to underwrite. Related to this issue are the qualifications of practitioners of a particular form of psychotherapy. For purposes of licensing and other forms of legislation, it is essential to develop criteria by which one may judge whether a practitioner meets specific standards of competence. The appearance of treatment manuals in our time, including that for TLDP, may be viewed as part of the clinical investigators' response to demands for greater specificity.

TLDP has continued to form the basis for our systematic studies of the psychotherapeutic process and its outcomes. However, we believe that we have gone beyond codifying a traditional form of therapeutic practice. Instead we have endeavored to integrate our understanding of psychoanalytic psychotherapy as it has evolved over the years and to present a contemporary model of that treatment modality. The model is intended as a blueprint of psychoanalytic psychotherapy that is broadly applicable irrespective of time limits.

Our research has called forceful attention to the overriding importance of the dyadic *interactions* between patient and therapist over the course of therapy, with special emphasis on the early phases. Thus, our approach forms part of a movement toward a greater integration of classical and interpersonal psychoanalytic theory and technique—in short, nothing less than a reconceptualization of transference and countertransference phenomena in interactional terms.

From a historical perspective, the forward-looking ideas of Franz Alexander and Thomas French (1946) have greatly influenced our thinking, as have the writings of specialists in time-limited dynamic psychotherapy (such as Malan, 1963, 1976a, 1976b; Sifneos, 1972, 1979; Davanloo, 1978, 1980; Mann, 1973; and Mann & Goldman, 1982). From a theoretical perspective we have profited greatly from the incisive contributions of Gill (1979, 1982), Klein (1976), Peterfreund (1983), Schafer (1976, 1983), Levenson (1972, 1982), and Epstein and Finer (1979). In developing TLDP, we have tried to stay close to clinical and observational data and to avoid as much as possible higher level inferences and complex theoretical constructions that have no apparent consequences for therapeutic activity. This has been a distinctive feature of our approach. Although techniques are crucial to the practice of psychotherapy, they are inextricably embedded in the interpersonal context of the relationship between patient and therapist. Beyond explicating this context, TLDP is designed to contribute to the training of thinking clinicians who view their profession as a disciplined activity evolving from clinical experience and scientific evidence.

SELECTION OF PATIENTS

While the theoretical foundation for TLDP is psychoanalytic, personality development and malfunctioning are viewed from interpersonal and object relations perspectives. The task in TLDP is to identify and examine certain themes from a person's internal object relations repertoire that are not responsive to current interpersonal realities and, therefore, may maladaptively influence that person's experiences and behavior in a variety of interpersonal settings (particularly with significant others). These themes take the form of maladaptive interpersonal patterns that press for enactment in current interpersonal relationships, including that with the therapist. Therefore, the therapeutic process involves (1) creating optimal (safe) conditions for the enactment of the patient's maladaptive interpersonal patterns; (2) allowing the patterns to be enacted within limits; (3) helping the patient to see what he or she is doing while doing it; and (4) encouraging the patient to identify and question the assumptions underlying maladaptive patterns. In this effort, TLDP relies primarily on examining transactions between patient and therapist as they occur.

This process presupposes that the patient's internal object relations and associated interpersonal patterns are sufficiently developed to be characterized by (1) coherent and identifiable interpersonal themes, (2) appreciation of the distinction between oneself and others, and (3) a capacity for concern and integrity in human relationships. Conversely, patients for whom TLDP would not be beneficial include those who are currently in a disorganized psychotic state and those whose affective experiences and object relationships are chronically incoherent, diffuse, and disorganized (Giovacchini, 1989). There are also patients whose modes of relating manifest identifiable patterns but who see no value in examining interpersonal relationships (or the therapeutic relationship) or who do not value honesty and integrity in human relationships.

The object relations capacities sought in potential TLDP patients may be detected across a broad range of formal diagnostic syndromes. Therefore, neither a presenting symptom picture nor the diagnosis of a specific personality disorder will itself justify exclusion from this form of treatment. It should be apparent that in most cases we do not advocate specific treatments for specific symptom pictures or personality disorders. We posit that for the range of patients previously defined, attention to correcting maladaptive interpersonal patterns will reduce psychopathology in whatever form it takes.

Since emphasis in TLDP rests on interpersonal concerns, it is important to elicit information on the extent to which the patient is able to recognize and discuss subjective experiences in interactions with significant others. Once forms of psychopathology that would contraindicate TLDP are ruled out, the attempt is made to formulate a salient maladaptive interpersonal pattern, identify life areas most affected by this pattern, and construct a general picture of the patient's interpersonal history of significant relationships. Most important is evidence of maladaptive functioning manifested in the immediacy of the therapeutic relationship. Then, in descending order, priority is given to functioning in current relationships outside of therapy and to recollections of past relationships extending back to childhood.

GOALS OF TREATMENT

The primary therapeutic goal of TLDP is to foster positive changes in interpersonal functioning. We believe that such changes will have beneficial effects on more circumscribed symptoms, such as affect and mood problems. In TLDP interpersonal problems are conceptualized in a specific format, which we have termed the Cyclical Maladaptive Pattern (CMP). Other short-term treatment approaches employ different constructs that serve functions similar to the CMP (for example, Luborsky, 1984; Davanloo, 1980; Malan, 1976a). The CMP is used as a heuristic that helps therapists to generate, recognize, and organize psychotherapeutically relevant information. It is not an absolute or final formulation of the problem, but rather it is used throughout the course of treatment as a tool for keeping the therapist focused on a remediable problem.

The CMP is a working model (Peterfreund, 1983) of a central or salient pattern of interpersonal roles in which patients unconsciously cast themselves; the complementary roles in which they cast others; and the maladaptive interaction sequences, self-defeating expectations, negative self-appraisals, and unpleasant affects that result.

This model is built upon an abstract format that aids in the construction of the model. The format of the CMP specifies four categories of information:

1. *Acts of self.* Included are both private and public actions (such as feeling affectionate as well as displaying affection). Acts of self vary in the degree to which they are accessible to awareness.
2. *Expectations about others' reactions.* These are imagined reactions of others

to one's own actions. Such expectations may be conscious, preconscious, or unconscious.

3. *Acts of others toward self.* These are observed acts of others that are
   viewed as occurring in specific relation to the acts of self. Typically,
   under the influence of a maladaptive pattern one tends to miscon-
   strue the interpersonal meanings of the other's actions in a way that
   confirms one's wished for or feared expectations.

4. *Acts of self toward self (introject).* This category of actions refers to how
   one treats oneself (for example, self-controlling, self-punishing).
   These actions should be articulated in specific relation to the other
   elements of the format.

The CMP should ideally encompass a pattern of interpersonal transactions that is both historically significant and also a source of current difficulty. Although currently enacted patterns are of primary importance,
the specific nature of these patterns may be ambiguous. Historical knowledge aids therapeutic understanding by providing a context in which confusing meanings of present events may be more easily interpreted. Typically, no single event can be characterized as the "presentation" of a focus
(CMP) to the patient. It is better to understand the process as one of
introducing the patient to the primary importance of interpersonal issues
and then collaboratively arriving at a shared view of what appears to be
the most salient and meaningful maladaptive interpersonal pattern currently troubling the patient. The goal of treatment is to ameliorate this
pattern.

THEORY OF CHANGE

TLDP is based on psychoanalytic conceptions and their extensions and
reformulations by contemporary theorists (see Sandler, 1976; Schlesinger,
1982; Gill, 1982). Accordingly, we assume that therapeutic change is pro-
duced by an interplay of intrapsychic and interpersonal activities and that
no particular therapeutic event is uniformly the most mutative. We also
appreciate that all dynamic conceptions of therapeutic change are hypothetical (indeed, the primary goal of the Vanderbilt studies has always
been empirically to explain the therapeutic processes associated with
change). Consequently, we have chosen interpersonal conceptions of therapeutic change as our primary framework because of their relevance and
utility for moment-to-moment clinical work. Our primary allegiance is
thus to an interpersonal perspective that is anchored in the theories of

Harry Stack Sullivan, other members of the neo-Freudian school (Karen Horney, Erik Erikson, and Edgar Levenson), and the contributions of modern interpersonal theorists (Anchin & Kiesler, 1982).

In our view, psychotherapy is basically a set of interpersonal transactions. It is a process that may become therapeutic because of the patient's unwitting tendency to cast the therapist in the role of a significant other and to enact with him or her maladaptive patterns of behavior rooted in unconscious conflicts. Through participant observation the therapist provides a new model for identification. He or she does so, in part, by limiting the kinds of attitudes and behavior (such as hostile, controlling) that the patient's maladaptive behavior tends to provoke. The therapist also attempts to grasp latent meanings in the patient's interpersonal behavior and communicates this understanding to the patient, thereby helping the patient to assimilate aspects of his or her experience that were hitherto unrecognized or disowned (repressed). To this end, the patient's experiences with significant others in his or her current and past life represent important sources of information that aid the therapist's understanding; however, they are secondary to the contemporary transactions between patient and therapist.

The foregoing implies that the patient's self-identity and interpersonal behavior are important functions of learning experiences during his or her formative years. Because of early deprivations, traumatic experiences, and the like, the patient is unable to gain sufficient gratification from his or her contemporary interactions with others and lacks adequate resources (or denies their existence) to mold his or her environment in accordance with his or her legitimate wishes and needs. The patient has unrealistic expectations of himself or herself and others, and frequently feels stymied. Patterns of dealing with changing life circumstances are rigid, and although their maladaptive character may be perceived, he or she feels unable to change them.

Essentially, the therapist uses the relationship with the patient as the primary medium for bringing about change. What the patient learns in psychotherapy, what conduces to therapeutic change, is acquired primarily in and through the dynamics of the therapeutic relationship. Identifying the recollected childhood origins of current psychological conflict and the unconscious fantasies and feelings associated with the continued influence of these early experiences probably make an important contribution to therapeutic change. However, in TLDP the most important change process is considered to be the recognition of patterns of interactions with others that continuously reinforce maladaptive attitudes and feelings about oneself and others (these attitudes and feelings are the object-relational manifestation of intrapsychic conflict). The sooner this recognition can be associated with the actual enactment of a maladaptive pattern, the greater is the potential for altering it. This is why identifying the influence of maladaptive patterns on the patient–therapist relationship is the primary strategy in TLDP.

In other words, therapeutic learning is experiential learning. The patient changes as he or she lives through affectively painful and ingrained interpersonal scenarios and as the therapeutic relationship gives rise to outcomes different from those expected, anticipated, feared, and sometimes hoped for. To promote these changes, the therapist, first, assiduously avoids prolonged engagement in activities that have the effect of perpetuating the conflicts that have resulted in the patient's interpersonal difficulties, and, second, actively promotes more satisfying experiences associated with productively collaborating in the solution of interpersonal problems.

With respect to the first, the therapist remains constantly attentive to the patient's unconscious attempts to elicit reciprocal behavior that meets the patient's wish for or expectation of domination, control, manipulation, exploitation, punishment, criticism, and the like. Such unwitting invitations may take the form of subtle seductions, requests for advice, special attention, extra hours, and many other maneuvers to which the therapist must be alert. The only way to avoid completely the impact of the patient's transference pressures would be for the therapist to erect barriers against any empathic involvement with the patient. A more therapeutic stance is to maintain a "free floating responsiveness" (Sandler & Sandler, 1978) to the patient's attempts to draw the therapist into a particular scenario. A therapist who cautiously goes along with the patient, while remaining alert to his or her own reactions, can obtain invaluable information about the nature of the self- and object-representational components of the patient's relationship predispositions.

With respect to the second, the patient must come to experience the therapist as a reliable and trustworthy ally who is in the patient's corner, and who, in a fundamental sense, has the patient's best interest at heart. To that end, the patient must become convinced that the therapist has something worthwhile to offer, that he or she has a genuine commitment to the patient as a person rather than a case, and that the therapeutic experience is manifestly helpful. These are the essential ingredients of a good therapeutic alliance, the prime moving force in all forms of psychodynamic psychotherapy. Conversely, unless these conditions are met early in therapy, a good outcome—certainly in time-limited psychotherapy—is seriously in question (Strupp, 1980).

If the therapist successfully fosters this process, the patient's salient CMP will be viewed with increasing clarity. The patient will gain a greater ability to question the previously accepted assumptions about his or her self-image and about the attitudes and intentions of others that lend the CMP its persistent influence. In turn, as the patient gains confidence in the beneficial effects of collaboratively examining maladaptive patterns, he or she is better able to confront emotions and fantasies associated with these patterns. The result is progressively more freedom to modify conflictual attitudes and behavior in the direction of more adaptive and flexible responses to changing circumstances and realistic opportunities for satisfying interpersonal needs. These changes typically are associated with improved overall functioning.

TECHNIQUE

The TLDP Process and Technical Goals

The basic working assumption in TLDP is that the patient will immediately enact a cyclical maladaptive pattern in the therapeutic relationship. In other words, the patient's behavior will be influenced by an amalgam of preexisting and long-established negative expectations of others, including of the therapist. Furthermore, he or she unconsciously seeks to induce the therapist to conform to the interpersonal scenarios dictated by those expectations. Thus, the overarching goal of technique in TLDP is the systematic and thorough examination of the patient's maladaptive action patterns and their effects on the interaction of the two participants. In common psychoanalytic terminology, the TLDP therapist's technical approach emphasizes the analysis of transference and countertransference in the here and now.

Guidelines for Understanding the Patient's Conflicts

The TLDP therapist seeks to identify the presence of a prepotent, conflictual interpersonal theme and organizes his or her observations within the framework of a CMP. Furthermore, the therapist is particularly attentive to indications of transference and countertransference reactions. Although in the psychoanalytic theory of therapy the examination of transference

144

is given a central role, our clinical and supervisory experiences have convinced us that transference analysis is frequently not well understood and is greatly underutilized in general practice.

Consonant with our view of the therapeutic relationship as an interactive dyadic system, we posit that conflict persists in the form of transference experience and behavior because circular interpersonal patterns confirm the patient's mistrustful expectations of others. Accordingly, the patient's transference experience and behavior are not simply representations of the past superimposed upon the therapist as "distorted" images. Rather, the patient has certain preexisting sets or fixed expectations with which he or she interprets the meanings of interpersonal events. The therapist proceeds on the working assumption that these plausible (from the patient's point of view) interpretations are always in response to something actually occurring (conscious or unconscious attitudes and behaviors of the therapist; or aspects of the therapeutic arrangements, such as office fixtures, fees, appointment times, and so forth). In other words, the patient's transference experience does not distort some consensual reality, but rather is based on rigid proclivities to interpret events in a certain way without the flexibility to consider alternatives (Gill, 1979, 1982; Hoffman, 1983). Furthermore, having turned to the therapist for help and being unconsciously prepared to relate to him or her as a significant other, the patient becomes exquisitely sensitive to everything that transpires in the evolving relationship. It follows that any clinical data, whether generated in the form of references to people and events outside the therapeutic relationship, the patient's mood and dreams, or the emotional climate of the interviews, must be viewed as "disguised allusions" to the transference (Gill, 1979, 1982). Whatever else they may represent, such data should always be scrutinized for what they might reveal about the patient's experience of the therapeutic relationship.

In TLDP, countertransference is defined as encompassing two types of reactions: first, therapist actions and reactions (including attitudes and behavior as well as thoughts, feelings, and fantasies) that are predictably evoked by behavior of the patient that is part of the enactment of a maladaptive pattern (transference); and, second, reactions of the therapist that express unresolved personal issues.* From this perspective transference and countertransference are ineluctably intertwined. Countertransference in TLDP terms may be described as a form of interpersonal empathy, in which the therapist, for a time and to a limited degree, is recruited

---

*We assume that the stimulus for most countertransference reactions contains a mixture of contemporary interpersonal and intrapsychic sources. However, in the routine work of the TLDP therapist, the former source is always investigated first.

to enact roles assigned to him or her by the patient's preconceived CMP. The therapist's empathy, however, encompasses more than an understanding of the patient's inner world—it can expand to include the first-hand experience of participating in that world as it is translated into interpersonal behavior. Thus, at the center of the therapeutic process in TLDP is the therapist's ability to become immersed in the patient's modes of relatedness and to "work his way out" (Gill & Muslin, 1976; Levenson, 1982).

There are times when it is extraordinarily difficult for the therapist to avoid enmeshment in the patient's scenarios. As we have stressed, patients are often impelled to force the occurrence of self-fulfilling prophecies by making the therapist a co-participant in their struggles. These pressures may be exceedingly subtle but they are vastly more pervasive than is commonly realized, particularly around the issue of hostility. The findings from our process/outcome studies (Vanderbilt I and II) have convinced us that even highly experienced therapists have great difficulty in therapeutically managing the hostility expressed by patients as well as their own reactive hostility. We have observed that even with extensive training to increase adherence to techniques for dealing with issues that arise in the patient–therapist relationship, therapists continue to be inconsistent in their management of hostility. This is a serious problem for the delivery of effective treatment. There is evidence that regardless of how much "warmth," "friendliness," and "support" may be present, if expressions of hostility (direct or indirect) are not effectively handled, there will be repercussions on the development of a positive therapeutic alliance and on outcome (Henry, 1986; Henry & Strupp, 1989; Kiesler & Watkins, 1989).

In each therapeutic hour the TLDP therapist attempts to identify a recurrent theme that in one way or another is related to the defined TLDP focus. In TLDP, the most important facet of a theme in any interview is its interpersonal manifestation in the therapeutic relationship. In order for the therapist to identify the general form of the patient's relationship predisposition, he or she must maintain constant alertness and curiosity about the state of the therapeutic relationship. At the same time, while attempting to understand the current interpersonal transactions, the therapist attends to other aspects of the patient's communications. Thus, any area of his or her life the patient chooses to discuss should be jointly examined.

The therapist must always begin a session by entering the patient's internal world at whatever point admittance is given. Needless to say, much can be gained by clarifying and interpreting conflicts that are manifested in relationships outside of therapy. Simultaneously, however, the therapist maintains a mental set aimed at applying what is learned about conflicts in other relationships to understanding the immediate state of the patient–therapist relationship. The translation is attempted when the therapist identifies a similarity between patterns of conflictual experience and behavior in other contexts and the transactions occurring in the therapeutic relationship.

Guidelines for Therapist Interventions

The TLDP therapist maintains with the patient a dialogue that is designed to help identify CMPs and to determine the affective meanings of these patterns. The paradigm guiding the therapist's interventions is as follows: first, the patient must act; then, with the therapist's help, he or she must step back and observe the action; finally, the meaning and purpose of the action must be explored. Typically, a patient spontaneously reports an interpersonal experience outside of therapy and his or her reactions associated with it. Patients clearly vary in the extent to which they can spontaneously report their interpersonal experiences. The TLDP therapist, through his or her interventions, seeks to obtain as detailed a picture as possible of the patient's interpersonal transactions and associated internal experiences. The CMP provides the format used to conceptualize these transactions. Five basic questions, based on that format, may serve as a guide to interventions:

1. How does the patient behave toward the other person, and what is the nature of his or her feelings toward the other?
2. What might be the patient's experience of the other's intentions, attitudes, or feelings toward him or her?
3. What might be the patient's emotional reactions to fantasies about and actions of the other?
4. How does the patient construe the relationship with the other, and how might his or her most recent reactions be a consequence of their previous interactions?
5. How does the patient's experience of the interactions and relationship with the other influence the manner in which the patient views and treats himself or herself?*

---

*We have observed that therapists tend to neglect detailed inquiry into the internal "relationships" (attitudes, thoughts, and feelings) that patients have with themselves. These internal relationships can be seen to mirror strikingly the maladaptive interpersonal patterns that are found in relationships with significant others (Benjamin, 1982; Sullivan, 1953).

At the same time, the therapist endeavors to make optimal use of all opportunities for exploring and explicating the patient's experience in the therapeutic relationship. To aid this effort, the five guiding questions can be reframed by substituting the first person "me" for "the other." In this form, the questions can be posed directly about conditions in the therapeutic relationship as well as about implications for the relationship that can be detected in reports of interactions outside of therapy.

Although most analyses of interpersonal patterns will deal with relationships outside of therapy, whenever possible the line of inquiry should return to examination of the therapeutic relationship, where the affective immediacy of the situation is most conducive to instilling in the patient an appreciation of affective and interpersonal patterns (Gill, 1982). As noted, the difficulty encountered by therapists in maintaining a consistent alertness to "disguised allusions to the transference" is often greatly underestimated (see Gill, 1979, 1982; and the authors' personal observations of supervisees and of experienced therapists participating in process/outcome studies).

Our emphasis is on therapeutic learning based on systematic examination of the transactions between patient and therapist. Accordingly, interpretive connections to current and past outside relationships can be helpful in placing a particular transference enactment in broader perspective *after* the enactment has been carefully explored in the immediacy of the patient–therapist relationship and the patient has gained an appreciation of its impact on his or her experience and behavior. Forging such links serves three primary functions: (1) to strengthen the patient's capacity to achieve emotional distance from stereotyped predispositions, (2) to reinforce the patient's awareness of the patterns' profound effect on the current relationship with the therapist, and (3) to help the patient achieve an understanding of how such maladaptive patterns may have developed.

The TLDP emphasis on experiential learning through analysis of transactions in the patient–therapist relationship should be thought of as a guiding strategy and as a mind-set that the therapist disciplines himself or herself to maintain. The actual extent to which transference interventions are used during any phase of treatment is determined by three factors: (1) the therapist's identification of material that can be understood as plausibly related to transference issues (Hoffman, 1983); (2) the patient's current receptiveness to examining his or her experiences of the patient–therapist relationship; and (3) the therapist's attentiveness to overt or disguised patient references to their relationship, as well as his or her attentiveness to countertransference reactions.

Preliminary findings from our latest process/outcome study indicate that the use of transference interventions per se is not tantamount to successful management of the therapeutic process, nor will it guarantee a positive outcome. Examination of transactions in the patient–therapist relationship represents use of a *type* of intervention. The utility of this intervention depends on the skill with which it is applied (Schaffer, 1982; Butler, Henry, & Strupp, 1989). Skill, in turn, is a function of such factors as how well the therapist times the intervention to coincide with the patient's readiness to address issues in their relationship, relevance of the content of the intervention to the patient's immediate concerns (Silber-schatz, Curtis, & Nathans, 1989), and the extent to which the manner of intervening serves to minimize enactments of maladaptive patterns within the therapeutic relationship. The question of whether primary reliance on analysis of the patient–therapist relationship, if skillfully conducted, will produce the most successful outcomes (at least with certain patients) awaits adequate empirical investigation.

CASE EXAMPLE

The following excerpt from a twenty-five session treatment illustrates some of the distinguishing technical features of TLDP. The therapy was conducted by one of us, Jeffrey Binder. The patient, Mr. A, was a man in his late thirties who sought treatment because of discomfort over insufficient emotional involvement with people. He was particularly distressed by the lack of intimate, pleasurable relationships with his wife and young child. In general, he felt that he did not fit in in most interpersonal settings and had a persistent feeling of depression. Mr. A came from an upper-middle-class family in which both parents were perfectionistic, critical, and emotionally constrained. As a teenager, Mr. A came into conflict with his parents by defying their expectations for his education. He married in his late teens; after ten years his wife precipitously divorced him. He drifted for a time before returning to school and remarrying. Subsequently, Mr. A had been vocationally successful (describing himself as a worka-holic). The primary diagnosis was dysthymic disorder, but there were also features characteristic of an avoidant personality disorder.

In the first few sessions the major theme involved the patient's belief that he hid selfish feelings and motives, of which others would be critical. More generally, he was very self-critical and expected the same harshly critical attitude from others if he were to expose his emotional life. He believed that his blameworthy feelings and motives contributed to his feeling out of place in most interpersonal settings. He was easily angered by human imperfections and would occasionally explode angrily at his wife or child. The influence of this pattern of criticism and blame directed toward and expected from others was quickly identified in the patient–therapist relationship: Mr. A felt that the therapist was dissatisfied with the low fee (arranged as part of the patient's participation in our research program). At the same time, Mr. A was impatient with the therapist for not providing sufficient direction.

The following passages are excerpts from the seventh session. At the beginning, Mr. A questioned how he and the therapist should address each other. Having explored Mr. A's motives and feelings about this issue (that is, its direct reference to the therapeutic relationship and its relevance for revealing the enactment of a CMP), the therapist eventually acknowledged that he routinely used last names.

PATIENT: OK. Well, that's all right with me. My main goal is just to know something.

THERAPIST: Well, in the context of what you've been saying about the implications of names, what reaction do you have to that?

PATIENT: My reaction is that it seems somewhat appropriate, in that your approach is to me a fairly distanced approach, quite analytical.

THERAPIST: True.

PATIENT: So it seems to me that . . . I don't know if that's a gut reaction . . . but that's my first reaction is, well, that makes some sense to me. Seems to go along with the rest of what I know about . . .

THERAPIST: How do you feel about it?

PATIENT: I'm a little uncomfortable with it, in the same way that I'm uncomfortable with the whole approach a little bit, somehow I feel like I'm *(nervous laugh)* always squirming slightly. And I am somehow always wishing that I could break through that feeling of reserve that I get from you.

THERAPIST: Can you elaborate on both of those experiences? You're feeling like you're squirming and you're also wanting to break through what you see as my reserve.

During the preceding interchange, the therapist used questions to encourage the patient to explicate his experience of their interactions around the issue of how to address each other. The technical strategy was to maintain a balance between encouraging spontaneous communication (free association) and keeping the therapeutic work focused on constructing a CMP. The therapist detected signs of a conflict between the patient's desire for closeness to a man, dissatisfaction with its absence, and concern that the therapist might be offended by his feelings. The therapist also silently formed the hypothesis that this issue recapitulated an old relationship pattern between the patient and his father. However, in TLDP the goal is to aid the patient in recognizing and appreciating the current existence of a CMP *before* links are made to childhood experiences.

As the session progressed, Mr. A continued gingerly to press the therapist to provide more guidance and to reveal his feelings about the patient. He admitted the desire to break through the therapist's "reserve" and to discover whether the therapist liked him. The therapist commented that Mr. A appeared to be increasingly sensitive about how the therapist felt about him and frustrated over having no clear indication. The therapist's encouragement to discuss these feelings resulted in Mr. A's voicing his first direct complaint: his goal of therapy was to learn how to relate to people, and if he did not have a comfortable relationship with his therapist, then therapy was failing. The patient went on to express concern over this "direct personal confrontation" with the therapist and continued to complain about not feeling closer to the therapist. This resulted in his "hanging back" and not sharing things.

THERAPIST: Why do you think you're doing that? What do you think holds you back?

PATIENT: Some kind of risk involved, and, I'm not wanting to make *(nervous laugh)* waves and feeling like, I would rather, to an extent, adjust to what your expectations are of the situation.

THERAPIST: Why? Especially since you feel that you're dissatisfied with it.

PATIENT: *(Chuckles)* Well, yes, I don't know. I mean all I can say is why would I be hanging back? It's because I feel like, like I said, with the thing with the names, that maybe it would develop organically. Then I wouldn't have to make a plan. And somehow that would be easier, I wouldn't have to bring up something that's uncomfortable, uh, risk your displeasure or making you uncomfortable or whatever.

THERAPIST: If we pull together some of the observations, the experiences you've described in the past few minutes, maybe it would help us understand particularly what makes you hold back. You see me as reserved and you see yourself as holding back because you're not sure what that's about and you feel at risk and anxious about it. You're also reluctant, like you said, to make waves. If you say you're dissatisfied, you don't want to make waves, you don't want to make it personal. It's hard for you to admit that you're dissatisfied with me.

And once you did, of course you said, "Well, it's not really you, it's me, too."

PATIENT: *(Chuckles.)*

THERAPIST: You're not going to put all the blame on me.

PATIENT: *(Chuckles.)*

THERAPIST: I wonder if you don't read something into my reserve. And that is, that I don't like you and that I don't want to be bothered by your feelings, particularly if you've got something to complain about or fuss about . . . any feelings, whether they are feelings of wanting to be closer to me or feelings of dissatisfaction, complaints, whatever. So that you feel you need to hold back, because otherwise I'll get mad or be offended, and our relationship will be ruined.

PATIENT: Uh, I think that's true. And I think that maybe I'm waiting for you to set the appropriate level of intimacy, so to speak. If you would complain about me, then I would feel free to complain about you. If your reserve wasn't there, then I feel like maybe I would be less reserved.

The therapist's interpretation was based on responses to the questions he asked about the patient's immediate experiences in their relationship and the therapist's understanding of similar features in the patient's recollections of his relationship with his father. At this point in the session, however, the therapist refrained from making a transference–parent link because he did not have clear evidence that the patient appreciated the immediate influence of a recurrent maladaptive interpersonal pattern. They were still in the midst of clarifying what the patient felt to be an issue solely between them. Furthermore, this issue involved subtle hostility toward the therapist. It was important to bring this attitude to the surface, because the patient already indicated that it inhibited his openness with the therapist.

Soon Mr. A expressed an awareness of what had been his unquestioned assumption that the therapist neither liked nor wanted to be bothered by him. "[It] wouldn't be my intellectual conclusion, but I think it would be my emotional conclusion, and the one that I've been acting on." Once the patient began to question how he was interpreting the patient–therapist relationship, the therapist sought evidence of similar experiences in other relationships. However, Mr. A retreated to intellectualized rationales, which the therapist gently confronted. When the patient again expressed an awareness of the maladaptive nature of his characteristic mode of relating to others, the therapist encouraged a search for the sources of this interpersonal pattern.

PATIENT: My father would have to be that source.

THERAPIST: Can you elaborate?

PATIENT: I think both in his actions and his reactions, my father . . . in his actions, he does not usually go out of his way to tell you anything that he's uncomfortable with. On the contrary, he'll withdraw usually if he's uncomfortable. And in his reactions, if he senses that you are coming to him with something that you're uncomfortable with, he'll also withdraw. So I guess that I picked up from those behaviors that is the right way to behave, both because it's a good way to get along with him, and also because that's the way he behaves.

THERAPIST: I was wondering about that, too. It sounded a lot like the way you describe your father and the relationship with him. But I wonder if it could be put more personally and more relevant to how you experience your relationships and how you act. He is prototypic of the other person who doesn't want to be bothered by your feelings, whatever they are. And maybe doesn't even like you. What I mean by not even liking you, look, you're growing up, you're a little kid and here you have this imposing figure, your father. And you're bursting with all kinds of things that you want to say and tell, reactions you want from your father. And he doesn't seem to want to listen or give anything. What conclusion can you draw from that? The obvious conclusion is he doesn't want to be bothered with you, doesn't like you, you're not worth bothering with. And I'm suggesting it's more than just speculation, because look at what you experienced with me today: that I'm reserved and that must mean I don't want to be bothered by your feelings, and maybe I don't even like you.

The patient indicated that this reconstruction was meaningful and proceeded to describe his unsuccessful attempts to remember childhood experiences with his father.

PATIENT: And I just couldn't come up with anything. And yesterday I lay down and I took a nap. And I had a . . . it wasn't really a dream exactly, but I remembered my fifth-grade teacher, a man by the name of Mr. M. And in this, remembering, it was as if I was just crying and crying, remembering this guy, because he was such an opposite from what my father was. He seemed so human, so approachable, he seemed to take such a concern with me. I was just remembering him, remembering his face. And it was just as if I was crying and crying. I wasn't really crying, because I was really asleep. But when I woke up from that and remembered it, I realized that I had finally remembered something from my childhood that was really significant to me, namely this other man who really did seem to care about me, more than my father did.

In this interchange the patient had acknowledged a particular set of expectations regarding the attitude toward him of important persons in his life. This acknowledgment was a sign to the therapist that the patient was ready to look for sources of this attitude. With only a little encouragement, Mr. A drew a connection (that is, the patient initiated a transference–parent link) between his current expectations of others and his childhood relationship with his father. At this point the therapist took the opportunity to offer an empathic rationale (reconstructive interpretation) for the patient's coming to expect significant others to be uninterested or disapproving. The therapist, then, sought to reinforce the current validity and relevance of his interpretation by linking it to the components of the interpersonal pattern that they both had identified as being enacted between them earlier in the session. Evidence supporting the utility of the therapist's interventions came from the patient's revealing more personal information, namely his intense longing for a close relationship with a man.

Patient and therapist continued to explore these newly emerged feelings of longing for a close relationship with a paternal figure and sadness over its absence. Mr. A observed that as he talked about these feelings they faded from his experience. The therapist focused attention on this reaction (a resistance) and emphasized the patient's active participation in his emotional disconnection from others. The patient was struck by this realization.

THERAPIST: As you're recalling [the semi-dream] now, does it stir up any feelings now?

PATIENT: Yeah, it, somewhat the same feeling of wishing that I could have a relationship like that and also be a person like that or just have that quality. I think in some ways he personifies to me what is lacking in my life.

THERAPIST: Is there any of the sadness right now?

PATIENT: Yeah, though just when I started describing it, I lost a bit of it, but if I think about it, if I just think about his face as I was imagining it, I can bring up that feeling. It's a feeling of longing and grieving that I have to go back to fifth grade to find that. And this sort of sense of empty years.

THERAPIST: You know, even as you're feeling some of it now, from the outside, you're very successful at keeping it well hidden inside.

PATIENT: I'm sorry. I am not being real successful in getting into it.

THERAPIST: As you said, even as you start talking about it, it fades. Which is kind of striking, because just as often, if not more typically, as you talk about feelings they become clearer. In the context of what we've been talking about today, I wonder if there's a part of you that feels that even as we're talking about assumptions about what you can share with other people you're still very much operating with them. As you begin to talk about feelings with me, there's a part of you that feels that you have to stifle them, that I don't want to be burdened with them.

PATIENT: I don't know if that is it or not, but I do know that this feels like it's a very deep thing. And it's very hard for me to stay in touch with it because of that. As you were talking, I started to get more in touch, and now as I start talking, I'm losing it again.

THERAPIST: So, as though you can't share it. And if that is what's happening, if as you begin to get closer to sharing these very personal feelings with me, you have got to stifle them. It is such a contrast to that dream where you so much want to be close and to share feelings with a man: the fifth-grade teacher, your father, me. You have the dream the day before we are going to meet again.

PATIENT: Un-huh.

THERAPIST: And that is what you . . . that is what you began with today.

PATIENT: Un-huh.

THERAPIST: There, by the way, is also something that I think would be important to look for in other relationships. The more you want to be closer to somebody, the more the feeling of it gets stifled . . . your wife, your child, other people.

PATIENT: All I can say is yeah. I know, I feel a bit dumbstruck, by the sort of strange, quirky nature *(nervous laugh)* of myself. I have been amazed during these two weeks that I can't remember anything about my relationship with my father as a child. And if I really try to think back to anything concrete, I can't really remember anything. And now if I'm trying to describe this experience or this feeling, I know that it's there, just like I know my father was there, I know I had a relationship with him.

THERAPIST: You know, I don't think . . . in the context of what we're talking about and how you experience the relationship with your father, it's not quirky or strange at all. It seems so reasonable that if you decided that your father did not want to be burdened with your feelings, with your needs for closeness, with your feelings whatever they were, and you obviously wanted to be approved of by him, loved by him, not be rejected by him. Then what else could you do but the more you wanted to be closer, the more you wanted to share, the more you had to stifle it. Because you felt that is what he wanted. Just like, again, earlier today you said you were going to hold back and wait and see what I approve of, what I will sanction.

PATIENT: Right now, all I can seem to say is that I believe that. It makes sense to me that it's there. Right now, it just seems like quite a dilemma. I wish that I was a more natural person and that I wasn't struggling with this.

The patient had been helped to see and genuinely appreciate the chronic and pervasive influence on his relationships of a particular mode of relatedness. He had seen evidence of it in his current relationships (the unhappiness associated with it was his original reason for seeking treatment), in recollections of the childhood relationship with his father, and in its influence on his relationship to the therapist. Although all areas of the "triangle of insight" (Malan, 1976a) had been examined, the line of inquiry always returned to the enactment of the maladaptive pattern in the immediacy of the patient–therapist relationship. At this point in their work, all components of the CMP had received some attention:

1. Acts of self. The patient maintained a wary, emotionally aloof stance toward others; he felt emotionally disconnected but yearned for closeness.
2. Expectations of others. He expected other people to not want to be bothered with his feelings and to not like him.
3. Reactions of others. Other people tended to react to his emotional aloofness with reserve, which the patient interpreted as proof that they did not want to be involved with him.
4. Acts of self toward self. The patient felt unappealing and uninteresting.

EMPIRICAL SUPPORT

Empirical support for the TLDP approach derives from a variety of sources, including accumulated research on patient, therapist, and interaction variables as well as the broad array of investigations concerned with therapeutic outcomes (Garfield & Bergin, 1986). More specifically, our research is based on the findings of two studies: Vanderbilt I, and Vanderbilt II, a major process and outcome study using the TLDP approach, for which data analysis is still in progress.

Vanderbilt I

Vanderbilt I (Strupp & Hadley, 1979) involved comparisons of a group of patients (male college students) treated by highly experienced therapists with a matched group treated by warm and empathic but untrained college professors. Major findings of central significance for the development of TLDP included the following.

Neither professional therapists nor college professors were notably effective in treating patients with longstanding maladaptive patterns of relating characterized by pronounced hostility, pervasive mistrust, negativism, inflexibility, and antisocial tendencies. On the other hand, professional therapists were most effective with patients who had personality problems in combination with high motivation and an ability to form a good therapeutic relationship (working alliance) early in treatment (Strupp, 1980; Hartley & Strupp, 1983; Henry, Schacht, & Strupp, 1986). This is not meant to imply that professional therapists were most effective with the least disturbed patients. Rather, these therapists were particularly effective with patients whose personality resources and capacity for collaboration allowed them to take maximal advantage of the kind of relationship and traditional techniques proffered by the therapists. These findings are in general agreement with the literature (Luborsky, Chandler, Auerbach, Cohen, & Bachrach, 1971), perhaps most notably with the results of the Menninger Project (Kernberg et al., 1972).

The quality of the therapeutic relationship, established early in the interaction, proved to be an important predictor of outcome. In particular, therapy tended to be successful if by the third session the patient felt accepted, understood, and liked by the therapist (Waterhouse, 1979). Conversely, premature termination or failure tended to result if these conditions were not met early in treatment. In addition, reasonably accurate predictions of process and outcome could be made from initial interviews, specifically in terms of judgments relating to the patient's motivation for therapy (Keithly, Samples, & Strupp, 1980) and quality of interpersonal relationships (Moras, 1979). Stated differently, there was no evidence that an initially negative or highly ambivalent patient–therapist relationship was significantly modified in the course of the therapy under study.

Furthermore, the patients' perceptions of the therapeutic relationship remained fairly stable throughout therapy and to the follow-up period.

There was no evidence that professional therapists adapted their therapeutic approach or techniques to the specific characteristics and needs of individual patients. Instead, the kind of relationship they offered and the techniques they employed were relatively invariant. Similarly, therapists did not tailor their techniques in specific ways to the resolution of specifically formulated therapeutic goals.

The quality of the therapeutic relationship appeared to depend heavily on the patient's ability to relate comfortably and productively to the therapist in the context of a traditional therapeutic framework. This capacity, in turn, seemed to be a function of the patient's personality resources and suitability for time-limited therapy. In short, there was compelling evidence that with therapists who maintained a relatively invariant stance toward patients the quality of the patient–therapist relationship was significantly, although not entirely, determined by patient variables.

Therapists, in general, had little success in confronting or resolving the markedly negative reactions characteristic of more difficult patients. Instead, they tended to react negatively and countertherapeutically to a patient's hostility, mistrust, inflexibility, and pervasive resistances, thereby perhaps reinforcing the patient's poor self-image and related difficulties. The result of such interactions tended to be negative attitudes on the part of the patient toward the therapist and therapy; premature termination; or a poor therapeutic outcome (no change or negative change).

We came to view these results as having significant implications for research and clinical practice. The following conclusions, therefore, were systematically applied to our formulations of TLDP (Strupp & Binder, 1984) and formed the basis for the Vanderbilt II study.

Conclusion 1.

In order for psychotherapy to meet more adequately the needs of patients as well as society, it is essential to focus attention upon patients who have typically been rejected as suitable candidates for short-term psychotherapy and to explore systematically the extent to which such patients can be treated more effectively by a well-defined, time-limited approach.

Conclusion 2.

Psychological assessments must be sharpened to include (a) evaluations of the patient's character structure; (b) estimation of the quality of the patient's participation in time-limited psychotherapy in terms of the criteria that have been identified as important prognostic indicators; and (c) reformulation of patients' presenting complaints in terms of central issues or themes that lend themselves to focused therapeutic interventions. In order to effect more specific treatment planning, these determinations must become an integral part of the assessment process. Through this step, a closer link will be forged between diagnosis, formulation of therapeutic goals, techniques, and outcomes.

Conclusion 3.

In order to realize the full potential of short-term dynamic psychotherapy, therapists should receive specialized training, with particular emphasis on the following elements.

1. Techniques should be optimally geared to the achievement of reasonably specific therapeutic objectives identified early in the course of treatment. Crucial here is the definition of a central issue or maladaptive interpersonal theme (Schacht, Binder, & Strupp, 1984).

2. The therapeutic situation should be designed to meet the unique needs of the individual patient, as opposed to the tacit assumption that the patient conforms to the therapist's notions of an "ideal" therapeutic framework. Techniques should be applied flexibly, sensitively, and in ways that are most meaningful to the patient.

3. Steps should be taken to foster a good therapeutic relationship (working alliance) from the beginning of therapy, thus enhancing the patient's active participation and creating a sense of collaboration and partnership.

4. Negative transference reactions should be actively confronted at the earliest possible time.

5. Concerted efforts should be made to help therapists deal with negative personal reactions, which are characteristically engendered by most patients manifesting hostility, anger, negativism, rigidity, and similar resistances.

6. Although time-limited psychotherapy poses particular challenges to all therapists (especially in its demands for greater activity and directiveness), they should resist the temptation to persuade the patient to accept a particular solution, impose their values, and in other respects diminish the patient's striving for freedom and autonomy.

7. Rather than viewing psychotherapy predominantly as a set of technical operations applied in a vacuum, therapists must be sensitive to the importance of the human elements in all therapeutic encounters. In other words, unless the therapist takes an interest in the patient as a person and succeeds

in communicating this interest and commitment, psychotherapy becomes a caricature of a good human relationship (the ultimate negative effect!). 8. Closely related to the foregoing, therapists should keep in mind that all good therapeutic experiences lead to incremental improvements in the patient's self-acceptance and self-respect; consequently, continual care must be taken to promote such experiences and to guard against interventions that might have opposite results.

Vanderbilt II

The Vanderbilt II study involved the systematic training of another group of experienced psychotherapists in the TLDP approach, in order to investigate the effects of this training on psychotherapeutic process and outcome. The preliminary analyses of Vanderbilt II data confirmed and extended our earlier results, as follows (Henry & Strupp, 1989).

Therapists can be trained to meet technical adherence criteria in a manual-guided training program in psychodynamic interpersonal psychotherapy (Butler, 1986). This result parallels similar findings by others (such as Luborsky, McLellan, Woody, O'Brien, & Auerbach, 1985; Rounsaville, O'Malley, Foley, & Weissman, 1988).

TLDP training as conducted in the Vanderbilt II study can enhance treatment outcomes, but the relationship is far more complex than had previously been assumed, due to a number of mitigating factors that should be addressed by further research leading to revised training efforts (Henry, 1987; Butler, Strupp, & Lane, 1987). A manual-guided therapy, taught using traditional training methods, did not result in "the therapist variable" actually being specified or controlled to the extent hoped for with the advent of the manual-guided approach to training and psychotherapy research.

When novices in a given approach apply technical interventions, they may do so in a forced, mechanical manner that may have deleterious effects on the therapeutic process despite meeting technical adherence criteria. Furthermore, less than skillful application of technical interventions may actually increase patient resistance and inhibitory processes (a result that is particularly problematic in time-limited therapy). We must consider the possibility that more specific and more focused therapeutic approaches may actually create some types of problems. Further research is necessary to better understand what happens when therapists attempt to apply techniques and to determine whether improved training can avert the observed problems.

The effects of training cannot be adequately understood without concurrent examination of personal qualities of the trainees, such as their own interpersonal histories. These qualities appear to interact with technical adherence, yielding complex process and outcome relationships (Butler, Henry, & Strupp, 1989).

Our central finding continues to be that experienced therapists often engage in countertherapeutic interpersonal processes with difficult patients, and traditional modes of instruction do not seem to rectify this problem, although they may have other benefits (Henry, 1986; Butler & Strupp, 1989). Put simply, the absence of poor process does not ensure good outcomes, but the presence of certain types of poor process is almost always linked to bad outcomes. This conclusion is consistent with an emerging body of empirical evidence pointing to the fact that even though dynamic approaches remain the principal theoretical approach to individual psychotherapy, interventions are often performed in ways that may not promote an optimal therapeutic process.

Further analyses of process–outcome links, with particular reference to in-session changes, are under way.

References

Alexander, F., & French, T. M. (1946). *Psychoanalytic therapy.* New York: Ronald Press.

Anchin, J. C., & Kiesler, D. J. (Eds.). (1982). *Handbook of interpersonal psychotherapy.* New York: Pergamon Press.

Benjamin, L. S. (1982). Use of Structural Analysis of Social Behavior (SASB) to guide intervention in psychotherapy. In J. C. Anchin & D. J. Kiesler (Eds.), *Handbook of interpersonal psychotherapy* (pp. 190–212). New York: Pergamon Press.

Bergin, A. E., & Strupp, H. H. (1972). *Changing frontiers in the science of psychotherapy.* Chicago: Aldine-Atherton.

Butler, S. F. (1986, June). *Vanderbilt II study: A progress report—TLDP training.* Paper presented at the meeting of the Society for Psychotherapy Research, Wellesley, MA.

Butler, S. F., Henry, W. P., & Strupp, H. H. (1989, June). *Therapeutic skill acquisition as a result of training in time-limited dynamic psychotherapy.* Paper presented at the Society for Psychotherapy Research, Toronto, Canada.

Butler, S. F., & Strupp, H. H. (1989). The role of affect in time-limited dynamic psychotherapy. In J. D. Safran & L. S. Greenberg (Eds.), *Affective change events in psychotherapy.* New York: Academic Press.

Butler, S. F., Strupp, H. H., & Lane, T. W. (1987, June). *The time-limited dynamic psychotherapy strategies scale: Development of an adherence measure.* Paper presented at the meeting of the Society for Psychotherapy Research, Ulm, Germany.

Davanloo, H. (Ed.). (1978). *Basic principles and techniques in short-term dynamic psychotherapy.* New York: Spectrum.

Davanloo, H. (Ed.). (1980). *Short-term dynamic psychotherapy.* New York: Jason Aronson.

Epstein, L., & Finer, A. H. (1979). *Countertransference.* New York: Jason Aronson.

Garfield, S. L., & Bergin, A. E. (Eds.) (1986). *Handbook of psychotherapy and behavior change* (3rd ed.). New York: Wiley.

Gill, M. M. (1979). The analysis of the transference. *Journal of the American Psychoanalytic Association, 27,* 263–288.

Gill, M. M. (1982). *Analysis of transference: Vol. 1. Theory and technique.* New York: International Universities Press.

Gill, M. M., & Muslin, H. L. (1976). Early interpretations of transference. *Journal of the American Psychoanalytic Association, 24,* 779–794.

Giovacchini, P. (1989). *Countertransference triumphs and catastrophes.* Northvale, NJ: Jason Aronson.

Hartley, D. E., & Strupp, H. H. (1983). The therapeutic alliance: Its relationship to outcome in brief psychotherapy. In J. Masling (Ed.), *Empirical studies of psychoanalytical theories* (Vol. 1). pp. 1–37. Hillsdale, N.J.: Analytic Press.

Henry, W. P. (1986, July). *Structural Analysis of Social Behavior (SASB): An application for the study of interpersonal process and change in short-term psychotherapy.* Paper presented at the meeting of the Society for Psychotherapy Research, Boston.

Henry, W. P. (1987, July). *The study of interpersonal process in psychotherapy.* Paper presented at the meeting of the Society for Psychotherapy Research, Ulm, Germany.

Henry, W. P., Schacht, T. E., & Strupp, H. H. (1986). Structural Analysis of Social Behavior: Application to a study of interpersonal process in differential psychotherapeutic outcome. *Journal of Consulting and Clinical Psychology, 54,* 27–31.

Henry, W. P., Schacht, T. E., & Strupp, H. H. (1990). Patient and therapist introject, interpersonal process, and differential psychotherapy outcome. *Journal of Consulting and Clinical Psychology, 58,* 768–774.

Henry, W. P., & Strupp, H. H. (1989, June). *The Vanderbilt Center for Psychotherapy Research: Aims of the research program.* Paper presented at the meeting of the Society for Psychotherapy Research, Toronto.

Hoffman, I. Z. (1983). The patient as interpreter of the analysis experience. *Contemporary Psychoanalysis, 19,* 389–422.

Keithley, L. J., Samples, S. J., & Strupp, H. H. (1980). Patient motivation as a predictor of process and outcome in psychotherapy. *Psychotherapy and Psychosomatics, 33,* 87–97.

Kernberg, O. F., Burstein, E. D., Coyne, L., Applebaum, A., Horowitz, L., & Voth, H. (1972). Psychotherapy research project. *Bulletin of the Menninger Clinic, 36,* 1–275.

Kiesler, D. J., & Watkins, L. M. (1989). Interpersonal complementarity and the therapeutic alliance: A study of relationships in psychotherapy. *Psychotherapy, 26,* 183–194.

Klein, G. S. (1976). *Psychoanalytic theory: An explanation of essentials.* New York: International Universities Press.

Levenson, E. A. (1972). *The fallacy of understanding: An inquiry into the changing structure of psychoanalysis.* New York: Basic Books.

Levenson, E. A. (1982). Language and healing. In S. Slip (Ed.), *Curative factors in dynamic psychotherapy.* New York: McGraw-Hill.

Luborsky, L. (1984). *Principles of psychoanalytic psychotherapy: A manual for supportive-expressive treatment.* New York: Basic Books.

Luborsky, L., Chandler, A., Auerbach, H., Cohen, J., & Bachrach, H. M. (1971). Factors influencing the outcome of psychotherapy: A review of the quantitative research. *Psychological Bulletin, 75,* 145–185.

Luborsky, L., McLellan, A. T., Woody, G. E., O'Brien, C. P., & Auerbach, A. (1985) Therapist success and its determinants. *Archives of General Psychiatry, 42,* 602–611.

Malan, D. H. (1963). *A study of brief psychotherapy.* New York: Plenum.

Malan, D. H. (1976a). *The frontier of brief psychotherapy: An example of the convergence of research and clinical practice.* New York: Plenum.

Malan, D. H. (1976b). *Toward the validation of dynamic psychotherapy: A replication.* New York: Plenum.

Mann, J. (1973). *Time limited psychotherapy.* Cambridge, MA: Harvard University Press.

Mann, J., & Goldman, R. (1982). *A casebook in time-limited psychotherapy.* New York: McGraw-Hill.

Moras, K. (1979, June). *Quality of interpersonal relationships and patient collaboration in brief psychotherapy.* Paper presented at the European conference of the Society for Psychotherapy Research, Oxford, England.

Peterfreund, E. (1983). *The process of psychoanalytic therapy: Models and strategies.* Hillsdale, NJ: Analytic Press.

Rounsaville, B. J., O'Malley, S., Foley, S., & Weissman, M. N. (1988). The role of manual-guided training in the conduct and efficacy of interpersonal psychotherapy for depression. *Journal of Consulting and Clinical Psychology, 56,* 681–688.

Sandler, J. (1976). Countertransference and role-responsiveness. *International Review of Psychoanalysis, 3,* 43–47.

Sandler, J., & Sandler, A. M. (1978). On the development of object relationships and affects. *International Journal of Psychoanalysis, 59,* 285–296.

Schacht, T. E., Binder, J. L., & Strupp, H. H. (1984). The dynamic focus. In H. H. Strupp & J. L. Binder, *Psychotherapy in a new key: A guide to time-limited dynamic psychotherapy* (pp. 65–109). New York: Basic Books.

Schaffer, N. D. (1982). Multidimensional measures of therapist behavior as predictors of outcome. *Psychological Bulletin, 92,* 670–681.

Schafer, R. (1976). *A new language for psychoanalysis.* New Haven, CT: Yale University Press.

Schafer, R. (1983). *The analytic attitude.* New York: Basic Books.

Schlesinger, H. (1982). Resistance as a process. In P. Wachtel (Ed.), *Resistance in psychodynamic and behavioral therapies.* New York: Plenum.

Sifneos, P. E. (1972). *Short-term psychotherapy and emotional crisis.* Cambridge, MA: Harvard University Press.

Sifneos, P. E. (1979). *Short-term dynamic psychotherapy: Evaluation and technique.* New York: Plenum.

Silberschatz, G., Curtis, J. T., & Nathans, S. (1989). Using the patient's plan to assess progress in psychotherapy. *Psychotherapy, 26,* 40–46.

Strupp, H. H. (1980). Success and failure in time-limited psychotherapy (in 4 parts). *Archives of General Psychiatry, 37,* 595–603, 708–716, 831–841, 947–954.

Strupp, H. H., & Bergin, A. E. (1969). Some empirical and conceptual bases for coordinated research in psychotherapy: A critical review of issues, trends and evidence. *International Journal of Psychiatry, 7,* 18–90.

Strupp, H. H., & Binder, J. L. (1984). *Psychotherapy in a new key: A guide to time-limited dynamic psychotherapy.* New York: Basic Books.

Strupp, H. H., & Hadley, S. W. (1979). Specific versus nonspecific factors in psychotherapy: A controlled study of outcome. *Archives of General Psychiatry, 36,* 1125–1136.

Sullivan, H. S. (1953). *The interpersonal theory of psychiatry.* New York: Norton.

Waterhouse, G. J. (1979, June). *Perceptions of facilitative therapeutic conditions as predictors of outcome in brief therapy.* Paper presented at the European conference of the Society for Psychotherapy Research, Oxford, England.

CHAPTER 7

Short-Term Dynamic Therapy of Stress Response Syndromes

Mardi J. Horowitz

The ideas in this chapter were developed for understanding the processes of symptom formation and change in the stress response syndromes. Stress response syndromes were selected because their anchoring in known and meaningful external events facilitated the study of change. Many of the suggested techniques are applicable to other disorders, since in any approach one should take into account the personality configuration of the patient and how he or she can master stress of external or internal origin.

ORIGINS AND DEVELOPMENT

Early in the 1970s, my colleagues and I conducted clinical investigations of persons who were struggling to master recent stressful events. At the time, there was no diagnosis of posttraumatic stress disorder (PTSD) in the official nomenclature, *DSM II*. Yet in our clinical observations we found that intrusive and repetitive thought, especially unbidden images, was a

Copyright 1989 Center for the Study of Neuroses, UCSF. Research on which this material is based has been supported by The Program on Conscious and Unconscious Mental Processes of the John D. and Catherine T. MacArthur Foundation and a Clinical Research Center and other grants from NIMH, each directed by the author.

This chapter appeared in slightly altered form in Horowitz, M. J. (1976, 1986). *Stress response syndromes.* (Northvale, NJ: Jason Aronson) and is reprinted here with the permission of the publisher.

distinctive symptomatic response to stress, and often occurred in conjunction with its apparent opposite, phases of ideational denial and emotional numbing related to the potentially traumatic experiences.

In a series of experimental studies we found that most people's subjective experience of intrusive thought increased after they experienced stress-inducing perceptions. Those experiments consisted of showing different types of subjects different types of films in laboratory settings with varied demand characteristics. In field studies, my colleagues and I also focused on a variety of persons who had recently undergone major life events. This led to the development of questionnaires that were specific to the subjective experiences that may increase after stress, such as found in the intrusion and avoidance measures on the Impact of Event Scale and in clinicians' equivalent rating scales, such as the Stress Response Rating Scale (Horowitz, Wilner & Alvarez, 1979; Weiss, Horowitz & Wilner, 1984).

Bolstered by the positive findings of our experimental and field investigations, we thought it wise to pursue the clinical investigations in more detail. Increased understanding of the mental processes involved in the integration of memories of traumatic events and of changes in personality structure that came with mastery of an experience such as mourning led us to formulate techniques specific to a kind of dynamic therapy for stress response syndromes. The outcomes of such therapies were found to be effective, as summarized elsewhere (Horowitz, 1986; Horowitz, Marmar, Weiss, DeWitt & Rosenbaum, 1984; Horowitz, Marmar, Weiss, Kaltreider & Wilner, 1986).

One advantage of selecting a stress response syndrome such as posttraumatic stress disorder for study is that part of the etiology is known. That is, the syndrome is, in part, a consequence of the experience of a major life event, usually an injury or loss, or a major threat. Because the event is known, one has a good tracer; memories of the stressful event do or do not gain conscious representation, with or without subjective volition. The goal is also fairly clear: to help the patient at least regain his or her preevent level of personality functioning. Larger goals are also possible—for example, to rework the predisposing conflicts that might have combined with the stressful event to lead to symptom formation.

SELECTION OF PATIENTS AND GOALS OF TREATMENT

Brief, time-limited psychotherapy has a distinct advantage for clinical psychotherapy research. The time between pretherapy evaluation and posttherapy follow-up evaluation is compressed. Knowledge of outcome can be gained in less than a year. This permits the researcher to change his or her mind, within a short time, about how to conduct the next step in a research effort. A time-unlimited psychotherapy could go on for some years before the outcome might be fruitfully assessed.

Time-limited psychotherapy is a useful technique if the traumatic event is fairly recent and if the person does not have an excessively conflictual or deficient personality structure. In the approach developed with my colleagues, we excluded persons with psychotic and borderline personality disorders, persons involved in litigation, and persons who had experienced a complex and long series of linked traumatic events. We focused instead on accepting for study persons who developed a neurotic level of illness.

THEORY OF CHANGE

The theory guiding the delineation of our brief therapy for PTSD, pathological grief, and other disorders precipitated by recent traumas involves three components: state theory, person schemas theory, and control process theory. These theories are discussed in my book *Introduction to Psychodynamics: A New Synthesis* (1988) and applied to a set of transcripts from a case of a pathological grief reaction in *States of Mind: Configurational Analysis of Individual Psychology* (Horowitz, 1987). A very condensed view will be given here.

States of Mind Theory

State theory describes how, after a serious life event, a person may begin to manifest different states, different state durations, and different state transition patterns than were present before the stressful event. During a stress response syndrome there is an increase in either undermodulated or overmodulated states, as in periods of intrusive experience or times of omission, denial, and numbing. The time that is given up to these under- or overcontrolled states is derived from well-modulated states, sometimes called working states. In the immediate clinical situation, the therapist observes increased phenomena of intrusions, as in undermodulated states, and takes from these topics for which gaining mastery in psychotherapy is important. The therapist also observes, and helps the patient approach, observable omissions of topics that would deal with the serious implications of a stressful event.

The patient's current state of mind makes a difference in therapy techniques; the therapist selects techniques to aid self-regulation for patients in undermodulated states, to reduce excessive controls such as topic inhibition in overmodulated states, and to confront contradictions and conflicts in well-modulated states.

Person Schemas Theory

Person schemas theory has to do with enduring but slowly changing views of self and of other, and with scripts for transactions between self and other. Each individual may have a repertoire of multiple self schemas. When a traumatic event occurs, there may not be appropriate schemas available for showing how to adapt to the event. Integrating the event into memory is a complex process that has to do in part with modifying schemas such as role relationship models so that the person's inner expectations of self as related to another will accord with new realities. An example of this is manifest in a mourning process, when a person must get used to the fact that he or she is no longer in a continuous real and living relationship with the deceased.

Achieving schematic change may require many repetitions in the effort to recognize new realities and practice new ways of thinking and acting. Change requires conscious and/or unconscious conceptual processing. After a traumatic event, the person must bring forth different themes related to a central focus, which is how the traumatic event relates to the self. A brief therapy may help the patient *start* schematic change; months later the change may have occurred. In psychotherapy, memories of the stressful event and personal reactions to it are reviewed. By the effects of the therapist's focusing attention, correcting distortions, making linkages, and counteracting defensive avoidances, a new working model of what happened and its implications to the self is developed. The repetition of a working model, gradually changed by more attention to the actual properties of the situations, gradually leads to schematic change. That schematic change is both epigenetic and characterized by the formation of schemas of schemas. Epigenetic development (Erikson, 1963) consists of new acquisitions that are grafted onto previous schemas. Thus the previous schema may gain new elements and more correctly approximate the characteristics of reality.

The schemas of schemas that may be formed are overarching or supraordinate forms. They integrate previous schemas. By integration, some of the properties of previous schemas can be softened. For example, a schema in which the other person is seen as critical can be softened by incorporating it into a higher symbolic form in which the other person is seen as sometimes helpful and sometimes critical. In other words, schemas change by evolution; they are not erased. The earlier forms remain available, but the more mature overarching forms have relative priority, and so may control the emergence of the less mature schemas. This construction is not the same as the corrective emotional experience; it has been termed a corrective relationship experience or a new learning experience (Horowitz et al., 1984).

Control Process Theory

Control process theory suggests that people use different types of controls to facilitate or inhibit conscious recognition or communication of conflicts between preexisting schemas and the new traumatic situation. A mismatch between old schemas and new situations leads to intense emotional responses. People use avoidance or inhibition to avoid entering distraught states of mind. They may improve work on the traumatic topic when they recover a sense of being in control and can stabilize a well-modulated state even while experiencing negative emotions and the pain of cognitive recognition of loss.

The therapist's choice of technique depends on what type of controls the patient is using, is capable of, or is capable of learning. As already mentioned, if the patient is exerting excessive control, one may want to use a variety of procedures to help him or her reduce the level of avoidance. The procedures include interpretation of what is warded off, why it is warded off, and how the patient might proceed in contemplating such a painful topic. This may help the patient accept the theme of emotional response to the stressful event in a dose-by-dose manner. If, however, the patient is unable to exercise control, then the aim of the therapy may be to help him or her do so; by careful deflection from the emotional heart of a topic, the therapist aims first at helping the patient to enter a working state in which he or she can deal with, rather than be overwhelmed by, memories or fantasies related to the traumatic event and preexisting schemas.

One also must consider fantasies and preexisting schemas because any traumatic event triggers various latent topics into activity. Responses are an array of different associations and concepts that incorporate magical belief systems as well as realistic knowledge schemas. The differentiation of reality and fantasy is an important technique, which elsewhere has been shown to be related to the outcome of brief therapies of stress response syndromes (Horowitz, Marmar, Weiss, DeWitt, & Rosenbaum, 1984).

The therapist must pay attention to setting different goals and to using different levels of interpretation with different types of patients. This issue of levels of interpretation is dealt with elsewhere (Horowitz, 1989), as is the technical variation of general principles with different types of personality styles (Horowitz, 1986; Horowitz et al., 1984). Here the general principles of a treatment approach are outlined by reprinting text from Horowitz (1986, pp. 122–146).

TECHNIQUES OF MODERN PHASE-ORIENTED TREATMENT

Although the various treatment techniques suggested in the past have had their efficacy, they have also had their hazards. Too often the techniques were applied by therapists in a stereotyped rather than a patient-specific manner. During World War II, psychoanalytically oriented psychiatrists tended to use abreactive hypnosis, and "directive organic" types of psychiatrists, as they were then called, tended to use rest and sedation. We now understand the importance of orientation to treatment not by schools but by the immediate situation as well as the phase of response and the character of the patient.

Phases are often determined by the current degree of control over a tendency toward repetition. In general, the rest and support types of treatment try to supplement relatively weak controls. The treatment staff takes over some aspects of control operations, and they reduce the likelihood of emotional and ideational triggers to repeated representations. In contrast, the abreactive-cathartic treatment reduces controls through suggestion, social pressure, hypnosis, or hypnotic drugs. The long-range goal of the abreactive-cathartic treatment is not to reduce controls, however, but to reduce the need for controls by helping the patient complete the cycle of ideational and emotional responses to a stress event.

Unfortunately, the repertoire of available techniques and theories has never been well classified, though a rudimentary attempt at phase-specific technique classification is presented in table 1, the goal being to convey a general idea, not to recommend particular treatment forms.

Completing integration of an event's meanings and developing adaptational responses are the goals of treating a stress response syndrome. One knows that this achievement is near when the person is freely able to think about or to not think about the event. These goals can be broken down

TABLE 1

Treatments for Stress Response Syndromes

States	
Denial-Numbing Phase	Intrusive-Repetitive Phase

Reduce controls
  Interpret defenses and attitudes that
  make controls necessary
  Suggest recollection
	Supply structure externally
	  Structure time and events for
	  patient when essential
	  Organize information
	Reduce external demands and
	stimulus levels
	Recommend rest
	Provide identification models, group
	membership, good leadership,
	orienting values
	Permit temporary idealization,
	dependency

Encourage abreaction	Work through and reorganize by clarifying and educative interpretive work

Encourage description
  Association
  Speech
  Use of images rather than just
  words in recollection and fantasy
  Conceptual enactments, possibly
  also role playing and art therapy
	Differentiate
	  Reality from fantasy
	  Past from current schemata
	  Self attributes from object
	  attributes
	Remove environmental reminders and
	triggers, interpret their meaning and
	effect

Reconstructions to prime memory and associations	Teach "dosing," e.g., attention on and away from stress-related information
Encourage catharsis	Provide support
Explore emotional aspects of relationships and experiences of self during event	Evoke other emotions, e.g., benevolent environment
Supply support and encourage emotional relationships to counteract numbness	Suppress emotion, e.g., selective use of antianxiety agents
	Teach desensitization procedures and relaxation

Source: M. J. Horowitz, *Stress Response Syndromes*, 2nd ed. (Northvale, NJ: Jason Aronson, 1986).

according to immediate aims that depend on the patient's current state. When the stress event is ongoing, aims may center on fairly direct support. When the event's external aspects are over, but the person swings between paralyzing denial and intolerable attacks of ideas and feelings, then the immediate aim is to reduce the amplitude of these swings. Similarly, if the patient is frozen in a state of inhibited cognitive-emotional processing, then the therapist must both induce further thought and help package these responses into tolerable doses (see table 2).

Treating Acute Patients in an Intrusive Phase of Response

Most patients seek help for stress response syndromes when they are overwhelmed with intrusive ideas and emotions. The reality of the traumatic events usually contributes, with the patient's sense of urgent need, to the therapist's wish to react rapidly and to provide help. For many physicians and psychiatrists, this urgency may translate into prescribing antianxiety or sedative agents. Although this is sometimes indicated, the availability of the care provider and the establishment of a treatment program are often sufficient. The act of talking about the events and personal reactions during an extended session often markedly reduces the sense of being overwhelmed. When insomnia is producing fatigue and lowering coping capacity, sedation with one of the antianxiety agents may be used on a night-by-night basis. Smaller doses of the same agent may be prescribed during the day, again on a dose-by-dose basis, if the patient's severely distraught, anxious states of mind challenge adaptive functioning.

The patient and persons close to the patient should be cautioned against using multiple mood control agents, especially against combining alcohol with prescribed medications. Alcohol in small doses may be a sufficient soporific and calming agent without additional medication, but for some patients it may lead to excessive self-dosages. Antidepressive agents should not be prescribed to relieve immediate sadness and despondent responses to loss, but they may be used for prolonged pathological reactions that meet the necessary diagnostic criteria for the major depressive disorders, if psychotherapy alone is not leading to clear, rapid, and progressive improvement.

In addition, in the acute phase of responding to a traumatic event, the patient may be advised, for a time, to avoid driving, operating machinery, or engaging in tasks in which alertness is essential to safety. Persons already under stress are more likely to have accidents because they have

TABLE 2

Priorities of Treatment

Patient's Current State	Treatment Goal
Under continuing impact of external stress event	–Terminate external event or remove patient from contiguity with it –Provide temporary relationship –Help with decisions, plans, or working-through
Swings to intolerable levels: Ideational-emotional attacks Paralyzing denial and numbness	–Reduce amplitude of oscillations to swings of tolerable intensity of ideation and emotion –Continue emotional and ideational support –Selection of techniques cited for states of intrusion in Table 1
Frozen in overcontrol state of denial and numbness with or without intrusive repetitions	–Help patient "dose" reexperience of event and implications that help remember for a time, put out of mind for a time, remember for a time, and so on. Selection of denial techniques from Table 1 –During periods of recollection, help patient organize and express experience. Increase sense of safety in therapeutic relationship so patient can resume processing the event
Able to experience and tolerate episodes of ideation and waves of emotion	–Help patient work through associations: the conceptual, emotional, object relations, and self-image implications of the stress event –Help patient relate this stress event to earlier threats, relationship models, self-concepts, and future plans
Able to work through ideas and emotions on one's own	–Work through loss of therapeutic relationship –Terminate treatment

Source: M. J. Horowitz, *Stress Response Syndromes*, 2nd ed. (Northvale, NJ: Jason Aronson, 1986).

lapses of attention, concentration, and sequential planning or because they have startle reactions that disrupt motor control.

During the intrusive phase, relatives and colleagues may also offer support. Advice that has been useful in the past to the patient can be extended directly or through such social support networks. The following paragraphs, which restate some of the principles already discussed, may be helpful.

1. Remember that the victim remains vulnerable to entering a distraught state of mind, even in states of safety and even weeks after the event. Such distraught states as pangs of searing grief, remorse, terror, or diffuse rage are attenuated or are less likely to occur if the victim is surrounded by supportive companions. The companions should be aware that being there is doing a lot and that helping may not require doing the impossible. Persons who have sustained the same type of trauma are sometimes especially helpful companions, and that is why self-help groups include persons who are at different phases of dealing with similar situations.

2. The more the person has been traumatized, the longer the phases of response will be. After a major loss, considerable revision is necessary in both daily life and inner views of life. This revision may mean that the person is not even relatively back to normal, in terms of usual mood patterns, for a year or two. This contrasts with the expectation in many work environments that the traumatized person should be back to usual functional levels within a week or two. The work place may provide sustaining interests and social supports so that the victim is not left isolated or encapsulated; yet some modulation of what is expected should extend for longer periods than has become the case in a society driven by work productivity and advancement.

3. Sleep disruption is a common part of posttraumatic stress disorders. The victim comes to associate efforts to relax and sleep with episodes of panic or vivid unpleasant imagery associated with the trauma, especially if it has occurred at times when the victim's guard has been lowered or concentration on daytime activities is reduced. It may be helpful to change habit patterns in whatever way strengthens the sense of safety that permits restful sleep. This may include leaving the room lights on or sleeping with a pet or with another person. In extreme cases, rest can be encouraged by telling the victim that a companion will stay awake and watch over him or her during sleep.

4. The person who has been traumatized may have cognitive impairments of which he or she is not aware. The victim may feel more effective, alert, and reflexively responsive than is actually the case and may be more at risk of accidents while driving or operating machinery. Any kind of drug, such as a single drink of alcohol, may have a more impairing effect on such persons than would usually be the case. For these reasons, advising the victim not to drive or engage in hazardous work tasks is advisable even

when the victim insists this is not necessary. Such limitations must be tactfully imposed so as to avoid anything that might encourage a transition to incompetent self-concepts.

5. Right after a traumatic event, the victim's relatives and friends rightfully cluster around and want to know all about what happened. The victim, often alone at the time of the event, now recounts the story again and again. There is here a paradox, because later on the victim will want to retell the story repeatedly but now, early, is when it is demanded. These many early repetitions may lead to an exhausting reliving of the still vivid experience with all its violent emotional responses. Later the relatives and friends may behave as if they were tired of hearing about it and may counter with their own similar tales of mishap and woe. The victim may then feel pent up with the need to repeat the traumatic experience and to communicate his or her conceptual and emotional responses to it. It is at these later stages that empathic listening, without trying to short-circuit the conversation, may be very useful. Then gradually the victim's attention can be brought first to the present and then to the future.

6. The victim expects to be upset after a trauma, and so when responses come later, after a period of restored good functioning, they come as a surprise and may lead to a fear of losing mental control and unnecessary doubts about recovery. Knowledge about the normal phases, including a return of intrusive ideas and emotions after a period of denial, can be very useful for the victim at this point. Sometimes, however, the victim will have a correct intuitive sense of being blocked in working through a trauma. This subjective sense may be usefully echoed by a relative or friend who also recognizes that the reaction is too intense, prolonged, complicated, or impacted. That social communication, in the context of a calm and straightforward discussion, may enable the victim to seek professional help when it is indicated.

In evaluating a patient in an acute, probably intrusive phase of response to a traumatic life event, the clinician should specifically inquire about intrusive experiences, as the patient may find them difficult to describe on his or her own. The clinician then may label symptoms as a normal response to stress in order to reassure the patient that he or she is not losing control of his or her mind. When the patient describes what is intruding into his or her experience, the clinician should encourage him or her to expand on the topic in order to develop further the meaning of the event. Usually nonspecific statements are helpful in encouraging this elaboration; for example, the therapist may ask, "Can you tell me more about that?" "Is there anything else?" "What was it like for you?" and so forth.

While listening to the patient expand on the topic, the clinician should be alert to blocks in thinking or feeling in the next step in a sequence that might lead to some kind of acceptance or closure of the event. For example, thinking about the event's implications may lead to ideas of what caused it. The patient may think that he or she did something that caused the event, which would lead to feelings of intense guilt, and so he or she may immediately block off this train of thought to avoid experiencing the guilt.

When the clinician discovers a block to working through reactions to a stressful event, he or she may help the patient by looking at the differences between realistic appraisal and fantasy appraisal. For example, if a patient feels that he has brought on a heart attack by harboring angry thoughts toward his boss, it may be important to indicate to him that this was not the cause of the coronary occlusion and that he does not have to blame himself for it. This is not meant to complete the therapy in a single visit but to move toward a hopeful focus for the treatment.

The clinician does not have to be a figure who restores what has been lost. But it is important to the patient that the clinician represent a person who is not overwhelmed by thinking about the implications of some illness, injury, or loss. The very presence of the clinician as a person who is able to contemplate these events and to think about them logically is often extremely reassuring to the patient during an intrusive phase. The denial phase is also an especially important one to consider in relation to treatment interventions. Denial may serve adaptive purposes, allowing the person to restabilize, but it may also interfere with important decisions that may have to be made at once. Health care choices are one example, as with a patient who has developed gangrene following an accidental electrical burn and must decide immediately how much amputation he will permit.

Time Pressure during a Denial Phase

Intellectualization may be openly advised for the patient as a way to make immediate decisions. For example, the patient may be told that although there will be many emotional reactions to the situation, for the time being it might be best to consider only those problems requiring an immediate choice and to talk them over in terms of advantageous and disadvantageous outcomes. The processes involved in denial may also be labeled so that the patient can understand why it is difficult to concentrate on making a decision. Sometimes it is necessary to accept the patient's inability to make a fully rational decision at the moment because of the specific stress disorder and to explain both the denial phase and the information pertinent to decision making to another person who is accepted by the patient as serving his or her best interests. When this is the case, the therapist should realize that this is a transient assignment, not one that should continue for a long time. Later the patient should be told how and why these decisions were reached.

No Time Pressure during a Denial Phase

Patients may be told that they are pushing away recognition of the event's implications and that this is a normal adaptive reaction. This should be done uncritically, indicating the acceptability of such defensive avoidances. If patients are not, on their own, progressing through a period of denial and numbness, it may be helpful to remind them of the need to make the next adaptive move. The patients may be encouraged to allow a conscious review of memories, and to experience ideas and feelings related to what has passed.

Patients may be urged to take a one-dose-at-a-time approach, contemplating the most immediate consequences of what has happened and perhaps putting off the next considerations for a while. This kind of reassurance indicates to the patients that they can tolerate some aspects of what has seemed intolerable but that they do not have to confront everything all at once. Patients may also be given realistic reassurance that they will eventually be able to tolerate what now seems overwhelming. The example of mourning may be given; it seems intolerable to accept a loss that has just occurred, but people come to accept it over a year or two. It is often helpful in this regard for the clinician to indicate that he or she will remain available to the patient as a support until the patient works through and accepts his or her experience.

TECHNIQUES SPECIFIC TO SHORT-TERM DYNAMIC THERAPY OF RESPONSE SYNDROMES

At the Center of the Study of Neuroses, University of California, San Francisco, my colleagues and I developed a brief psychotherapy for stress response syndromes (Horowitz, 1973, 1976; Horowitz & Kaltreider, 1979; Horowitz et al., 1984). This procedure uses a time limit of twelve sessions which can be varied as required by individual circumstances, characteristics, and responses. A sample of what tends to happen in such therapies is given in table 3.

When a person seeks help, the therapist establishes a working alliance through which he or she assists the patient in working through his or her reactions. In addition, efforts may be directed at modifying preexisting conflicts, developmental difficulties, and defensive styles that made the person unusually vulnerable to traumatization by this particular experience.

Therapy begins by establishing a safe and communicative relationship. This, together with specific interventions such as an analysis of defensive avoidances and an identification of warded off contents, alters the status of the patient's controls. The patient can then proceed to reappraise the serious life event and the meanings associated with it and make the necessary revisions of his or her inner models of the self and the world. As this reappraisal and revision take place, the person moves into a position to make new decisions and to engage in adaptive actions. The patient can follow any altered behavior patterns until they become automatic. As he or she is able to achieve new levels of awareness, this process is repeated and deepened. That is, as the patient can relate more closely, he or she can modify controls further and assimilate more warded off thoughts about the current stress. There is then the necessity of working through the reactions to the approaching loss of the therapist and the therapy.

Within the time limits of a brief psychotherapy, the therapist works to establish conditions that will help process the painful event. There is an early concern by the patient for both the safety of the relationship and the therapist's ability to help him or her cope with the symptoms. These symptoms can seem less overwhelming when the therapist offers support, suggests some immediate structuring of time and events, and prescribes medication if anxiety or insomnia are too disruptive.

Introducing plans for terminating the therapy several sessions before the final one leads to a reexperience of the loss, often with a return of the symptoms. But this time the loss can be faced gradually, actively rather than passively, and within a communicative and helping relationship. Specific interpretations of the link of the termination experience to the stress event are made, and the final hours center on this theme. At termination, the patient will usually still have symptoms, both because of the time needed to process a major loss and because of anxiety about the loss of the relationship with the therapist.

Patients sometimes become aware during these brief therapies of a particular style they have for *not* thinking about events, and they are able deliberately to alter that avoidance. It may be possible for them, by con-

TABLE 3

Sample Twelve-Session Dynamic Therapy for Stress Disorders

Session	Relationship Issues	Patient Activity	Therapist Activity
1	Initial positive feeling for helper	Patient tells story of event	Preliminary focus is discussed
2	Lull as sense of pressure is reduced	Event is related to previous life	Takes psychiatric history. Gives patient realistic appraisal of syndrome
3	Patient testing therapist for various relationship possibilities	Patient adds associations to indicate expanded meaning of event	Focus is realigned; resistances to contemplating stress-related themes are interpreted
4	Therapeutic alliance deepened	Implications of event in the present are contemplated	Defenses and warded off contents are interpreted, linking of latter to stress event and responses
5		Themes that have been avoided are worked on	Active confrontation with feared topics and reengagement in feared activities are encouraged
6		The future is contemplated	Time of termination is discussed
7–11	Transference reactions interpreted and linked to other configurations; acknowledgment of pending separation	The working through of central conflicts and issues of termination, as related to the life event and reactions to it, is continued	Central conflicts, termination, unfinished issues, and recommendations all are clarified and interpreted
12	Saying goodbye	Work to be continued on own and plans for the future are discussed	Real gains and summary of future work for patient to do on own are acknowledged

Source M. J. Horowitz, *Stress Response Syndromes*, 2nd ed. (Northvale, NJ: Jason Aronson, 1986).

tinued work on their own after therapy, to live out changes that may gradually modify their habitual defenses and attitudes. In this manner, the brief therapy of stress response syndromes follows the techniques of focal dynamic therapy, as described by Malan (1979), Basch (1980), Strupp & Binder (1984), and Luborsky (1984), and may also use special imagery techniques, as described by Singer & Pope (1978) and Horowitz (1983).

When people experience the impact of a serious life event, such as a loss or injury, their most advanced, adaptive role relationships can be threatened. They may regress to earlier role relationships, or the meaning of the life event itself may create some new role relationship, perhaps with unattractive, dangerous, or undesirable characteristics. Such persons may then enter a series of painful, strongly affective states based on altered self-concepts and role relationship models. As a consequence of the therapeutic facilitation of normal processes, these disturbing role relationships or self-concepts can once again be subordinated to more adaptive, more mature self-concepts and role relationships. Intensive work using this type of brief therapy model may change the symptomatic response to a stressful life event and may facilitate further progress along developmental lines.

Realignment of Focus

Patients will usually have presented painful symptomatology or problematic states as the chief complaint or motivation for seeking help. The first focus or agreement between patient and therapist will be to help attenuate these symptoms or states or to avoid reentry into them. Problematic states will be seen in relation to other states of experience and behavior. A broader analysis of the situation with the patients will include examining the reasons for entering the problem states and other, even more threatening states that are warded off. As painful symptoms are ameliorated, the emphasis may shift to exploring when and why the patient enters these painful states. This revised focus often pertains to particular self-concepts and inner models of relationships. If this shift in focus is not made at the right time, the patient may move toward termination or avoidance of treatment when he or she achieves enough control to enter a relatively stable denial phase. Separation from treatment at this time may be an error because the patient has not worked through some of the most difficult parts of his or her stress response and may not do so on his or her own.

Example: From a Bereavement Case

The patient was a young woman in her mid-twenties. She sought help because of feelings of confusion, intense sadness, and loss of initiative six weeks after the sudden, unexpected death of her father. Her first aim was to regain a sense of self-control. This was accomplished within a few sessions, because she had found a substitute for the idealized, positive relationship with her father in the relationship with the therapist and realistically hoped that she could understand and master her changed life circumstances.

As she regained control and could feel pangs of sadness without entering flooded, overwhelmed, or dazed states, she began to wonder what she might further accomplish in the therapy and whether the therapy was worthwhile. The focus gradually shifted from recounting the story of her father's death and her responses, to understanding her past and current inner relationship with her father. The focus of therapy became her vulnerability to entering states governed by defective, weak, and evil self-concepts. These self-concepts related to feelings that her father had scorned her in recent years because she had not lived up to his ideals. He died before she could accomplish her goal of reestablishing a mutual relationship of admiration and respect through her plan to convince him that her own modified career line and life style would lead to many worthwhile accomplishments.

This image of herself as bad and defective was matched by a complementary image of her father as scornful of her. She felt ashamed of herself and angry with him for not confirming her as worthwhile. In this role relationship model, she held him to be strong, even omnipotent, and in a magical way she saw his death as a deliberate desertion of her. These ideas had been warded off because of the intense humiliation and rage that would occur when they were clearly represented. But contemplation of such ideas in therapy allowed her to review and reappraise them, revising her view of herself and of him.

Every person has many self-images and role relationship models. In this patient, an additional important self-image was of herself as a person too weak to tolerate the loss of a strong father. As is common, no life event occurs in isolation from other life changes but is almost invariably part of a cluster of events and effects. After this woman returned from her father's funeral, she turned to her lover for consolation and sympathy. She had selected a lover who, like her father, was superior, cool, and remote. But when she needed compassionate attention, he was unable to provide it, and they separated. Establishing a therapeutic alliance thus provided much needed support, but its termination threatened her once again with the loss of a sustaining figure. In the midphase of therapy, it therefore was necessary for her to focus on those weak self-images in order to test them against her real capability for independence.

To recapitulate, early in therapy this patient rapidly established a therapeutic alliance around a working focus to relieve her of the acute distress of the intrusive phase of a stress response syndrome, in this case an adjustment disorder. This alliance led to a rapid attenuation of the problematic states of mind. With this symptom reduction, the focus shifted to the aim of working through various aspects of her relationship with her father. In addition to the primary meanings of her grief, that is, the loss of a continued relationship with her father and the hope of changing it, she had to work through several additional themes: herself as scorned by her father, herself as too weak to survive without her father, and herself as evil and partly responsible for his death.

These important self-concepts, present before the death, were worked on during the midphase of therapy. They were related to role relationship models that pertained not only to her father but also to other past figures (mother and siblings), current social relationships, and transference themes. As she contemplated and worked with these themes, her focus expanded from past and current versions of these constellations to include additional issues. Were she to maintain these self-concepts and views of role relationships, she might either reject men altogether or continue with a neurotic repetition of efforts to regain her father and convert him to the ideal figure she remembered from early adolescence. This prospective work also included examining her reaction to separation from the therapist and how she would in the future interpret that relationship.

Interpreting Defenses and Transference for a Particular Event

All patients will have a combination of reactions to stress events and their prestress problems. Therapists therefore should attend to the manifestations of characteristic defensive styles and the emergence of transference even during the comparatively brief treatment of a stress response syndrome. What do therapists do with this information? Do they interpret defenses, interpret and try to work through transference? Or do they work around defense and transference to bring the stress-event reactions to a point of completion? Each patient–therapist pair can arrive at a satisfactory end point by means of different routes. Nonetheless, using the gestalt of the stress event can be one of the guiding principles. This means that defensive modifications and self–object dyad interpretations can be made and that they can be centered on the specific contents of the stress-event memories.

Example of Connection-Forming Interventions.

A young woman had attacks of incapacitating anxiety for months after she was raped. She had flirted with the man and encouraged his advances, but when she wished to go no further in the sexual encounter, he forced her, with threats of violence, to have intercourse. She decided not to report the matter to the police or to a physician. She came for help later because of increased anxiety.

The first work involved her telling the story of how she was traumatized by this man's vicious behavior. This, plus the establishment of a therapeutic relationship, helped reduce her anxiety, but an unclear sense of her own participation remained and required further therapeutic attention.

During psychotherapy she was generally vague in her verbal communication. Nonverbally, there were bodily gestures to which the therapist did not respond but that he found somewhat erotically stimulating. When the therapist failed to show interest in her physical attributes and movements, the patient seemed to feel hurt; she looked dejected, withdrew, and talked in a self-depreciating manner. Despite this reactivity, the patient did not appear to be conceptually aware of her bodily gambits, the therapist's lack of attention to them, or her hurt responses.

Through many such observations of process, the therapist made two inferences. One was that the patient had a repressive/denying and dissociative style. The other concerned a pattern for interpersonal relationships in which she offered an erotic surrender to a domineering other person and expected attention and care in return.

These inferences were not interpreted directly or in terms of the transference manifestations. Instead, they were used as information to help reconstruct the rape and preceding events. The rape was seen as a pattern contributed to by the real but unrecognized assaultive nature of the man involved, her general pattern of relating to men, and her method of avoiding appraisal of this particular man.

In this way, some aspects of the fear, anger, guilt, and shame evoking ideas about the event were worked through. In addition, the therapeutic process allowed some progressive change in the patient's self- and object concepts. For example, one unconscious attitude present before the stress event was that an erotic approach was the only way to get attention because she herself was so undeserving. She must give her body in order to get attention. In work on the meaning of the rape, she became aware of this defective self-concept and related rescue fantasies. She was able to revise her attitudes, including her automatic and unrealistic expectations that dominant others would feel guilty about exploiting her and then be motivated by guilt to be concerned and tender.

The relatively clear contents of the stress-event memories provided a concrete context for this work. The focus of discussion was outside the therapeutic relationship, although there was a tendency toward a compulsive repetition of the "rapist–raped" relationship in the transference situation. The therapeutic alliance was maintained but might have been disrupted by the anxiety that would have occurred if interpretation of the same self–object transactions had been directed to the transference situation.

At some point, if advisable, it may be possible to extend recognition of the same patterns to the transference, to childhood relationships, and to current interpersonal relationships. That is, this focus on the stress events does not mean that the interpretation of transference is omitted from a stress-focused treatment. But there is no intent to allow a transference neurosis to evolve, and transference interpretations will usually focus on negative responses that are likely to impede therapy.

Example of a Blend of Transference Recognition Focusing on a Recent Stressful Event.

A young woman patient broke her leg in a fall from a ladder while helping her father paint his house. A partial paralysis complicated matters and disrupted her plans to accept a teaching position on graduation from college. She came to therapy because of a reactive depression. One of the dormant psychological complexes activated by her injury was hostility toward her father for not taking good enough care of her. The relevant theme of the stress event was anger that her father had given her a rickety, second-class ladder while he used a good one. She had, in the past, been unable to recognize her own ambivalence toward her father, even when he gave her good cause to be hostile. Awareness of her anger was warded off at the time treatment began.

During one treatment hour, the emotion closest to the surface was anger at the therapist because he would not prescribe sleeping pills for her insomnia. Though the therapist was able to infer this emotion, it was not recognized or expressed clearly by the patient.

We shall now artificially dichotomize the immediate problem of whether the therapist should interpret the anger in terms of the transference or in terms of the stress event. A therapeutic rule of thumb is to focus on negative transference reactions, such as surfacing anger at the therapist; negative reactions interfere with other therapy processes, and the patient might even quit or withdraw. The problem is not only how to deal with negative transference feelings, so that they are reduced enough for the therapy to progress, but also how to use the information gained to work through the stress event. One way to decide whether to focus on the emergent anger is the therapist's diagnostic impression of the patient's strength. If the patient is capable of tolerating it, the therapist can interpret what is going on. But if the patient is in danger of fragmentation, as in severe narcissistic and borderline characters, the therapist may not interpret the anger directly, but instead may deal with it in a counteractive way or give it a peripheral interpretation in relation to characters outside the treatment situation.

If the therapist decides to interpret the anger in a fairly direct manner, he or she still must decide which line of interpretation will be the most therapeutic. For example, the therapist can choose among four lines of approach:

1. You are angry with me because you feel that I am not taking care of you, just as your father did not take care of you (interpretation of the transference link to father).
2. You are angry with me and are afraid to express it or even know it (interpretation of the fear of being angry).
3. You are angry with me, and so you withdraw (interpretation of the defensive maneuver).
4. You get angry when your dependency needs are not met (interpretation of underlying wishes).

These are, of course, not the wordings of the interpretations but a shorthand illustration of the various possible directions. In a full segment of work, each aspect of the interpretation may be made.

Whichever type of interpretation is made first, it may be possible to link the exploration of the anger to the recent stress event, even though the focus remains on working through the immediate negative sentiments toward the therapist. For example, the interpretation may be worded as follows, except that it would be given in short phrases rather than all at once:

THERAPIST: You are angry with me right now because I am not meeting your need for a sleeping pill, just as you are still angry with your father because you feel he took poor care of you by giving you a lousy stepladder.

The principal advantage of this type of wording, which links current transference to the model of the stressful event, is that it maintains a conceptual clarity regarding the treatment's goals and priorities. If the focus is on only the transference meanings of a patient–therapist transaction, the transference will be accentuated as a topic of interest to the therapist. Doing some transference work creates more transference work because the therapist's interest in the transference aspects of treatment has an intrinsic transference-evoking effect, a paradoxical cycle. The tendency is toward a character analysis (Oremland, 1972) rather than working through the life event and then terminating or establishing some other therapeutic contract.

Example of Depression after the Death of a Loved One.

During the first three interviews the work focused on a young male patient's feeling that his mother had left him alone by dying. As a result of this work, his feelings of intense loneliness decreased. The pain and threat of his loss had been reduced to a level at which his available defensive and coping strategies could inhibit further emotional responsivity. During the ensuing interviews, his feelings of sadness and ideas of being left were absent.

Despite the symptomatic relief, the therapist inferred that the stressful event had not been completely worked through but, rather, had only been worked on to the point that denial and numbness had become possible. At this point in treatment, as is common, the patient searched for topics to discuss because he did not want to lose the therapist through treatment termination. That is why in one hour he brought up a current problem, an argument the night before with his girlfriend.

There was no doubt that the emotion nearest the surface was anxiety about the argument, and the therapist gave his attention to this situation. But in his interventions he chose not to explore in detail the relationship between the patient and his girlfriend because he felt it would deflect the therapeutic path to interpersonal relationships in general and from there into a long-term therapy. Instead, he linked the patient's fears of losing his girlfriend to the recent loss of his mother by saying, "Another loss might be very hard for you to contemplate right now."

This remark was enough to link the young man's current emotional state to the incompletely processed stress event. Through such maneuvers, it was possible to avoid diffusion of the therapy to many topics. With this patient, a decision to attempt a general characterological revision might be made after more work on the loss.

These case examples do not mean that the work of relating the meaning of subsequent occurrences to the stress event can be forced. In some patients, especially adolescents or young adults, loss of a parent or sibling may be worked on only to a point that denial can set in. Then the implications of the loss are vigorously inhibited, and attempts at connection, such as illustrated here, will not succeed. In such instances, the therapeutic goal must be reconsidered, the defenses accepted, and the patient either seen over a considerable period of time with a therapeutic strategy or terminated until later work is indicated.

EMPIRICAL SUPPORT

My colleagues and I have developed a series of measures useful for assessing the outcome of such treatments, the disposition of patients, the process of therapy, and the interaction of these variables. These include the Impact of Event Scale, which offers specific stress measures for self-report (Horowitz, Wilner & Alvarez, 1979; Zilberg, Weiss & Horowitz, 1983); the Stress Response Rating Scale, which measures the clinician's assessment of current stress levels (Weiss, Horowitz & Wilner, 1984); and the Patterns of Individualized Change Scales (PICS), which assess social and work functions as well as self-esteem and specific stress symptoms (Kaltreider, DeWitt, Weiss & Horowitz, 1981; DeWitt, Kaltreider, Weiss & Horowitz, 1983; Weiss, DeWitt, Kaltreider, & Horowitz, 1985).

The therapeutic process measures pertinent to this approach to psychotherapy include assessments of the therapeutic alliance (Marziali, Marmar & Krupnick, 1981; Marmar, Marziali, Horowitz & Weiss, 1986) and the assessment of specific therapist interventions on a therapist actions scale or checklist (Hoyt, 1980; Hoyt, Marmar, Horowitz & Alvarez, 1981). These process scales, the assessment of patients' motivations for dynamic psychotherapy (Rosenbaum & Horowitz, 1983), and the developmental level of the self-concept (Horowitz, 1979; Horowitz, Marmar, Weiss, DeWitt, & Rosenbaum, 1984) rely on independent opinions of judges reviewing videotapes, audiotapes, or transcripts and have been found to be reliable at satisfactory levels.

Using all such measures in the study of fifty-two cases of pathological grief reactions after the death of a family member, we examined the results of a twelve-session, time-limited brief dynamic psychotherapy of the kind just described (as reported in detail in Horowitz et al., 1981). Before treatment, this sample had levels of symptoms comparable with those of other outpatient samples in treatment research. The SCL-90 is perhaps the most widely used measure of symptomatic distress and thus provides a valuable benchmark. The mean total pathology score at intake on the SCL-90 for the sample was 1.19 (SD = 0.59). This level is almost identical with the figure of 1.25 (SD = 0.39) reported by Derogatis, Rickels, & Rock (1976) for a sample of 209 symptomatic outpatients analyzed in a validation study of this measure. The mean depression subscale score in our sample at intake was 1.81, and in the Derogatis et al. study it was 1.87. The scores for anxiety were also comparable: 1.39 in our sample and 1.49 in the sample of Derogatis et al.

A significant improvement was seen in all symptomatic outcome variables when pretherapy scores were compared with follow-up levels. These findings are given in table 4. The results are also expressed in terms of the standardized mean difference effect-size coefficient recommended by Cohen (1979) for before-and-after data. He defined a large effect as 0.80 or greater. Our large effect sizes were in the domain of symptoms and ranged from 1.21 to 0.71. Changes in work and interpersonal functioning (PICS relationship composite) and the PICS capacity for intimacy were more moderate.

The approach to brief dynamic therapy described here was also successfully adapted to the treatment of depression by Thompson, Gallagher, and Breckenridge (1987). In their study, brief dynamic therapy reduced depressive symptoms in elderly adults significantly and was equal in effectiveness to both cognitive and behavioral treatment conditions.

Time-Unlimited Psychotherapy

Complex, delayed, or chronic stress response syndromes are probably best treated within a time-unlimited format. The same applies to persons with posttraumatic stress disorders in the context of a personality disorder, especially those personality disorders characterized by vulnerability to the coherence and stability of self organization. Even in such extended psychotherapies, however, a focus on working through the traumatic events and the reactions to them may be usefully preserved. This brings into question the level of interpretation to be used during such therapies.

TABLE 4

Outcome Variable Means at Time of Pretherapy and Posttherapy Follow-up Assessments

Primary Distress Measures	Pretherapy Score, Mean	(SD)	Posttherapy Score, Mean	(SD)	No.	t	p	Effect Size (SD Units)
Self-report								
Stress specific								
Intrusion (IES)	22.1	(7.6)	12.9	(8.0)	48	8.53	< .001	1.2
Avoidance (IES)	19.1	(9.8)	8.7	(8.5)	49	5.15	< .001	0.9
General								
Anxiety (SCL)	1.4	(0.8)	0.7	(0.6)	48	6.40	< .001	0.9
Depression (SCL)	1.8	(1.0)	1.0	(0.8)	48	6.41	< .001	1.0
Total pathology (SCL)	1.2	(1.6)	0.7	(0.5)	48	6.90	< .001	0.9
Evaluating Clinician Report								
Stress specific								
Intrusion (SRRS)	17.6	(9.9)	9.7	(8.1)	49	5.15	< .001	0.7
General								
Total neurotic pathology (BPRS)	15.6	(5.4)	11.0	(6.2)	49	5.03	< .001	0.7
PICS, Independent Clinician Judgments								
Stress symptoms composite	3.6	(0.6)	4.7	(1.1)	43	−6.56	< .001	1.0
Relationship composite	4.2	(1.1)	4.6	(1.0)	44	−2.29	.027	0.4
Intimacy capacity	3.4	(1.6)	4.1	(1.6)	42	−3.65	.001	0.6

Note: IES indicates Impact of Event Scale; SCL, 90-item Hopkins Symptom Checklist; SRRS, Stress Response Rating Scale; BPRS, Brief Psychiatric Rating Scale; and PICS, Patterns of Individual Change Scales.
Source: M. J. Horowitz, *Stress Response Syndromes*, 2nd ed. (Northvale, NJ: Jason Aronson, 1986).

190

In general, the approach advised is one that begins at the surface, is anchored to the traumatic events, and gradually extends to related issues at a pace that is tolerable and useful to the patient.

Levels of Interpretation

Levels of interpretation range from surface to depth, as shown in table 5. At the top of the table the first of eight levels from surface to depth is called "Stressors and stress responses" and at the bottom of the table is "Warded off unconscious scenarios and impulsive agendas." In general, the shorter the therapy is and the more disturbed the patient is in his or her organizational level of inner working models of self and relationships, the longer the therapist must deal with the surface levels.

Any of the levels of attention that the therapist uses in helping the patient establish a focus and goals for the treatment and in organizing sequences of his or her own interventions may focus on current situations, the in-treatment situation, and/or past historical and developmental events. Some aspect of the focus at a given level is also offered for each of these sectors in table 5.

Crisis intervention (Caplan, 1961; Jacobson, 1974; Kutash & Schlesinger, 1980) often successfully enables a patient to get through a crucial strain while staying at the top level of table 5. Establishment of the connection also enables the patient to examine experiences in a way that was too overwhelming to do alone or in an existing social network. Usually, dynamically oriented psychotherapy, however brief, advances to at least the next level of analysis, at which pending coping choices and conscious scenarios are examined. This includes a variable attention to current situations outside and inside the therapy and to varied clarifications of previous patterns. However it is done, this level of interpretation requires confrontation with conflicts: conflicting aims regarding how to master and integrate the recent stressors, dilemmas regarding how much to expose to the therapist, and possibly how goal conflicts and habitual conundrums relate to a current impasse in progressing toward the completion of reaction to a recent trauma.

As the patient can tolerate it and requires it to achieve maximal adaptation to a traumatic event, the therapist can deepen the analysis of conflicts. Frequently, especially in chronic or blocked passage through the phases of response to stressful life events, the patient will require some interpretation and confrontation with avoidance of the adaptive challenges carried from the event to current life-plan decisions. The threats projected to

TABLE 5

Levels of Interpretation

| Content Areas | | Level of Analytic Focus | |
	Current Situation	Therapy Situation	Past
1. Stressors and stress responses	Intentions of how to respond	Expectations of treatment	Relevant experiences of previous stress events
2. Pending coping choices and conscious scenarios	Conflicting aims of how to respond	Dilemma analysis of what to deal with first	Longstanding goals and habitual conundrums
3. Avoidance of adaptive challenges	Threat and defense	Resistance to working through a conflicted issue	History of self-impairing character traits

Link between external situation and personal responses

TABLE 5 *(Continued)*

| | Level of Analytic Focus | | |
Content Areas	Current Situation	Therapy Situation	Past
4. Repertoire of states of mind	Triggers to entry into problem states or exit from symptomatic states	States of therapeutic work and nonwork	Habitually problematic and desired states
5. Expressed irrational beliefs	Differentiation of realistic from fantastic associations and appraisals		
6. Repetitive maladaptive interpersonal behavior patterns	Interpersonal problems and self-judgments	Difference among social alliances, transferences, and therapeutic alliances	Abreaction or reconstruction of traumas and strains in relationship
7. Self-concept repertoires and role relationship models	Views of self and others	Differences among social alliances, transferences, and therapeutic alliances	Development of role relationship models
8. Warded off unconscious scenarios and impulsive agendas	Urges, dreams, and creative products	Regressive, intense transferences	Episodes of regression that uncovered warded off aims in the past

Link between current problems and longstanding, individualized personality patterns

Source: M. J. Horowitz, *Stress Response Syndromes*, 2nd ed. (Northvale, NJ: Jason Aronson, 1986).

occur, were these avoidances set aside, can be analyzed with a focus on external situations. The resistances to discussing topics and emotions during the therapy can be interpreted, and when indicated, these can be related to enduring and self-impairing character traits. Often, with the development of a sense of safety based on evolution of a therapeutic alliance, the patient alone will set aside many avoidances and resistances, but the linking of these to enduring character traits usually requires accurate observation and labeling by the therapist as the facilitator.

Unless the stress response syndrome is relatively simple, most dynamic psychotherapists will find it advantageous to deepen the level of interpretive work to include the patient's repertoires of mental state, irrational beliefs, and repetitive interpersonal behavioral patterns, insofar as these relate to (1) predispositions to the person's reaction to the event, (2) the actual current signs and symptoms of the stress response syndrome, and (3) current impediments to optimal adaptive life changes set in motion by the event.

Examining the patient's repertoire of states of mind allows the patient to put the symptoms of the stress response syndrome in a broader personal context and to study the specific triggers to activating the state of mind that contains the symptom. The importance of doing this in instances of chronic stress response syndromes cannot be overemphasized, because it leads the way to understanding the link between the past trauma and current realities and the occasional use of the past trauma as a screen that both depicts current conflicts and yet symbolically obscures aspects of their immediacy.

Example of a Screening Function

The patient was a seventy-year-old man who had been a civilian worker in the Philippines at the time of the Japanese invasion in World War II. He was interned in a concentration camp throughout the war, where he both experienced and witnessed atrocities. For several periods he helplessly anticipated his own death with panic and anguish. He also felt murderous rage states well up in him, but he had to contain any sign of hostility in response to provocations, in order to increase his chances of survival. Periodically, in the nearly forty years that had passed since his release, he had nightmares in which he relived aspects of these experiences. These usually were accompanied by panicky feelings but occasionally had surges of raw hatred as their affective components. Recently, the nightmares had increased in frequency, and he had other depressive symptoms.

When these mental states were analyzed, he was found to vary in the degree to which he would enter a state of anger in which he struggled to control hostile expressive urges. His retirement had placed him in family circumstances in which he was goaded and humiliated by a son-in-law who wanted him to move out of a room he had in his daughter and son-in-law's house. When this happened, he was more likely to have the nightmares of his World War II experiences. Treatment did not eliminate these nightmares but did attenuate the overall situational difficulty, symptom picture, and frequency of sleep disruption.

The longer the time is from the stressor event to the present therapy, the more likely it is that the stress-event syndrome will involve complex problems of maladaptive interpersonal behavior patterns. There is a lock-in across levels of interpretive work, so that work at the surface levels will help maladaptive patterns based at the organizers of meaning at deeper levels. Early work in therapy may lead to improved interpersonal relationship patterns without proceeding to interpretive work at the level of self-concepts; role relationship models; and unconscious fantasy scenarios, scripts, and life agendas. Nonetheless, in complex cases the work is often necessary, and complex cases are the ones most often seen by dynamically trained psychotherapists; the simpler ones have already been treated. Thus, in the middle phase of therapy, the therapist may reformulate the case in terms of what has been learned thus far and deepen the level of interpretive work. This will mean exploring the usually unconscious meaning structures involved in forming views of self and others, including self-critical functions and their derivatives from developmentally important relationships.

SUMMARY

The treatment of stress response syndromes is centered on completing the information-processing cycles initiated by the stress event. The phase of stress response is recognized in an informed interview for signs and symptoms, and the treatment techniques are used according to the current phase, in order to move forward. Sometimes this includes facilitation of warding off maneuvers, just as at other times the patient will be helped to set aside unconscious defensive operations. Transference and core neurotic conflicts will be a part of the therapeutic work but will often be interpreted according to their real relationship to the current stress. This will permit a clear focus for brief therapy. The nuances of the therapy technique, beyond the general strategies, will depend on the patient's and the therapist's character styles.

References

Basch, M. (1980). *Doing psychotherapy.* New York: Basic Books.

Caplan, G. (1961). *An approach to community mental health.* New York: Grune & Stratton.

Cohen, J. (1979). *Power analyses for the social and behavioral sciences.* New York: Academic Press.

Derogatis, L. R., Rickels, K., & Rock, A. F. (1976). The SCL-90 and the MMPI: A step in the validation of a new self report scale. *British Journal of Psychiatry, 128,* 280–289.

DeWitt, K., Kaltreider, N., Weiss, D., & Horowitz, M. (1983). Judging change in psychotherapy: The reliability of clinical formulations. *Archives of General Psychiatry, 40,* 1121–1128.

Erikson, E. (1963). *Childhood and society.* New York: Norton.

Horowitz, M. J. (1973). Phase-oriented treatment of stress response syndromes. *American Journal of Psychotherapy, 27,* 606–615.

Horowitz, M. J. (1976). *Stress response syndromes.* 2nd. ed. 1986. Northvale, NJ: Jason Aronson.

Horowitz, M. J. (1979). *States of mind.* New York: Plenum.

Horowitz, M. J. (1983). Post-traumatic stress disorders. *Behavioral Sciences and the Law, 1,* 9–23.

Horowitz, M. J. (1987). *States of Mind: Configurational analysis of individual psychology* (2nd ed.) New York: Plenum.

Horowitz, M. J. (1988). *Introduction to psychodynamics: A new synthesis.* New York: Basic Books.

Horowitz, M. J. (1989). *Nuances of technique in dynamic psychotherapy.* Northvale, NJ: Jason Aronson.

Horowitz, M. J., & Kaltreider, N. (1979). Brief therapy of stress response syndromes. *Psychiatric Clinics of North America, 2,* 365–378.

Horowitz, M. J., Krupnick, J., Kaltreider, N., Wilner, N., Leong, A., & Marmar, C. (1981). Initial psychological response to parental death. *Archives of General Psychiatry, 38,* 316–323.

Horowitz, M. J., Marmar, C., Krupnick, J., Wilner, N., Kaltreider, N., & Wallerstein, R. (1984). *Personality styles and brief psychotherapy.* New York: Basic Books.

Horowitz, M. J., Marmar, C., Weiss, D., DeWitt, K. N., & Rosenbaum, R. (1984). Brief psychotherapy of bereavement reactions. *Archives of General Psychiatry, 41,* 438–448.

Horowitz, M. J., Marmar, C., Weiss, D., Kaltreider, N., & Wilner, N. (1986). Comprehensive analysis of change after brief dynamic psychotherapy. *American Journal of Psychiatry, 143,* 582–589.

Horowitz, M. J., Wilner, N., & Alvarez, W. (1979). Impact of Event Scale: A study of subjective stress. *Psychosomatic Medicine, 41*(3), 209–218.

Hoyt, M. (1980). Therapist and patient actions in "good" psychotherapy sessions. *Archives of General Psychiatry, 37,* 159–161.

Hoyt, M., Marmar, C., Horowitz, M. J., & Alvarez, W. (1981). The Therapist Action Scale and the Patient Action Scale: Instruments for the assessment of activities during dynamic psychotherapy. *Psychotherapy: Theory, Research, and Practice, 18,* 109–116.

Jacobson, G. F. (1974, June). The Crisis Interview. In *Comparative psychotherapies.* Symposium conducted at the University of Southern California School of Medicine, Department of Psychiatry, Division of Continuing Education, San Diego.

Kaltreider, N., DeWitt, K., Weiss, D., & Horowitz, M. J. (1981). Pattern of individual change scales. *Archives of General Psychiatry, 38,* 1263–1269.

Kutash, I. L., & Schlesinger, L. B., (1980). *Handbook of stress and anxiety.* San Francisco: Jossey-Bass.

Luborsky, L. (1984). *Principles of psychoanalytic psychotherapy: A manual for supportive-expressive treatment.* New York: Basic Books.

Malan, D. H. (1979). *Individual psychotherapy and the science of psychodynamics.* London: Butterworth.

Marmar, C., Marziali, E., Horowitz, M. J., & Weiss, D. (1986). The development of the therapeutic alliance rating system. In L. Greenberg & W. Pinsoff (Eds.), *Research in psychotherapy.* New York: Guilford.

Marziali, E., Marmar, C., & Krupnick, J. (1981). Therapeutic alliance scales: Development and relationship to therapeutic outcome. *American Journal of Psychiatry, 138,* 361–364.

Oremland, J. D. (1972). Transference cure and flight into health. *International Journal of Psychoanalytic Psychotherapy, 1,* 61–75.

Rosenbaum, R., & Horowitz, M. (1983). Motivation for psychotherapy: A factorial and conceptual analysis. *Psychotherapy: Theory, Research and Practice, 20,* 346–354.

Singer, J. L., & Pope, K. S. (Eds.). (1978). *The stream of consciousness: Scientific investigations into the flow of human experience.* New York: Plenum.

Strupp, H. H., & Binder, J. L. (1984). *Psychotherapy in a new key: A guide to time-limited dynamic psychotherapy.* New York: Basic Books.

Thompson, L. W., Gallagher, D., & Breckenridge, J. S. (1987). Comparative effectiveness of psychotherapies for depressed elders. *Journal of Consulting and Clinical Psychology, 55,* 385–390.

Weiss, D., DeWitt, K., Kaltreider, N., & Horowitz, M. (1985). A proposed method for measuring change beyond symptoms. *Archives of General Psychiatry, 42,* 703–708.

Weiss, D., Horowitz, M., & Wilner, N. (1984). Stress Response Rating Scale: A clinician's measure. *British Journal of Clinical Psychology, 23,* 202–215.

Zilberg, N., Weiss, D., & Horowitz, M. J. (1982). Impact of Event Scale: A cross validation study and some empirical evidence. *Journal of Consulting and Clinical Psychology, 50,* 407–414.

CHAPTER 8

Brief Adaptive Psychotherapy

Jerome Pollack, Walter Flegenheimer, and Arnold Winston

HISTORY AND CONCEPTUAL FRAMEWORK

Brief Adaptive Psychotherapy (BAP) was developed at Beth Israel Medical Center in New York in the early 1980s (Pollack & Horner, 1985). BAP was designed for patients with personality disorders, similar to those whom psychotherapists in private practice generally treat. Our patients meet the *DSM III-R* criteria for avoidant, dependent, histrionic, obsessive-compulsive, and passive-aggressive personality disorders. These are people who have problems in the areas of intimacy and work, generally with difficulties in forming lasting relationships and in realizing their vocational potential.

BAP is a short-term psychotherapy based on a psychoanalytic understanding of character, conflict, and defense (Reich, 1949). We have defined character as patterns of beliefs and behavior, adaptive or maladaptive. We chose to help patients change their major maladaptive patterns of beliefs and behaviors—those that cause pain or a lack of gratification—into a more adaptive framework. As a brief therapy, BAP differs from classical psychoanalysis in its techniques; instead of free association, the therapist actively maintains the focus, and instead of encouraging the transference neurosis, deals consistently with transferences as they appear within the pattern.

Heinz Hartmann's (1939) work on adaptation also provided a theoretical framework for our approach. He saw adaptation as the integration by the ego of beliefs, wishes, needs, and impulses with the demands of the external world and of the superego. The core issue of adaptation is reality (inner and outer)—a knowledge of reality and acting in accord with it to achieve the most gratification with the least pain. The failure of this integration by the adult ego leads to maladaptive patterns of behavior, which, in some cases, lead to the formation of a personality disorder.

Personality *traits* are not considered mental disorders. They may include such factors as innate temperament or cognitive style. *DSM III-R* defines personality traits as "enduring patterns of perceiving, relating to and thinking about the environment and one's self" (American Psychiatric Association, 1987, p. 335). However, these traits may become rigid in the service of an attempt at adaptation. When they become inflexible and maladaptive they are referred to as personality *disorders.* BAP was designed not to eliminate or radically change basic personality traits but to extricate these traits from their maladaptive rigidifications. When the traits serve adaptation, all is fine, but when they add to maladaptive patterns, they must be loosened and altered to serve reality. Maladaptive patterns manifest themselves through inflexible cognitive and emotional functioning, primarily within interpersonal relationships.

Adaptation takes place under the aegis of the ego. The ego, as used in this approach, is a psychological construct based on a structural division of the psychic apparatus into ego, id, and superego (Freud, 1958). The ego serves a number of psychological functions, such as relation to reality, defense, impulse control, and object relations (Hartmann, Kris, & Loewenstein, 1946; Bellak, 1958). The overall function of the ego is to organize, synthesize, and structure the demands of the inner and outer worlds of the individual and in this sense is the organ of adaptation (Hartmann, 1939). BAP is an ego psychological approach, exploring how the ego deals with wishes, beliefs, needs, and impulses, both adaptively and maladaptively. The ego in patients selected for BAP is a relatively healthy one. Thus, the patients bring to the therapy an ego doing essentially what it is supposed to do in the adaptation process, although it is working with thoughts, perceptions, feelings, beliefs, or wishes that have an element of conflict and reality distortion in them. Although these aspects of the system may have served adaptation at one time, they no longer do. Since the data the ego is dealing with are distorted in relation to the reality of the here and now, the attempted adaptation will also be distorted—that is, maladaptive.

The goal of BAP is to acquaint patients with their maladaptive patterns, enabling them to achieve insight into the origins and development of these patterns and to become aware of how the patterns prevent the achievement of their goals in life. In this sense BAP is a cognitively based treatment.

However, it was not clear at the outset how this primarily cognitive insight was going to help patients make the necessary changes in their lives. Examining the elements of the pattern in detail, and not settling for vague answers to confrontational questions, was found to be a useful technique for ultimately producing change. Insisting that the pattern be examined in detail resulted in resistance by the patient to the therapist's confrontations; this in turn, made the relationship between therapist and patient the central area of the treatment. The work of Merton Gill (1982), stressing the centrality of the patient–therapist relationship, became an important influence on the developers of BAP. We began to emphasize the patient-therapist relationship so that early resistance could be recognized, challenged, interpreted, and resolved. It became apparent that it was in the transference that the maladaptive pattern could be most clearly seen, explicated, and understood. It is in the transference that the patient's pathology will be most apparent to the patient and most available for real work.

THEORY OF CHANGE

We believe that a cognitive and affective understanding of the operations and origins of the maladaptive pattern (insight) allows patients to change enough so that they can construct more adaptive patterns and are better equipped to face adult lives and new relationships.

It is the task of the therapist to show the patient that the maladaptive pattern is not just something to be cognitively understood; it is the way the patient lives his or her life. As an active system that originated in the past, the maladaptive pattern is alive in the important relationships in the patient's current life and—most important for BAP—in the patient–therapist relationship.

The major work in BAP is in the transference. The transference work has an emotional impact on the patient, affording him or her the opportunity to see, to feel, and to change the aspects of the pattern that stand in the way of healthy adaptation. The therapist gives the patient the opportunity to experience cognitive and emotional conflicts and memories in a more benign setting that allows for a corrective emotional experience (Alexander & French, 1946). The transference is the stage on which the patient enacts the pattern, where both the therapist and the patient are the main dramatis personae, and where the maladaptive pattern provides the basic plot of their improvisations (Arlow, 1969a). Working in the transference lends affective strength to the insights that are developed about current relationships and the linkages to the origins of the maladaptive pattern in the past. Transference work allows patients to develop enough control over the operations of the pattern so that the pattern loses its rigidity and new situations can be approached more flexibly. Patients can develop newer patterns that are better suited to current reality. We try to give patients the sense of having choices, so that rather than respond to a new relationship in the old manner they can stop, think, and choose other ways of responding. For example, patients who have always accommodated to the needs of others by putting aside their own needs, can now, having been helped to look at their motivations, act in a way that leads to satisfaction, as opposed to what generally ensued when their needs were put aside.

SELECTION OF PATIENTS

BAP was developed to provide a brief psychotherapy for the treatment of personality disorders. In our initial work, patients were limited to those who met the criteria for Axis II diagnoses of the Cluster C type, such as avoidant, dependent, obsessive-compulsive, and passive-aggressive, and the histrionic diagnosis in Cluster B *(DSM III-R)*. We excluded those with more severe personality disorders, such as borderline and narcissistic patients. Other exclusion criteria were: a history of suicide attempts, a history of substance abuse, current psychoactive medication, organic mental impairment, and any Axis I diagnosis except for anxiety or affective disorders of mild to moderate severity.

BAP was designed to help patients develop insight into the operations of their maladaptive pattern. This works quite well with patients who have histrionic personality disorders. They use repression as a major defense, causing gaps in their understanding of the origins and operations of the maladaptive pattern. The affective side of the pattern is generally clear and rarely presents problems. These patients will often repress historical and cognitive elements underlying the maladaptive pattern, but the repressed material often emerges during the course of treatment. As David Shapiro (1965) has pointed out, their style is characterized by their failure to put the pieces of their lives together so that insight can be attained. Therefore, a cognitively based therapy such as BAP would seem to be the treatment of choice for histrionic patients.

Obsessional patients use more cognitive styles of defense such as intellectualization, rationalization, and reaction formation. Often, these patients will say that they "understand it all" and will give the therapist a complete history, full of details, concerning the origin and operation of the maladaptive pattern. The therapist is inundated with unnecessary details and, along with the patient, may miss the forest for the trees. The task of the therapist is to concentrate on the affective aspect of the insight. In treating the obsessive-compulsive patient it is necessary that the therapist immediately relate the intellectualizing defenses to the therapeutic relationship. The therapist looks for affect as confirmation of the accuracy of interpretations.

We are now attempting to study the efficacy of BAP with narcissistic and borderline patients. Theoretically, it is possible to take as a focus of treatment such phenomena as splitting, overidealization of the other, identification, excessive needs for attachment, and some forms of merging. The therapist must be more cautious and somewhat less confrontational than with healthier patients. A positive relationship with the patient is formed during the early sessions, and the patient's defenses are carefully pointed out to the patient as they are perceived. It is possible that courses of brief therapy alternating with planned periods without treatment may be successful for some of these patients. This type of treatment plan may afford patients some distance from the therapist, and thus help them cope with the fears of merging that often complicate ongoing treatment.

We have treated patients with mild to moderate depression who have not been actively suicidal. The technique has been the same: uncovering the pattern and making this the focus of therapy. With these patients the therapist must monitor the severity of the depression; though suicidal thoughts may emerge, these can often be dealt with as part of the pattern, but they must be explored thoroughly to evaluate the suicidal risk.

TECHNIQUES

BAP is a psychoanalytically based psychotherapy that uses the standard techniques of brief dynamic psychotherapy (Marmor, 1979). These include the maintenance of a focus, early and repeated work in the transference, and a high activity level on the part of the therapist. The focus is maintained by keeping the patient from straying from the major maladaptive pattern. The pattern is always an interpersonal one and is explored in the present, in the past, and in the patient–therapist relationship. These three areas are repeatedly connected to one another through the use of questions, clarifications, confrontations, and interpretations. These interventions, especially clarification and confrontation, are used to intervene whenever resistance begins to interfere with the therapeutic process.

Sessions are fifty minutes long, face-to-face, once a week; the maximum is forty sessions. The rule of abstinence and therapeutic neutrality is followed (Greenson, 1967). The therapist does not self-disclose, reveal elements of his or her life, or give advice.

Evaluation

The goals of the evaluation session are to make a diagnosis, to exclude those patients who cannot tolerate a confrontational psychotherapy, and to explore the interpersonal relationships of the patient so that the major maladaptive pattern can be formulated. The therapist attempts to establish a positive therapeutic relationship and begins the exploration of the patient–therapist interactions. At the end of the evaluation the rules of the psychotherapy are discussed and a contract is made with the patient.

Although the evaluation often involves two separate meetings of about an hour each, it is better done in one session. This allows more continuity in obtaining a history of the present difficulty and past history. The longer interview is more stressful and provides a better picture of the patient's defensive structure. The task of the therapist is to get the history as directly as possible and not allow the patient to stray or become vague. When straying does occur, the therapist must confront the patient and his or her evasive tactics. This confrontation generally increases the level of resistance, and these new resistances must then be confronted by the therapist. The questioning and confrontation of resistance serves to illuminate the patient's defenses and the maladaptive pattern within the patient–therapist relationship. When the defenses become clearer the therapist can begin to link the defenses with the pattern, at first in a general way—for example, "You seem to have trouble telling me the details of what happens between you and your wife. Does this also happen in other circumstances?" Or "Did it also occur in the past when you had trouble telling your parents what your wishes were or what you were feeling?" This interaction can also proceed in the opposite direction. If a patient is talking about difficulties that arise in current and past relationships, the therapist should bring up how those difficulties are present in the therapeutic relationship. An example might be: "You have difficulty when you are angry with your wife and when you were angry with your mother. How will that work here when you get angry with me?"

The therapist does not specifically seek affect, as in some short-term therapies (Davanloo, 1980). The use of repetitive challenges and confrontations as used by Davanloo is not a part of BAP. It is expected that affect will follow if the transference is made an integral part of the treatment.

It is important during the evaluation to get as much information as possible about the major maladaptive pattern. The therapist looks for links between the way the patient interacts with the major figures in his or her life and the way the patient interacts with the therapist. The patient may avoid aggression or sexuality, distance from others, intellectualize and avoid feelings, accommodate to whomever he or she is relating to, withdraw when certain issues are discussed, or behave in an excessively passive and dependent manner. The therapist must point out these mechanisms to the patient during the evaluation and then attempt to determine what underlies them. One looks for the wishes that these defenses oppose and the conflicts that exist, with the goal of finding the primary unconscious fantasy system (Arlow, 1969a, 1969b). Trial interpretations (Malan, 1976) are used to evaluate the patient's responses. A positive response from the patient might be an introspective, pensive glance, further information related to the pattern, questions as to whether he or she does the same thing in other situations, some obvious affect, or even disagreement that is not excessive, such as, "I don't think that applies, but I'll think about it." Agreement by the patient without elaboration may indicate compliance or passivity, rather than an ability to work with the material. Clinically it is our impression that patients who respond favorably to trial interpretations during the evaluation process will do well in BAP.

Once the pattern is relatively clear to the therapist it is presented to the patient. It is not expected that all the elements of the pattern will be known by the end of the evaluation process. Indeed, the pattern is elaborated and enriched throughout the course of the treatment.

Therapeutic Contract

At the end of the evaluation or at the beginning of the first session, the therapeutic contract is discussed. Therapists are instructed to use their own words in establishing the contract; the following statement is one example.

THERAPIST: Our goal will be to explore the pattern you have used and are using in your personal relationships. These are patterns that have not worked well for you, have gotten you into difficulty in your life, and have led to your coming here. By examining these patterns in detail, we will be able to see them more clearly and help you to develop new patterns that will work better for you and thus give you the opportunity to make changes in your life.

During our work together, thoughts and feelings will emerge that are important. It is critical that you express them to me in as open a manner as possible. If there is something that is difficult for you to tell me, at least report the reluctance, if not the actual material. What you are reluctant to talk about may have to do with your reactions to me. This should be discussed, because your reactions to me are often related to the very patterns that we want to examine.

We will set a fixed hour each week for which you will be responsible. Each session will last fifty minutes and there will be a maximum of forty sessions.

Do you have any questions or reactions so far?

Treatment

The therapeutic work proceeds directly from the evaluation. As was done in the evaluation session, the details of the maladaptive pattern and their underlying elements are explored. This work inevitably leads to the patient's resisting, generally using elements of the pattern, that is, the defensive structure. The therapist confronts the resistance, linking it to the pattern, especially in the transference. This serves two purposes. First it makes clear to the patient that the relationship between patient and therapist will be subject to exploration in the therapy. Second, it lends more immediacy to the treatment. It is easier for the patient to intellectualize if the therapy deals only with external and past relationships. Intellectualization may preclude the integration of cognitive and emotional issues and thus diminish the likelihood of insight. However, if there is pressure to explore the patient's pattern in the transference, distancing is less likely and the insight that is achieved is more likely to be both cognitive and affective.

Linking at least two examples of the pattern in an interpretation appears to be advantageous. An example of this is: "Whenever we talk about your relationship with your father and your anger at him, you become withdrawn, just as you do with your husband when he makes demands that infuriate you." As much as possible, interpretations of present and past relationships should come after examples have been explored in the transference. It is critical that the therapist be aware of the state of the transference at all times and that when possible he or she channel interpretations through the transference, for example: "Whenever we get close, you start becoming anxious and passive, just as you used to do with your parents."

Confronting the resistance generally reveals additional elements of the pattern, enabling the patient to get to underlying fantasies or beliefs and the conflicts they engender. The pattern usually is not fully elicited early in the therapy. Often in the beginning, it is rather sketchy, as in a tendency to avoid conflicts or a need to accommodate to another's wishes. As exploration of the pattern proceeds, especially within the transference, specific details about when and how the pattern operates begin to emerge. These may be elements such as: the patient avoids conflict of a particular nature or with a particular person; the patient may accommodate in an aggressive situation and be more assertive in a sexual situation; the patient may function at an adult level in a dyadic situation but became defensive when triadic or oedipal issues come to the forefront. The therapist must always work at connecting the elements of the pattern until the unconscious fantasy system becomes clearer.

As BAP unfolds it is important to look for changes in the way the patient relates to the therapist and to other persons in his or her life. A common problem has been the reluctance of a patient to change, often because the patient refuses to change for the therapist's sake, in the same way as changing for the parent implied some loss of autonomy. This refusal to change often comes up during the middle of therapy and can be the basis of much of the later therapeutic work.

If the therapist adheres to the technique with a patient who meets the criteria for BAP, termination should pose no major problems. As in most therapies, the maladaptive aspects of the pattern often return in full force toward the end of treatment. When this occurs, it must be explored, interpreted, and linked to the transference and the impending termination. There are no clearly distinct phases in BAP. The therapy proceeds from the defense to the wish and from superficial to deeper levels as does any psychoanalytic therapy.

A problem with any short-term therapy is the lack of time to work through the insights achieved. The working through in BAP is part of the ongoing treatment. After an interpretation patients will often respond either with affect or with data that support the correctness of the interpretation. The therapist then asks about other situations where this insight might apply, attempting to get the patient to apply what has been learned to other situations and to generalize the insight that has been gained. We have found that patients are able to do a good part of the working through on their own, between sessions and after terminating the therapy.

CASE EXAMPLE

The following case example demonstrates how treatment progresses in BAP. The material was transcribed from videotaped sessions.

The patient, a forty-year-old divorced woman who worked as an administrator in a law firm, sought treatment because she felt she had lost her energy, optimism, and sense of expectation following the break-up of a relationship she had had three years earlier. The man with whom she had the relationship was described as melancholic and gloomy. He was a Vietnam War veteran whose life reminded her of her early years in postwar Europe. She was more involved with his depression than she thought was appropriate, and she herself also became depressed. She did not understand why this man affected her so much and hoped that treatment would help her understand herself better.

The patient stated she "dabbled" in life and was unable to make any lasting commitment or develop her full capabilities. She had had two previous experiences with therapy. One was practical and helpful when she came to the United States and needed to learn how to operate in a different culture. The other was three years before she came to us, when she saw a therapist several times. She felt he wasn't strong enough to help her, so she left treatment.

The patient was born to thirty-nine-year-old parents near the end of World War II in France. She remembered the poverty and destruction of the 1950s. She believed her particular cultural heritage was a gloomy one. She described both parents as having been overprotective and infantilizing, and she continued to experience them this way. Her mother was described as a charming and gracious person socially, but bitter, negative, and caustic within the family. Her father was talented but never really succeeded, ending up as a middle-level civil servant. The patient stated that her parents sent a double message to her and her younger brother: they were talented and special children, but they shouldn't try to do anything, as they would not succeed.

The patient had earned a teaching degree in France. She had been married and divorced and remained friendly with her ex-husband and his girlfriend. The patient had long-term friendships with a number of women. At the time she had a boyfriend; they were sexually intimate on a regular basis, but shared few other interests or activities. The patient tended to be flamboyant in her style of dress and in the way she spoke. At the same time she was a perfectionist who devoted herself to her work and yet was often indecisive. She was compliant in her relationships with others and constantly worried about being rejected. The diagnosis was mixed personality disorder with histrionic and compulsive features.

The major maladaptive pattern was determined to be as follows: the patient ran from personal conflicts and from issues that were important to her. She did this by accommodating to others and by avoiding what was of importance to herself. Elements of this pattern could be seen in her difficulty sharing her emotions with others and in her seeking secrecy rather than openness. Underlying the pattern was a belief that others would disappoint and abandon her.

In the course of the evaluation, the therapist presented the patient with the following intervention: "You put things off socially and workwise. What is that all about?" The patient responded to this intervention with statements about feeling unsure of herself and her abilities, relating this to her basic insecurity. The therapist, to get the patient to be more specific, added, "Do you often feel you won't measure up?" The patient replied, "In social relationships I always get a vague feeling in the back somewhere, ever since I was a little girl." The therapist, having seen the patient's feelings of insecurity in interpersonal relationships in the present and past, asked, "How do you feel about showing *me* your feelings of insecurity?" The patient agreed that it might be difficult. She continued talking about her reactions in many different relationships during her past. She then stopped and expressed the fear that she might be confusing the therapist. The therapist replied: "You seem to be so worried about confusing me and my getting confused. Are you afraid that I, like the others in your life, will give up on you?" The patient responded affirmatively and the therapist then broadened the issue: "Do you often worry about others more than yourself?" At this point tears began to flow, the patient nodding in assent.

The therapist's repeated references to the transference throughout the evaluation interview enabled the patient to examine her relationship with the therapist from the beginning of their encounter, helping to clarify the pattern and showing the patient that the pattern was operative in *all* her relationships. Another example of this can be seen in an exchange at the end of the first evaluation session, after the time had been set for the next meeting.

PATIENT: Do you like your work?
THERAPIST: What do you mean?
PATIENT: Just a simple question.
THERAPIST: What does it mean to you?
PATIENT: I'm thinking . . . can you handle it. . . . Maybe I'm afraid I can't handle it.
THERAPIST: Will I be able to measure up . . . to look at what has to be looked at? Or will I fail you, abandon you?
PATIENT: I have felt abandoned at certain times.

THERAPIST: Like during the crisis with your ex-boyfriend and often during your childhood.

PATIENT: I have felt abandoned and totally on my own.

Toward the end of the evaluation the therapist presented the pattern to the patient. "I've observed that you have a tendency to move away from things and push them aside. You don't think through things yourself. The other thing is your strong sense of secrecy. It works here today and in your life. We have to understand this more fully."

The maladaptive pattern was agreed upon and the therapy begun. There were further interchanges on the themes of the patient's avoiding conflict and accommodating to others, but the underlying fantasy remained elusive at the beginning.

In the second therapy session the patient talked about her relationship with her ex-boyfriend. She made the point that when he would speak to her in a nasty way she would get a pain in her chest rather than be direct with him. The therapist then pointed out how the patient had difficulty being direct with her, giving examples of her boyfriend's nastiness, instead of speaking of her own complaints about the therapist. At this point the patient complained of experiencing the pain in her chest. The therapist asked her feelings about the pain.

PATIENT: Like I want to grasp for air, like it's very belittling, cutting, cutting down.

THERAPIST: *(Trying to relate the pain to the transference)* Where do you think the belittling is coming from right now?

PATIENT: From the memory of that time I spent with him and the way it made me feel at that time *(avoiding the immediacy of the transference)*.

THERAPIST: Therefore you have difficulty remembering something for that reason . . . is that what you're implying?

PATIENT: Yeah, like I haven't thought about it for a while. I finally have managed to put it out of my mind instead of being obsessed with the whole thing . . . so the sharp edges of the whole experience are gone. Things are blurred. The whole thing was a break in my life. . . . It has something to do with my parents.

The therapist used this opportunity to link the anxiety with the defenses, showing the patient how they were operative in the relationship with the therapist and with her ex-boyfriend and how their origins had something to do with her parents. The therapist did this by using a reference to what was going on, saying: "Yet when I ask the question you can't answer, you get a pain and can't talk, like in the past."

The therapist continued to confront the patient with her reluctance to talk about matters of importance to her. The patient then started talking about her relationship with her parents and the deprivation she experienced with them. They did not provide her with an environment to come home to. They did not encourage her to go out into the world. The therapist then asked for a specific memory of when her parents could have given her more help:

PATIENT: I remember a very, very old memory when I was little, before I was in school. I had a great desire to write. I would scribble things and ask my mother to tell me what it meant. She would just tell me it was nonsense, "You are too little to be able to write." She would completely do away with it. That's the earliest. Later, when I wanted to do things . . . when I was eight or nine I was dying to take ballet lessons, and my mother told me I had no talent and she didn't want to waste money on it. That was something I really wanted. She had no confidence in me, and I was cut off.

The patient went on to talk about her sadness. The therapist's only intervention was to point out her need to avoid feelings, especially sadness. The patient went on talking about her lack of confidence. She stated that she avoided sadness because she had to leave the session to go to work: "Outside, right after the session. I have to go to work. I don't want to have that vulnerable feeling there. It's a predatory environment and people just jump on you. I won't be able to defend myself." The therapist again pointed out her avoidance of feelings. The patient went on, "When I was growing up I would have the feeling, I never acknowledged it, but I always wished my mother would die, but then I felt guilty. They decided what was good for me. They were powerful . . . but they can't help the way they are. But they paralyzed me. I was furious. Can I express my rage at them for not making me a free person?" The therapist answered that the patient had the opportunity to work on these conflicts in treatment, and then added, "But you feel I also won't provide the right environment here so that you could go out into the world . . . just like your mother." The patient stated, "It's a problem of trust and confidence. I can tell you I trust you, but . . ." The therapist then compared trusting her with trusting her mother and that her mother was not there for her, so she now held back with the therapist and with the world. The fantasy and belief systems were beginning to be unearthed, the pattern was clearer to the patient, and she was starting to work with the material. The emphasis of the treatment was the examination of the pattern and its operation in the transference, in the here and now, and its origins in the past.

The therapy continued and more details of the pattern were understood. At about the middle of the treatment, session 19, problems with the patient's reluctance to change came to the fore:

THERAPIST: What did you want to say when you said, "How can I . . . ?" You didn't finish the sentence.

PATIENT: What can I do to make the switch in my old brain, that part that is holding me back.

THERAPIST: When you ask that, I feel you're asking me and I should be able to give you an answer.

PATIENT: For this and that and that and that. *(Laughing)*

THERAPIST: A couple of minutes ago you said you were waiting for a miracle. *Waiting for,* is the important point. You waited for your mother to get you out into life, but she said life is hard and she retreated. You did the same thing, and you sit and wait for someone to come, a guy, the authority you talked about last week, something here . . . me to take you somewhere and yet we know you're not of the age where any of us could take you anywhere. I can't speak to where you can go, but I can speak to what stops you from moving. You look to me and you look to other people.

PATIENT: I know that, I look to other people. I know that. I know what's wrong and what I should be doing. Yet I feel so totally powerless to change myself . . . to jump into the behavior more appropriate to the situation.

THERAPIST: What do you mean, you feel powerless?

PATIENT: I feel . . . very . . . I feel I don't have the strength and the energy. I feel very old.

THERAPIST: Not young? I expect you feel very young.

PATIENT: No. I feel very old.

THERAPIST: That's how you describe your mother . . . too old and tired, not having any spunk.

PATIENT: I feel that same way. It's funny . . . that's the weird thing. . . . I always thought I didn't want to be like my mother because I really don't like her and . . . I know I'm not like her but it's like part of me is like her.

THERAPIST: Staying like her is a way of hanging on to her. Hang on to that and you stay little—powerless, depressed, and defeated.

PATIENT: Well, I just want to know what I have to do to get rid of that situation.

THERAPIST: You are looking for me to be your mother; I can't. You say, "My mother was old and tired," so you want me to take over. You wait for a miracle instead of changing what's inside of you.

The patient went on to talk about feeling sorry for her mother and other old ladies. She talked of her mother's unfulfilled life with a great deal of affect.

The therapist in this interchange confronted the patient with her fear of change and her feeling that change had to do with trying to eliminate her identification with her mother, who was old and tired. This was tantamount to killing her mother, and the patient had not been able to do that. Later in the therapy, the therapist was able to show the patient how in all important relationships she had played the part the other had chosen for her, rather than participate actively in the relationship.

The remainder of the therapy dealt more and more with the patient's taking responsibility for her life and starting to make commitments. Once the patient was able to show her feelings, she was able to form a close relationship with the therapist. The therapist was able to use the transference to help the patient understand, both cognitively and affectively, how she had been dependent on the outside world for her self-esteem and how she had kept to herself, as the patient put it, "in a cocoon, waiting for the right person to break it open and commit myself to life." Whether the instrument of this hatching was insight, a corrective emotional experience, or an identification with a new object cannot be stated with any certainty. We feel that insight into the operations of the pattern and its origins contributed to a favorable outcome that was still present at follow-up four years later.

THE TRAINING OF THERAPISTS

We have trained psychiatrists, psychologists, and social workers who expressed an interested in learning the technique. For our research program we trained clinicians with an average of thirteen years' experience, but we have also trained psychiatry residents and psychology interns.

Our program consists of attending a weekly one-and-a-half-hour seminar where different videotaped sessions are reviewed and discussed. Each trainee receives one hour of individual supervision for each therapy session on his or her first two cases. We find that with the current training program, it generally takes one to two years for a person to become proficient in the technique.

COMPARISON WITH OTHER BRIEF DYNAMIC THERAPIES

BAP appears to be similar to Time-Limited Dynamic Psychotherapy as formulated by Hans Strupp and Jeffrey Binder (1984), although the two therapies were developed independently. Though both therapies make extensive use of the transference, BAP appears to make more transference linkages to both past and current relationships. A comparison of BAP with Habib Davanloo's (1980) Short-Term Dynamic Psychotherapy reveals an equal emphasis on the transference. However, in general the Davanloo approach is a more active and confrontational therapy than is BAP, although both these forms of brief psychotherapy are quite active and confrontational relative to standard therapeutic techniques. BAP is a more cognitive therapy and uses the interpretation of resistance as it relates to the major maladaptive pattern, while Davanloo's approach focuses on confronting defensive behavior and eliciting affect.

BAP resembles Peter Sifneos's (1979) Short-Term Anxiety-Provoking Psychotherapy in being somewhat cognitively based. Sifneos handles the transference differently, quickly intervening so as to avoid the transferential resistances. He avoids the dependent transference, but thereby must leave untouched the longstanding characterological difficulties that BAP was designed to work with. Sifneos puts less emphasis on the patient's understanding of defensive operations than does BAP. In addition, Sifneos's focus is primarily an oedipal one; BAP is not limited to such a focus.

Most brief dynamic psychotherapies are of shorter duration than BAP. We believe that it is important for our therapy to be longer than the usual twenty sessions. Our patients all suffer from personality disorders and require a longer course of treatment to alter longstanding characterological patterns.

EMPIRICAL SUPPORT

The efficacy of BAP has been examined in a pilot study comparing a group treated with BAP with a waiting list control group (Pollack, Winston, McCullough, Flegenheimer, & Winston, 1990). Fifteen patients with long-

TABLE 1

*Analysis of Covariance for Global Outcome Measures
between BAP and Control Group*

	BAP N = 15 (39 weeks)	Control N = 16 (20 weeks)	Analysis of Covariance
Target Complaint One			
Admission mean	10.60	11.44	F = 26.60
Termination mean[a]	6.40	10.88	P = .000
Target Complaint Two			
Admission mean	9.80	10.88	F = 8.02
Termination mean[a]	6.80	10.25	P = .008
Target Complaint Three (N = 14)			
Admission mean	8.71	10.88	F = 3.10
Termination mean[a]	6.71	9.81	P = .09
SCL-90 Global Scale			
Admission mean	44.55	47.37	F = 13.29
Termination mean[a]	36.27	44.06	P = .001
Social Adjustment Scale			
Admission mean	2.06	2.15	F = 8.64
Termination mean[a]	1.74	2.17	P = .007

[a]Termination measures taken one month after actual termination.
Source: Pollack, J., Winston, A., McCullough, L., Flegenheimer, W., & Winston, B. 1990. Brief adaptational psychotherapy. *Journal of Personality Disorders, 4*, 244-250. Used with permission.

standing personality disorders primarily of the *DSM III-R* Cluster C (avoidant, dependent, obsessive-compulsive, passive-aggressive, and mixed personality disorder) and histrionic disorder were compared with sixteen control patients. Significant differences at termination of therapy were found between the BAP and control group on two of three target complaints, the SCL-90, and the Social Adjustment Scale (see table 1). In addition, the BAP patients improved further on two of three target complaints from termination to follow-up at one to five years (mean follow-up time was 2.6 years) (see table 2).

In another study (Winston et al., 1991) BAP was compared with Intensive Short-Term Dynamic Psychotherapy (ISTDP), based on the work of

TABLE 2

*Matched t-test of Termination Versus Follow-up
for Target Complaints*

	t-test (n)	Analysis of Covariance
Target Complaint One		
Termination means	6.40 (15)	F = 3.11
Follow-up means	4.86 (14)	P = .10
Target Complaint Two		
Termination means	6.80 (15)	F = 9.54
Follow-up means	3.71 (14)	P = .009
Target Complaint Three		
Termination means	6.71 (14)	F = 7.06
Follow-up means	5.00 (13)	P = .02

Note: Termination measures taken one month after termination; follow-up measures taken one to five years after termination (mean = 2.6 years).
Source: Pollack, J., Winston, A., McCullough, L., Flegenheimer, W., & Winston, B. 1990. Brief adaptational psychotherapy. *Journal of Personality Disorders, 4*, 244-250. Used with permission.

Davanloo (1980) (see table 3). BAP and ISTDP patients showed significant improvement on target complaints, SCL-90, and the Social Adjustment Scale compared with waiting list control subjects. Effect sizes for BAP ranged from .70 to 1.23. The two therapy groups were similar in overall outcome, but showed differences on several subscale measures. BAP patients' outcomes were significantly better on the anxiety and the phobic anxiety subscale of the SCL-90 while ISTDP patients' outcomes were significantly better on the depression subscale. These findings may indicate that a more cognitively based therapy such as BAP lowers anxiety more than ISTDP, which tends to focus more on affect.

The results of these studies are encouraging since they indicate that BAP produces significant change in patients with longstanding personality disorders.

We examined a number of therapist and patient process variables using a coding system developed for videotaped psychotherapy sessions (McCullough, Trujillo, & Winston, 1985). BAP therapists are quite active, making approximately one intervention a minute. BAP therapists address current and past relationships an average of 11.5 times a session and the patient–therapist relationship an average of 8.3 times a session. These data

TABLE 3

*Admission and Termination Means and Effect Sizes for
Global Outcomes across Groups*

	BAP (N = 17)	ISTDP (N = 15)	Controls (N = 17)	Analysis of Covariance
Target Complaint I [a]				
Admission	10.47	10.08	11.69	F = 12.46
Termination	6.67	5.91	10.25	P = .0001
Effect Size	1.23	1.35	.46	SD = 3.10
SCL-90 Global Score [a]				
Admission	44.55	43.77	47.38	F = 4.84
Termination	36.27	36.62	44.06	P = .01
Effect size	1.11	.96	.45	SD = 7.45
Social Adjustment Scale [a]				
Admission	2.06	2.13	2.15	F = 6.68
Termination	1.74	1.76	2.18	P = .003
Effect size	.70	.80	−.07	SD = .45

Note: Effect size was computed by subtracting the termination mean (measured one month after actual termination) from the admission mean and dividing by the standard deviation of the combined control and experimental groups.
[a]The scores of the two groups given therapy were significantly different at termination from those of the control group (p < 0.05, Duncan Multiple Range Test).
Source: Winston, A., Pollack, J., McCullough, L., Flegenheimer, W., Kestenbaum, R., & Trujillo, M. (1991). Brief psychotherapy of personality disorders. *Journal of Nervous and Mental Diseases, 179*, 188-193, © by Williams & Wilkins, 1991. Used with permission.

indicate an interpersonal focus and active use of the transference; the results are in accord with the design of BAP and may help explain its efficacy.

CONCLUSION

We believe that BAP is an effective form of brief psychotherapy with wide applications. Because it is essentially a modification of standard psychotherapy techniques, BAP is generally well accepted, both by patients and by therapists wishing to learn brief psychotherapy. We hope that our ongoing research will help in clarifying the essential elements of the technique as well as in identifying those patients for whom BAP will be the treatment of choice.

References

American Psychiatric Association. (1987). *Diagnostic and statistical manual of mental disorders: DSM III-R.* Washington, DC: American Psychiatric Association.

Alexander, F., & French, T. M. (1946). *Psychoanalytic therapy.* New York: Ronald Press.

Arlow, J. A. (1969a). Unconscious fantasy and disturbances of conscious experience. *Psychoanalytic Quarterly, 38,* 1–27.

Arlow, J. A. (1969b). Fantasy, memory, and reality testing. *Psychoanalytic Quarterly, 38,* 28–51.

Bellak, L. (1958). *Schizophrenia: A review of the syndrome.* New York: Grune & Stratton.

Davanloo, H. (Ed.). (1980). *Short-term dynamic psychotherapy.* New York: Jason Aronson.

Freud, S. (1958). The ego and the id. In J. Strachey (Ed. & Trans.), *The standard edition of the complete psychological works of Sigmund Freud* (Vol. 19, pp. 3–66). London: Hogarth Press. (Original work published 1923.)

Gill, M. M. (1982). *Analysis of transference: Vol. 1. Theory and technique.* New York: International Universities Press.

Greenson, R. R. (1967). *The technique and practice of psychoanalysis* (Vol. 1). New York: International Universities Press.

Hartmann, H. (1939). *Ego psychology and the problem of adaptation.* New York: International Universities Press.

Hartmann, H., Kris, E., & Loewenstein, R. (1946). Comments on the formation of psychic structure. *Psychoanalytic Study of the Child, 2,* 11–38.

Malan, D. H. (1976). *The frontier of brief psychotherapy.* New York: Plenum.

Marmor, J. (1979). Short-term dynamic psychotherapy. *American Journal of Psychiatry,* *136,* 149–155.

McCullough, L., Trujillo, M., & Winston, A. (1985). *A video-coding manual of psychotherapy process.* Unpublished manuscript, Department of Psychiatry, Beth Israel Medical Center, New York, NY.

Pollack, J., & Horner, A. (1985). Brief adaptation-oriented psychotherapy. In A. Winston (Ed.), *Clinical and research issues in short-term dynamic psychotherapy.* Washington, DC: American Psychiatric Press.

Pollack, J., Winston, A., McCullough, L., Flegenheimer, W., & Winston, B. (1990). Brief adaptational psychotherapy. *Journal of Personality Disorders, 4,* 244–250.

Reich, W. (1949). *Character analysis.* New York: Farrar, Strauss and Cudahy.

Shapiro, D. (1965). *Neurotic styles.* New York: Basic Books.

Sifneos, P. E. (1979). *Short-term dynamic psychotherapy: Evaluation and technique.* New York: Plenum.

Strupp, H. H., & Binder, J. L. (1984). *Psychotherapy in a new key: A guide to time-limited dynamic psychotherapy.* New York: Basic Books.

Winston, A., Pollack, J., McCullough, L., Flegenheimer, W., Kestenbaum, R., & Trujillo, M. (1991). Brief psychotherapy of personality disorders. *Journal of Nervous and Mental Diseases, 179,* 188–193.

CHAPTER 9

Dynamic Supportive Psychotherapy

Henry Pinsker, Richard Rosenthal, and Leigh McCullough

ORIGINS AND DEVELOPMENT

Supportive psychotherapy is widely practiced and may in fact be the treatment provided to most psychiatric patients. In the early years of psychoanalysis, it was generally assumed that anyone who studied psychoanalysis could automatically do psychotherapy. Since the 1950s it has been recognized that psychotherapy should be systematically taught as a modality apart from analysis and that it should be conceptualized on its own terms, not as a lesser form of analysis. However, supportive psychotherapy has seldom been taught.

It seems to be assumed that if one masters psychodynamic therapy, one is able to do supportive therapy, which has generally been seen as a therapy that requires less skill and is appropriate primarily for patients who are less intelligent, less well motivated, or less interesting (Winston, Pinsker, & McCullough, 1986). The consequence of this assumption has been that supportive psychotherapy is often conducted with the objectives and techniques of expressive therapy as the model. Paul Dewald (1971) described expressive therapy and supportive therapy as the poles of the continuum of dynamic psychotherapies. Most patients receive a therapy that incorporates both supportive and expressive elements. There is a model for the expressive, or psychoanalytic, end of the continuum. Supportive psychotherapy has been described primarily as a body of techniques and in terms of subtraction of certain elements of expressive therapy, so there has been no model for the supportive end of the continuum.

Two rather different definitions of supportive therapy are current in the literature. Supportive psychotherapy is sometimes presented as a treatment for patients who are too fragile or too unmotivated to participate in therapy that is intended to bring about lasting personality change. Otto Kernberg (1984) has characterized as supportive therapy any therapy that is not primarily expressive. If one accepts his narrow view of expressive therapy, then supportive psychotherapy is what many practitioners think of simply as psychoanalytic psychotherapy. Lester Luborsky (1984) describes a continuum of psychotherapies. Between the poles of supportive and expressive therapies, he places expressive-supportive and supportive-expressive. In each instance, supportive psychotherapy is conceptualized primarily as a modified and truncated version of expressive therapy.

Our clinical and research psychotherapy group at Beth Israel Medical Center has attempted to define a separate supportive psychotherapy. We have codified and structured a stand-alone set of concepts, rules, and techniques embodying a treatment that may be useful for a wide range of patients and that may be tested within a brief psychotherapy research mode. We have not invented a new modality of treatment. We believe we are making concrete and teachable an area of psychotherapy that has been widely practiced but not adequately articulated. Although it is not a new therapy, it is a new way of thinking about psychotherapy, and it may make it possible for new therapists to grasp more quickly the large body of clinical wisdom that most experienced therapists have discovered. We began by conceptualizing the essential elements of the supportive treatment provided to the most impaired patients. We then realized that psychotherapy based on this definition was appropriate for a much broader range of clinical problems.

The objective of expressive therapies is generally to bring about change in the patient's personality. Perhaps the most explicit statement that the objectives of expressive therapy must be the objectives of all therapy is the assertion that "if it is supportive it isn't therapy" (Crown, 1988, p. 266). We do not define supportive therapy as being intended to produce personality change, but we believe that if an individual's habitual responses and habitual ways of feeling are altered, personality change has occurred.

Here is our definition of supportive psychotherapy: individual dynamic supportive psychotherapy is a dyadic treatment characterized by use of direct measures to ameliorate symptoms and to maintain, restore, or improve self-esteem, adaptive skills, and ego function. To the extent necessary to accomplish these objectives, treatment may use the examination of relationships, real or transferential, and both past and current patterns of emotional response or behavior. Ego functions include relation to reality, thinking, defense formation, affect regulation, synthetic function, and others as enumerated by Beres (1956), Bellak (1978), and so on. What we term ego functions could alternatively be called psychological functions, since they are addressed by behavioral therapists and cognitive therapists, whose formulations do not include the ego as a component of mental apparatus. By adaptive skills we mean almost anything a person does to function more effectively. The boundary between ego function and adaptive skill is not sharply defined. The patient's assessment of events is ego function; the action taken in response to the assessment is adaptive skill. Ego function looks inward. Adaptive skill looks outward. Supportive therapy uses direct measures to accomplish these objectives. It does not assume that benefits will flow from greater maturity, insight, or the resolution of intrapsychic conflict.

Each of the three objectives must be addressed: self-esteem, adaptive skills, and ego function. If the therapy does not address each of these, it may be useful—it may be just what the patient needs—but it is not supportive therapy. Behavioral therapy, for example, may focus on adaptive skills and nothing else. Some patients—those who are most fragile and narcissistic—may need a supportive relationship and derive benefit from it, but if the therapy has no other ingredients, it cannot be called supportive psychotherapy. Some such patients, after a prolonged supportive relationship, become able to participate in supportive therapy.

Lawrence Rockland (1989), in an important new book on supportive therapy, defined supportive therapy as focused on improving ego function and adaptation. Attention to self-esteem, an explicit component of supportive psychotherapy in our definition, is characterized by him as appropriate transference gratification.

Various psychotherapies can be conceptualized as being a continuum, with the most expressive, psychoanalysis, at one end, and the most supportive at the other. Various blends of supportive-expressive or expressive-supportive occur at the middle. Some treatment techniques may be found at any point on the continuum. For example, examination of patterns from the past may be part of any treatment, although this is not the major focus for the low-functioning patient, with whom it is often more useful to concentrate on current circumstances. The treatment techniques that are associated with the two ends of the spectrum cannot be randomly applied at the intermediate points of the spectrum. The therapist is real to the patient or not. Transference is the major focus or it is not. Fantasy is encouraged or not encouraged. Character defenses are attacked or accepted. Just as inappropriate support may be a contaminant in expressive therapy, the techniques of expressive therapy—which have been taught to most of us as universal techniques of *therapy*—may be contaminants in supportive therapy.

Conventional practice has been to depart from the model of pure expressive psychotherapy to the extent necessary to meet the patient's needs. It is our thesis that supportive psychotherapy should be conducted with the supportive psychotherapy model uppermost in mind, deviating in the direction of expressive therapy only to the extent necessary to meet the patient's needs, always recognizing departures from the supportive psychotherapy model. For example, in expressive therapy, making a direct answer to the patient's question, without exploring its meaning, is a departure from the model. In supportive dynamic psychotherapy, nonresponse to a question is the departure from the model.

Rockland's supportive therapy is based upon the model of expressive therapy. He permits silence, recognizing it as resistance, but it is resistance to the work of supportive therapy, not resistance to uncovering.

SELECTION OF PATIENTS

Expressive therapy has been widely accepted as the default therapy—the therapy to be provided unless there is some reason to do something else. Supportive therapy has been dismissed as a treatment for those who cannot or will not engage in what has been seen as the more substantial therapy. This is, perhaps, a legacy of Freud's (1919/1955) description of psychoanalysis as "gold" as compared with the "copper" of suggestion.

Recent work has been more critical, with clinical assessment no longer based primarily upon global attractiveness. It is now recognized that being bright, verbal, and introspective does not really predict success in treatment. According to David S. Werman (1984), the typical patient for whom supportive therapy is indicated demonstrates some degree of ego deficit or insufficiency. Clinical characteristics include inability to introspect, alexithymia, inability to tolerate suffering, poor object relations, prominence of such primitive defenses as projective denial and splitting, weakness in trust, somatoform problems, and deficient energy. These are presented as indications for supportive therapy because they preclude expressive therapy.

According to Peter Buckley (1986), the following factors are indications for supportive therapy: (1) primitive defenses such as projection and denial predominate; (2) object relations are impaired and characterized by an

223

absence of capacity for mutuality and reciprocity; (3) and in more extreme cases, inability to recognize the object as being separate from the self; (4) failure to adequately modulate affect, particularly aggression; (5) overwhelming anxiety around separation/individuation issues.

Rockland (1989) endorses the view that patients who have chronic neurotic or borderline character pathology of moderate severity and who also have adequate intelligence, motivation, and psychological mindedness should be in exploratory psychotherapy. But even these patients, should they seek treatment during an acute crisis, should have supportive psychotherapy. Only after resolution of the crisis should the prospect of exploratory therapy be considered.

We believe serious consideration must be given to the proposition that treatment based upon the principles we have delineated as the foundation of supportive psychotherapy should be the basic or default approach. We propose that it is expressive psychotherapy, not supportive, that should be prescribed only when specifically indicated. It is beyond the scope of this chapter to explore indications for expressive treatment or for psychoanalysis. These indications probably include the presence of oedipal-level development, an assessment of remediable character pathology, and the presence of repeated ego-dystonic behavior. The basic treatment model should be supportive, with only as much expressive technique as necessary. This is the reverse of the usual practice, which is to provide only as much support as necessary.

The style of supportive therapy is more conducive to continued effort for most patients. The discipline of therapist nonresponse that characterizes good expressive therapy is chilling to many patients, and it is hardly a desirable model for human relationships.

Supportive therapy for the higher-functioning patient is, of course, not the same as supportive therapy for the low-functioning patient, as, for example, the chronic schizophrenic. With a low-functioning patient, patient–therapist conversation focuses on adaptive skills and self-esteem. With the higher-functioning patient, the content is more likely to be relationships and patterns of response, with room for exploration of the meaning of the patient's words. We are not suggesting that the therapy of the high-functioning patient involve unnecessary attention to life skills or to such ego functions as reality testing and impulse control.

There appear to be certain populations of patients for whom supportive psychotherapy is the treatment of choice. Edward Kaufman and Joseph Reoux (1988) have suggested that supportive psychotherapy is indicated for substance abusers who are in the initial stages of sobriety. This treatment may need to be continued indefinitely, with expressive elements added as needed within the patient's capacity for tolerance. Expressive therapy is generally contraindicated until the patient has developed a firm therapeutic alliance and has both a support system and a concrete means for maintaining sobriety. Premature use of anxiety-provoking psychotherapeutic strategies aimed at character change will tend to push the patient back into drug use as a means of modulating strong affect.

While there is little controversy about the prescription of supportive therapy for the low-functioning patient, therapists have not been as comfortable with the prescription of supportive psychotherapy for the higher-functioning patient for whom expressive therapy has been the traditional treatment of choice. Since the traditional model for much of psychotherapy has been expressive therapy and since commonplace supportive psychotherapy has been derived by the removal of expressive elements from the traditional model, it is not surprising that there is an intuitive resistance to indicating supportive psychotherapy as the default treatment for high-functioning patients.

GOALS OF TREATMENT

A clear mandate of the supportive therapy process is to set explicit goals and a clear agenda. These are not required in traditional expressive treatment. The agenda may be set either by the patient or by the therapist. The therapist may set an agenda in order to follow through on an unfinished topic or to teach therapeutic process. Reduction of anxiety is a goal of supportive therapy, so it is important to consider ways in which the routine practices of conventional psychotherapy create anxiety. Allowing the patient to see the map before exploring the territory reduces anxiety and emphasizes that therapy is a rational collaborative process.

The therapist should have many ideas about the patient's dynamics, the dynamics of the patient–therapist relationship, and his or her planned tactics. The therapist does not make a point of sharing everything with the patient, but in contrast to the traditional model that has taught to give as little as possible, the supportive psychotherapy model mandates a meeting of the minds about goals between patient and therapist. It is often helpful to make explicit how the topic at hand is connected to self-esteem, to a specified ego function, or to a specified adaptive skill. The patient who works at therapy extensively on his or her own often gains the most, so it is important that the patient understand the tactics of therapy. Since our model of supportive therapy is not conceptualized as the application of a theory of development or a theory of symptom formation, the supportive end of the supportive-expressive continuum involves only those goals that patient and therapist have agreed upon. In general terms, the goals are embodied in our definition of supportive therapy. To the extent that treatment is a mixture of supportive and expressive elements, there may be additional goals derived from theoretical positions.

Time-limited or brief therapy must be undertaken with realistic goals. It is reasonable to anticipate relief of specific symptoms, such as anxiety or depression. When longstanding personality characteristics are a major problem, the goal of brief treatment is for the patient to become able to formulate the problem; to understand how various symptoms, behaviors, or feelings are manifestations of this problem; and to gain command of strategies for coping with it. The analogy of school is pertinent. School does not go on interminably. Each course has discrete organization, with a beginning, a middle, and an end. A period of therapy is like a course. The student who has a worthwhile experience is likely to return for more. It is not suggested that the outcome of therapy will be a new personality. It is suggested that at some time in the future, the patient may be able to benefit from another time-limited therapeutic endeavor.

In the Beth Israel Psychotherapy Research Program, brief treatment is defined as up to forty weekly sessions.

THEORY OF CHANGE

The theory of change in traditional expressive therapy is character transformation through the resolution of core neurotic conflicts and abandonment of maladaptive characterologic defensive strategies. This is achieved through the conduit of emotional insight into the transference.

The concept in supportive psychotherapy is that change stems from learning and from identification with or introjection of an accepting, well-related therapist, not through resolution of unconscious conflicts. Change is not a product of discovering reasons for the existence of the behavior or feelings, but rather it is a direct consequence of better self-esteem and improved adaptive skills. Poor self-esteem is associated with helplessness and unwillingness to try new ways. If nothing new is tried, nothing can change. Low self-esteem is associated with demoralization and unwillingness to attempt anything new. Improved self-esteem, through a good (although uninterpreted) relationship with the therapist, may make it possible for the patient to make the conscious effort to change. Successful efforts then make for improved self-esteem. Distortions about self and others are corrected by education, not by removal of defenses.

The criteria for positive outcome in supportive psychotherapy relate to quality of life issues. Thus, a good outcome of therapy is increased self-esteem, reduction in experienced anxiety or dysphoria, and a resultant stabilization or increase in adaptive functioning. Character change per se is not our hallmark of successful supportive therapy, but it may be a positive effect of treatment. Self-understanding is not central to the treatment, and it is pursued only to the extent that it supports the accomplishment of patient goals and therapist objectives. It is not necessary for the unconscious to become conscious, and it is not essential that linkages be made between current and past figures. By a collaborative effort of the patient and the therapist, patterns of interpersonal or other behavior or of feeling responses are identified and strategies for changing them are devised to the extent possible.

Theory of the Therapeutic Process

Traditional expressive psychotherapy recognizes that there are two general categories of interpersonal dynamics in the exchanges between patient and therapist. One, recognized mostly by therapists with a psychodynamic viewpoint, is the transferential relationship, which in latent or manifest form is the pattern of reflexive attitudes, thoughts, and emotional responses that are currently maladaptive and related directly to intrapsychic processes from an earlier time in psychosocial development. In expressive psychotherapies, it is this relationship that is deemed to be of paramount importance for revealing conflicts, and it is to the essentially noncognitive process of working through these transferential relationships that therapeutic gain is ascribed.

The second relationship is universally recognized and forms the context of all treatment, including expressive therapy. This is the "real" relationship that is manifested in the therapeutic alliance and coexists with, and is to some extent reflective of, the transference relationship. For example, what appears on the surface to be a positive therapeutic alliance may be bolstered, out of the patient's awareness, by the fact that dependency needs are gratified in the transference relationship.

In figure 1, we illustrate the way in which the two types of relationship—real and transferential—are recognized by expressive and supportive therapies. It is the amount of emphasis upon each relationship that distinguishes these two forms of dynamic treatment.

In expressive treatment, the real relationship becomes a background or context within which the therapist responds mostly to the transference

Figure 1

Differing Emphasis Upon Real and Transferential Relationships

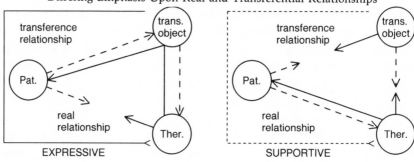

nature of the interpersonal process. There is a conscious minimization of real information about the therapist in the therapist's statements to the patient. Thus, much of the real relationship and therapeutic alliance depends upon the acceptance by the patient of the rules and agreements on the conduct of treatment and its relationship to the therapist.

Supportive psychotherapy, on the other hand, emphasizes the real relationship, as reflected in the therapeutic alliance. This process is a more globally recognizable and acceptable one, as it is based upon overt mutuality in the conduct of therapy. The relationship between therapist and patient is a mirror of other current relationships. This is contrasted to the socially unusual and anxiety-provoking neutral stance of the therapist in expressive treatments. The therapeutic alliance in supportive therapy is enhanced through the use of accurate empathic responses, validation of feeling states, and so on, but development of transference neurosis is avoided. To that end, there is a minimization of focus upon transferential material, and regression in the service of ego is not fostered. The fact that transference is not discussed does not mean that it is not recognized. Negative transference can threaten the alliance and the treatment, so the therapist must be vigilant about recognizing it and dealing with it. With higher-functioning patients, clarification of evidence of negative feelings or thoughts may be productive. With lower-functioning patients, it may be necessary for the therapist to change his or her stance, as people usually do when talking with someone who is becoming angry or distant.

In Short-Term Dynamic Psychotherapy, as described by Habib Davanloo (1980), the development of transference neurosis is avoided by constant interpretation of the transference. Supportive therapy does not confront defenses unless they are grossly maladaptive—for example, primitive projection, splitting, and the like.

While supportive psychotherapy is dynamic, and attention is paid to transference material by the therapist, responsiveness of the therapist is most likely to be within the domain of the real relationship. It is essential that negative transference be recognized and dealt with and that primitive defenses be recognized and refuted. Clearly, to understand psychodynamic principles is necessary within our model of supportive therapy, but it is not sufficient for the conduct of treatment.

Interpersonal versus Intrapsychic Approaches

Expressive therapies have a primarily intrapsychic focus with respect to the therapist's attention to and interaction with patient material. The therapist and patient examine the conflicts between the patient's mental constructs of id, ego, and superego, or, stated in developmental terms, conflicts between the inner representations of self and others. The therapist's persistent attention to these conceptual frames during the process of treatment assists the patient in being aware of and then consciously contributing to material with this focus in mind.

In contrast, supportive psychotherapy has a predominantly interpersonal focus in that adaptive strategies, coping skills, and anxiety reduction are attended to within a frame of reference that looks at patterns of interpersonal behavior. In current usage, the term interpersonal psychotherapy refers to a variety of treatment approaches extending from the classic work of Harry Stack Sullivan (1953) to more recent work by Jack Anchin and Donald Keisler (1982). The relationship between the patient and the therapist is used to teach the patient about difficulties in transactions with other people, with the intent of improving the quality of the patient's relationships. The focus of an interpersonal psychotherapy model developed for research purposes by Gerald Klerman is on social and interpersonal functioning, morale, and coping with stress (1984).

Approach to Defensive Structures

It is necessary for the therapist to have an awareness of the patient's object relations, defensive structures, and conflictual issues. The therapist makes hypotheses about the patient's core conflicts and defensive structure, then responds with these specific hypotheses in mind. In this way, therapist responses can be modified to strengthen relatively adaptive defenses— such as healthy narcissism; reasonable, possibly soothing rationalization;

and esteem-protecting generalization—or to sidestep anxiety-provoking transference-linked postures. In general, the therapist conveys implicit respect for the character structure as presented.

TECHNIQUES

Our model of supportive therapy is applicable to both higher-functioning and lower-functioning patients. With markedly impaired individuals direct measures are used to improve self-esteem and to improve function. These measures include reassurance, praise, encouragement, and so on, techniques customarily enumerated as the constituents of supportive therapy. With higher-functioning patients, direct supportive measures are less frequently used because sessions deal—as in expressive therapy—with relationships, self-concept, and patterns of feeling, rather than defective coping skills or poorly contained symptoms.

The following discussion of techniques addresses first approaches applicable to all patients, then techniques that become more important with the lower-functioning individual.

Reduction of Anxiety

The style of supportive psychotherapy is conversation. It is remarkable how much of the style of conventional psychotherapy keeps the patient off balance and out of control. Patients learn to tolerate the style, but they do not benefit from it, unless it is specifically indicated to raise anxiety as a motivational strategy from within the model of expressive therapy. Silent listening is appropriate only when the patient prefers it. We make interjections or comments as we would do in a social situation. We might ask a question just to show that we are listening. If we ask a question and the patient answers, we acknowledge in some way what has been said. Conversational style does not mean that therapy is ordinary conversation, for in therapy, it is never the therapist's turn to take the floor. Whatever the therapist says is intended to be useful for the patient. The therapist's responses are not limited to simple conversational devices. Leston Havens (1986) provides a treatise on the therapeutic use of language, and most of his illustrations are brief responses.

Fred Pine (1984) has written about techniques for reducing anxiety in the analytic situation. He points out that if an interpretation or other comment is made, the patient is called upon to respond. This is experienced as a challenge. To avoid challenging the patient, which would increase anxiety, the interpretation can be embedded in other comments so that the patient is not forced to respond immediately. Another of Pine's suggestions is to warn the patient that you are about to say something that might be upsetting, and ask the patient if he or she is willing to go on with it. This gives the patient a measure of control, and does allow postponement when the patient feels it necessary. When the patient becomes upset, it may be helpful to wait until the emotion has died down before discussing the matter, which is, as Pine says, to "strike when the iron is cold."

If we want to reduce anxiety and increase the patient's sense of control, then we explain what we are doing and we do everything possible to allow the patient to be prepared for what will happen. Medical students learn to do this while conducting a physical examination. In the psychiatric setting, this might take the form of a statement such as: "I have some questions that may make you anxious. Do you think you can handle this now?" or "I'd like to talk about medication sometime soon."

It is especially important to have thorough and extended discussions about medication. The psychotherapeutic stance of collaboration is often suspended when medication is the topic, and the psychiatrist reverts to the authoritarian medical role. Medication then becomes a power issue instead of a shared concern. Kernberg (1984) has pointed out that medication should be an integral part of a treatment plan and not be introduced haphazardly when the patient fails to improve. Bad response to medication, he has said, is often a manifestation of negative transference.

Enhancing Self-Esteem

Many psychotherapists undoubtedly work with a supportive style, but the field of psychotherapy has not given the formal attention to measures for protecting the self-esteem of their patients that salesmen use to protect the self-esteem of their prospects. For example, Tom Hopkins's best-selling book *How to Master the Art of Selling* (1982) details ways in which the salesman may lose control of the situation by stimulating negative responses. He lists three precepts that every "champion" lives by. Two of them are: (1) don't argue—it's trying to beat the prospect down, and (2) don't attack them when you overcome their objections. Of course, the therapist has the patient's interests at heart, whereas the salesman's goal is to sell. However, as Hopkins points out, the customer is paying for something that will be of benefit. Although the therapist and the salesman have different objectives, the patient and the customer both seek to benefit.

Hopkins instructs the salesman to avoid asking a question that the prospect cannot answer and to avoid questions to which the answer might be no. It is important not to destroy the positive feeling that is essential to make the sale.

Medical students learn to take a history by asking questions. The patient doesn't know the intent of a question or the implications of the answer. It is like being cross-examined in court, or giving a deposition, for the traditional style of medical history taking is attacking.

With practice, one can reduce the number of questions that have a challenging or attacking impact. Most questions that begin with the word *why* are challenges or criticisms. People learn during childhood that when a parent or teacher asks *why* they did something, the implication is, "You shouldn't have done that!" If it is hard for the patient to talk about something, consider asking, in a nonchallenging way, "How can we talk about this without increasing your anxiety or without making you feel that you're being pressured?" It may be that the patient will not be able to answer in a useful way, but at least you will have had another chance to demonstrate that you understand, and this has implications for self-esteem and empathy. When a patient misses a session, any attempt to discuss the absence may be experienced by the patient as criticism. The therapist must decide whether it is more important to explore the patient's defensive avoidance or more important to abstain from sounding critical. Helping the patient to see that his or her actions are responsible for the way people respond to him or her is a regular technique of psychotherapy. For some narcissistic patients, the idea is intolerable. At times, talking about patterns of behavior is palatable when it is linked to concrete steps for improvement or change.

With higher-functioning patients, the therapist's interest and responsiveness may provide a suitable degree of gratification. With those who are significantly impaired, it may be appropriate to be more active, as described by Leopold Bellak: "Implicit support is provided by the therapist's statement of his availability or by feeding a variety of possible oral gifts: cigarettes, coffee, cookies, fruit, etc. to foster the incorporation of the therapist as a benign introject" (1978, p. 87).

The essence of supportive therapy is not specific supportive actions but continuous concern about self-esteem and anxiety and deliberate effort by the therapist to avoid subtle actions that might lower self-esteem or increase anxiety.

Respecting Defenses

Expressive therapy has, as one of its objectives, getting rid of character defenses so that the core neurosis can be exposed. In supportive psychotherapy adaptive defenses and the patient's personal style are generally respected. The individual whose defense is maintaining control over emotions should not be too quickly asked to relax this control. For example, one often sees this in a treatment plan: "Encourage patient to verbalize feelings." Sometimes this is the right treatment and sometimes it is the wrong treatment. The advice that "it's all right to cry" may be the wrong intervention with a person who has a great need for control and who, with a little support, may be enabled to regain control. A businessman who was accustomed to overcoming all obstacles by taking decisive action described in his first meeting with a therapist an unusual combination of external events that had created stresses that he could not master by his usual methods. He had to wait until others acted. When tears welled up in his eyes, the therapist changed the topic, calculating that the patient would overcome the problem by use of his usual mastery and that his self-esteem would be further lowered by crying in the presence of a stranger. Although defenses in general are to be supported, this support stops when the defense is maladaptive or pathological, such as regression or most projection. Pathological defenses, such as projection, maladaptive denial, and grossly unrealistic planning, should be challenged.

Denial, when adaptive, is compatible with good emotional health and is therefore supported. For most of us, if we are to live in the real world, it is not love that makes the world go round, but denial. If a patient says about something important, "I don't want to think about it," the therapist might ask: "Does it work? Have you found that not thinking about something is an effective way of coping with it?" Because if the patient believes that not thinking about it has been an effective way of reducing anxiety, the therapist could never succeed by attacking the defensive denial. Chances are, asking the question, which shows respect for the defense, will open the way to useful discussion of the problem. The more mature defenses—repression, reaction formation, rationalization, and intellectualization—are generally encouraged. Even immature defenses, as Rockland (1989) has pointed out, may be supported if they are adaptive.

233

Dreams may be discussed, but they are used as indicators of the patient's concerns, not as undefended glimpses of the unconscious.

Clarification, Confrontation, and Interpretation

Clarification, confrontation, and interpretation are useful in supportive psychotherapy, but not with the requirement that the unconscious be made conscious or that full linkage be made with impulses or affects connected with genetic figures.

Clarification is used extensively in supportive psychotherapy. This means summarizing, paraphrasing, and organizing the patient's statements, without elaboration or inference. These techniques have the supportive effects of providing the patient first with evidence that the therapist understands and then with a frame of reference within which to understand the patient's patterns of thought, feeling, and action.

Clarification promotes interpersonal communication in the therapeutic process. Since the model of process in supportive psychotherapy specifies that the style is conversational, and since the therapist is obligated to obtain feedback on his or her understanding of the patient's utterances, the use of these techniques can facilitate the therapeutic alliance.

Confrontation, which brings to attention a pattern of behavior or something that the patient is avoiding or not attending to, can be useful as a technique within the setting of supportive psychotherapy, but needs to be put into a specific context (for example, to increase adaptive skills). Although the objective of supportive psychotherapy is not analysis of defenses, it is correct to discourage the use of maladaptive defenses, such as the projective blaming of others, rationalization of inactivity, excessive attention to detail, power struggles, an unrealistic sense of entitlement, or an obfuscatory style of speaking. Even the most supportive treatment has the objectives of increasing the patient's awareness of the relationship between his or her behavior and the responses of other people; to improve the patient's ability to sort out cause-and-effect relationships; and to foster the patient's appreciation on a manifest level of the connection between past and current patterns. When unrecognized anger is an issue, it is usually necessary for the patient to recognize it and to develop strategies for dealing with it.

As previously described, interpretations or clarifications may be postponed until the affect is no longer intense, shifting emphasis from the feeling to the thought; or the patient may be protected by being warned that something potentially anxiety-provoking is about to take place. The therapist can make an "incomplete interpretation," which may leave out the genetic references or may generalize the subject to reduce the experienced demand for response. This is related to but differs from Ernest Glover's (1931) inexact interpretation, which protects the fragile patient by offering an explanation about impulses or behavior that is plausible but not the whole truth about infantile fears. For example, the therapist might explain unacceptable homosexual wishes to the patient as a defense against heterosexual fears. In making an incomplete interpretation, the therapist might interpret anxiety around pursuit of a love object as fear of competition without localizing it to the original oedipal triangle, even if the genetic references are clear from the latent content of the patient material.

Robert Langs (1973) elaborated on interpretation upward, on devaluing primitive fantasies, and on other supportive techniques for dealing with especially terrifying material in the course of psychoanalytic psychotherapy. An example of interpretation upward would be statements by the therapist to a highly narcissistic patient that he is enraged and wants to punish a particular person who frustrates him, when the latent content indicates that the fantasy is primitive oral rage in which the patient wants to tear apart and consume his tormentor. These techniques are useful as well in supportive psychotherapy proper, when interpretation is indicated. Interpretations of transference may incorporate genetic figures if specifically indicated within the context of treatment, if the patient is clearly aware of the connections and is "running with the ball." The therapist must be relatively sophisticated in order to give partial interpretations that at the same time support and increase emotional awareness, where the full interpretation might bring increased anxiety or the use of more primitive defenses.

In anxiety-raising therapies, a patient might be challenged for being vague. In supportive psychotherapy, the patient would be urged to be more specific. The goal is not to explore the motivation for vagueness, but rather to guide the patient to more effective communication. Only when this strategy is proven ineffective do the previously mentioned specific indications for a more anxiety provoking style of therapy become relevant.

Rationalization

Politics, religion, and self-help books all teach rationalizations and intellectualized formulas for helping people get through life. Psychotherapists have done this, too, but often the therapist is ashamed of doing it. Yet rationalization is a legitimate technique if done knowingly and for a reason. The adult patient who dwells excessively on what his or her parents did wrong may benefit from a statement like, "Your parents seem to have been very rigid and cold, but you know, they were doing what the experts taught was the most scientifically correct way to raise children in the 1930s; they may have been doing the best they could." The parent who broods about his disappointment in an adult child may be helped by being told, "You do the best you can, but you can't always determine how your children will grow up." We remind the disappointed parent that Benjamin Franklin's son was the royal governor of New Jersey and that he tried to guide the British to Washington's encampment.

Reframing

Reframing is a cognitive technique that can be used to assist the patient in diffusing or sidestepping painful affects or negative self-references, thus enhancing self-esteem. In addition, the therapist can reframe a maladaptive behavior in order to make it ego dystonic, a standard psychotherapeutic technique, if it fits into the basic format of supportive psychotherapy.

Encouragement

Encouragement may include reassurance, praise, and the empathic comments and subtle encouragements that are part of everyday life among people who have good feelings about each other. Most therapists have learned to offer empathic comments as responses to particularly difficult circumstances. "That must have been hard for you." "That was rough." "You must have felt terrible." "You must have been frightened." "Anyone would be frightened if that happened." Or "I would have been frightened (or angry) if that happened to me." We try to go further and find opportunities to add words that tell the patient something good about himself or herself. "It sounds like that was a brave way to handle it." "That took courage." "You must be very determined (or tough) to have kept going so long when you were that anxious and had voices after you all the time." Milton Viederman wrote, "It is rare to find a patient who does not reveal something that can evoke admiration. . . . The support of self-esteem is such a central issue in any supportive therapy that one would think it barely deserves mention. However, young psychiatrists with a sense of constraint are reluctant to 'flatter the patient' and in particular 'to feed the narcissism' " (1984, p. 151).

It is very important, though, when offering praise, that it be based on facts, that it be directed to something the patient considers worthy of praise. Defective praise undercuts the patient. It raises the suspicion that the therapist is impersonal, inattentive, or false. Defective praise may damage the therapeutic relationship. Most patients who are new to therapy or new to the therapist appreciate being told that they are doing it right.

Just as praise must be expressed in terms that are meaningful to the patient, so must reassurance. As every physician knows, reassurance can be powerful, but if the reassurance fails, credibility may be lost forever. It is reckless to say, "This medicine will make you feel better." It is more prudent to say, "This medication makes most people feel better," or "It usually helps people with conditions like yours." The best reassurance draws on what the patient has already demonstrated that he or she can do. "Yes, you have recurrences, but you always get over them—your spirit doesn't seem to have been destroyed." Reassurance based on expert knowledge may be useful, provided it is accurate. Reassurance is a direct means of reducing anxiety. It also fosters the therapeutic alliance.

Suggestion was a popular tactic when psychiatrists dealt with dramatic symptoms in hysterical patients. However, when it fails, the healer's power is lessened. If it succeeds and the patient learns of it, the patient may feel deceived.

Advising

Advice must be factual, related to the therapist's expert knowledge, and limited to the topics of therapy. With lower-functioning patients, every aspect of daily life may be within the scope of the therapy. Advice may be relevant if it is designed to help the patient act in a way that will enhance his or her self-esteem, to improve adaptive skills, or to improve ego function. The basis and rationale for the advice must always be stated. Not "You should work," but "Most people who stop working don't feel better—not working protects you from some stresses, but it's usually bad for self-esteem." It is the therapist's expertise, not his or her authority, that is crucial. Identification with the therapist—as a focused, reasonable professional—may be an important aspect of treatment. It is well to remember, however, that in all forms of therapy, patients have a habit of construing as advice almost anything the therapist has said.

Modeling

In any therapy the therapist may, intentionally or unintentionally, provide a model of behavior and responsiveness. Our concept of supportive therapy does not include activity outside the therapeutic encounter—social activity with the patient, for example. Many descriptions of supportive therapy have included the notion that the therapist lends his or her ego to the patient. One might think that this refers to modeling, but the phrase seems to be a jargon metaphor for counseling and for applying to the patient's problems the therapist's problem-solving skills and knowledge of individual and social behavior.

Rehearsal or Anticipation

Anticipatory guidance is a technique that allows the patient to move through new situations hypothetically, considering the possible events and ways of responding to them. This allows the patient to become acquainted with the context of the future event, reducing some of the anticipatory anxiety associated with it. Rehearsal further allows the patient to work out more appropriate or even novel ways to participate in future events, thus adding to his or her repertoire of adaptive skills. Anticipatory guidance is used early in therapy with patients who are likely to drop out, instead of waiting for negative attitudes to become evident.

Responding to Ventilation

Ventilation, or "getting it off your chest," may be useful to the patient when a traumatic event is experienced or when something important has been unexpressed. The fact that the therapist has heard the patient's story and does not reject him or her may be the essence of support for some. The therapist's active responses may include tracking (indicating that he or she is following the patient), universalizing (making it clear that many people have similar feelings, wishes, or problems), or decatastrophizing (minimizing issues or problems that the patient has exaggerated). The patient may be permitted to recount events at length, without interruption, but the objectives of supportive therapy cannot be achieved by passive listening.

Techniques Not Used in Supportive Psychotherapy

A resident told her supervisor that she had been talking with her new patient, a depressed elderly woman, about things that the patient liked. The patient said, "I like opera." The resident replied, "I do, too." She asked the supervisor, "Was that a mistake? I've been told you shouldn't do that in psychotherapy." Over the years, the techniques of expressive psychotherapy have become the model for all psychotherapy. One of the most commonplace examples is the practice of not answering questions. The patient asks, "Are you married?" The therapist replies, "Do you think I am married?" or "Does it matter whether I am married or not?" The public has come to believe that this is the way psychiatrists talk.

The techniques of psychoanalysis were developed to accomplish specific purposes. The analyst presents as little of himself or herself as possible in order to maximize the chance that the patient will invest the therapist with feelings and reactions that originated in past relationships—transference. The therapist does not answer questions because the development of fantasy is encouraged and the tension or anxiety generated by this lack of gratification helps to maintain the therapeutic process.

Expressive therapy presumes that the therapy is the central point of the patient's life; supportive therapy assumes that it is just one of the patient's activities. In fact, if the patient misses a session, his or her explanation may be accepted at face value, although the therapist must be alert to the possibility that unconscious motivations may have to be explored, since missing a session can be part of a pattern of maladaptive behavior.

Central to expressive therapy is the principle of free association. Furthermore, the patient always speaks first. Again, skillfully practiced supportive therapy does not employ technical maneuvers that were invented for the specialized psychoanalytic situation and that have become erroneously institutionalized as universal rules of psychotherapy. At the same time, supportive psychotherapy requires that the therapist limit what he or she says to that which is useful for the patient. To do otherwise would be to exploit the patient.

Edwin Wallace summarized the thesis that the practice of supportive psychotherapy is more difficult than the practice of uncovering therapy:

> There is a wider range of responses by the therapist, and it is difficult to decide which response is correct. You cannot wait for the patient to make connections. . . . you must decide . . . now to come down on the side of expressiveness, now of restraint, now to confront his

intellectualization or reaction formation, now to support it, now to analyze the transference, now to utilize it as a suggestive reinforcing lever . . . now to ask him what goes into his question, now to answer it immediately and directly, now to gratify his request for coffee or advice, now to analyze it. (1983, pp. 345–346)

CASE EXAMPLE

The following vignette illustrates supportive techniques. The patient was a young woman who began treatment because she felt depressed, was dissatisfied with her life, and had been vacillating about continuing the relationship with her boyfriend. It became clear as therapy got under way that she saw herself as indecisive and uncertain about everything. In this session the patient discussed having taken a second job, a night job at a bar, which she quit after a few days.

PATIENT: At first I felt bad to start and quit. It wasn't as good as I thought it was going to be, and I was very tired the next day. It's more important that I do well at my regular job.

THERAPIST: *(Clarifies)* You felt bad about quitting, but only a little bad.

PATIENT: Yeah. I felt a little bad because I could make money if I stuck it out, but I realized it was going to be hard. If people stayed late, I'd have to stay, too. And they wanted me to work on nights when I had school.

THERAPIST: *(Asks for confirmation of his understanding of the patient's statements)* Well, would I be correct if I said that you still think an extra job to make some money is a good idea, but that this isn't the way to do it?

PATIENT: I just realized I didn't have time for school. The best thing about it is that now I value my time more. After that, now my schedule seems great.

THERAPIST: *(Fact-based praise)* Well, you made this decision without a lot of uncertainty.

PATIENT: No, I was pretty sure.

THERAPIST: *(Asks for feedback about accuracy of praise)* It sounds to me like taking the job was a reasonable thing to do, and getting out as soon as you saw that it wasn't good was also a reasonable thing to do. Would you agree?

PATIENT: Yeah.

THERAPIST: *(Reminds patient of their agenda and attempts to enhance self-esteem by reinforcing patient's awareness of good adaptive function)* Since I'm always coming back to the issue of self-confidence—what did it do for your self-confidence that you made a decision to do it and then you made a decision to stop doing it?

PATIENT: Yeah, it was OK. At first I thought I was copping out because I didn't think I'd be able to handle it, but by the third night, I was catching on . . . so last week was a tough week.

THERAPIST: *(Makes empathic conversational response)* It sure sounds like it!

PATIENT: *(Sets a different agenda)* There's something I wanted to talk about . . . going home and seeing my parents. It was very upsetting.

THERAPIST: *(Asks a focusing question, potentially reducing anxiety by interrupting the beginning of an intensely felt expression)* When did you do that?

PATIENT: I went home Wednesday night. My parents picked me up. This was the worst time I can remember with my mother in a long time. She was horrible.

THERAPIST: *(Asks another question, maintaining conversational style, again intending to mitigate intensity)* What happened?

PATIENT: I couldn't deal with it in my usual way. I was, I wouldn't say antagonistic, but I reacted to her. I couldn't believe what was coming out of her mouth!

It's upsetting to me that at this point I still can't deal with her at all.

THERAPIST: *(Focuses, without confronting defensive postures)* Let's have some specifics.

PATIENT: The first thing she said was "How's Jerry? I guess you're not seeing Jerry any more." I tried to explain the situation to her. I told her I'd gone out with Ben, that she'd met him, that I have a great time with him. Right away she asks, "What kind of people are these? Drug addicts?" How can you infer this from what I'm saying? Do I look like I hang around with people who take drugs? He didn't fit her cookie-cutter mold and instantly she assumes there's something wrong with him. She hears that he's an artist and assumes I'm hanging around with a bad crowd. She moved from one thing to another. She made some ridiculous comment about "What do they expect if they buy you dinner? Sexual favors?" Mom, I can't even be in this conversation because you don't know what you're talking about. She has no idea who I am. She has no faith in my judgment.

THERAPIST: *(Makes a clarification and supports the therapeutic alliance)* So, you're not only single, but you're doing bad things, and nothing you say to her gets through.

PATIENT: The fact that she assumes this makes me not want to talk to her.

THERAPIST: *(Asks about adaptive skills rather than focusing on affect)* You didn't tell her that it isn't so?

PATIENT: I kinda got that across.

THERAPIST: *(In conversational style)* What did you say to her? How did you go about trying to present yourself?

PATIENT: She started on the attack right away, so I was just trying to defend myself. But in the case of Jerry, I didn't have a good answer, so I can see where she might have had a point in being confused.

THERAPIST: *(Clarifies)* She may be confused about what's going on between you and Jerry, but does that make it correct for her to impute that you are involved with drug users who buy you dinner and immediately want sex?

PATIENT: I don't know where she dreams up the world she's living in.

THERAPIST: *(mildly confronts the patient's prior selling herself short, focusing on adaptive strategies)* These are familiar stereotypes, but these stereotypes are not you. Did you explain that to her?

PATIENT: I couldn't even comment.

THERAPIST: *(Proposes clarification)* It's understandable that when something is outrageous, that you don't know how to think. I wonder if you felt anger at the same time?

PATIENT: Yes, I was furious.

THERAPIST: *(Cushions confrontation to avoid forcing patient to agree or disagree)* Maybe anger plays a part in some of the feeling of uncertainty you describe at other times. That's not the only possible explanation, but it could play a part.

EMPIRICAL SUPPORT

Supportive psychotherapy has not been thought of as a potent modality of treatment, so it is not surprising that it has not been the subject of many studies. Psychotherapy research has paid much attention to the concept of therapeutic alliance, and although supportive psychotherapy involves more than maintaining a supportive relationship (Winston, Pinsker & McCullough, 1986), the repeated finding that therapeutic alliance is a crucial variable is relevant.

Supportive maneuvers have been shown to be at least as helpful as drugs or other therapies (such as cognitive, behavioral, or insight-oriented therapy) in the treatment of coronary artery disease (Razin, 1982), opiate addiction (Woody et al., 1983), phobia (Klein, Zitrin, Woerner, & Ross, 1983), and "anxious depressives" (Schwab, 1984).

Probably the strongest support for the value of supportive therapy has come from the findings of two large studies. One involved several years of treatment of chronic schizophrenic patients (Carpenter, 1984), and the other was the forty-year Menninger Clinic study of psychotherapy with severely disabled nonpsychotic patients (Wallerstein, 1989). Contrary to their predictions, supportive psychotherapy proved at least as effective as expressive methods, and in some cases, more so. On the other hand, Horowitz, Marmar, Weiss, DeWitt, & Rosenbaum (1984), in a study of psychotherapy of patients with bereavement reactions, observed that supportive actions by therapists were positively related to better outcome for patients who had low development-level scores, while there was a negative relationship for those who had high development-level scores.

Process research is now beginning to examine supportive maneuvers. Hill et al. (1988) showed that interventions intended as supportive are rated as not helpful by therapists, but are rated as moderately helpful by patients.

The Beth Israel Psychotherapy Research Program is continuing Hill et al. (1988) and Elliot et al.'s (1987) style of intensive process analysis, using videotaped sessions and the Psychotherapy Interaction Coding System (McCullough, in press), which codes both therapist and patient behaviors for each minute of a fifty-minute session. A preliminary analysis of data comparing individual dynamic supportive psychotherapy with Intensive Short-Term Dynamic Psychotherapy (see chapter 4, by Laikin, Winston, & McCullough), a confrontional therapy based on Davanloo (1980), and Brief Adaptational Psychotherapy (BAP) developed at Beth Israel (see chapter 8, by Pollack, Flegenheimer, & Winston) has been completed. Therapists in the supportive mode were significantly more likely to give information, make directive statements, or use self-disclosure than were the therapists providing more insight-oriented or expressive therapies. They were less likely to use confrontation. The groups did not differ in the number of clarifications or interpretations. However, the content of interpretations was significantly different in the supportive condition. Defensive maneuvers were interpreted only one-fourth as often, and no transference or patient–therapist issues were interpreted in the sessions analyzed so far. Although the number of actual supportive interventions is relatively low in the supportive group, it is significantly different from the other conditions, in which support rarely occurs. The supportive therapists used many more informational interventions (eighteen per session, compared with one per session in the other groups) and much less confrontation (four per session, in contrast to twelve to thirty per session).

The patients in the supportive group showed differences from the ISTDP and BAP groups, whereas the ISTDP and BAP patients' responses were more similar to each other. Defensive responding is the most notable difference because of the higher frequency of intermediate responses (nineteen per session, compared with nine) and the reduced number of immature responses. The brief anxiety-provoking therapies seem to elicit more immature responding, while the ego-building supportive therapy allows or even encourages intermediate defensive responses (such as intellectualization and rationalization).

Outcome research is beginning to demonstrate the efficacy of supportive interventions, and process research is beginning to intensively examine these interventions in relation to other interventions and other aspects of treatments.

CONCLUSION

We believe that the efficacy of supportive psychotherapy can be enhanced and the satisfaction of the therapist increased if the therapy is conceptualized as a distinct modality of dynamic psychotherapy and if it is appreciated that doing it well requires considerable skill. Supportive psychotherapy is usually recommended as the treatment of choice for the lower-functioning patient. We believe it should be the treatment of choice for most patients. There is ample precedent in medicine for holding the more invasive and more expensive treatments in reserve for use only when the gentler treatment has been found ineffective.

References

Anchin, J. C., & Kiesler, D. A. (Eds.). (1982). *Handbook of interpersonal psychotherapy.* New York: Pergamon Press.

Bellak, L. (1978). *Emergency psychotherapy and brief psychotherapy.* New York: Grune & Stratton.

Beres, D. (1956). Ego deviation and the concept of schizophrenia. In *The Psychoanalytic Study of the Child* (*11*, 164–236).

Buckley, P. (1986). A neglected treatment. *Psychiatric Annals, 16*, 515–521.

Carpenter, W. T. (1984). A perspective on the psychotherapy of schizophrenia project. *Schizophrenia Bulletin, 10*, 599–603.

Crown, S. (1988). Supportive psychotherapy: A contradiction in terms? *British Journal of Psychiatry, 152*, 266–269.

Davanloo, H. (Ed.). (1980). *Short-term dynamic psychotherapy.* New York: Jason Aronson.

DeLeo, D. (1989). Treatment of adjustment disorders. A comparative evaluation. *Psychological Reports, 64*, 51–54.

Dewald, P. A. (1971). *Psychotherapy: A dynamic approach* (2nd ed.). New York: Basic Books.

Elliot, R., Friedlander, M., Hill, C., Mahrer, A. R., Margison, F. R., & Stiles, W. B. (1987). Primary therapist response modes: Comparison of six rating systems. *Journal of Consulting and Clinical Psychology, 55*, 218–233.

Freud, S. (1955). Lines of advance in psychoanalytic therapy. In J. Strachey (Ed. & Trans.), *The standard edition of the complete psychological works of Sigmund Freud* (Vol 17, pp. 157–168). London: Hogarth Press. (Original work published 1919.)

Freyberger, H., Kunsebeck, H. W., Lempa, W., Wellman, W., & Avenarius, H. J. (1985). Psychotherapeutic interventions in alexithymic patients, with special regard to ulcerative colitis and Crohn's patients. *Psychotherapy and Psychosomatics, 44,* 72–81.

Glover, E. (1931). The therapeutic effect of inexact interpretation: A contribution to the theory of suggestion. *International Journal of Psycho-analysis, 12,* 397–411.

Havens, L. (1986). *Making contact: Uses of language in psychotherapy.* Cambridge, MA: Harvard University Press.

Hill, C. E., Helms, J. E., Tischenor, V., Spiegel, S. B., O'Grady, K. E., & Perry, E. S. (1988). Effects of therapist response modes in brief psychotherapy. *Journal of Counseling Psychology, 35,* 22–233.

Hopkins, T. (1982). *How to master the art of selling.* New York: Warner.

Horowitz, M., Marmar, C., Weiss, D., DeWitt, K. N., & Rosenbaum, R. (1984). Brief psychotherapy of bereavement reactions. *Archives of General Psychiatry, 41,* 438–448.

Kaufman, E., & Reoux J. (1988). Guidelines for the successful psychotherapy of substance abusers. *American Journal of Drug and Alcohol Abuse, 14,* 199–209.

Kernberg, O. F. (1984). *Supportive psychotherapy in severe personality disorders: Psychotherapeutic strategies.* New Haven, CT: Yale University Press.

Klein, D. F., Zitrin, C. M., Woerner, M. G., & Ross, D. C. (1983). Treatment of phobias. Behavior therapy and supportive psychotherapy: Are there any specific ingredients? *Archives of General Psychiatry, 40,* 139–145.

Klerman, G. L. (1984). *Interpersonal psychotherapy of depression.* New York: Basic Books.

Langs, R. (1973). *Techniques of psychoanalytic psychotherapy.* New York: Jason Aronson.

Luborsky, L. (1984). *Principles of psychoanalytic psychotherapy: A manual for supportive-expressive treatment.* New York: Basic Books.

McCullough, L. (in press). An overview of the psychotherapy interaction coding system. *Social and Behavioral Science Documents.*

Pine, F. (1984). The interpretive moment. *Bulletin of the Menninger Clinic, 48,* 54–71.

Razin, A. M. (1982). Psychosocial intervention in coronary artery disease: A review. *Psychosomatic Medicine, 44,* 363–387.

Rockland, L. H. (1989). *Supportive therapy: A psychodynamic approach.* New York: Basic Books.

Schwab, J. J. (1984). Anxiety in depression. *Clinical Therapeutics, 6,* 536–545.

Sullivan, H. S. (1953). *The interpersonal theory of psychiatry.* New York: Norton.

Viederman, M. (1984). The active dynamic interview and the supportive relationship. *Comprehensive Psychiatry, 25,* 147–157.

Wallace, E. R. (1983). *Dynamic psychiatry in theory and practice.* Philadelphia: Lea & Febiger.

Wallerstein, R. S. (1989). The psychotherapy research project of the Menninger Foundation: An overview. *Journal of Consulting and Clinical Psychology, 57,* 195–205.

Weissman, M. M. (1979). The psychological treatment of depression: Evidence for the efficacy of psychotherapy alone, in comparison with and in combination with pharmacotherapy. *Archives of General Psychiatry, 36,* 1261–1269.

Werman, D. S. (1984). *The practice of supportive psychotherapy.* New York: Brunner/ Mazel.

Winston, A., Pinsker, H., & McCullough, L. (1986). A review of supportive psychotherapy. *Hospital and Community Psychiatry, 37,* 1105–1114.

Woody, G. E., Luborsky, L., McClellan, A. T., O'Brien, C. P., Beck, A. T., Blaine, J., Herman, I., & Hole, A. (1983). Psychotherapy for opiate addicts. *Monographs of the National Institute of Drug Abuse Research, 43,* 59–70.

CHAPTER 10

Brief SASB-Directed Reconstructive Learning Therapy

Lorna Smith Benjamin*

GUIDING PRINCIPLES

Undergoing the process of psychotherapy is like learning to ski: to the beginner, the task is both attractive and frightening, and one must be strongly motivated to undertake this intimidating activity. In both skiing and psychotherapy, the novice can see that there are many folks who seem to enjoy the endeavor, and that they are willing to spend amazing amounts of money on it. But the process is not for everyone. There are those who have certain handicaps that interfere with development of the needed skills for mastery. On the other hand, there are adaptations and variants to the basic approach which can be implemented by certain creative and highly motivated handicapped persons.

The fundamental principles of learning to ski and of learning in psychotherapy are relatively simple to state, but not so easy to execute: take lessons and practice, because they will help you develop good form, and that will serve you well in the difficult spots. The would-be therapist/instructor should expect to become quite skilled in what is being taught and know that certification involves an extended, usually painful learning process. Even after therapist learning has reached high levels, expert thera-

*Thanks are expressed to friends and associates who made helpful comments on an earlier draft of this paper: Hans H. Strupp, Paul Crits-Christoph, Jacques Barber, and the patient identified as SDPD.

pists, like expert skiers, know there always will be times when they fall, and they need not attempt to deny this vulnerability.

The analogy between psychotherapy and learning to ski is particularly apt when discussing the increasingly popular concept of brief psychotherapy. After killing the third-party goose that was laying golden eggs for years, psychotherapists and patients have been confronted with demands for (often very) brief psychotherapy. Under the learning model, brief psychotherapy can make sense: goals can be set, principles articulated, and a few basic skills imparted; then the person can then go off on his or her own to practice. As with the skier, the psychotherapy student is at some point ready to come back for another series of lessons, to correct recurrent bad habits, or to learn new skills in order to go on to higher levels.

The comparison of psychotherapy to learning a complicated skill like skiing is sharply discordant with the medical model, which dominates current thinking. The medical model holds that mental disorders are diseases transmitted by defective genes, and that they are best treated by chemicals or other physical interventions such as electroshock or surgery. Even though there is a long and venerable tradition in the literature of seeing psychotherapy as a learning process (Marmor & Woods, 1980), clinicians and researchers have been reluctant to make the comparison explicit. Perhaps if psychotherapy were defined as a problem in learning, third-party payments would be withheld, and eventually therapists might be reimbursed as teachers, a group that is notably underpaid.

Despite the economic and political risks, a view of psychotherapy primarily as a learning experience offers many advantages, not the least of which is provision of a frame of reference within which it is possible to construct testable theories about causes of mental disorders and to develop logically related psychosocial treatment plans. Moreover, the learning frame can relate directly to the definition of mental disorder offered in the official nomenclature of the American Psychiatric Association, the *DSM III-R*. There, mental disorder is defined as a "behavioral or psychological syndrome or pattern that occurs in a person and that is associated with present *distress* (a painful symptom) or *disability* (impairment in one or more important areas of functioning) or with significantly increased risk of suffering, death, pain, disability, or an important loss of freedom" (American Psychiatric Association, 1987, p. xxii).

The view presented in this chapter is that successful psychotherapy, no matter what its theoretical basis, helps the patient to learn about his or her interpersonal and intrapsychic patterns and to develop better alternatives—both more adaptive in the here and now and both associated with less subjective distress. Because it directly addresses the two key aspects of mental disorder, maladaptivity and subjective distress, the learning interpretation of psychotherapy is in fact as relevant to the medical definition as are the more purely somatic approaches based on a "disease" model. It should be added that the description of psychotherapy primarily as a learning process does not rule out use of medications normally associated with the disease model. Practitioners of psychotherapy can and should refer to qualified professionals for the prescription of drugs, which can provide needed biochemical support in times of crisis or offer relief to individuals with certain limitations. Just as it is widely assumed that genes affect athletic ability, a learning view of psychotherapy also naturally acknowledges major contributions from inherited factors.

Ideally, the psychotherapist who uses a learning model selects from any of the hundreds of available therapy approaches (Goldfried, Greenberg, & Marmar, 1990) to optimize the learning for a given patient at a given stage of psychotherapy. The critical elusive questions for this somewhat self-evident analysis of psychotherapy as a learning experience are these: How does one precisely define patterns that are maladaptive and associated with subjective distress? How does one select an approach that will be optimally effective in changing these patterns at any given moment? and How does one evaluate the effects of the intervention?

At this point the present approach departs noticeably from many others, answering the questions how to define maladaptive interactive and intra-psychic patterns and how to assess the effects of interventions through the Structural Analysis of Social Behavior, or SASB (Benjamin, 1974, 1984). The key proposition is that each of the mental disorders in the *DSM III-R* is hypothetically associated with specific SASB-codable interpersonal and intrapsychic patterns. This thesis has been explicated for the *DSM III-R* Axis II personality disorders in a forthcoming monograph (Benjamin, in press) wherein the SASB model is used to describe each personality disorder in terms of characteristic interpersonal and intrapsychic patterns. The SASB model also provides hypotheses about specific associated interpersonal learning experiences presumed to contribute to the disorder; the analysis has specific implications for learning experiences needed to change the patterns characteristic of the respective disorders. Comparable SASB-based hypotheses for the Axis I disorders are undergoing informal clinical field trials.

In addition to providing descriptions of characteristic patterns for disorders and their hypothetical interpersonal antecedents, SASB codes of patient responses to a given intervention can provide information about whether the intervention has reinforced old patterns or whether it has moved the patient in the direction of a more adaptive orientation. The use of the SASB model to define patterns and to plan and assess interventions is called SASB-directed Reconstructive Learning (SASB-RCL).

Since learning and dynamic therapy approaches have historically been placed in opposition (Mischel, 1973; Wachtel, 1973), it is important to clarify how the SASB-RCL approach to psychotherapy can be characterized as dynamic even though it explicitly invokes principles of learning. Gordon Allport defined personality as "the dynamic organization within the individual of those psychophysical systems that determine his unique adjustments to his environment" (1937, p. 48). When he used the word *dynamic,* Allport referred to the person's goals and purposes. The SASB-RCL approach also centers on the concept of goals because interpersonal wishes and fears must carefully be assessed and addressed before therapeutic change can occur. These interpersonal goals may or may not be unconscious, and they are assumed to function just as do more traditional reinforcers such as money, food, or sex. If, for example, a person wishes to have the approval of a withholding and critical parent, then the patient is likely to engage in actions that he or she imagines might generate approval from that parent. Each therapy plan considers possible unconscious interpersonal reinforcers, and standard psychoanalytic procedures such as free association and dream analysis are used to observe the unconscious. Also consistent with the psychoanalytic viewpoint is the belief that insight and understanding facilitate the change process.

The dynamic therapy described here can be brief since the length of the therapy can be determined arbitrarily. It can last until hospital discharge, or for the number of sessions permitted by the patient's HMO, or for a number of sessions set by any other contingencies. As long as there can be a single session, there can be learning. On the other hand, to ask when the therapy is finished is like asking when has one learned to ski, or to play the piano, or to speak French. The answer is relative to the starting level and to desired goals. If the task of therapy is to start with a patient with personality disorder who has already been unsuccessfully treated with medications, multiple hospitalizations, and various psychotherapies, and to finish with a reconstruction of the personality that includes no more suicide attempts and that permits the person to function consistently well in love and at work, then a long period of learning and practice is required. Two to four years of SASB-RCL therapy meeting at least once a week, with some periods of more frequent contact, would be reasonably brief compared with the normative expectation that this type of disorder could require continual support for decades, perhaps even for a lifetime.

Ideally, SASB-RCL continues until there has been a "reconstruction," meaning the problem patterns are no longer very likely to emerge and new and more adaptive patterns are the ones usually experienced by the individual and observed by the people who know him or her well. For patients with personality disorders, a therapy that implements such a reconstruction within a year is quite brief.

When resources are limited either by patient or therapist contingencies, then the therapy can be far more brief, provided the goals are reduced to specific targets. An example would be to set a limited goal during hospitalization of helping the patient specifically and concretely understand how his or her perceptions and feelings do make sense, and to understand which specific interpersonal changes can be implemented with further work. Brief inpatient therapies also can focus on a quintessential issue with the hope that subsequent natural processes will help the patient follow the new directions marked by this issue. For example, a young person presenting with schizophreniform disorder could be helped to respond better to medications or to "outgrow" the crisis by a brief inpatient psychotherapy concentrating exclusively on self-definition relative to enmeshed parents. The therapist could support the vital signs of differentiation, for example, by affirming the patient's own choice of lipstick color despite her admirably groomed mother's insistence that another color is better for her. Such validation of the patient's right to discover her own person, if delivered before the schizophrenic life style has evolved, might make the difference between a schizophreniform episode and a lifetime of schizophrenia.

Brevity, then, is relative to the task and to the norms for the task. Brevity is implemented by sharpness of focus, and by consistency in adhering to the selected goals. A brief therapy is defined when the therapy has been effective in reaching its specific goals, and when no time or money has been wasted on maintaining old maladaptive wishes or fears.

HISTORY OF THE DEVELOPMENT OF THE METHOD AND ORIGIN OF THE IDEAS.

The SASB-RCL method consists of two aspects: (1) the interpretation of psychotherapy as a learning experience, and (2) the use of the SASB model to describe patterns, etiology, wishes, fears, treatment interventions, and the effects of interventions. The history of each aspect will be reviewed separately.

Psychotherapy as a Learning Experience

The present version of a learning approach to psychotherapy describes problems, etiologies, interventions, and outcomes in terms of SASB codes. In that effort, there is heavy reliance on the work of many others, starting with Freud (1896/1959), who convincingly argued that childhood experiences have a profound impact on the adult personality. Freud's ideas about the development of mental disorders were given interpersonal emphasis by Henry Stack Sullivan (1953), and, to a lesser but still noticeable extent, by modern object relations theorists (Greenberg & Mitchell, 1983).

Meanwhile, using an entirely different approach based initially on studies with rats and pigeons, B. F. Skinner and his colleagues (see Keller & Schoenfeld, 1950) effectively identified important learning principles that can be seen to be omnipresent during psychotherapy. The most useful of these include the concepts of positive and negative reinforcement, punishment, reinforcement schedules, extinction, fading, shaping, stimulus generalization, and discrimination. The idea of connecting the learning literature to psychoanalysis was introduced as early as 1940 by Herbert Mowrer. The application of concepts from the operant conditioning literature to the psychotherapy process is especially effective if the contingencies are described in terms of SASB codes of interpersonal and intrapsychic patterns.

The SASB-RCL learning view of pathology and of therapy assumes that mental disorder represents an *adaptation* to previous interpersonal dilemmas, rather than a "breakdown." From the point of view of the patient, the patterns characteristic of the disorder must have been reinforced at some time, and must continue to make internal sense. The psychotherapist's task is to help the patient learn how his or her apparently maladaptive or subjectively uncomfortable patterns evolved and how they once served adaptive purposes. Then the patient must assess whether the patterns are still adaptive, and if convinced they no longer work, begin the task of learning patterns that are more adaptive in the here and now.

Consider the seemingly maladaptive behavior of a person with self-defeating personality disorder (SDPD). One might ask how negating the self can be seen as adaptive. How can self-defeating behavior sustain itself through reinforcement? In an actual case of self-defeating personality disorder (SDPD), which will be cited throughout this paper, how can one say that it is adaptive for a woman whose husband has just left her for another woman to invite him to come to her home for brunch and bring the other woman? How can one say it is adaptive for this person to maintain a pattern of dutifully shopping for groceries for her adult sons, each of whom lives in his own apartment, and each of whom mocks, degrades, and refuses her if she requests that he go along with her to the store? How can her patterns at work be adaptive, if she puts in astonishing numbers of extra hours evenings and weekends in order to meet unreasonable deadlines? How can it have been adaptive for her to stay in a work place where she is denied appropriate support staff and where she does not receive adequate compensation either in money or in acknowledgment?

The answer lies in a careful assessment of her early history and present unconscious or preconscious views of herself. By taking the perspective of Sullivan's (1953) participant observer, it is possible to discover that the self-defeating behavior of this woman can be seen as adaptive according to a learned complex of family rules. These are not apparent to the outside observer, but they can be discerned by an empathic interviewer who listens while making the assumption that all interactions make sense from an internal perspective.

This woman with SDPD had been taught that she, the only healthy child of three, was responsible for the care of her needy and overstressed mother and her two siblings: a sister who was brain damaged, and a brother who suffered from chronic mental illness. This future SDPD patient had been so obviously neglected that she was often invited (and permitted) to take meals and sleep over at a neighbor's home. The demands that she have no needs of her own, that she devote herself to the care of others, were reinforced by a religious orientation that held that the highest moral value is to be humble, to sacrifice oneself for the sake of others, and to show no anger. In light of this background, the woman's tendency to ignore her own feelings and needs, to minister faithfully to her alcoholic husband and his other woman, to cater to her demanding sons, and to try to satisfy her exploitive bosses can be seen as a continuation of striving for the approval of her parents and of God. According to *her understanding* of the rules of good personhood, self-defeating behavior was a maximally adaptive ideal.

The SASB model provides a sharply focused but broadly applicable description of key aspects of intrapsychic and interpersonal patterns in the past and makes the parallels to the present more obvious. Events that seem to have only distant relationships to one another can be connected directly if they can be shown to have the same underlying SASB dimensionality. It will become clear in the next section that the SASB codes for the patient's mother, her siblings, her alcoholic husband, her sons, and her bosses were all the same, even though her specific interactions with these people differed. Consistency can be seen in her pervasive guilt and in the fact that in each relationship she was compliant as she delivered nurturance and

254

sought affirmation, which rarely was forthcoming—and which made her uncomfortable if it was offered. There also were implicit accusations of others in her recounting of the details of their demands. The self-negating patterns were nothing more or less than repetitions of the way it was in childhood, and they were maintained in adulthood by her supposition of their continuing validity.

The idea that mental illness is an adaptation maintained by reinforcing contingencies is not new. Certainly Freud's notion of thanatos, circular though it may have been, represented acknowledgment that maladaptive patterns must be maintained by some force. Sullivan (as in 1953, pp. 113–122), who reflected carefully on the infant's efforts to avoid anxiety in relation to the "mothering one," invoked principles of interpersonal learning to account for mental disorder. Many other theorists, one of the more notable having been Theodore Millon (1982), have also used the concept of social reinforcers in understanding mental disorders.

Uses of the SASB Model

The SASB model is atheoretical with respect to schools of therapy. In addition to being used to guide the present learning-based view of psychotherapy, the SASB model can be used to code process and outcome from a variety of therapeutic approaches. It is being used in the European Collaborative Study of Psychotherapy to compare and contrast Gestalt, client-centered, and psychoanalytic psychotherapy (Klaus Grawe, personal communication, 1990). The only requirement for use of the SASB model is that the material to be analyzed must be interactional: something or someone must interact with something or someone else. The interaction need not be explicitly interpersonal. One can use the SASB model to code the patient's relationship with abstractions: his headache, her trust fund, the welfare agency, her psychotherapy, his medications, and so on.

The history of the SASB model has been reviewed elsewhere (Benjamin, 1974, 1984). In brief, the model was based first on Earl Schaefer's (1965) factor-analytic circumplex model of parenting behavior validated in a variety of cultures, and then extended to incorporate the interpersonal circumplex proposed by Timothy Leary and his colleagues (1957). The latter was based on Henry Murray's (1938) description of basic human needs. Although its predecessors were in the form of a single circumplex, the SASB model consists of three surfaces. Among the advantages offered by the three-surface version are its ability to link intrapsychic patterns to interpersonal experience and its capacity to define differentiation. The ability to define friendly differentiation, to articulate the notion of a self that is clearly defined yet maintains attachment (see Berlin & Johnson, 1989),* is crucial to the capacity to define normal behavior as qualitatively different from pathological behavior. A simplified version of the SASB full model, the cluster version, appears in figure 1.

The algorithm for cluster names is simple. Clusters located on the top surface of the model all begin with 1; those on the second, with 2; and those on the third, with 3. The second part of the cluster number ranges from 1 to 8, starting with 1 at twelve o'clock and proceeding clockwise to cluster 8. For example, in figure 1, Cluster 1-4, nurturing and protecting, is on the first surface, and it is the fourth one down from the top.

Consider the SASB cluster codes for the woman with SDPD described above. For research purposes, the SASB coding of a clinical description or narrative is usually done phrase by phrase (Humphrey & Benjamin, 1989; Grawe-Gerber & Benjamin, 1989). In clinical practice, the coding can be more selective, focusing on prototypic statements. The SASB model will be explained by showing how it can be used to describe the prototypic behaviors of the woman with SDPD as she tried to take care of relatives who criticized her for being selfish and stubborn and difficult.

SASB coding begins by designating two interactive *referents:* in this case the patient, X, who is acting upon others (mother, siblings, husband, bosses), Y. Coding proceeds from the point of view of X and starts with consideration of whether X is (1) focusing on Y, (2) focusing on himself or herself in relation to Y, or (3) directing an action inward upon himself or herself. These three types of focus are represented by the stick figures at the top of figure 2 and by the three diamonds on figure 1 respectively labeled other, self, and introjection. In this example, the patient, X, focuses on her mother (and/or siblings or sons), Y, as she cleans the house, prepares the meals, runs errands, and tries to help in every way possible. The decision that she is focused on others means that the coding of her efforts will be on the top, or transitive, surface of figure 1.

The second coding decision is whether the transaction is friendly or hostile; this is represented on the horizontal axis of the model, shown at the center of figure 2. The patient's efforts to take care of her mother and the others are friendly, say +5 on the horizontal scale.

The third coding decision is whether the transaction is interdependent or independent, as represented by the vertical axes of figure 2. The vertical scale runs between different poles depending on which surface of the

---

*The use of the SASB model to define differentiation and attachment is discussed at length in Benjamin (in press).

Figure 1

The Cluster version of the SASB Model. The text shows that the illustrative case of SDPD prototypically engaged in behaviors coded at Cluster 1–4, Nurturing and Protecting plus Cluster 2–6, Sulking and Scurrying. Reprinted by permission from Benjamin (1987), copyright 1987 the Guilford Press.

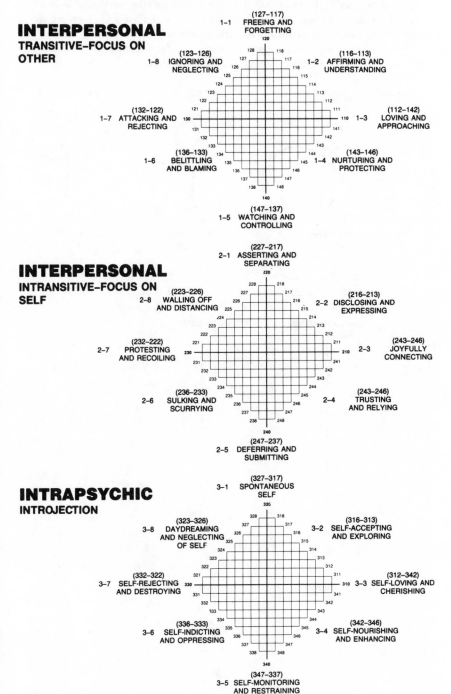

Figure 2

The Three Dimensions of the SASB Model. Therapy content and process expressed in interactional terms can be coded in terms of the three dimensions: focus (the three surfaces of Figure 1), love vs. hate (the horizontal axes of Figure 1), and interdependence (the vertical axes of Figure 1). Viewing all relationships in terms of these dimensions makes parallels among early and current relationships more apparent. Reprinted from Benjamin (1986), by permission of the Guilford Press.

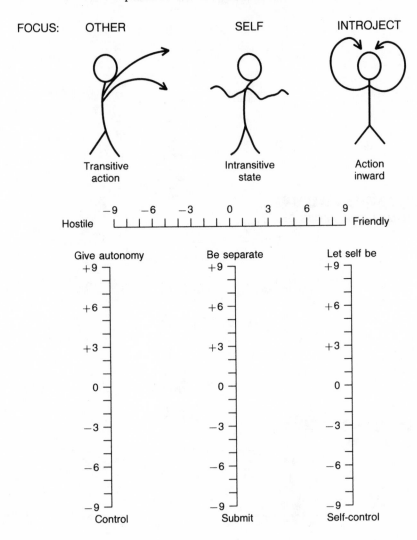

model describes X's position. In this example, the SDPD who takes care of others, the behaviors are transitive, so figure 2 shows that the interdependence judgments will range from control to give autonomy. The patient's role in the family involves some influencing, say 5 units in the controlling direction on the transitive vertical scale (−5).

The final SASB classification is determined by the three judgments: focus (surface), affiliation (horizontal axis), and interdependence (vertical axis). The patient's prototypic set of behaviors has been judged to be transitive (which locates the code on the first surface in figure 1), friendly (+4), and moderately controlling (−5). These judgments create a vector: transitive (+4, −5). On figure 1, a vector drawn to 4 units to the right on the horizontal axis and 5 units downward on the vertical scale projects through Cluster 1-4, Nurturing and protecting. In general, the point at which the underlying vector crosses the boundary of the model yields the SASB code. On the full SASB model, which requires the use of each of the nine points in the scales in figure 2, there are 108 possible classifications, while in the simplified version of figure 1, there are only 24 final categories (eight clusters on each of three surfaces). The underlying geometry and the logic for classification is the same for the full model, the cluster version, and the even simpler quadrant version of SASB (see Benjamin, 1984, for a discussion of the three levels of complexity).

The SASB code of the accusations of mother, husband, sons, bosses (X) toward the patient (Y) were transitive, hostile (−5), and controlling (−4). A vector representing these judgments is transitive (−5, −4), and it crosses the surface's boundaries at Cluster 1-6, belittling and blaming.

Like these two examples, any event, whether it is in the narrative of psychotherapy or in the therapy process itself, can be SASB coded as long as there are two interactive referents (X, Y), and as long as the example is specific enough that there can be readings of friendliness versus hostility (horizontal), and enmeshment versus independence or differentiation (vertical) dimensions.

Predictive Principles

In addition to offering a generic descriptive frame of reference within which relationships can be compared and contrasted, the SASB model has a number of predictive principles, which facilitate identification of patterns and their interpersonal antecedents. The principles that are most useful in identifying connections between early learning and problematic adult patterns are (1) introjection, (2) opposition, (3) complementarity, and (4) similarity.

Introjection.

The third surface of the SASB model describes Sullivan's concept of introjection by recording intrapsychic events that stem from directing transitive action inward. The stick figure at the right-hand side of the top of figure 2 shows that X is directing an action inward upon him or herself. As the illustrative person with SDPD criticized herself, she (X) directed an action inward upon herself (X). For example, in her first session, this patient stated that she wanted to learn to be more "grown up," and documented the need for improvement with a tale of an afternoon when she avoided saying hello to her sons at an athletic event because they were accompanied by their father and the "other woman." The SDPD patient berated herself for not being mature enough to nurture her sons in that context. The SASB code for this self-critical attitude is: introject (the patient directs action inward upon herself), unfriendly (-4), and controlling (-5). The resulting vector $(-4, -5)$, drawn on the third surface of figure 1, crosses the boundary at Cluster 3-6, self-indicting and oppressing.

SASB introject theory suggests that the patient's self-degradation is a result of internalization of the belittling and blaming (Cluster 1-6) she received from her mother, and later, from her husband, sons, and bosses. The treatment implication is that she will need to develop a different perspective on her relationships with these people or on their internal representations in order to stop her self-degradation.

Opposition.

Opposition, described by points located at 180-degree angles on the model, is another important SASB predictive principle. For example, it can be seen on figure 1 that the opposite of 1-6, belittling and blaming, is 1-2, affirming and understanding. For a long time in therapy, this person with SDPD had difficulty accepting the therapist as affirming and understanding. Instead, there was a strong tendency to assume that the therapist was secretly judgmental and hostile. On the Berrett-Lennard relationship inventory, measures of the patient's perception of the therapist, the patient marked "?" for the item "I feel appreciated by her *(therapist)*," and penciled in: "Appreciated for what? I think of this as a transitive verb." In short, this person with SDPD was so accustomed to hostile control that it was difficult for her to perceive its opposite: friendly respect for her as a separate, competent person.

The treatment implication is that the transference will likely be negative, and the therapist must be active showing genuine affirmation (1-2, affirming and understanding) to overcome the patient's tendency to see its opposite (1-6, belittling and blaming).

Complementarity.

This illustrative patient with SDPD continually scurried to please demanding others. These behaviors are coded on the intransitive surface shown in the middle of figure 1 because the emphasis was on X and what she was doing or failing to do, rather than on Y. Her intransitive position was tension-laden (-3 on the horizontal axis), and quite submissive (-6). The vector ($-3, -6$) drawn on the middle surface of figure 1 crosses the boundary at Cluster 2-6, sulking and scurrying.

Her scurrying to please illustrates *complementarity,* another important SASB predictive principle. Complementarity is present if a given interpersonal behavior (coded anywhere on either of the top two surfaces of figure 1) is matched by a behavior at the same location on the other interpersonal surface. Scurrying, 2-6, is the complement of blaming, 1-6. For another example, if the therapist provides the desired affirmation (1-2, affirming and understanding), complementarity theory states that the patient is more likely to respond with its complement (2-2, disclosing and expressing). Robert Carson (1969) was an early proponent of the idea that complementarity can be defined among behaviors described by a circumplex model.

It should be noted that no causal direction is implied by descriptions of complementarity. Blaming (1-6) will elicit scurrying (2-6), but it is also true that scurrying (2-6) will elicit blaming (1-6). Affirming (1-2) will elicit disclosure (2-2), and disclosure (2-2) pulls for affirming (1-2).

Similarity.

Similarity, or identification, is manifest when a person acts like an important earlier figure. For example, this SDPD patient dreaded identifying with her oppressors, but in fact she did show similar attitudes when she privately despised (1-6, belittling and blaming) their inconsiderate ways.

This brief exposition has reviewed how to use the SASB model to describe interpersonal and intrapsychic patterns and how to understand connections between early learning and problematic patterns in adulthood by using the predictive principles. The illustrative case has demonstrated that a few SASB codes can describe the structure of interpersonal and intrapsychic space for a person with personality disorder. Starting in childhood in relation to parents and siblings, this woman's early patterns extended in adulthood to her relationship with her husband, her sons, and her bosses. In all these relationships, she was aptly described by a prototypic position of hustling (2-6, sulking and scurrying) to take care of others (1-4, nurturing and protecting). Because her caregiving (1-4) was inextricably mixed with appeasement (2-6), her final prototypic code is recorded as: [1-4 + 2-6], and is called complex. It is a complex code because this person did not at times nurture and at times comply; rather, she always combined the two positions. Her acts of nurturance were always accompanied by resentful compliance with the assumed demand that she nurture. Her nurturance was locked into a context of exploitation and abuse.

SELECTION OF PATIENTS

SASB-RCL therapy is appropriate only if the patient and therapist both speak the same language—normally English in the United States.

The model is collaborative, and patient and therapist must be able to agree that the therapy has the goal of building personal strength. The acceptance of a learning model and a willingness to focus on and work with the self are required. In cases where the therapy is court ordered or if other kinds of noncollaborative coercion are involved, the therapist's first task is to provide experiences that encourage trust and collaboration and that can stimulate the desire to build personal strength. These preliminary and vital tasks do not comprise the therapy itself. Paradoxically, in cases of unwilling clients, once collaboration appears so that therapy can begin, major constructive changes already will have been made!

Persons who cannot, after a reasonable trial period, enter the collaborative mode to enhance their personal strength also cannot be successfully treated by SASB-RCL. Examples of such inappropriate cases are people who cling to the "wrong patient syndrome"—those who cannot resist blaming and complaining about others and who are utterly unwilling to work on enhancing their own strength. Persons who abuse alcohol and other drugs frequently have the wrong patient syndrome. Referral to Alcoholics Anonymous or Narcotics Anonymous, where powerful and enlightened group process can take place, can sometimes prepare such people for SASB-RCL.

Requests for therapy that violate the therapist's personal norms rule out the necessary collaboration. For example, I once declared myself unsuitable to work with a highly successful and altogether engaging person whose therapy plan was to receive help with time management. His presenting problem was that he was unable to keep both his mistress and his wife and family happy, because they all demanded that he spend considerable time with them, and his professional commitments also were substantial. He insisted that he needed help to maintain all relationships while remaining fully committed to his career.

Normal developmental crises are also inappropriate for SASB-RCL psychotherapy. The college student worried about normal career and relationship decisions should not have his or her lessons in living contaminated by professional input. Similarly, normal existential dilemmas are not appropriately solved in SASB-RCL psychotherapy. An example would be when a person wonders whether to take a new job that offers more money but involves unwanted changes in life style. SASB-RCL psychotherapy cannot help a person make such value choices. In brief, SASB-RCL helps people learn about their maladaptive interpersonal and intrapsychic patterns, and then helps them develop better patterns. Ideally, this learning in psychotherapy clears the way so that the individual has appropriate insight and skills for making his or her own developmental and existential decisions.

Of course, therapy should not be used to manipulate someone without his or her knowledge and consent. One example would be "treatment" geared to "cure" a college student of homosexuality when the person is content with the adaptation. Another would be to engage in attempts to convince a person that he has an incurable, genetically based psychological illness, so that he must accept that his mind is diseased, give up his "inappropriate" attempts to receive an education and find a profession, and come home to receive "proper" care and attention as a mentally handicapped person.

It is possible to use outpatient SASB-RCL psychotherapy with difficult cases that involve chronic threats of suicide or homicide or abuse of drugs and alcohol. However, it is not appropriate to continue with the therapy if these destructive behaviors are not sharply curtailed after an initial trial period of about three months. In other words, the SASB-RCL therapist can agree to try to help a properly motivated person overcome these difficult patterns, but since the patterns are often dangerous and interfere with learning in a major way, there must be unequivocal behavioral evidence that the approach is going to be effective in order for a person to continue in treatment. Similarly, SASB-RCL psychotherapy can be used with persons vulnerable to psychotic thought processes, but only if they show an ability to contain auditory hallucinations most of the time by the use of neuroleptics or by their own will as it is strengthened in therapy.

Certain other disabilities make individuals ineligible for a learning psychotherapy—for example, those with organic brain damage that interferes significantly with their ability to learn about patterns and their consequences. Nor could persons benefit who utterly lack attachment to other human beings. Some of these individuals might be prepared for SASB-RCL therapy by the creation of unconventional learning experiences designed to address the major deficiency. For example, young antisocial personalities might benefit from a carefully structured wilderness camping experience designed to teach them rudiments of trust and trustworthiness.

GOALS OF TREATMENT

After hearing the patient's view of the problem and its desired solution, the therapist explains that SASB-RCL therapy will offer a "chance to learn what your patterns are, where they came from, what they were for, and whether they are worth continuing."

If interested in this task, patients are invited to take the Intrex (SASB) questionnaires. These give the patient an opportunity to rate himself or herself and important others, such as spouse and parents, in terms of the SASB model. The long-form Intrex questionnaires (used in this case) include an item to represent each point on the full SASB model, while the short-form Intrex questionnaires provide a single item for each cluster in figure 1. Raters can assign a number from 0 to 100 to each item, and they are asked to think of ratings of 50 or more as indicating "true." For both versions, the computer program INTERP provides feedback to the patient in terms of the perceived patterns for each relationship. The algorithm suggests whether the patient is maintaining a pattern of complementarity with an oppressive earlier figure, identifying with him or her, or neither. For example, after rating herself in relation to her husband, her mother, and her father, the SDPD patient described above was shown the output from INTERP. The key ratings related to the self-defeating pattern are shown in figures 3 and 4, which respectively present her introject at worst and her reactions to her husband at worst.

A glance at the introject pattern presented in the left-hand side of figure 3 shows that this person with SDPD was very self-attacking at worst. The long lines of plus signs on the left-hand side indicate strong endorsement of self-destructive items. The pattern coefficients, explained in Benjamin

(1984), can range from −1.00 to +1.00 and indicate the degree to which the rater's endorsements of the items conform to the theoretically underlying dimensionality. A positive attack pattern coefficient (ATK) indicates a hostile orientation, while a negative ATK coefficient suggests friendliness. A positive control pattern coefficient (CON) marks enmeshment, while a negative CON suggests differentiation. Positive conflict pattern coefficient (CFL) suggests conflict about enmeshment versus differentiation (vertical axis), while negative CFL shows conflict about love versus hate (horizontal axis). The self-attack in figure 3 is summarized by an ATK pattern coefficient of .895.

The right-hand side of figure 3 suggests that the patient's self-attacking attitudes were associated with her experiences with her husband and her mother. This woman's husband provided the interpersonal antecedents of blaming (1-6), attack (1-7), and neglect (1-8), which, according to SASB introject theory, antedate self-blame (3-6), self-attack (3-7), and self-neglect (3-8). The figure also suggests that the self-restraint (3-5) and self-belittling (3-6) were enhanced by mother's control (1-5) and blaming (1-6).

Figure 4 shows that this woman recoiled from her husband at worst (pattern coefficient = .833) with an especially strong tendency to scurry (2-6) in complementary relation to his blaming (1-6). The right-hand side of figure 4 also suggests that her tendency to scurry while under the control of others has its early beginnings in her relationship with her mother because the complementary relationship with mother suggests that the patient was loving (2-3), trusting (2-4), deferential (2-5), and scurrying (2-6) as mother was warm (1-3), nurturant (1-4), controlling (1-5), and belittling (1-6).

In the early stages of therapy, output like that in figure 3 can demonstrate to the patient that there are "reasons" for poor self-concept, although it by no means conveys the meaning of the introjective process in all of its complexity. Output like that of figure 4 can help the patient understand his or her interpersonal patterns and their antecedents. Usually, with some explanation from the therapist, a patient can understand the output from INTERP and feel reassured to see that the patterns do make sense. As therapy progresses, the goals can be deepened as the patient's understanding increases. For example, after trust in the therapeutic relationship is well established, the possible erotic elements of the self-defeating patterns can be discussed in terms of simple associative learning. Such understanding can help the patient stay in a new relationship with a kinder partner, and try to "reprogram" herself, even though he is not at first as interesting sexually as the abusive partner.

Figure 3

Output from INTERP for the Introject Ratings of SDPD at the Beginning of Therapy. The Attack, control and conflict pattern coefficients are explained briefly in the text, and in detail in Benjamin (1984). This part of the output from program INTERP shows that the patient was very harsh on herself at worst, and that this self-criticism was encouraged by the criticism she received from her husband and from her mother.

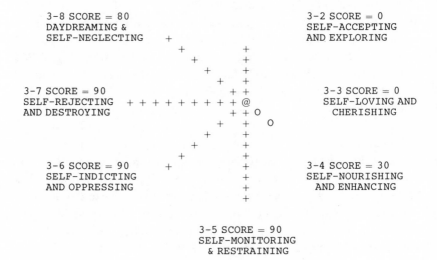

MY INTROJECT OR HOW I SEE MYSELF AT WORST

3-1 SCORE = 50
SPONTANEOUS
SELF

3-8 SCORE = 80
DAYDREAMING &
SELF-NEGLECTING

3-2 SCORE = 0
SELF-ACCEPTING
AND EXPLORING

3-7 SCORE = 90
SELF-REJECTING
AND DESTROYING

3-3 SCORE = 0
SELF-LOVING AND
CHERISHING

3-6 SCORE = 90
SELF-INDICTING
AND OPPRESSING

3-4 SCORE = 30
SELF-NOURISHING
AND ENHANCING

3-5 SCORE = 90
SELF-MONITORING
& RESTRAINING

+ SHOWS THE ITEM WAS MARKED TRUE; O THAT IT WAS FALSE

THE MAXIMUM CORRELATION WAS = .895 WITH PATTERN PROFILE 2
WHICH MEANS THIS RELATIONSHIP IS BEST DESCRIBED AS
  SUICIDAL

ATTACK PATTERN = .895 (PROFILE 2)
CONTROL PATTERN = −.432 (PROFILE 8)
CONFLICT PATTERN = .235 (PROFILE 9)

THEORY OF CHANGE

Mental illness is conceived as an adaptation to social contingencies presented in childhood and recapitulated in adulthood, superimposed upon temperamental factors. The theory of change is that the patient must learn to recognize his or her patterns and understand their payoffs (insight),

ASPECTS OF SELF CONCEPT LISTED IN THE LEFT COLUMN MAY BE
RELATED TO SOCIAL EXPERIENCE LISTED IN THE RIGHT COLUMN

MY INTROJECT OR HOW I SEE MYSELF AT WORST

SPONTANEOUS SELF
        MAY HAVE BEEN INCREASED BY:
        MY SIGNIFICANT OTHER AT BEST (HE OR SHE IS RATED)
            WHEN HE OR SHE WAS:
            FREEING AND FORGETTING
    STATISTICS: R = −.928 (6DF); DIFFERENCE IN Z SCORES = .278

SELF-INDICTING AND OPPRESSING
SELF-REJECTING AND DESTROYING
DAYDREAMING & SELF-NEGLECTING
        MAY HAVE BEEN INCREASED BY:
        MY SIGNIFICANT OTHER AT WORST (HE OR SHE IS RATED)
            WHEN HE OR SHE WAS:
            BELITTLING AND BLAMING
            ATTACKING AND REJECTING
            IGNORING AND NEGLECTING
    STATISTICS: R = .750 (6DF); DIFFERENCE IN Z SCORES = .874

SELF-MONITORING & RESTRAINING
SELF-INDICTING AND OPPRESSING
        MAY HAVE BEEN INCREASED BY:
        MY MOTHER WHEN I WAS AGE 5-10 (SHE IS RATED)
            WHEN HE OR SHE WAS:
            WATCHING AND CONTROLLING
            BELITTLING AND BLAMING
    STATISTICS: R = −.036 (6DF); DIFFERENCE IN Z SCORES = 1.997

decide whether to give them up, and learn new ones. The answer to the question How does awareness lead to change? is as elusive for this approach as for any other. For the present, the answer rests simply on the observation that when people are aware of what they are doing and why, they have more—but not necessarily complete—choice and control over whether to continue.

A therapist using an SASB-based reconstructive learning therapy consistently attempts to understand important events from the perspective of the patient, in terms that are object relational (that is, allow definition of referents X and Y), and that are concrete and specific enough to use figure 2 to code degrees of love and hate (horizontal dimension), and degrees of enmeshment and differentiation (vertical dimension). The therapist's assumption is that social or intrapsychic stimuli and responses are adaptive from the perspective of the patient and that they follow ordinary principles of learning. Specific experiences shape specific symptoms, and mental processes replay original object relations. Diagnosis is in terms of SASB codes of present patterns, and the etiological assumption is that present

Figure 4

Output from INTERP for the Ratings of SDPD with Her Husband. The output
shows that she was very deferential to his attack, and that this was
reminiscent of her position with her mother. Showing patients such output at
the beginning of therapy can help them understand their interactive patterns
and their origins, and assist in setting interpersonal goals.

AS I SEE MYSELF IN RELATION TO MY SIGNIFICANT OTHER AT WORST (I AM RATED)
WHEN IN AN INTRANSITIVE STATE

```
                              2-1 SCORE = 30
                              ASSERTING AND
                              SEPARATING


       2-8 SCORE = 40                          2-2 SCORE = 20
       WALLING OFF                             DISCLOSING AND
       DISTANCING                              EXPRESSING

                              O      O
                           O     O
       2-7 SCORE = 40         O  O  O          2-3 SCORE = 30
       PROTESTING AND  O  O  O  O @ O  O  O     JOYFULLY
       RECOILING              +  O  O           CONNECTING
                           +     O    O
                        +        O
                     +           O

       2-6 SCORE = 50                          2-4 SCORE = 30
       SULKING AND                             TRUSTING AND
       SCURRYING                               RELYING


                              2-5 SCORE = 40
                              DEFERRING AND
                              SUBMITTING
```

+ SHOWS THE ITEM WAS MARKED TRUE ; O THAT IT WAS FALSE

THE MAXIMUM CORRELATION WAS = .833 WITH PATTERN PROFILE 4
WHICH MEANS THIS RELATIONSHIP IS BEST DESCRIBED AS
   HOSTILE INTRANSITIVE STATE OR REACTION

HATEFUL RECOIL PATTERN = .833 (PROFILE 4)
SUBMIT PATTERN = .445 (PROFILE 6)
CONFLICT PATTERN = .167 (PROFILE 18)

patterns represent (1) continuation of earlier positions (sustained complementarity) or (2) identification with (similarity to) important early
figures.

The goal of SASB-RCL therapy is to develop contextually appropriate
interpersonal flexibility within a baseline of friendliness (Clusters 2, 3, and
4), and differentiation (Clusters 1 and 2). In the case of the woman with

INTRANSITIVE STATES OF THE RATER LISTED ON THE LEFT INCREASE LIKELIHOOD OF
THE TRANSITIVE ACTIONS OF THE PERSON RATED ON THE RIGHT—AND VICE VERSA

AS I SEE MYSELF IN RELATION TO MY SIGNIFICANT OTHER AT WORST (I AM RATED)
SULKING AND SCURRYING

       MY STATES WERE MATCHED BY:
       MY SIGNIFICANT OTHER AT WORST (HE OR SHE IS RATED)
              BELITTLING AND BLAMING
       STATISTICS: R = .794 (6DF); DIFFERENCE IN Z SCORES = .740

               ****

INTRANSITIVE STATES OF THE RATER LISTED ON THE LEFT INCREASE LIKELIHOOD OF
THE TRANSITIVE ACTIONS OF THE PERSON RATED ON THE RIGHT—AND VICE VERSA

AS I SEE MYSELF IN RELATION TO MY MOTHER WHEN I WAS AGE 5-10 (I AM RATED)
JOYFULLY   CONNECTING
TRUSTING AND   RELYING
DEFERRING AND SUBMITTING
SULKING AND   SCURRYING

       MY STATES WERE MATCHED BY:
       MY MOTHER WHEN I WAS AGE 5-10 (SHE IS RATED)
              LOVING AND   APPROACHING
              NURTURING AND PROTECTING
              WATCHING AND   CONTROLLING
              BELITTLING AND BLAMING
       STATISTICS: R = .851 (6DF); DIFFERENCE IN Z SCORES = .550

               ****

SDPD, the friendliness was in place, but she needed to learn about differentiation, including how to become angry if appropriate. For this person, the goal of differentiation was explained in simple language: she was told she needed psychologically to separate herself more from the views of those inconsiderate other people.

Interventions in therapy are successful if they block maladaptive patterns or if they enhance new, better patterns. The general approach is to choose interventions that will optimize the chances that the patient will understand, reconsider, and decide to give up old interpersonal and intrapsychic patterns in favor of learning new patterns more appropriate to the here and now.

The most elusive phase of psychotherapy is arriving at the *decision* to give up the old patterns. This vital act of will is facilitated when the patient comes to understand how the patterns are maintained by wishes or fears about his or her relationship with beloved others or their internalized representations. New learning can follow if and only if there is a decision that it is no longer worth it to be directed by the old wishes and fears. This decision need not be conscious, but awareness usually helps. The woman with SDPD, for example, was moved to give up her self-sacrificing ways in relation to her husband, mother, and bosses as she came to realize how angry she was at their outrageous expectations and as she accepted that she never would receive their approval. She did, however, remain in the self-sacrificing mode in relation to her handicapped siblings because she wanted to do so out of an internally directed moral sense of herself.

Occasionally, confrontation of that key underlying organizing wish can occur in a single session. For example, a woman who had suffered a two-year-long intractable depression, which had been unreliably responsive to medication and psychotherapy, sought brief consultation. She was divorced from an apparently self-centered, controlling, and abusive man, and was now in a wonderful new relationship; but she remained depressed, unable to enjoy it. The consultation ended with the interviewer's comment that the patient should bring her ex-husband in for marital therapy. The interviewer observed that maybe he had given up his drug abuse, and maybe he had learned to be more concerned about others; the patient definitely shouldn't miss the chance to recapture this wonderful relationship. The patient left the session thoughtfully, and a few months later called back just to say she felt much better and "empowered." Although she actually had called her ex-husband to see if he would come to such a session, and he had agreed, her subsequent reflection upon this unrealistic wish to recapture her original marital fantasy had freed her to go on and develop the new relationship.

Usually the reconstructive process occurs in about six stages. (1) A collaborative relationship develops between patient and therapist. (2) The patient learns to identify his or her interactive patterns, and where they came from. (3) Unconscious wishes and fears are faced, and directly or indirectly, the patient decides whether it is worth continuing to try to fulfill the wishes and honor the fears. (4) Stages of grief follow the decision to give up the old ways. These resemble the bereavement process described by Kübler-Ross (1969). (5) Panic and chaos follow implementation of the decision to reorganize. Patients say, in effect, "If I am not this, then I don't exist." Being in a massively new and unstructured state typically is terrifying. (6) A new self emerges. At this point, the therapist becomes a midwife, and enjoys the rebirthing process, while remaining on standby to help guard against regression.

TECHNIQUES

Techniques in SASB-RCL therapy must facilitate constructive learning. They are selected and evaluated in terms of whether they block destructive patterns and/or build constructive new ones. Since therapy is a complicated learning process, many different techniques are appropriate at different times.

A Baseline of Empathy

The baseline therapist position in SASB-RCL includes the Rogerian positions of empathic understanding, positive regard, and personal congruence. These are well represented by the SASB, Cluster 2, and the corresponding Intrex short-form items: Therapist 1-2, affirming and understanding—"X likes Y and tries to see Y's point of view even if they disagree." The patient complement is 2-2, disclosing and expressing—"X warmly and openly states his innermost thoughts and feelings to Y." Internalization of the therapy experience is 3-2, self-accepting and exploring—"understanding his or her own faults as well as strong points, X lets him or herself feel good about him or herself 'as is.' "

However, the positive regard is not unconditional, because the therapist does not affirm destructive patterns. The therapist at times takes a powerful position to block reenactment of pathological patterns and to facilitate the development of new ones. This is SASB coded as: 1-4, nurturing and protecting—"With much kindness, X comforts, protects and teaches Y."

Observing the Unconscious

In the middle stages of therapy, the understanding of connections with the past and the uncovering of wishes and fears are priority experiences. These are facilitated by classical analytic techniques such as free association, dream analysis, tracking the stream of consciousness, and so on. The Gestalt derivatives of analysis, such as two-chair techniques, and discussions of "adult" and "child" are also helpful in pattern recognition.

SASB codes of these materials facilitate the identification of connections (see Benjamin, 1986). The therapist does not use SASB language in the session, but the sharp delineation by SASB of the underlying dimensionality of the patterns aids the therapist in choosing metaphors that are usually quite accurate.

In a sense, the SASB formulations of patterns and connections among relationships serve as *clarifications* or *interpretations* in the classical analytic sense. However, unlike the analytic interpretations, the clarifications and interpretations in SASB-RCL therapy are always interpersonal or SASB codable intrapsychic and they are based on patient recollections of very specific interpersonal experiences. If, for example, patient and therapist agree that there is probably is a pattern resembling the classical Oedipus complex, the patient must be dreaming, fantasizing about, or actually recalling clearly romantic contact with a parent. The therapist and the patient can agree that such contact was likely even though no clear memories remain. In this case, both see the oedipal hypothesis as a provisional hypothesis until further evidence emerges. No "interpretation" is maintained without patient collaboration.

It should be noted that many analytic techniques for uncovering were developed under the guidance of the cathartic model. The classical view is that these techniques serve to get out unconscious material, and that in itself is thought to be curative. An extended discussion of the differences between the SASB-RCL model and the cathartic model as applied to the expression of anger appears in Benjamin (1989). There, examples are given to show that encouraging the expression of anger can, in many instances, enhance maladaptive patterns, and in so doing can be iatrogenic. The SASB-RCL approach holds that it is important, when encouraging the expression of buried affect, to be sure that the experience is in the service of changing maladaptive patterns or building constructive new ones.

The Observing Ego

Intense and consistent focus on patient learning about key patterns is the constant objective for the SASB-RCL therapist. The maintenance of relevance makes the therapy briefer. Each intervention is evaluated in terms of whether it enables personal strength by working on problem patterns or enhancing new and better ones. Hypnosis, the use of sodium pentathol, and other methods for gathering unconscious information without active collaboration from the patient's observing ego are usually not invoked in SASB-RCL therapy. Such techniques are vulnerable to encouraging the patient's dependent wishes to merge with an all-powerful magical therapist, and this move toward enmeshment is antithetical to the goals of a learning model.

Helping Patients Observe Themselves

One particularly useful technique for breaking logjams in individual therapy is to hold a single family conference and record it. The goal of this conference is to elicit family perceptions of, wishes for, and fears of one another, and there is an attempt to facilitate understanding and communication. Unfortunately, family members usually approach such conferences with the agenda that others should "shape up," and they are not pleased with any other result, particularly one that might validate the perspective of those others. In fact, a single family conference is unlikely to successfully work out longstanding differences between the patient and others. However, the tape recording of the single conference can be used in subsequent individual sessions to help with pattern recognition. Typically, the resulting tape provides a frightening but potent stimulus for any family members who are in individual therapy. As the patient and therapist listen to the tape together, the bare bones of the interaction patterns are starkly apparent. As the patient listens to himself or herself in the family milieu, the patient's own objective third-party observing ego may be moved toward change, because as the patterns become clear, it is easier to give up fantasies about what can happen.

If an actual family conference cannot be arranged, an alternative is to concentrate on developing an observing ego just prior to a family visit. Taking the mental set of watching for patterns and reflecting on them during the visit, rather than being drawn into useless repetitions of old habits, can give the patient an effective new sense of differentiation. The woman with SDPD was able to use this approach to come to understand that no matter how self-sacrificing her nurturant acts of good will might be, her mother would never approve of her.

SASB Coding of Concepts

All patient–therapist exchanges in SASB-RCL must be SASB codable. This means that at a minimum they must be object relational and quite concrete. Codable material is elicited by liberal use of the question: "Would you please give me an example of that?" repeated until the basic material is at the level of "He said . . . and I said. . . ." Greater specificity enhances clarity and there is evidence that therapies with more uncodable exchanges have poorer outcomes (Mueller, 1985).

Negative Transference

Negative transference offers a wonderful opportunity for new learning. Since the patient and therapist are engaged in a collaborative process, negative feelings must be recognized and discussed as soon as they arise in SASB-RCL therapy. The reasons are: (1) that little learning can occur in an atmosphere of tension and suspicion, and (2) in all likelihood, the negative transference invokes key problematic interactional patterns. Discussion of negative transference assures that the therapist and patient are focusing on basic issues.

Countertransference

Since awareness facilitates choice, and since choice enhances the likelihood that participants will remain at their task, the therapist must be aware of his or her own countertransference feelings and perceptions. If the therapist's special sensitivities can enhance the patient's needed learning, they are not a problem. If, for example, the patient struggles with issues that the therapist has mastered, the therapist may have unusual compassion, which could help rather than hurt the process. However, it is more likely that distortions, overdetermined interest, and so on will interfere, and so they must be known and avoided. The therapist is responsible to identify these vulnerabilities, and either master them or not attempt to work with people who touch on them. A ski instructor who can't handle moguls, for example, would be foolish to give a mogul lesson.

In SASB-RCL the therapy relationship itself can have a central or a peripheral role in the treatment. The personal relationship between the therapist and patient is totally confined to the office and it does not involve physical contact; but within those limits, the relationship can be a major medium for learning. For example, the patient may learn that even though he or she engages in monumentally provocative behavior, the familiar consequences of attack, or seduction or rejection, and so on, do not follow. Such new personal experiences can be vital to the formation of new patterns. But they are not required, for learning can occur in many different ways. Some skiers can learn a great deal by simply watching videotapes, while others need a strong supportive personal relationship with the instructor.

The "White Heat of Relevance"

"Confrontation" and "pointing out" are not characteristic of SASB-RCL therapy because of the high risk that they will be experienced by the patient as 1-6, *belittling and blaming.* Nonetheless, to make therapy brief and effective, every intervention must be meaningful in the sense that it enhances collaboration, patient awareness of patterns, patient will to change, or patient learning of adaptive patterns. By making nearly every statement SASB codable interpersonal or intrapsychic, SASB-RCL therapy usually develops a "white heat of relevance." Sessions are intense and draining on both therapist and patient. A therapist would no more be able to maintain concentration in SASB-RCL for eight sessions in a row than an Olympic skier could safely make championship runs all day long without resting.

CASE EXAMPLE

The woman with SDPD previously discussed was treated for nine months behind a one-way mirror, viewed by senior psychiatric residents as part of a seminar. The criteria for patients selected for that seminar were that the chief complaint had lated for at least ten years and that there had been least two previous failed therapies.

Space limitations preclude full explication of the treatment of this woman with SDPD. Two key and frequently very difficult junctures of her therapy have been selected for illustration: (1) avoiding the draw to enable the negative transference, and turning it instead to self-discovery; and (2) addressing the underlying goals that drove the maladaptive patterns.

Using Negative Transference Interpretation

Maintaining the collaborative relationship is vital, and the therapist must actively block transference distortions in a collaborative, nonjudgmental way. Careful use of humor is one means to discuss negative transference. The following exchange occurred about five months into the therapy, and found the patient in a depressed condition, castigating herself for not being tougher, and commenting bitterly on her destiny as an "adult" who had to cope with an abusive husband, a negligent lawyer, demanding sons, and exploitive bosses. She had just decided she would be unable to take a planned vacation because she had so much to do. (Unfortunately, the quality of the audiotape was very poor, and so there are gaps in the transcript indicated by [unclear].)

THERAPIST: When you think about feeling bad about yourself, what are your thoughts? What do you feel badly about?

PATIENT: I guess like I hate myself for not managing it better, you know, being a little bit stronger emotionally, tougher.

THERAPIST: Managing it, being what?

PATIENT: Well, [unclear] moving through life . . . being tougher . . . I mean like a lot of energy just goes into trucking on, you know, getting up in the morning [unclear] and there's not enough energy to be able to [unclear].

THERAPIST: Yeah, so you're not taking care of yourself and you're feeling that [unclear].

PATIENT: Well, I mean I'm smoking [unclear], I feel pretty out of control in the sense that I know I could have more control, do it.

THERAPIST: So the solution is you should be stronger and tougher, get yourself together.

PATIENT: Uh-huh. Pull myself by the bootstraps . . .

THERAPIST: By the bootstraps, you say?

PATIENT: Yeah. This is called adult life . . . and if you can't enjoy it, it's your own fault.

THERAPIST: OK. We've reviewed the problems and your solution.

PATIENT: Yes.

THERAPIST: Let's see—I guess I could bring a whip next time.

PATIENT: I already have one.

THERAPIST: I noticed.

Here, the therapist marked the fact that the patient was engaged in extensive self-blame (3-6), and with warm humor suggested an outrageous form of therapist blame (1-6), the hypothetical antecedent to introjected self-blame. This immediate result was that the patient reflected on her tendency to self-flagellate. This was followed by examination of her worry that her new lover would become critical of her because he "notices everything":

THERAPIST: And you're worried about that?

PATIENT: I'm worried that that's a very nice thing that's happening.

THERAPIST: Uh-huh.

PATIENT: But you know, with everything else, I'm not sure that I can handle it.

THERAPIST: What does that mean?

PATIENT: Well, maybe it means that I'm not sure I'll let myself enjoy it.

THERAPIST: Yeah. Can you say more about that?

PATIENT: No. But I don't understand myself [unclear].

THERAPIST: You recognize that you might undermine yourself.

PATIENT: Uh-huh.

THERAPIST: And you might take away from yourself the thing you really
need the most . . .

The conversation continued in this vein; the patient was able to stay for
a long time in this new relationship, which presented her with unfamiliar
attentiveness, kindness, and consideration.

Addressing the Underlying Goal

In a different session, the patient reflected on her reaction to the suggestion
that she think about the therapy and how she felt about it.

PATIENT: . . . but I still feel puzzled about what it is I think I want, and
you had said last time that I should think about that. And I took that
to mean, you know, you need to decide who you want to be, what's
your mind-set and emotional-set, what needs to be what you want
to do. I have thought about that and I realize that perhaps one of the
reasons I've had a problem is that, and I've—that I guess I really do
want my life to go, to be in a certain way [unclear]. That may be
overly romanticized . . . that I still value it very much. . . . But time
and again it does conflict with, with other goals or things in the real
world . . . [My husband] used to say I was just a pussycat, and it used
to make me really mad because I . . . care very much about the notion
of people loving one another, taking care of one another, you know.
Life isn't all roses, and people need each other.

THERAPIST: Let me be sure I'm hearing what I think I'm hearing.

PATIENT: OK.

THERAPIST: We're talking about, I asked you how you felt about what
we're doing, you said "I know I need to do something, I don't know
what. You asked me to think about it." Now I think I hear you saying
you're really quite content with what you are and with your ideas,
but you're afraid they won't do in the real world. Is that what you're
saying?

PATIENT: Yes. That they will set me up [unclear] with failing to achieve them, or realize them.

THERAPIST: So you have very high standards but the world can't live up to them. So you're doomed to failure whenever you interact with the world. Is that an accurate statement?

PATIENT: I guess. I guess that's the way I feel also.

THERAPIST: So, to the extent then, that . . .

PATIENT: So you can't, yes, you can't force other people . . . to live your way or adopt your standards. You look for people who share things [unclear].

THERAPIST: Well, so what that means, then, is if in therapy you are to change at all, what we need to do is degrade you, or lower you to a level of the rest of the world.

PATIENT: Yeah, I guess what I worry about is that I've been sort of stubborn and, and maybe afraid to change, too. I haven't thought about, you know, about changing my ideas. . . . I have clung to them over the years, and not wanted to change the way I am.

There followed an exchange during which the patient recalled that her husband mocked her for her high ideals, and the therapist elicited the transference feeling that she was also being mocked in the above exchange. Following the therapist's inquiry about why she still wore her wedding ring, she became very tearful about the loss of her marital relationship. That led to a discussion of her fear of being hurt in her new relationship. The therapist suggested that her injuries in marriage were related to early learning.

PATIENT: Yes, I suspect that a lot of what the behaviors that I have now that have been nurtured over the years in this marriage are old relics that, you know, were convenient in the environment of marriage, [unclear] that would not be convenient if I'm ever to, you know . . .

THERAPIST: So what we're talking about is in your family of origin you had some patterns which you took to the marriage and which you don't want to take with you from here on. Now if we work on that, would that be a degrading agenda?

PATIENT: No.

THERAPIST: OK. All right, then we're agreed. We'll work on that.

PATIENT: I'll need lots of help to see it, because I don't trust myself to be objective.

THERAPIST: No?
PATIENT: I feel really confused.

This crucial session confronted the idea that the patient's moral goals might be driving the self-defeating behaviors that were maintaining her pain. She was able to understand that early patterns had been repeated in her marriage, and that she was vulnerable to repeating them again in her next relationship. She was confused about whether she would need to diminish her moral standards in order to achieve a more comfortable interpersonal adjustment.

Ultimately, in therapy she resolved the conflict by accepting and legitimizing her anger at exploitation, valuing her own contributions, and giving up the noncontingent self-negating nurturance of her husband, her sons, her mother, and her bosses. But she retained her sense of moral obligation to take care of her handicapped siblings, and later on made good on that promise. In short, this kind woman learned to expect and receive decent treatment in her everyday exchanges, while retaining her moral standards to give to others. The change amounted to learning that she herself was worth decent treatment and that she should not suffer exploitation, while at the same time she still could identify contexts in which self-sacrifice was indeed appropriate.

APPLYING SASB TO SPECIFIC POPULATIONS

The general SASB-RCL approach of identifying key patterns, their roots, and their goals, then facilitating goal change and fostering the learning of new patterns, applies to all populations meeting the inclusion/exclusion criteria. For the different populations, different therapist techniques are chosen during each session depending on the nature of the problematic interpersonal and intrapsychic patterns and on the developmental stage of the therapy.

In the monograph identifying prototypic SASB-coded patterns for each of the *DSM III-R* Axis II personality disorders (Benjamin, in press), there is a discussion of typical transference problems as well as of a list of new patterns recommended for the respective disorders. One consequence of this pattern analysis is that therapists have a guide for determining which technique is good for which person at which phase of therapy. To illustrate briefly, while persons with SDPD have difficulty accepting therapist affirmation (1-2, affirming and understanding), persons with narcissistic personality disorder demand it, even when they are engaged in destructive transference reactions. These differences in patient expectations suggest that in cases of SDPD, the therapist needs to maintain the position of benign affirmation more often in order to introduce a new experience and to inspire more self-affirmation. By contrast, in the cases of narcissistic personality disorder, gentle but firm confrontations need to be offered more often (in a supportive way, of course) if there is to be constructive change.

EMPIRICAL SUPPORT

The SASB questionnaires and coding system have been used to describe process and outcome from a number of different theoretical perspectives (Henry, Schacht, & Strupp, 1986; Quintana & Meara, 1990; Grawe, personal communication, 1990). SASB-RCL itself has been formally studied in only three cases, all treated in the one-way mirror, year-long therapy context described above. All three cases met the criteria of a ten-year-long problem and failed previous therapies. All three showed major improvement according to SCL-90 (Derogatis, 1977), MCMI (Million, 1982), and Intrex (Benjamin, 1984) ratings. Selected data from the person with SDPD discussed above appear in figures 5 through 7.

Figure 5 presents changes in SCL-90 ratings for the person with SDPD. It shows she began therapy with quite high scores for obsessive compulsive symptoms, depression, and psychoticism, and all of these exhibited dramatic decreases over the nine-month treatment period.

Figure 6 presents the changes in the MCMI during the same period of time. The MCMI measures are in terms of base rate (BR), which compares scores to known cases and sets 75 percent as a cut point that optimizes the ratio of valid positives to false positives. The upper part of the figure, which depicts the MCMI scales theoretically measuring Axis II personality disorder, shows that this person started therapy with positive classifications (BR > 75) for narcissistic and obsessive compulsive personality disorder. The scores for histrionic and for antisocial personality disorders were close to the boundary for diagnosis. By the end of therapy, all scales for Axis II were comfortably below the critical mark of 75.

The lower part of figure 6 includes Millon's clinical scales. None of these was above the 75 mark at the start or at the end of therapy. It is not clear whether the apparent increases in clinical scores (anxiety, hypomania, alcohol abuse, and psychotic depression) should be interpreted. The pa-

Figure 5

Changes in SCL-90 Scores. These self ratings of traditional psychiatric
symptoms suggested marked improvement during therapy (Derogatis, 1977).

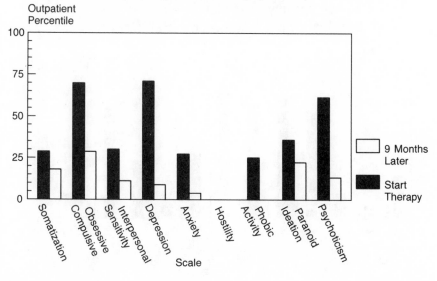

tient's experience of some anxiety and her use of evening cocktails were
discussed in interviews, but neither was defined as a problem.

Figure 7 shows the SASB attack and control pattern coefficients for this
person's major relationships as she experienced them at the beginning of
therapy and at nine months.

Inspection of the figure shows that the patient's pattern of liking herself
a lot at best and attacking herself a lot at worst did not change much from
the beginning to nine months of therapy. Although there was no formal
measure, her worst moments were less frequent later on in therapy. The
only really noticeable changes in the attack patterns themselves were in
some aspects of her relationship with her husband: over the nine months
of treatment, she became somewhat friendlier. Divorce proceedings were
fully under way by the nine-month point in therapy.

Lack of friendliness was never a key issue. Rather, the problem at the
outset was the patient's expression of love in self-defeating ways. Accordingly, the bottom part of figure 7 shows that the major interpersonal
change was from clear enmeshment with her husband to differentiation
from him. The control pattern changes for her relationship with her

Figure 6

Changes in MCMI Scores. At the beginning of therapy, the woman with SDPD scored above the critical base rate of 75, and qualified for the labels narcissistic and compulsive personality disorders. After nine months, she was well below this range. In clinical scales, she did not exceed the critical rate either at the beginning of therapy or at nine months (Millon, 1982).

Changes in MCMI
Personality Disorder Scales
Self Defeating Personality (SDPD)

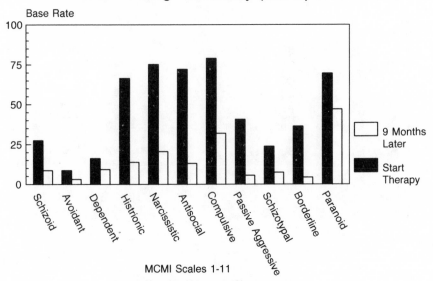

MCMI Scales 1-11

Changes in MCMI
Clinical Scales
Self Defeating Personality (SDPD)

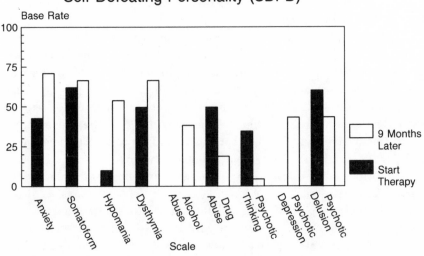

Scale

Figure 7

Changes in SASB Attack and Control Pattern Coefficients. I = introject; B = best state; W = worst state; S = spouse; M = mother. Ratings: 1 = other's (spouse's or mother's) transitive focus on the rater; 2 = other's intransitive reaction to the rater; 3 = rater's transitive focus on other; 4 = rater's intransitive reaction to other. At the beginning of therapy, this woman perceived and showed hostility only toward herself (IW), and in her relationship with her husband at worst (SW). There were no marked remarkable changes in her baseline of friendliness during the nine months of therapy. However, she did show a major change from enmeshment to differentiation in ratings of herself with her husband at worst (SW3,SW4) (Benjamin, 1984).

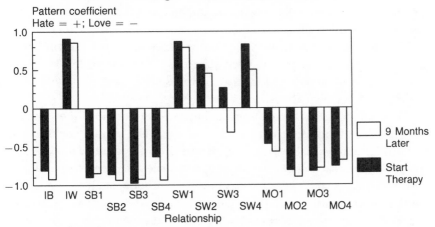

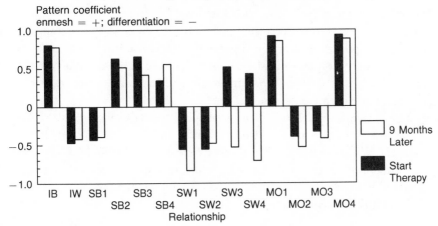

husband at worst shifted from clear interdependence to clear separation for both types of focus (SW3, SW4).

A third SASB parameter, the conflict coefficient, suggested a shift from an attachment conflict to an intimacy–distance conflict in her perception of her husband and in her memory of her mother. Her self-descriptions did not change, but her views of these other key persons did: she came to see them as conflicted over whether they wanted to be close or distant to her, rather than over whether they loved or hated her.

Her ratings of her new relationship with a kind, attentive man were very positive. Theoretically, the internalization of that good new relationship should help her soften the harshness of her introject at worst. The SASB-RCL view is that much interpersonal learning goes on outside of the therapy session, and it is important to identify and facilitate relationships that enhance the goals of therapy.

The patient became more assertive at work, insisting on receiving suitable support services and an appropriate raise. She worked less often on evenings and weekends and instead allocated more discretionary time to activities of her own choosing.

The patient viewed herself as much improved at the end of the seminar, but she asked to continue her work in the therapist's private practice. She did this for another half a year, but unfortunately there are no final ratings available. She asked not to make them, and since assertiveness was a part of the therapy goal, the matter was dropped without comment. At termination she was quite comfortable and, according to her own conversational report five years later, maintained her new adjustments reasonably well.

One might ask: Did she get better or not? Did her patterns change or not? But this is like asking: did she learn to ski or not? It is clear that there was definite improvement. It is also apparent that more learning is needed. SASB-RCL therapy makes no claim to "cure" or to implement "complete change." There is, however, the opportunity to make significant changes that will improve a person's relationship with himself or herself and important others. Without question, this patient broke her rigid devotion to self-defeating patterns and became more skillful in asserting herself on behalf of her own rights and interests.

The current research plans are to obtain funding to validate the SASB diagnoses of the personality disorders, and following that, it is hoped that there can be a project to study the effectiveness of the SASB-RCL approach in a broader way. Other than the three aforementioned cases, the validation of the SASB-RCL approach now rests only on testimonials of patients and therapy trainees.

References

Allport, G. W. (1937). *Personality: A psychological interpretation.* New York: Henry Holt.

American Psychiatric Association. (1987). *Diagnostic and statistical manual of mental disorders: DSM III-R.* Washington DC: American Psychiatric Association.

Benjamin, L. S. (1974). Structural Analysis of Social Behavior. *Psychological Review, 81,* 392–425.

Benjamin, L. S. (1984). Principles of prediction using Structural Analysis of Social Behavior. In R. A. Zucker, J. Aronoff, & A. J. Rabin (Eds.), *Personality and the prediction of behavior* (pp. 121–173). New York: Academic Press.

Benjamin, L. S. (1986). Operational definition and measurement of dynamics shown in the stream of free associations. *Psychiatry: Interpersonal and Biological Processes, 49,* 104–129.

Benjamin, L. S. (1987). Use of the SASB dimensional model to develop treatment plans for personality disorders: I. Narcissism. *Journal of Personality Disorders, 1,* 43–70.

Benjamin, L. S. (1989). Interpersonal analysis of the cathartic model. In R. Plutchik & H. Kellerman (Eds.), *Emotion: Research and experience* (Vol. 5, pp. 209–229). New York: Academic Press.

Benjamin, L. S. (in press). *Structural analysis of interaction patterns in personality disorders.* New York: Guilford Press.

Berlin, S., & Johnson, C. (1989). Women and autonomy: Using Structural Analysis of Social Behavior to find autonomy within connections. *Psychiatry, Interpersonal and Biological Processes, 52,* 79–95.

Carson, R. (1969). *Interaction concepts of personality.* Chicago: Aldine.

Derogatis, L. R. (1977). *SCL-90 administration, scoring and procedures manuals for the revised version.* Baltimore: Leonard R. Derogatis.

Freud, S. (1959). On the psychical mechanism of hysterical phenomena. In E. Jones (Ed.), *Collected papers of Sigmund Freud* (Vol. I, pp. 24–41). New York: Basic Books. (Original work published in 1896.)

Goldfried, M., Greenberg, L. S., & Marmar, C. (1990). Individual psychotherapy: Process and outcome. *Annual Review of Psychology, 41,* 659–688.

Grawe-Gerber, M., & Benjamin, L. S. (1989). *SASB coding manual.* Psychologisches Institut, University of Bern, Switzerland.

Greenberg, J. R., & Mitchell, S. A. (1983). *Object relations in psychoanalytic theory.* Cambridge, MA: Harvard University Press.

Henry, W. P., Schacht, T. E., & Strupp, H. H. (1986). Structural Analysis of Social Behavior: Application to a study of interpersonal process in differential therapeutic outcome. *Journal of Consulting and Clinical Psychology, 54,* 27–31.

Humphrey, L. L., & Benjamin, L. S. (1989). *An observational coding system for use with Structural Analysis of Social Behavior: The training manual.* Unpublished manuscript, Northwestern University, Chicago.

Keller, F. S., & Schoenfeld, W. N. (1950). *Principles of psychology.* New York: Appleton-Century-Crofts.

Kübler-Ross, E. (1969). *On death and dying.* New York: Macmillan.

Leary, T. (1957). *Interpersonal diagnosis of personality: A functional theory and methodology for personality evaluation.* New York: Ronald Press.

Marmor, J., & Woods, S. M. (Eds.). *The interface between the psychodynamic and behavioral therapies.* New York: Plenum.

Millon, T. (1981). *Disorders of personality DSM-III: Axis II.* New York: Wiley.

Millon, T. (1982). *Millon Clinical Multiaxial Inventory manual* (2nd ed.). Minneapolis: National Computer Systems.

Mischel, W. (1973). On the empirical dilemmas of psychodynamic approaches: Issues and alternatives. *Journal of Abnormal Psychology, 82,* 335–344.

Mowrer, O. H. (1940). An experimental analog of "aggression" with incidental observations on "reaction formation." *Journal of Abnormal Psychology, 35,* 56–87.

Mueller, H. P. (1985). *Therapist–patient interaction and therapy outcome in different therapy conditions.* Paper presented at the meeting of the European Society for Psychotherapy Research, Louvain à Neuve, 1985, September.

Murray, H. A. (1938). *Explorations in personality.* New York: Oxford.

Quintana, S. M., & Meara, N. M. (1990). Internalization of therapeutic relationships in short-term psychotherapy. *Journal of Counseling Psychology, 37,* 123–130.

Schaefer, E. S. (1965). Configurational analysis of children's reports of parent behavior. *Journal of Consulting Psychology, 29,* 552–557.

Sullivan, H. S. (1953). *The interpersonal theory of psychiatry.* New York: Norton.

Wachtel, P. L. (1973). Psychodynamics, behavior therapy, and the implacable experimenter: An inquiry into the consistency of personality. *Journal of Abnormal Psychology, 82,* 324–334.

CHAPTER 11

Shorter-Term Psychotherapy: A Self Psychological Approach

Howard S. Baker

Our patients present us with an overwhelming amount of data that we must understand. Whether we know it or not, we have a theory, an organizational schema, that we use to make sense of the information. The theory, *whatever* one we choose, will clarify some things about our patients; but it will obscure other things. James Gustafson put the dilemma this way: "I say there is no universal method of brief psychotherapy. . . . Every observing position has its advantages, its successes, and its dangers. Every position has a periphery, where important phenomena will occur and be missed, because of the center of interest of that position" (1986, p. 7). This limitation holds as well for the contributions of self psychology. Nevertheless, I believe that the contributions of Heinz Kohut and his followers are particularly thought provoking and useful. The purpose of this chapter is to show how self psychology can provide a helpful organizational framework to guide brief therapy.

ORIGINS AND DEVELOPMENT OF SELF PSYCHOLOGY

The beginning of self psychology is generally given as 1971, when Heinz Kohut published his first book, *The Analysis of the Self*. Several of his earlier

287

papers had anticipated what was to come (especially 1957, 1966, and 1968), and he was to alter his thinking regularly and substantially until his untimely death in 1981. His colleagues and followers have continued this evolutionary process, and there is every reason to believe that the discipline will continue to develop. This chapter continues previous efforts (Ornstein & Ornstein, 1972; Baker, 1979; Ornstein, Gropper, & Bogner, 1983; Deitz, 1988) to improve the effectiveness of brief psychotherapy by adding a self psychological perspective.

Although self psychology has been summarized elsewhere (Baker & Baker, 1987; Wolf, 1988), it is not widely understood. It is necessary, therefore, to offer a brief summary of central aspects of its theory. Four elements are essential: (1) the empathic perspective, (2) the concept of the selfobject, (3) the supraordinate position of the self in motivating behavior, and (4) the role of symptoms as the patient's best efforts to restore self-cohesion.

For self psychology, empathy is not being nice to someone. Nor is it putting oneself in another's shoes. Rather, empathy is an accurate cognitive and affective grasp of what others experience—what *they* feel in *their* shoes. Kohut thought that the empathic responsiveness of early caregivers was essential to the formation of a healthy personality, and that these responses indelibly colored normal sexual and aggressive drives and determined conflictual issues. He stated unequivocally that clinically significant Oedipus complexes occurred because the developing child's normal drives and conflicts were distorted and intensified by unattuned parental responses.

For self psychologists, the role of empathy is crucial to both the developmental and the therapeutic process. Kohut thought that change could occur only when the patient

> feels that the state of his self has been accurately understood. . . . It is one of the basic tenets of psychoanalytic self psychology as therapy . . . that understanding must precede explanation—indeed, that even completely accurate explanations may be useless if they have not been preceded by the establishment of a bond of accurate empathy between the analysand and the interpreting analyst. (Kohut, 1983, p. 406)

Kohut believed there were two elements in effective analysis: communicating understanding and *then* interpreting.

Kohut thought his main contribution to psychoanalytic thinking was the concept of the selfobject. At first, this concept routinely confuses people; but actually it is not very complicated. A selfobject is something or someone else that is experienced and used as if it were a part of one's own self. Metaphorically, it is as if the other is a part of one's own body. They become an "organ" that is responsible for sustaining certain vital psychological functions. Just as the lungs are necessary to maintain oxygenation, others function as necessary intrapsychic organs that help us to maintain self-esteem and to regulate tension and affect. For example, imagine an actor who looks to people in the audience for applause. Their positive response affirms the work he does. It is as though they are the organ that regulates his self-worth. In self psychological terminology, someone or something that we use to regulate self-esteem is called a *mirroring selfobject.* The term draws the analogy that the "reflection" the actor saw in the "mirror" of the audience ruled his self-esteem. If the audience's response is sufficient, he is able to use the audience as a mirroring selfobject. If people were to hiss or boo, he could not use them as a selfobject, he could not use them to consolidate his experience of himself, and the narcissistic injury would probably create severe distress. He might feel that he was falling apart and be overwhelmed with fragmentation anxiety. Likewise he might fall into a depleted depression.

The extent to which our actor would rely on the audience may or may not be absolute. This would depend on (1) whether he has other sources of selfobject support and (2) his *intrapsychic* capabilities to maintain his self-esteem. If only some in the audience were bored, he might focus on the others. If his wife were there and nodded her approval, that too would help. These reassuring others could be used as mirroring selfobjects to stabilize the actor's self-esteem. He may also have internal dialogues with parents, friends, colleagues, and others. Sometimes those "conversations" with remembered others calm him and pull him back together. Then the intrapsychic construction, the memory of the other, can be used as a selfobject that encourages him and makes him feel better.

He would also have habitual patterns or theories to process information about the audience's response, and these patterns would be crucial in determining his well-being. If, for example, he could not regard his performance as satisfactory unless the entire audience was highly enthusiastic, if one or two bored women fell asleep and he focused primarily on them, his organizational theory would lead to repeated insults. Even a good response could not be used to meet mirroring selfobject needs, and he would regularly feel humiliated and rarely gain support for his self-esteem.

Likewise, all therapists can think of patients who "know" that we do not really care about them, that our positive regard is merely a part of our job. The result is that they cannot organize our responses to them in a way that consolidates their self-esteem. They cannot, in other words, use us as a mirroring selfobject.

In summary, what happens to any of us and what we think happens to us are not always the same. Michael Basch notes that "strange as it sounds at first blush, theory comes before facts. . . . Sensory input that finds no established ordering framework is just noise, not information; that is, it is not and cannot be organized" (1983, p. 223). The way we organize information is crucial in determining our well-being. Furthermore, our organizational theories or patterns have a way of confirming themselves. The way we construct reality tends to create the reality that we confront. For example, therapists also have patients who "know" that they will be angry at them for something they do. This may lead the patients essentially to pick a fight with the therapist. If they succeed, their theory is proven; and they will be unable to use the therapist as a selfobject. They may also try to hide some provocative thing they did. Then they will never disconfirm that the therapist is angry, and their belief will persist.

It is important to note that a selfobject is not someone or something outside the self that is used as if it were an extension of the self. Rather, a selfobject is the intrapsychic representation of that person or thing that the self uses to maintain self-esteem and regulate affect. The internal construction of the other may or may not correspond to external reality. Constructivist (as opposed to realist) epistomology argues that external reality cannot be known. It holds that we always interpret data according to a framework or theory (recall Basch above). That theory determines what fraction of the theoretically available data is actually observed. Self psychologists are in general agreement that it is the intrapsychic construction of relationships that function as selfobjects, and they also agree that these constructions follow patterns that do not necessarily match generally (that is, consentually) accepted reality. External reality is certainly not irrelevant, but intrapsychic reality supercedes external reality in determining internal states and behavior.

Most of us, however, have a variety of ways of seeing things. Sometimes a slight will seem trivial, whereas at other times an essentially identical insult will feel devastating. Perhaps the most important contribution of self psychology is that it has shown that the way we organize input, whether an affront feels denigrating or irrelevant, is largely determined by whether or not we feel securely enough held by the selfobject aspects of our environment. When we feel supported, we brush things off; when we feel isolated, minor problems become unbearable. Our intrapsychic structuring activities are determined partly by our past and partly by our ongoing relationships. This has crucial implications for the process of psychotherapy.

Kohut thought that our embeddedness in a sufficiently empathic selfobject surround determined both our developmental and our ongoing ability to establish sufficient self-sustaining capacities. It is the early caretakers' delight in the child (metaphorically, the gleam in the mother's eye) that provides the foundation for the development of healthy self-esteem. Their happy response facilitated our enjoyment, and their encouragement authorized our appropriate self-assertion and ambition. We can recruit memories (consciously or unconsciously) of those responses, and the intrapsychic construction of those experiences can be used to shore up our self-esteem throughout our life. Additionally, early experiences are organized by the infant (Stern, 1985) into patterns of expectation. As noted above, these patterns will determine future interactions with others in ways that are likely to be self-confirming. The infant who is treated with empathic respect and understanding is likely to grow into an adult who likes himself or herself, enjoys human interaction, and will be able to find an abundance of selfobject support. By contrast, the abused or developmentally deprived child will understand relationships in unhelpful ways, often behaving in a manner that garners continued painful responses (Lichtenberg, 1983, 1989).

Parents, of course, are never perfect; and perfection is not necessary. At least with children who do not have biological vulnerabilities, all that is required is reasonable consistency—in Donald Winnicott's (1965) term, the "good enough mother." But if parents are regularly critical, disappointed, or inhibiting, the developing child cannot create satisfactory intrapsychic self-sustaining capabilities to maintain self-esteem, enjoyment, or ambitions. There will be deficits and distortions in intrapsychic structure. Shane and Shane (1989) have recently summarized the developmental research that substantiates the self psychological developmental theory.

When a sufficiently empathic environment is not present, the child is not able to develop capacities to maintain self-esteem. He or she *cannot* organize information about relationships in ways that grant support; the necessary conditions are simply not present. You cannot breathe in a room with no oxygen, and a person cannot develop self-esteem in an environment that denies the mirroring needs of the developing child. Rather, the deprived child will formulate enduring patterns of understanding that lead him or her (1) to find the negative elements in most interactions and (2) to ignore the positive as if it were transparent.

These deficits and distortions will inevitably lead to both intrapsychic and interpersonal conflicts, but self psychology believes that these are not the normal stuff of life. Instead, clinically relevant conflicts are the product of empathic failure. When the developmentally deprived child grows up, he will be unable to sufficiently maintain his self-esteem internally. Consequently he is forced to turn to others excessively. His dependence may terrify him, leading him to flee from relationships. But his inability to care for himself draws him back in a way that some would consider greedy. Thus we see an intrapsychic conflict, and we can predict that his needs will provoke interpersonal conflicts. No amount of clarification of the rapaciousness of his needs or the false nature of his independence will help because he simply does not have the intrapsychic capability to care for himself. This is why self psychologists focus on deficit rather than conflict.

There are other opportunities for developmental success and failure. In addition to mirroring selfobject needs, we all have what Kohut called idealizing selfobject needs. We all require others to function as selfobjects to help us regulate or contain our affects. The developmental paradigm for this is the child who stumbles and scrapes her knee. She returns home to mommy and *then* bursts into tears. As if by magic, mother's kiss calms and soothes her, teaching that others are available for help and that she, too, will eventually be able to manage her own upsets. If the mother's response is regularly nonempathic, either agitation or disinterested neglect, the developing child will have difficulty forming intrapsychic capacities to contain affect and channel and regulate sexual and aggressive tensions.

We also have so-called alter-ego or twinship selfobject needs. It is necessary to feel like others, to maintain a sense of connectedness. Kohut believed that this aspect of relationships facilitates our ability to turn latent talents into usable skills.

In summary, we use selfobjects to maintain or restore an internal experience of consolidation and organization and to promote psychological growth. For self psychology, object relations do not merely activate the feeling tone of past conflicted relationships (the traditional view of transference). Object relations also activate the endopsychic experiences of wholeness, vigor, self-esteem, tension regulation, ambitions, goals, and skills by providing selfobject experiences.

The intricate interactions between the child's biological endowment and the responsiveness of the selfobject milieu leads to a variety of skills, memories, and perceptual patterns (which self psychologists call self-sustaining structures). These structures tend to impact each other; and they, in turn, are organized into a supraordinate organization or scheme. This suprastructure is what self psychologists call the *self.*

Figure 1 provides a schematic representation of the self. Depending on the flexibility and usefulness of the constituent parts, and depending on how the parts impact one another, the structure of the self may be effective and harmonious—or it may be weak and vulnerable and contain elements that are incompatible. Under stress, one structure may fail to function. Sometimes a breakdown in function will be relatively circumscribed. For example, if loop A remains intact, if memories of maternal love and comfort are securely available, then self-organization may be preserved relatively easily. But if several structures are vulnerable and loop A is barren, if it contains no happy memories because of serious deprivation, the unraveling of self-structure may progress.

Figure 1

Interlocking Self-Sustaining Systems (The Self)

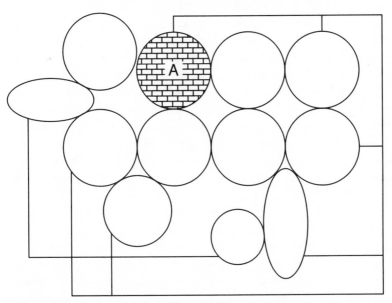

1. The various structures interact with each other.
2. One structure may impact some or all of the other structures.
3. One structure may impact another directly, or it may impact another only through another, or it may do both.
4. Loop A is particularly important and impacts nearly all loops. It might be thought of as either (a) the way that the person organizes information that concerns crucial, core relationships, ambitions, and goals or (b) memories of parental love and reassurance that can be retrieved (consciously or unconsciously) under stress.

If there is sufficient disintegration of self-structure, the internal experience can be one of severe depressed depletion, or what Kohut called fragmentation anxiety. That anxiety is considered to be the most powerful terror known to humans, and people will do almost anything to avoid it. A patient once illustrated fragmentation in a terrifying dream he had after he finished studying organic chemistry. The dream consisted of nothing but organic compounds that were being twisted and torn. As they ruptured, blood gushed from the broken molecules. This was precisely the way that he experienced his life at the time of the dream: his life and his inner experience were disintegrating and he was filled with profound and disorganizing anxiety and dread. He turned to his therapist and felt that his predicament was understood. The interaction enabled him to use the therapist as a selfobject, and the patient was able to repair his self-structure, at least temporarily.

Although this patient's needs were extreme, Kohut was certain that we all have needs for selfobject support to maintain and sustain the self throughout the entire life cycle. This is true for healthy individuals as well as for the severely troubled. Depending on the success of our self-sustaining capabilities (our relative degree of health), the way we understand our relationships, and the amount of stress that we are experiencing, selfobject needs may be (1) intense (or archaic) and difficult to meet or (2) relatively benign (mature) and easily met. The ability to find and effectively use relationships that meet our selfobject needs is essential to the psychological health of us all, although the extent of the need varies. Selfobject failures and successes, then, occur not only in infancy and early childhood but throughout life. For the healthy self, selfobject needs are modest, techniques to meet them are well established, and there are only occasional times when the environment fails to meet the needs. For those with weakened self-structure, the needs are intense, techniques to meet them are strident and ineffective. Failure to sustain the self is frequent and symptomatic efforts to restore the self are often necessary.

Stress imposed by disruptions in self–selfobject relationships, narcissistic injuries, or traumas are the precipitant causes of loss of self-cohesion. The extent to which self-cohesion is lost may run the spectrum from mild upset through to profound fragmentation anxiety and depleted depression. The ultimate motivation for most symptomatic behavior and psychopathology is either (1) to avoid or terminate those unbearable affective states or (2) to gain some modicum expression of core needs of the self. For example, a schizoid adjustment may be an effort to avoid the threat of lost selfobject support. What isn't present can't be lost, and the danger is avoided. Such a person might be devoted excessively to a dog, because the pet responds with greater consistency and fewer demands than any human. The patient gains some expression of the self in the relationship to the dog. His devotion might expand to fervent vegetarianism and caustic antivivisectionist activism (I do not mean to imply that all vegetarians or antivivisectionists are so motivated). Likewise, a young woman may indulge in a binge-purge cycle in an effort to invigorate a self depleted by a disruption in her relationship with her mother (who had been functioning as a centrally organizing selfobject).

Symptomatic behavior follows this sequence: (1) disruption of a self–selfobject relationship, trauma, and/or narcissistic insult, leading to (2) loss of self-cohesion, leading to (3) fragmentation anxiety, rage, and/or depleted depression, leading to (4) efforts at self-restoration. These efforts may be healthy, such as turning to a loved one for support or performing a task one does well, or they may be symptomatic, such as addictive behavior. The goal usually is not mere gratification of a conflicted drive need (although such needs may indeed be met). It is restoration of self-cohesion.

Symptoms fall into three general categories: (1) direct affective expression of the loss of self-cohesion, such as panic disorder, rage reactions, or depression; (2) intrapsychic defenses, such as splitting or obsessional thoughts; and (3) symbolic or manipulative behaviors designed to restore the self, such as addictive sexuality, drug abuse, and suicidal gestures that are a call for help. The symptoms may be shortsighted, but they are the patient's best effort to restore self-cohesion. If loss of self-cohesion is severe, it feels like an absolute emergency. If something with long-term negative consequences will function to restore the self temporarily, it may be used despite its long-term consequences. The current state must change.

Even under severe stress, most people do not undergo such a complete loss of self-cohesion that they resort to such thoughtless actions as drug abuse. Self psychology postulates a spectrum of self pathology that runs from adjustment reactions through to psychosis. In adjustment reactions, there is a transient and relatively limited disorganization of the patient's self-structure. Generally, this is precipitated by either a serious narcissistic insult, a traumatic event, or a disruption in a relationship that is meeting important, but circumscribed, selfobject needs. Returning to figure 1, a breech in a self–selfobject relationship has disrupted the functioning of an intrapsychic self-sustaining structure (one of the loops in the figure) that is peripheral and not intricately interconnected to the deepest layers of the core self. The effects of this breakdown do not expand rapidly and weaken other areas. We might suspect that for most of these patients, development had proceeded well and that problematic failures in important self-

selfobject relationships were relatively circumscribed. As a child, the patient was able to find needed selfobject support in most areas; and failures that did occur happened at a relatively late phase, perhaps even in adolescence. Consequently, the patient is vulnerable in only a few aspects of personality, and most of the self-sustaining structures have been sufficient to meet the demands imposed by normal stress. Because the patient is able to recruit memories of positive self–selfobject interactions from the past, he or she is able form new object and self–selfobject relationships with relative ease—and he or she can also establish a good therapeutic relationship quickly.

When the loss of self-cohesion is of longer duration and is more pervasive (eventually moving from disorganization to fragmentation), the diagnosis moves through neurotic disorders to narcissistic character and behavior disorders, to borderline conditions (Kohut & Wolf, 1978). In the more severe disorders, the organization of the self is more vulnerable and prone to fragmentation. Again referring to figure 1, the number of loops that fail is greater, and the entire self-structure is more likely to collapse under less stress. Kohut and Wolf believed that schizophrenics were still worse off and had failed to construct any reliably integrated self at all.

SELECTION OF PATIENTS

In theory, following a careful evaluation of a patient, indications and contraindications for treatment are assessed on the basis of the diagnosis, and the best treatment is prescribed and provided. Economic realities, however, add another dimension. Brief interventions may be the only possible treatment even when more extended treatment might be optimal. Happily, many people get some relief from their symptoms, some through an appropriate series of several time-limited interventions over a period of several years (see, for example, Siddall, Haffey & Feinman, 1988).

For many patients, however, short-term psychotherapy is either the treatment of choice or at least a very good option. There is surprising agreement on the positive indications for brief psychotherapy. In general, self psychologists concur with the indications voiced by Davanloo, Malan, Sifneos, and Strupp at the 1975 and 1976 International Symposia on Short-Term Dynamic Psychotherapy (Davanloo, 1978). Self psychologists are encouraged when a patient has a genuine motivation to change and shows a relatively effective self-structure, with significant strengths that are handicapped by weakness in only some areas (in figure 1, only a few loops). If the patient has a history that includes positive self–selfobject interchanges with early caregivers, it is likely that memories of those past interactions can be recruited and built upon in the therapeutic setting, allowing him or her to establish an effective therapeutic alliance rapidly (Charles Jaffe, personal communication, October 1990). Reasonably good intelligence and an interest in self-understanding also help. Jeffrey Deitz may have summarized the thinking of many with his opinion that "time-limited psychotherapy is an especially useful approach . . . [when] both patient and therapist agree that the goal of treatment is reconstitution to a previous state of psychic equilibrium" (1986, p. 295).

By contrast, brief interventions are unlikely to do more than palliate the difficulties of those with major self pathology. Because they have undergone severe deprivation or trauma, they are limited by a paucity of memories that they can recruit to gain selfobject support. Protracted psychotherapeutic work is generally required for them to risk opening themselves to the sort of human interactions that are necessary for them to make genuine changes in the structure of their personality. For them, prolonged, intensive psychotherapy or a self psychological psychoanalysis is the treatment of choice.

In addition to assessing the extent of the patient's personal self pathology, it is also important to determine the actual quality of his or her interpersonal relationships. Because one goal of treatment is to enhance the patient's ability to use his or her ongoing relationships to meet self-object needs, patients who have a circle of reasonably positive relationships are likely to profit most from brief therapy. By contrast, some people are locked into unhealthy relationships. A spouse may have more pervasive psychopathology than the index patient. A marital interaction may have developed that meets absolutely vital selfobject needs for that spouse; and when the patient begins to change, the partner is threatened and must undermine treatment. Sometimes this problem can be overcome by punctuating an individual treatment with occasional marital or family counseling.

Finally, careful assessment of possible biological factors is essential. Combined psychopharmacological and psychotherapeutic interventions may be ideal.

There are some contraindications to brief therapy. Of course, patients with bipolar disorders or other psychoses, addictions, severe character disorders, and the like are not appropriate candidates for brief treatment. For some, setting a time limit may encourage magical hopes for major life changes that will certainly be thwarted; this may leave them even more demoralized and unwilling to seek further treatment. Brief techniques may also enhance pathological defenses, creating a more brittle self-structure that is increasingly vulnerable to fragmentation. This requires that the patient try to maintain ever more ironclad control over relationships or that he or she self-protectively withdraw from all human interaction.

Serious damage may also befall patients who develop regressed selfobject transferences if the therapist's personal, technical, or financial limitations prevent him or her from sustaining the therapeutic relationship through to its necessary and time-consuming resolution. Borderline patients and those with serious narcissistic disorders are most vulnerable to rapidly establishing regressed selfobject transferences. Fortunately, their defenses (particularly their tendency to provocatively test limits) generally protect them from stumbling into this unwanted situation. If a patient develops such a transference in brief treatment, and if more intensive treatment is not possible, every effort should be made to direct attention to ongoing outside relationships and away from therapist–patient interactions.

In summary, except for the danger created by the development of a selfobject transference that cannot be resolved, self psychological brief treatment indications and contraindications are essentially similar to the guidelines that others use. We do, however, have a different explanation why these guidelines hold.

GOALS OF THERAPY

The process of framing the therapeutic situation begins when the patient calls for an appointment, but this becomes more specific at the beginning of the first appointment. It is usually best to clarify that the first visits are to evaluate the patient's problems and determine what is likely to help him or her.

Generally within the first two appointments a standard psychiatric examination should be completed. It is particularly useful to assess the patient's ability to relate. Is there a potential for her to use interactions in her life to meet selfobject needs? Does the interaction with me predict whether a positive therapeutic alliance will develop? If not, does this say something about our particular interaction? If it does, then referral elsewhere is mandatory. If our interaction reflects her problems in relating, can the reasons be addressed in brief therapy?

If it is possible to offer a suggestion about why the patient is experiencing her symptoms, this should be offered very early on. For example, I might suggest, "When you sit down to study, you often encounter material that you don't understand. This makes you feel stupid, and you avoid that feeling by doing something else. Maybe you have some ideas about the kinds of things you use to avoid that stupid feeling." Notice that I suggested she avoids feeling stupid—*an affect*—not studying—*a behavior.* A comment like this serves partly to assess the accuracy of the interpretation. But a more important use is that it may give an idea of the extent to which she is interested in self-understanding and how well she can put such information to use.

Following the evaluation, the patient deserves an explanation about the duration and cost of treatment, the nature of the symptoms, what psychotherapy is like, and what can reasonably be hoped for.

Duration of Treatment

A generally agreed upon time framework should be established. Sometimes, external realities such as graduation from college or an anticipated move to another city create an absolute time limit. In general, we plan twenty to thirty weekly appointments, with the understanding that treatment may be a little shorter or a little longer. If there is a crisis, frequency may need to be increased.

Jeffrey Binder (1979) reported the successful treatment of a patient with serious narcissistic problems that suggests a disadvantage of a firm time limit. He had set (imposed?) a firm twelve-visit limit. Following standard procedure, he related much of the patient's material to the termination. At a follow-up interview several months after termination, the patient believed that he got the majority of his benefits during the first six visits. After that he felt that the therapist's focus on termination prevented him from doing more work. Perhaps the selfobject bond to the therapist was needlessly disrupted and further reorganization of the self stopped. I do not, therefore, make termination such a central focus of brief therapy.

Nature of the Symptoms

What the patient wants to change is, of course, a central goal for therapy. If his wishes are impossible, then we must try to restructure them into something relatively discrete and attainable. I might well explain something like: "I think that you would like to change the way you do your schoolwork. It seems you are a champion procrastinator and that, even if you do sit down to study, you are often distracted and quit. We may discover some other problems, but I think that is the major thing you would like to change. Does this make sense to you?"

What Therapy Is Like

Many patients really have no idea what to expect in psychotherapy. I think Martin Orne (1968) is correct when he states that it is important to explain the process to them. I will often suggest something along these lines:

> THERAPIST: You have ways of understanding your relationships and what happens to you that aren't very helpful. Since it's pretty hard to change something you don't know is happening, I'll try to help you understand those patterns. That means I won't give you much advice. Instead I'll try to help you understand what interferes with your making up your own mind. We'll want to look again and again at what happened at the moment you decided to eat three bags of cookies. That may be just before you do it, or it may be ten hours before you could find the opportunity. What is important is the thing that precipitated the decision. Sometimes it may even be something I did. If that happens, you probably won't want to tell me; but that sort of thing will be especially helpful to talk about. Any feeling you have toward me—whether it makes you feel better or worse—is important, because I think you'll find it is similar to what gets you in and out of trouble out there. Is that fairly clear?

The Therapist's View of the Goals

From a theoretical perspective the goal of therapy is to help patients change their intrapsychic patterns so that they are less vulnerable to either the loss of selfobject support or narcissistic insults. This means they (1) expand their repertoire of sustaining selfobject memories (perhaps including thoughts of the therapist) and (2) change the way they process information about what is happening to them. We therapists try to help them more usefully organize input about their relationships, affects, drives, cognitions, and motivations. For example, they may realize that every time they are ignored the other person is not trying to deliberately humiliate them, or that all of their mistakes are not serious. When troubled, they may have an imaginary conversation with the therapist that calms or encourages them. All of this would be expected to help them maintain their self-esteem more effectively. Additionally, they may come to develop new skills at managing relationships, affects, drives, cognitions, and motivations. Perhaps they will turn to a friend or to practicing an instrument to calm themselves when they are upset rather than going out and getting drunk. These two aspects work synergistically—affects that spring from a slight that is understood as accidental are easier to learn to manage than the pain of what is perceived as a deliberate insult.

THEORY OF CHANGE

Self psychologists agree that success in therapy requires that dysfunctional intrapsychic structures be changed or compensating new structures be added. (I suspect that most therapists, whatever their orientation, would agree with this, although some would change the language). Although there are differences among self psychologists about what causes change, there is general agreement on essential points. All agree with Kohut's (1984) position that change occurs via a two-step process: understanding and then interpretation.

Understanding is fundamental to developing an effective selfobject transference. This transference serves numerous functions: (1) It restores a sense of self-cohesion, and this alone reduces pain and suffering. (2) The therapeutic selfobject relationship also functions to sustain the self while old structures are reorganized and new structures are built. This happens in two ways: it helps the patient contain intense affects so that they can be worked through; and it sustains the overall integration and coherence of the self while various elements are being reorganized and reintegrated into a new, perhaps considerably different, overall self-organization. It is as though the therapist's accurately empathic responses were reliable, strong hands that support the self system (recall figure 1) during the reorganization. (3) Because the therapist's response is empathic, it is in fact different from previously traumatizing interactions. As such, the relationship provides a corrective emotional experience (Alexander & French, 1946). It confronts patients with a new reality that demonstrates that the present and future need not be endless repetitions of the past.

Understanding is accomplished through careful empathic immersion in the patient's experience. Kohut regularly referred to empathy as "vicarious introspection," intending to emphasize that the therapist must grasp the patient's life both affectively and cognitively from the patient's own particular perspective. This understanding is then communicated to the patient. In essence, the therapist clarifies how the patient *constructs* the cognitive, affective, and interpersonal elements of his life. Until a selfobject relationship is firmly in place, the therapist does not try to correct what seems to be distortions or inconsistencies in the patient's views. That is to say, the therapist does not try to deconstruct their view of reality, because to do so might prevent the development of the selfobject transference.

Self psychologists believe that genuine change occurs only in the context of a relationship that sufficiently sustains the self-organization (the selfobject transference). Without that relationship, the patients may appear to alter behavior and thinking; but, all too frequently, this change proves to be mere compliance with what they believe are the therapist's wishes. Furthermore, in the context of a sustaining selfobject transference, patients routinely change their own minds about how they are thinking. Interpretations then solidify the changes—after the fact. When patients are unable to change dysfunctional patterns in the presence of a selfobject relationship, interpretations are offered. At that point, interpretations are less likely to fall on deaf ears. This helps explain why timing is so important.

The content of most interpretation would not be directed toward correcting "reality distortions" of dysfunctional thinking or the irrationality or shortsightedness of symptomatic behavior. Instead, attention would be directed to the context in which problematic thinking or behavior occurs. We usually find that difficulties occur when the patient feels dropped from a needed self–selfobject relationship, narcissistically wounded, or otherwise traumatized.

Although this technique contains elements that are similar to Alexander's (1946) corrective emotional experience, Kohut insisted that what was corrective was the therapist's accepting and tolerant stand, that is, remaining empathically immersed in the patient's experience no matter how painful that experience might be. He eschewed Alexander's recommendation to deliberately respond to the patient in a way that is opposite to childhood traumatic experiences. It seems obvious that if we hope to help our patients find new ways of understanding themselves and others, they cannot do so unless they actually have experiences that are affectively intense and different than what they believe to be "just the way things are." Whether it is acknowledged or not, I believe that some sort of corrective emotional experience is a part of every effective therapeutic experience.

Where controversy arises in self psychology may be summarized by Kohut's description of the therapeutic relationship as optimally frustrating and Bacal's (1985) term, optimally responsive. It is clear that, even in formal analysis, the analyst's focus on the selfobject transference creates an atmosphere that is more gratifying than what is generally understood under the rubric of the rule of abstinence. In the context of psychotherapy, especially relatively short-term psychotherapy, most practitioners probably deviate even further from the rule of abstinence and occasionally allow quite direct expressions of support, pleasure, and concern.

The following vignette of a twenty-nine-year-old executive in intensive psychotherapy may provide clarification of the gratification versus abstinence controversy as well as demonstrating other principles of how change occurs. At one point in the hour, I said: "During our last hour, you very much wanted me to express my delight about your promotion. If I had, you would have felt proud and motivated to work extra hard; and when my response seemed insufficient, you felt hurt, frustrated, and angry; and you got drunk in an effort to calm yourself down." At least in an analytic setting, I do not know whether Kohut would have thought it appropriate to add, "But, of course, I was pleased as punch about it." He might have thought that comment would prevent optimal frustration. Indeed, if I had made that comment during the previous hour, the material in this hour might not have emerged. As the hour continued, I added, "It seems now that you particularly wanted me to do that because Sam [a friend] seemed to ignore it or even seemed angry at you." And later I added, "This all fits with the way you sensed so little pride from your parents for your accomplishments." By relating the transference interaction to the patient's current life situation and developmental experiences, the triad of an ideal interpretation was completed. Over time I tried to help this patient understand that thwarted mirroring needs precipitated feelings of narcissistic rage (Kohut, 1972), that this fury led directly to assessing his friend's response to be competitive or hostile, and that these affects overwhelmed his ability to calm himself without the use of alcohol.

The point is that the patient longed for someone outside of himself (his therapist) to perform the self-sustaining functions of maintaining self-esteem and motivation. He was unable to accomplish this for himself because he did not have the intrapsychic structures to sustain himself any more than he had the ability to fly. The patient's inability to gain sufficient mirroring responses precipitated some loss of self-esteem and self-cohesion, which resulted in anxiety and rage. These precipitated affects are the stuff of pathogenic conflict and are what Kohut called breakdown products. They are normal affects intensified by the absence of a needed selfobject response. Moreover, this combination of selfobject failure and affect (a breakdown product of the disruption he had experienced in our relationship) led the patient to intensify habitual and dysfunctional patterns of understanding relationships. He saw the hostile and competitive aspects of his friend's response, and he probably failed to recognize his friend's pleasure at his promotion. He turned to alcohol because it provided temporary, albeit illusory, wind that made him believe he could fly.

This patient had three intrapsychic problems. First, he could not experience pleasure at his promotion unless another also delighted in him (a deficit in the intrapsychic ability to maintain self-esteem). Second, because of the way the patient organized his understanding of the responses of those around him (both therapist and friend), he was unable to internalize the normal mirroring responses that were available—he actually experienced less mirroring than was within reach (a developmentally based distortion of information processing). Third, he wanted more mirroring than he would be likely to obtain from a typical environment (an unmeetable need). To reduce that demand would require that he become more capable of independently enjoying himself. But he could not do that because he had an intrapsychic deficit. He simply could not regulate his motivation and self-esteem at that time. It would only have added insult to his deficit to point out his neediness, and he eventually came to the realization on his own as his intrapsychic limitation subsided.

My combined understanding without either criticism or specific gratification of his wish would have provided Kohut's optimal frustration. Again going back to figure 1, the understanding would have allowed the patient to use the therapist as a selfobject—to have the therapist function in place of a self-sustaining loop. Without gratification of the wish for praise, the patient still needed to create his own intrapsychic capabilities to perform the function of that loop. He would need to work out a way to maintain healthy pride and motivation intrapsychically, and not rely on the presence of the therapist to function as a selfobject that maintained self-esteem. But because of the therapist's presence, the task would be one of manageable proportions, not one that was entirely beyond his capabilities.

For Kohut, change consisted of building or reorganizing intrapsychic self-sustaining capabilities through "transmuting internalization." He thought of this as a process by which the patient (or developing child) took aspects of the way he or she was sustained by a variety of others and combined these aspects into his or her own endopsychic capabilities to maintain a vigorous experience of self-cohesion. Kohut compared this process to the way the body builds protein by digesting other proteins into amino acids, absorbing them, and then rebuilding new proteins from the amino acids. Transmuting internalization works best in circumstances of optimal—not traumatic or excessive—frustration.

As noted above, some in the self psychological arena (Bacal, 1985; Terman, 1988) have questioned whether change occurs because it is propelled by optimal frustration. Instead, they believe that transmuting internalization is part of a person's normal developmental thrust. They realize that the frustrations in the therapeutic work are unavoidable, that these disjunctions clarify what goes wrong for the patient; but they think that growth occurs principally during the times in therapy when the patient feels enclosed in a secure selfobject milieu. Particularly in briefer psychotherapy, they might have congratulated the patient described above for his promotion and have assumed that the essential material would have arisen in some other way.

Self psychologists agree that the treatment focus is on the following sequence: (1) a disruption in a salient self–selfobject relationship or a narcissistic insult (whether this occurs in the transference or in the patient's outside life), leading to (2) a diminution in self-cohesion, leading to (3) affect that the patient very much wants to terminate (such as anxiety, depression, or rage), leading to (4) an effort to reduce affect and restore self-cohesion. Just as in analysis, the brief therapist clarifies this sequence through interpretation given in a context of an understanding and kindly relationship. The relationship catches the patient as he or she falls, providing a needed selfobject bond that prevents (or at least minimizes) further loss of self-cohesion. In that circumstance of improved self-cohesion, reorganization of the events that precipitated the symptomatic outburst can occur. The differences between analysis and brief approaches are that the shorter methods concentrate more attention on discrete areas of the patient's personality and behavior (that is to say, the treatment is more focused on particular issues) and on self–selfobject interactions in the patient's outside life as much as interchanges within the transference. The result is that there is far less regression in the therapeutic relationship.

In figure 1, the self was represented by a number of interlocking loops. In patients for whom brief therapy is the treatment of choice, one might conceive of problems in only one or two of the loops. Those loops, moreover, are not so interconnected to the core of the patient's being that general disorganization occurs when they are disrupted. The patient is afforded an opportunity in the transference for the therapist to function temporarily as one of the loops.

For example, although she functioned well in most areas, a college student sought treatment for studying difficulties that affected her grades. She felt stupid when she didn't understand the difficult course material almost immediately. This was especially obvious when she did her calculus homework. A loop involved with maintaining self-esteem was regularly broken when she studied. In most other aspects of her life, she maintained her self-esteem in a healthy, reasonable way. When the following inter-change occurred, she was able to use the therapist as a substitute loop. This happened because he was interested, remained nonjudgmental, and stayed relatively close to her viewpoint. In other words, he was empathic and tactfully suggested that she organized her experience in a nonhelpful way, even using some lighthearted humor.

THERAPIST: You didn't get those problems, and you decided you were stupid—not that the problems were really hard.

PATIENT: They weren't hard. It's just that I never get how to do them.

THERAPIST: Then you felt stupid and hopeless and quit trying.

PATIENT: Yeah, there's no use. Well, no, I didn't get up and go to Marge's room. I kept trying.

THERAPIST: You kept sitting there with the books. Did everyone else get the problems?

PATIENT: All the smart ones.

THERAPIST: Just the dummies like you messed it up.

PATIENT: . . . Well, maybe a few kids who weren't dumb didn't get it.

THERAPIST: How did that happen?

PATIENT: . . . Well, I guess they didn't study.

THERAPIST: They studied a lot less than you did.

PATIENT: That's right—I studied three and a half hours!

THERAPIST: Gee, most people can't study that long without a break. How'd you do that?

PATIENT: I always do it.

THERAPIST: You can concentrate for three and a half hours! I'm impressed.

PATIENT: And look at all the good it does.

THERAPIST: Doesn't your mind wander?

PATIENT: Well, sure, a little.

THERAPIST: You mean you daydream some.

PATIENT: Yeah.

THERAPIST: I wonder, could you think back? Did you daydream for a few minutes, or did your mind wander off quite a bit?

PATIENT: Well, I'm not sure. I don't remember. . . .

THERAPIST: What are you thinking?

PATIENT: I was remembering. I was thinking about going to law school, and then I thought about having this wonderful apartment. I think about that place a lot.

THERAPIST: What's it like?

PATIENT: *(Proceeds with a long description of an attractive, spacious apartment.)*

THERAPIST: It sounds wonderful. It must have made you feel better to think about it rather than to frustrate yourself with the calculus.

PATIENT: Boy, that's for sure.

THERAPIST: But, you know, if you were thinking about that, you must have spent a lot of that time with the books not studying.

PATIENT: Yeah, I guess so.

THERAPIST: I call that the librarian theory of study.

PATIENT: Huh?

THERAPIST: Well, you know, librarians spend all day around books. If being near books was all that was necessary, they'd know more than anyone in the world. *(Patient laughs.)* In other words, did you spend all that time near the books or studying?

PATIENT: I guess I spent a lot of time near the books.

THERAPIST: You said that the other kids who didn't get the problems didn't study. I wonder if you were really one of the other ones who didn't study?

PATIENT: . . . You know what else—I was thinking about Joe [a boyfriend at a distant school]. He didn't call me.

THERAPIST: Why?

PATIENT: I don't know.

THERAPIST: Were you thinking it's because he's losing interest in you?

PATIENT: No. . . . Well, I don't know. I worry about that.

THERAPIST: And when he doesn't call, does that make you worry more?

PATIENT: Sure.

THERAPIST: Well, let's look back. You were worried when Joe didn't call. You tried to study, but instead you spent a lot of time daydreaming; and, surprise, you didn't learn very much, but the daydreams made you feel a lot better—at least for a little while.

In this interchange we see a relatively complete sequence. The patient felt dropped from an important relationship that served selfobject functions. In addition, she felt narcissistically injured when she didn't understand the problems. She wandered off into a self-reparative fantasy, which worked for the moment but prevented her from doing any real work. Because the therapeutic relationship could grant her a temporary self-cohesiveness, she was able to reorganize the narcissistic insult. She went on to think that it was possible that the problems were really quite difficult and that only the smartest students got them all. Eventually, she could see that she had an established habit of processing all studying difficulties as evidence for her stupidity. She also came to see that she tended to do this most when she felt lonely or rejected. In metapsychological terms, when she felt a disruption in a mirroring self–selfobject relationship, a relatively circumscribed weakness in her self-esteem-regulating structures became evident. Because the therapist's attitude helped restore her self-esteem and self-cohesion, she was able to reorganize her routine perceptions about her intellect. She also began to realize when she was particularly vulnerable to trying to restore self-esteem through ineffective means like withdrawing into daydreaming. She began to take alternative steps (for example, calling Joe rather than sulking if he forgot to call her). The result was better study habits, which yielded better grades, which further consolidated her reorganization of her attitudes about her intelligence.

Because the developmental process normally occurs throughout life, if a patient improves the quality of her self–selfobject relationships outside the therapeutic setting, she can use those relationships to enhance growth. The patient just described had a basically good relationship with Joe; but her tendency to sulk nearly ruined it. As she came to understand this, she changed and the relationship improved. Perhaps this could further sustain her so that, if they should break up, she would not collapse.

In summary, the theory of change stresses the establishment of, disruptions of, and repairs of self–selfobject relationships both in the transference and in the patient's outside world. Disruptions clarify what precipitates symptomatic behavior, and the effective functioning of the relationships meets the patient's selfobject needs. The selfobject experience (1) restores self-cohesion, thereby alleviating pain and suffering; (2) provides a corrective emotional experience that allows the patient to realize new potentials for his or her life; and (3) supplies an environment that allows the patient both to reorganize dysfunctional self-structures and to develop and integrate new structures.

TECHNIQUES

People are very complicated amalgams of affects, needs, conflicts, deficits, cognitions, motivations, and relationships. Although the basic theory of self psychology is quite straightforward (I like to think parsimoniously elegant), its application is anything but simplistic. There is always a very intricate interaction between a multitude of variables that regularly test the psychological integrity and strength of therapists. Even this relatively austere theory is best learned with careful supervision and after a considerable amount of personal self psychological analysis.

Although both brief and intensive self psychological treatment techniques flow from the same theoretical groundwork, there are important differences in what the therapist does and does not do. For intensive work, the development of robust, often highly regressed selfobject transferences is an essential part of the change process. These will unfold best—or perhaps only—if the therapist is able to remain within the empathic perspective, eschewing correcting the patient's cognitive distortions and following the patient's thoughts and associations wherever they lead. Because of their personal histories, patients dread the risk involved in opening themselves to such powerful transferences, and deviations from analytic technique tend to intensify rather than resolve these resistances. Once such a relationship is allowed to develop, careful attention is paid to disruptions in the transference, the patient's reactions to these breaches, and the ways that the relationship is repaired.

In short-term approaches, it is necessary to focus attention on one or two areas that are particularly problematic for the patient. Greater attention is directed toward breaks in the self–selfobject relationships in the patient's outside life. The therapist must attend to the patient's immediate problems, but this sacrifices the potential for developing full selfobject transferences. For practitioners who do both brief and intensive therapy, it can be very difficult to shift between these two very different therapeutic stances.

Both approaches focus attention on the four-step symptomatic sequence that I have stated above. This concentration on the intricate interaction between the degree of self-cohesion and the self–selfobject relationship surround is what differentiates self psychological approaches from other systems. Keeping clear attention on one or two themes in the patient's life is essential and differentiates brief work from intensive psychotherapy.

To clarify how self psychologists work, I will briefly contrast self psychology to several other methodologies. Although comparing what I might have said to what others report they said is risky, I think it is important to do.

Although self psychologists help patients alter cognitive distortions and build more useful ways of understanding what is happening to them, the technique is extremely different from the procedures of cognitive therapists (Beck, Rush, Shaw, & Emery, 1979). Their very logical interventions attempt to alter the patient's problematic thinking patterns directly. By contrast, because so much attention is paid to the interpersonal context in which the cognitive distortions occurred, self psychologists find the almost

309

obsessional cognitive techniques unnecessary. In fact, patients regularly correct their own distortions when they feel genuinely contained in a sustaining relationship.

The technique is also very different than that recommended by neo-Freudians such as Peter Sifneos (1979) or Habib Davanloo (1978), who seem to almost hammer the patient into awareness of their drive-related (generally oedipal) conflicts. Because self psychologists would focus on how patients deal with disruptions in self–selfobject relationships, the content of the interpretations obviously would be different. There would also be a more gentle quality to the interactions, because confrontational techniques often lead to serious ruptures in the selfobject aspects of the relationship. It seems, however, that Davanloo and Sifneos personally are able to sustain the relationship through these confrontations. I would suggest, therefore, that they are able to sustain a rather effective self–selfobject relationship through what many others would find impossibly assaultive techniques. Self psychologists might attempt to understand how confrontational techniques work for these two talented therapists.

Likewise, there is considerable difference with the procedures recommended by post-Kleinians such as Michael Balint (Balint, Ornstein & Balint, 1972) or Malan (1976). Gustafson (1986) provides a transcript of much of an appointment with a young woman whom he treated using the Balint/Malan model. He tried to help her confront her "true feelings" rather than bury them in order to maintain a so-called necessary relationship. A self psychologist might understand the same pattern of behavior using different terms. The patient may suppress feelings to maintain a self–selfobject relationship that is necessary to avoid fragmentation. Thus far, the difference might seem to be a trivial variation in terminology. However, from a self psychological perspective, the feeling is sacrificed to maintain a relationship; and this is done because the patient simply does not have the intrapsychic capabilities to manage the feeling if the relationship is disrupted. Consequently, what would happen in therapy is different.

The patient Gustafson described was a college student who had a panic attack when she thought about her boyfriend, Sam. During the hour, she realized that she panicked because she was "mad as hell" at him because he had left her and gone on an extended trip. The goal of therapy was to help her uncover her tendency to become enraged and then to help her try to contain it by redefining it as mere anger. Gustafson emphasizes this by italicizing three places in the transcript (I have deleted the italics):

THERAPIST: But being mad and being in a fight are not the same thing.

PATIENT: I know they're not. They're different.

THERAPIST: But you tend to run them together.

PATIENT: Yeah. . . .

THERAPIST: [The anger] either wrecks you or wrecks him. . . .

THERAPIST: And what you're dealing with is not only anger. You want to punish him, until he says uncle. (Gustafson, 1986, pp. 143–150)

From the rest of the transcript, there seems no question that his assessment of what the patient does is correct—she does fall into rages that she cannot control. His therapeutic intent is to get her to understand that the rages happen, and it also seems that if she stops denying the rage she will be able to contain the intensity of her affect and convert rage to manageable anger. However, she has avoided the rage precisely because she neither understands its origins nor possesses established intrapsychic capacities to govern it.

Why can't she manage it? We learn that she can—if she is with Sam. When she gets angry at him, he does not become defensive. Rather, he accepts that she has some justification for her feelings, and he says he'll try to be more responsive to her needs. Gustafson does not, however, comment on this or explain to her that her anger might not escalate to unmanageable rage if she were able to express it in a way that the other person could comprehend; nor does he wonder what keeps her in relationships with other people who respond defensively and push her from anger into rages. In other words, he does not examine the contexts, the drops from selfobject relationships, that precipitate the rage. Nor does he help her see how some relationships can help her contain and usefully express her anger.

Why does she have this particular vulnerability? We also learn that her mother regularly flies off the handle. The patient says that she does not like losing her temper because it makes her "feel like my mother." His response is that she is "tempted to be like [your mother]" and that "children identify with their parents," and then he switches the subject to his belief that she enjoys "sock[ing] it to" Sam. The problem is that she hates to sock it to him; but she is unable to stop herself because she apparently doesn't really know why she's mad at him, and because she simply has never been able to establish intrapsychic structures that would help her contain her rage. Her family could not help her develop techniques to manage anger; they could not help her because they themselves were unable to direct their own rage. She was not motivated to be as out of control as her mother—she could not help herself because of an intrapsychic deficit.

A self psychologist would have, first, commented on her contained response when Sam responded thoughtfully; second, wondered what it meant that she could sometimes control herself; and, third, sympathized with her frustration about her inability to control herself when she got angry. The therapist might have added that it was fairly clear why she was never able to develop the capacity to contain her anger, and he or she would certainly have tried to get a better grasp of precisely what about Sam's trip made her so angry. For example, did she feel insulted that he didn't stay with her? Did she feel that she couldn't keep herself together without him? Did she just miss him? I would also have wondered what Sam would have thought about her anger, perhaps suggesting that he might see that at least a part of it was understandable. She had, after all, been left behind.

In summary, it is not a sufficient goal of therapy to open up the patient's "true feelings." Doing that may only leave the patient overwhelmed with affect that cannot be managed. Rather, it is more useful to examine the origins of the feelings. This tends to reduce their intensity to a level at which the patient can begin to develop defenses to manage them. As the defenses gradually build up, greater levels of affect can be experienced safely.

Finally, I think there is a significant parallel between the self psychological approach and Lester Luborsky's (1984) Core Conflictual Relationship Theme (CCRT) method (see chapter 5). The wish expresses what the patient wants from the relationship. I would simply add that this is one way to explain what selfobject need the patient obtains when the relationship succeeds. The expectation of the other expresses how the patient expects the other to fail to meet selfobject needs. The expectation also organizes the relationship in a way that tends to be self-fulfilling and self-defeating. The response of the self expresses what happens to the patient when he or she feels dropped from the relationship.

CASE EXAMPLE

Mike was a twenty-two-year-old, single, white, Roman Catholic man who was completing his last year of undergraduate studies before going on to professional school. He presented complaining of depression and anxiety that would occasionally escalate to moderate panic attacks. He was terrified that he would be unable to perform satisfactorily in his graduate education, although he understood that his undergraduate average of 3.9 and his admission examination scores indicated that he would do well.

Several months earlier, he had responded to a newspaper ad and participated in a no-fee psychopharmacology study at a nearby medical center. He had gotten little help during the course of the study, and on follow-up he was diagnosed as having an atypical depression and given a monoamine oxidase inhibitor. The treating physician relied on the medication as the sole treatment mode. Mike did feel better, but he had stopped the drug because he feared (with some justification) that taking a medication would reduce his chances for getting the scholarship he needed.

On further examination, he showed a considerable amount of obsessional thinking with some ritualization. There were no signs of overt psychosis. Although he had enough friends, he was concerned about his heterosexual relationships. Several months previously, he experienced his only sustained relationship, but he and the girl had mutually agreed to break up after several months. His only sexual experience had been with her. It was successful but not very satisfying because he felt extremely guilty about it and believed that God would surely punish him for his transgression.

Mike's family life was troubled. His father, an engineer in his midforties, had been laid off from his job and had moved the family from the area in search of a better job. He remained unemployed for several months and had gotten a satisfactory job only weeks before the patient began treatment with me. Although the father had moderated his drinking, there was a history of alcoholism that led to frequent verbal and occasional physical abuse of most members of the family, including the patient.

Mike's mother was a deeply religious woman who worried incessantly. When confronted with problems, her solution was to pray or undertake some unrelated good deed in hopes that God would intercede on behalf of her or her family. Proof that her methods worked included that the father had indeed gotten a job before the family finances collapsed.

The patient had two younger siblings toward whom he directed the sort of contemptuous hate that is normally relinquished by college age.

He needed treatment for his depression, anxiety, and obsessional and narcissistic character problems. Not being an ideal candidate for brief therapy, he could, I thought, benefit from long-term psychotherapy; but this was not possible. With massive educational bills to come, there were no financial resources to support it. He planned to leave college in three months, live with his family for several more months, and then begin professional school in a distant city. We agreed on twelve weekly appointments, after which he would leave town.

Mike was eager to understand himself and rapidly formed a strong positive therapeutic alliance. His depression lifted almost immediately, and his anxiety decreased substantially. An unusual focus emerged from his first appointments: his relationship to God. I pointed out that he thought of this relationship the same way that he understood his relationship to most people. God was not a source of comfort and help, someone to turn to in times of trouble. Rather He was a critic to be placated in hopes of avoiding punishment. It also seemed to Mike that if he pleased God, He might grant some special favor. From my perspective, Mike could not use God, me, or anyone else as an idealizing selfobject to help calm and soothe him when he was upset. This, in turn, necessitated a need for absolute control lest his emotions gain the best of him. He also could not enjoy any accomplishment because he was unsure whether he had earned it or whether it was the result of some special dispensation from God. My point in addressing these matters was not spiritual. Rather, we used Mike's relationship to God as a metaphor that showed how he organized his understanding of all of his interactions: no help was gladly given and only supplication could possibly gain a favorable response. This omnipresent judgment left him chronically enraged, frightened, and depressed.

After Mike's God metaphor was clarified, he rapidly realized that interactions with me did not conform to those organizing principles. When we discussed his fears that he would fail in his future education, he saw that he expected the faculty to be like his avenging God. I took some pains to point out that most of them would be helpful, but that he shouldn't use the genuinely nasty ones as proof of his fears. We succeeded in Kohut's two-step recommendation: Mike felt understood, and then I was able to interpret the unhelpful way that he organized most interactions.

During his fifth appointment, he talked about a young woman whom he had met. He liked her and she seemed to like him, but he couldn't understand why.

PATIENT: You know, I'm covered with hair. Women think it's disgusting.

THERAPIST: All women think that?

PATIENT: Yes. Even my friends make fun of me. They call me "bear man."

THERAPIST: I have to tell you that some women like vanilla ice cream and some like chocolate. I don't think all women hate body hair.

PATIENT: Yeah, well none of them like hairy ice cream, and you'll never convince me of that.

THERAPIST: I don't think that's really the point, anyway. You think Sarah will take one look at your hair and be disgusted. That makes her kind of like God—looking for a flaw. And when she finds it, she'll throw you away because of it.

PATIENT: But my hair is really gross.

There were several rounds on this subject; when the hour ended, Mike left convinced that his hair was revolting but perhaps, maybe, possibly, some woman could like him in spite of it.

During the sixth appointment he said that he had asked Sarah out and that she had accepted. The expected date was to come before our next meeting. He began the seventh appointment by saying there was good news and bad news. The good news related to his future education, the bad to Sarah canceling the date. She had left a message on his answering machine that she needed to go home, but that there was a possibility that she might be back early enough on Sunday for the date and would call him. She never called, and Mike was furious.

PATIENT: There was some way she could have called.

THERAPIST: So what do you make of her not calling?

PATIENT: I don't care. She's written off. If she wanted to, she would have called.

THERAPIST: Sounds like you feel put down.

PATIENT: You bet. The dumb ——— could damn well have called.

THERAPIST: Little angry, huh?

PATIENT: You bet.

THERAPIST: So what are you going to do?

PATIENT: Nothing. She can call me.

THERAPIST: And if she does?

PATIENT: *(Snarling)* I'll tell her, "Thanks for calling Sunday."

THERAPIST: And how will she take that?

PATIENT: I don't care. Don't you think she could have called?

THERAPIST: I don't know, but you sure do. *(This leads to several interchanges about what could have excused her failure to call, all of which he had considered and dismissed.)* So you want to get even with her for humiliating you like that.

PATIENT: You bet. She deserves it. . . . Well, don't you think so?

THERAPIST: That's up to you, but I think what you really hope will happen is that she'll say she's sorry and almost plead with you to go out.

PATIENT: Sure, I guess so.

THERAPIST: Well, if that *is* what you want, I mean if you want to find out if she likes you, then it seems to me that if you sort of snarl "Thanks for calling," it might screw things up.

PATIENT: Yeah, but she deserves it. She didn't call and there's no excuse.

THERAPIST: I understand what you're saying, that if she put you down she deserves to get it and you deserve to get even. But if you talk to her like that, that doesn't come for free. You'll have an effect on her—and that effect will screw up finding the answer to the Does she really like you? question.

PATIENT: I don't understand. She deserves it.

THERAPIST: That may be, but if you snarl at her when you're trying to find out if she likes you, you're changing things. Look, it's sort of like doing an experiment. The experiment has two parts. One is to find out if she likes you and the other is to get even. But the get even part is sort of like spitting into a petri dish when you're doing a microbiology experiment. If bugs grow there, you don't have any idea why because you spit in the dish. Your experimental technique fouled up the experiment.

PATIENT: You mean, if I say, "Thanks for calling," she takes offense?

THERAPIST: *(laughs)* Well, yes, wouldn't you?

PATIENT: Yes, I suppose. But she deserves it and I wouldn't.

THERAPIST: *(Both chuckling)* Of course, you'd never make a mistake. But the point is that when you do that, you'll probably make her want to say, "Screw him." And then you'll never find out why she didn't call, and you'll never find out if she likes you.

PATIENT: Well, I suppose.

THERAPIST: And it's kind of like with God. You don't trust Him, and you approach Him in a way that makes it hard to find out about Him.

PATIENT: Well, what should I do? I mean, what should I say to her?

THERAPIST: I think you could figure that out if you realize that you're angry because you feel rejected. That makes you want to get even, and then you're likely to treat her in a sort of nasty way. If you do that, it has an effect that is likely to screw up your ability to find out why she didn't call or if she really would like to go out with you.

PATIENT: You mean I'm not supposed to get angry.

The exchange led to a discussion of how he could express some anger without getting so angry that he spoiled his chances to find out what he wanted to know. We also thought more about the source of the anger—his feeling rejected—and how what he did next would either clarify or obscure his finding out if he was, indeed, rejected. I told him: "This is a tough message. You want to get even and to find out if she likes you. There may not be a way to do both, so you have to make a choice." It was important not to contradict his belief that he was wronged, sticking instead to the idea that there might be another explanation or that he might, in fact, be right.

When he left, he was determined to ask Sarah what happened and to say that he felt bad about her not calling. He returned the next week saying that I would be angry at him. He had spoken to Sarah, she had come over to his apartment, and they had ended up in bed. This led to another opportunity to explore his expectation that my opinions would be the same as God's. We began to relate this expectation to other relationships, making particular reference to what he might anticipate when he went to professional school in the fall. He thought that he had learned a general principle from the interaction with Sarah.

The goal had been to help Mike understand that when he felt dropped from a relationship that met mirroring selfobject needs, he felt a narcissistic insult that precipitated rage. This fury led him to want to get even, but he realized that he needed to exercise some caution about how he expressed anger lest he create a self-fulfilling prophecy that proved no one liked him or would help him. These and the other main themes of his treatment were explicitly reviewed during his last appointment. At that time we also agreed that he should continue to think about these concepts.

When he terminated he felt better, and, more important, he had some understanding of how he dealt with relationships. A consistent focus and a supportive relationship that acted as a splint for his self-esteem combined to enable him to reorganize much of his thinking in a remarkably short time.

EMPIRICAL SUPPORT

There have been scores of excellent case studies on self psychology, and self psychologists are generally agreed that this theory has yielded superior results. We have found that we are able to help most patients more effectively and that we can treat patients previously considered unreachable. However, there are no experimental outcome studies, and all descriptions of the therapeutic process are merely anecdotal. There are several reasons for this serious shortcoming. Self psychology is a relatively young area, and most of its practitioners have been engaged in psychoanalytic or other intensive treatment approaches. Research on long-term therapy is, of course, fiendishly difficult. There has been little systematic work applying the theory to brief models of treatment, and there is no manual that defines the method.

Despite this regrettable situation, several facts derived from existing research beg for a self psychological analysis. Many researchers (for example, Strupp, 1989; Luborsky, Crits-Christoph, Mintz, & Auerbach, 1988) find that a positive therapeutic alliance correlates with a good outcome. Does the concept of the selfobject transference help clarify this most consistent and robust finding of existing research? Robert Wallerstein (1986) comprehensively studied the intensive psychoanalytic individual treatment of forty-two seriously troubled patients. He found that some of those who gained great insight did well, but others with good insight did not do at all well. Still others with superior outcomes had gained little insight. These data raise the serious question whether traditional psychoanalytic insight (insight related to drive-based conflict) produces therapeutic gain.

Crits-Christoph, Cooper, and Luborsky (1988) have found that there is a good correlation between positive outcome and Core Conflictual Relationship Theme (CCRT) interpretations that are accurate. The content of CCRT interpretations is at least similar to what self psychologists might say. Did their patients gain insight from these interpretations? If so, one could also speculate that CCRT insight is, in fact, useful. At the least, accurate CCRT interpretations help create a sense of being understood that enhances the empathic bond; and the empathic bond is central to all self psychological theory. Does the self psychology help explain why the CCRT works, and might the modest alterations that self psychologists could add yield still better outcomes?

These questions are pregnant with research promise, but the best that can be said is that the answers remain a gleam in the eyes of some self psychologists.

CONCLUSION

The great German physicist Werner Heisenberg (1958) realized that it was possible to locate an electron in space *or* to determine the amount of energy it contained—but that the process of establishing one destroyed the possibility of finding the other. Both procedures uncover elements of the "truth" while simultaneously obliterating other "facts." Whatever procedure we undertake to examine anything, even an atom, irreparably alters it. We destroy one aspect of reality as we clarify another.

The same holds for psychotherapeutic interventions and theories. Although some hypotheses (such as phrenology) uncover very little useful information, others (such as traditional Freudian and self psychological metapsychologies) hold considerable explanatory power. Whatever theory we use to understand our patients clarifies some elements of their lives and renders other facets opaque.

In this chapter, I have provided a description of how self psychological principles can guide brief psychotherapy. I have found this perspective useful—I think more useful than alternate approaches. Yet I am convinced that others have helped their patients with entirely different techniques. Robert Wallerstein (1986) demonstrated that psychoanalysis does not exist in a pure form in clinical practice. Likewise, I suspect conceptual purity is routinely abandoned in brief psychotherapy and that we all should and do borrow from other methods in order to meet the particular needs of individual patients.

Nonetheless, the Heisenberg principle applies: whatever approach we use inevitably alters the course of therapy. Patients may obtain positive outcomes from many different approaches. But these are different outcomes with different benefits and different shortcomings. It remains for future research to determine whether one approach is always best or is best for particular patients. Perhaps we will also discover that therapists have inherent styles that determine which methods they can use and which they do well to avoid.

References

Alexander, F., & French, T. M. (1946). *Psychoanalytic therapy.* New York: Ronald Press.

Bacal, H. (1985). Optimal responsiveness and the therapeutic process. In A. Goldberg (Ed.), *Progress in self psychology* (Vol. 1, pp. 202–227). New York: Guilford Press.

Baker, H. (1979). The conquering hero quits: Narcissistic factors in underachievement and failure. *American Journal of Psychotherapy, 33,* 418–427.

Baker, H., & Baker, M. (1987). Heinz Kohut's self psychology: An overview. *American Journal of Psychiatry, 114,* 1–9.

Balint, M., Ornstein, P. H., & Balint, E. (1972). *Focal psychotherapy: An example of applied psychoanalysis.* London: Tavistock.

Basch, M. (1983). The significance of self psychology for a theory of psychotherapy. In J. Lichtenberg & S. Kaplan (Eds.), *Reflections on self psychology* (pp. 223–238). Hillsdale, NJ: Analytic Press.

Beck, A. T., Rush, A. H., Shaw, B. F., & Emery, G. (1979). *Cognitive therapy of depression.* New York: Guilford Press.

Binder, J. L. (1979). Treatment of narcissistic problems in time-limited psychotherapy. *Psychiatric Quarterly, 51,* 257–270.

Crits-Christoph, P., Cooper, A., & Luborsky, L. (1988). The accuracy of therapists' interpretations and the outcome of dynamic psychotherapy. *Journal of Consulting and Clinical Psychology, 56,* 490–495.

Davanloo, H. (Ed.). (1978). *Basic principles and techniques in short-term dynamic psychotherapy.* New York: Spectrum.

Deitz, J. (1988). Self-psychological interventions for major depression: Technique and theory. *American Journal of Psychotherapy, 42,* 597–609.

Gustafson, J. P. (1986). *The complex secret of brief psychotherapy.* New York: Norton.

Heisenberg, W. (1958). *Physics and philosophy: The revolution in modern science.* New York: Harper.

Kohut, H. (1957). Introspection, empathy, and psychoanalysis: An examination of the relationship between mode of observation and theory. In P. H. Ornstein (Ed.), *The search of the self: Selected writings of Heinz Kohut, 1950–1978* (Vol. 1, pp. 205–232). New York: International Universities Press.

Kohut, H. (1966). Forms and transformations of narcissism. In P. H. Ornstein, (Ed.), *The search of the self: Selected writings of Heinz Kohut, 1950–1978* (Vol. 1, pp. 427–460). New York: International Universities Press.

Kohut, H. (1968). The psychoanalytic treatment of narcissistic personality disorders: Outline of a systematic approach. In P. H. Ornstein (Ed.), *The search of the self: Selected writings of Heinz Kohut, 1950–1978* (Vol. 1, pp. 477–509). New York: International Universities Press.

Kohut, H. (1971). *The analysis of the self.* New York: International Universities Press.

Kohut, H. (1972). Thoughts on narcissism and narcissistic rage. In P. H. Ornstein (Ed.), *The search of the self: Selected Writings of Heinz Kohut, 1950–1978* (Vol. 2, pp. 615–659). New York: International Universities Press.

Kohut, H. (1983). Selected problems of self psychological theory. In J. Lichtenberg & S. Kaplan (Eds.), *Reflections on self psychology* (pp. 387–416). Hillsdale, NJ: Analytic Press.

Kohut, H. (1984). *How does analysis cure?* Chicago: University of Chicago Press.

Kohut, H., & Wolf, E. (1978). The disorders of the self and their treatment: An outline. *International Journal of Psychoanalysis, 59,* 413–425.

Lichtenberg, J. (1983). *Psychoanalysis and infant research.* Hillsdale, NJ: Analytic Press.

Lichtenberg, J. (1989). *Psychoanalysis and motivation.* Hillsdale, NJ: Analytic Press.

Luborsky, L. (1984). *Principles of psychoanalytic psychotherapy: A manual for supportive-expressive treatment.* New York: Basic Books.

Luborsky, L., Crits-Christoph, P., Mintz, J., & Auerbach, A. (1988). *Who will benefit from psychotherapy? Predicting therapeutic outcomes.* New York: Basic Books.

Malan, D. H. (1976). *The frontier of brief psychotherapy.* New York: Plenum.

Ornstein, A., Gropper, C., & Bogner, J. Z. (1983). Shoplifting: An expression of revenge and restitution. *The Annual of Psychoanalysis, 11,* 311–331.

Ornstein, P., & Ornstein, A. (1972). Focal psychotherapy: Its potential impact on psychotherapeutic practice in medicine. *Journal of Psychiatry in Medicine, 3,* 311–325.

Orne, M. (1968). Anticipatory socialization for psychotherapy: Method and rationale. *American Journal of Psychiatry, 124,* 88–98.

Shane, E., & Shane, M. (1989). Mahler, Kohut, and infant research: Some comparisons. In D. Detrick & S. Detrick (Eds.), *Self psychology: Comparisons and contrasts* (pp. 395–413) Hillsdale, NJ: Analytic Press.

Siddall, L. B., Haffey, N. A., & Feinman, J. A. (1988). Intermittent brief psychotherapy in an HMO setting. *American Journal of Psychotherapy, 42,* 96–106.

Sifneos, P. E. (1979). *Short-term dynamic psychotherapy: Evaluation and technique.* New York: Plenum.

Stern, D. (1985). *The interpersonal world of the infant.* New York: Basic Books.

Strupp, H. H. (1989). Can the practitioner learn from the researcher? *American Psychologist, 44,* 717–724.

Terman, D. M. (1988). Optimum frustration: Structuralization and the therapeutic process. In A. Goldberg (Ed.), *Learning from Kohut: Progress in self psychology* (Vol. 4, pp. 113–126). Hillsdale, NJ: Analytic Press.

Wallerstein, R. S. (1986). *Forty-two lives in treatment: A study of psychoanalysis and psychotherapy.* New York: Guilford Press.

Winnicott, D. W. (1965). *The maturational process and the facilitating environment.* New York: International Universities Press.

Wolf, E. (1988). *Treating the self.* New York: Guilford Press.

CHAPTER 12

Comparison of the Brief Dynamic Therapies

Jacques P. Barber and Paul Crits-Christoph

The multitude of brief dynamic psychotherapies puts a burden on practitioners and researchers about how to distinguish between them, which form to choose, and for which purpose. In this chapter, we compare the various approaches and outline the clinical implications of their differences.

The chapter is organized according to the major issues and parameters that define brief dynamic psychotherapy. We begin by reviewing the criteria presented by the various theorists for the selection of patients for their specific brand of treatment. We continue by discussing the issue of the length of treatment. Then we review the various stages of the therapeutic processes.

In the second part of the chapter, we turn to how the theorists conceptualize therapeutic change. Intertwined in those descriptions is an attempt to explain the psychological processes involved in the various forms of brief dynamic psychotherapy. We discuss what changes during treatment, the specific techniques used to induce change, and how change occurs. Issues regarding the key concepts of insight and transference are discussed in detail.

In our review, we make use not only of the material presented in the collection of chapters of this book but also of other writings by the authors of these chapters as well as other theorists not represented here. Furthermore, we examine the views given in the original writings of important brief dynamic theorists such as David Malan and Habib Davanloo, although aspects of their approaches are presented in chapter 4, by Michael Laikin, Arnold Winston, and Leigh McCullough.

SELECTION OF PATIENTS

In brief therapy, whether dynamically oriented or not, a complete and detailed assessment and formulation of the patient's problems is crucial for selecting the most appropriate candidates for this demanding journey. The therapist who cannot make such an assessment or formulation within the first few sessions is unlikely to be able to focus treatment well enough to perform brief dynamic therapy. In contrast, during psychoanalysis the analyst has ample time to define and refine patients' formulations. Thus, in brief therapy the initial sessions have the dual goal of selecting the appropriate patients and defining the focus of treatment.

Short-term dynamic psychotherapists have suggested a wide range of applicability for their techniques. Some have argued that their methods are applicable to a delimited group of patients, while others believe their methods can be used with a wide range of pathology. James Mann's therapy (chapter 2), for example, has been designed for a specific group of patients, well-functioning neurotic patients, although obviously some of the techniques could be applied to other kinds of patients. Horowitz's Short-Term Dynamic Therapy for Stress Response Syndromes, or STDP-SRS, (chapter 7) was developed to treat a specific diagnostic category, patients who have encountered major stresses. Brief Adaptive Psychotherapy, or BAP (chapter 8, by Jerome Pollack, Walter Flegenheimer, and Arnold Winston) was also developed for specific populations of mild neurotics and patients with Cluster C types of personality disorders (avoidant, dependent, obsessive-compulsive and passive-aggressive personality disorders). It seems worth mentioning that Pollack, Flegenheimer, and Winston limited their inclusion criteria for research purposes, and they are currently examining whether patients with relatively more serious problems can benefit from BAP. In contrast, Laikin, Winston, and McCullough (Intensive Short-Term Dynamic Therapy or ISTDP, chapter 4; Davanloo, 1985), Lorna Smith Benjamin (chapter 10), and Lester Luborsky and David Mark (Supportive-Expressive (SE) Psychotherapy, chapter 5; Luborsky, 1984) suggest that their therapy might be used successfully with a wide range of patients. Therapists using ISTDP or SE psychotherapy nevertheless exclude psychotic disorders and borderline personality disorders. Originally, Luborsky (1984) did not exclude such patients. In addition,

Luborsky presents a specific rule based on psychiatric severity, that is, the more severe the patient's condition, the more supportive and the less expressive the psychotherapy should be.

Luborsky's SE Psychotherapy therapy has been examined with a difficult patient population, that is, opiate addicts at a VA hospital. It has been shown that SE in addition to drug counseling was as effective as cognitive therapy in the treatment of opiate abusers (Woody et al., 1983). Woody and his colleagues have also shown that patients with antisocial personality disorders without concurrent major depression are not helped by psychotherapy.

The selection criteria for the short-term dynamic therapies do not necessarily follow *DSM III* diagnostic categories since psychodynamic and personality factors are considered at least as important as the specific diagnosis. The authors do not view formal diagnosis as sufficient for selecting patients since their goals often consist of improving interpersonal or intrapsychic functioning (or both). Even Horowitz's (chapter 7) focus on stress response syndromes does not follow the *DSM* diagnostic classification since a variety of diagnoses are included under the umbrella of stress response syndromes.

In many forms of brief dynamic therapy, the most important criterion seems to be the therapist's appraisal of the patient's potential to create a collaborative relationship with her or him. This potential is assessed during the first few sessions by an extensive psychiatric (diagnostic) and psychodynamic interview (Karin Barth and Geir Nielsen, chapter 3; Sifneos, 1979) and/or by observing how the patient handles trial intervention (see Strupp & Binder, 1984; Laikin, Winston, & McCullough, chapter 4; Davanloo, 1985). One also has to remember that current diagnostic nosology does not assess the severity of a disorder. Moreover, psychological health has been shown to be an important predictor for outcome (Luborsky, Crits-Christoph, Mintz, & Auerbach, 1988), together with similarities between patient and therapist on demographic and attitudinal characteristics. *DSM III*'s lack of a severity index might partly explain why these theorists often include additional criteria for selecting patients.

In chapter 3 Barth and Nielsen list the various personality and ego functions that make patients more suitable for brief dynamic treatment. In their view, the patient's ability to define a "circumscribed chief complaint" is indicative of ego strength, reality testing, tolerance of frustration, and capacity for delaying gratification. These ego functions are deemed necessary for focal treatment. Finally, Barth and Nielsen operationalize "motivation for change," which has often been a murky concept. In order to decide whether a patient is motivated for change, the therapist should answer positively five out of the seven criteria listed in their chapter (see also Sifneos, 1972).

Despite these advances in conceptualizing and operationalizing psychoanalytic terms related to patient selection, additional work remains to be done in regard to concepts such as multiple focus (several conflicts) and oedipal pathologies, used by therapists such as Davanloo. These terms and others need to be better related to the more specific and explicit criteria employed in modern nosologies. But this process should not proceed in one direction only; phenomenological nomenclatures like the *DSM*s could be improved by incorporating some of what has been learned in dynamic therapy. For example, the degree of interpersonal pathology, although barely appreciated in *DSM III*, seems to be important for predicting how a patient will do in these therapies. To a large extent, Benjamin's (in press; see also chapter 10) work on the classification of various psychiatric disorders using the Structural Analysis of Social Behavior (SASB) is a first and sophisticated step in that direction. It will be interesting to examine whether levels or types of interpersonal functioning predict treatment outcome (predictive validity); this is an important dimension for assessing the validity of a diagnostic group (Kendell, 1975).

The selection criteria employed by most theorists included in this book imply that patients who do not present what one might vaguely define as a particular personality organization (a highly motivated patient who has the ability to create relatively good relationships) are not appropriate for brief treatment. Such predictions have not yet been systematically examined, and more research needs to be performed before such a large segment of the patient population is excluded (see also Strupp & Binder, 1984, p. 24). Nonetheless, many theorists (Benjamin, chapter 10; Laikin, Winston, & McCullough, chapter 4; Luborsky & Mark, chapter 5) suggest that brief treatments might be more helpful than sometimes thought, even for patients presenting with relatively more serious psychopathology.

Although many ISTDP practitioners view the severity of the pathology and the level of premorbid functioning as essential criteria for patients' selection, other ISTDP therapists, such as Davanloo, have reportedly shown how patients previously considered too severely disturbed for short-term treatment can be helped by such treatments. Based on Malan's earlier work and on his own experience with difficult patients, Davanloo concluded that the best predictor for outcome is the patient's ability to handle trial therapy. Patients who develop disabling levels of anxiety, fragmentation, identity confusion, or paranoid ideas during the evaluation interviews are not suitable for ISDTP (Laikin, Winston, & McCullough, chapter 4). Unfortunately, the trial therapy method of selection is rather circular: patients who are selected for ISTDP are the ones who respond positively to a concentrated and very brief version of the therapy. It is noteworthy that Davanloo does not necessarily require that the patient approaching treatment present all the required aspects of what we may call the ideal personality organization (access to feelings, enabling the therapist to learn something about previous relationships, willingness to recognize the relationship between those earlier relationships and the transference) before the onset of therapy. Similarly, Hans Strupp and Jeffrey Binder (1984) also experiment with patients who present less ideal characteristics, such as hostility and negativism. Nonetheless, independent criteria would be very helpful at determining in advance which patients can be helped by various forms of treatments.

One of the reasons some of the authors exclude more severe forms of personality disorders is the expectation that these patients might develop psychotic transference reactions—in Howard Baker's (chapter 11) language, "regressed selfobject transferences." Another reason for exclusion is related to the short-term focus of treatments. For most authors, the exclusion of patients with a severe diagnosis is linked to their beliefs that long-term treatments are the most suitable for such patients.

In summary, therapists diverge on the types of patients they deem appropriate for brief dynamic psychotherapy. Among the patients' qualities most commonly emphasized by these theorists, we found a history of at least one good interpersonal relation, some level of psychological mindedness, some willingness to change beyond the level of symptoms, and a positive response to the therapist's early interpretations. Patients for whom most of the reviewed forms of treatment are not intended include patients with alcohol and drug problems, patients who tend to decompensate into psychotic states or who have severe personality disorders, and patients who have a tendency toward frequent acting out of their feelings and impulses. These criteria are summarized in table 1.

LENGTH OF THERAPY

Of course, brief dynamic therapists all agree that treatment should be relatively limited in time. We will address two issues: Is length of treatment determined from the onset of treatment? What are the considerations for deciding on the length of treatment?

TABLE 1

Criteria for Patient Selection

Theorist/Therapy	Inclusion Criteria	Exclusion Criteria
Malan	Strict psychiatric and dynamic criteria Capacity to be open and responsive Positive response to trial interpretations	Addictions, serious suicide attempts, severe major depression, severe acting out
Nielsen & Barth/STAPP	Intelligence, psychological mindedness History of meaningful relationships Appropriate affect during interview (emotional expressiveness and flexibility) One major and specific complaint Motivation for change, beyond symptom relief	Psychosis, major affective syndromes, addictions, suicidal tendencies and acting out, severe character pathology
Mann/TLP	Good ego strength: capacity for rapid affective involvement and disengagement Definable central focus Mild neurosis and personality disorders, including borderline with effective neurotic defenses	Psychosis, schizoid and severe obsessional personality disorders, severe psychosomatic disorders
Laikin, Winston, & McCullough/ISTDP	Wide range Pass trial therapy	Psychosis, severe major depression, brain impairment, significant suicidal and acting out tendencies, addictions "Decompensation" during or following trial therapy

TABLE 1 *(Continued)*

Theorist/Therapy	Inclusion Criteria	Exclusion Criteria
Pollack, Flegenheimer, & Winston/BAP	Positive response to trial interpretations	Severe personality disorders, psychotic states, substance abuse, medication, organic brain impairment, and any Axis I diagnosis except mild to moderate anxiety and/or affective disorders Patients who cannot tolerate confrontative psychotherapy as revealed during the evaluation interview
Pinsker, Rosenthal, McCullough/Dynamic supportive	Wide range, including psychosis Therapy tailored to patients' level of functioning Contraindication for expressive treatment	
Luborsky & Mark/ Supportive-Expressive		Psychotics, borderline personality disorders, suicidal acting out, antisocial personality disorders without affective disorders
Binder & Strupp/ Vanderbilt TLDP	Coherent and identifiable interpersonal themes Distinction between self and others Capacity for human relationships Ability to form collaborative relationship with therapist	

TABLE 1 *(Continued)*

Theorist/Therapy	Inclusion Criteria	Exclusion Criteria
Benjamin/SASB-RCL	Willingness to learn and focus on oneself	Lack of capacity to be collaborative Unwillingness to enhance strength, e.g., addictions Value conflict with therapist Normative life crisis Inability to keep acting behavior under control within three months of treatment Psychotic, cannot keep hallucinations under control Brain impairment
Baker/Self Psychology	Motivation to change Effective self-structure Positive past interpersonal relations Intelligence Interest in self-understanding	Severe self-pathology, psychosis, addictions, severe personality disorders
Horowitz/STDP-SRS	One or few recent traumatic events	Excessive conflictual or deficient personality, psychosis, borderline personality disorders, involved in litigation

Number of Sessions

Crucial to the definition of brief therapy is Simon Budman and Alan Gurman's distinction between brief therapy by default and brief therapy by design. Conducting brief dynamic therapy involves planning to have a limited time to achieve specific goals and is not the "commonly occurring unplanned brief therapy by 'default' " (Budman & Gurman, 1988, p. 6).

Related to the issue of length of therapy is the question whether the number of sessions is specified at the beginning of treatment. Almost all theorists are flexible in terms of the number of sessions they recommend. A notable exception to this rule is Mann, who sees patients for only twelve sessions irrespective of the severity of problems and the patients' difficulties with termination. In his view, the brief time frame and definite termination enables the working through of universal, existential separation issues. Furthermore, the knowledge that treatment will last only for twelve sessions reinforces the patient's view that he or she is not in such bad shape. Others, like Mardi Horowitz (chapter 7), seem to adhere to a strict number of sessions mainly for research-related reasons.

Most therapists will decide on a termination date or number of sessions after a therapeutic focus has been agreed upon (see Binder & Strupp, chapter 6) or after having gained comprehensive knowledge of the patient's psychopathology (for example, ISTDP therapists such as Davanloo). Still other theorists (such as Baker, chapter 11; Luborsky, 1984) offer more open-ended forms of therapy in which termination is collaboratively decided upon once the specific goals have been achieved. In contrast to others, Luborsky (1984) and Horowitz (chapter 7), for example, offer both time-limited and open-ended versions. But most therapists would not view the open-ended version of their treatments as versions of brief dynamic therapy.

Deciding the Length of Treatment

Obviously, the length of treatment should be related to its goals. Some therapists try to achieve only symptom reduction (for example, Horowitz, this volume), while others target the complete resolution of the oedipal conflict (for example, Davanloo, 1980). Because of this divergence in the scope of treatment, the definition of length of treatment as a criterion for brief dynamic therapy cannot be made independently. Therefore, treatments lasting even forty sessions are included in our review, although in Gregory Bauer and Joseph Kobos's (1987) opinion traditionally brief treatment includes a smaller number of sessions (fifteen to twenty-five).

The reasons for the divergence regarding length among the short-term dynamic psychotherapists and between them and traditional dynamic therapists rest on the following considerations: (1) A short treatment minimizes the development of regression or dependence on the therapist and facilitates the patient's working through of separation and loss issues. (2) Therapists may need longer to work on the central conflict and to repeat the work several times (work through); it may be necessary to address a range of severity levels in pathology, as well as to achieve more than symptomatic relief (that is, to accomplish some personality change).

Some of the therapists (Sifneos, Mann) are what we might call true believers of short-term treatment; others (Baker, chapter 11) seem to resort to short forms of treatment because of external constraints such as insurance payment limits. Baker, for example, adopts the view that brief treatment is palliative and is helpful at returning the patient to a previous homeostasis. Others, such as Laikin, Winston, and McCullough (chapter 4) view dynamic treatment not as accomplishing a simple return to a previous level of functioning but rather as inducing personality change.

Length of treatment—summarized in table 2—seems to depend on the definitions of the patient's characteristics, the targets of therapy, and the issues deemed central by the theorist. Moreover, different theorists have emphasized various strategies concerning how early the therapist should introduce the issue of termination. Some view termination in the context of what is achieved during the course of treatment or of what has been agreed upon as a treatment plan, while others view it independently of the patient's improvement (for example, Mann, 1973). Finally, brief therapies were developed to achieve more limited goals than psychoanalysis within briefer periods of time. Davanloo (1980) claimed that widespread changes are possible using his form of therapy. Nevertheless, all brief therapists seem to share the belief that treatment should focus on a limited set of issues, in most cases on one central issue.

STAGES IN TREATMENT

Some therapists in the framework of brief therapy have realized that in order to make the most of the limited amount of time they have, a detailed description of the stages of treatment can be very helpful. Furthermore, such a description is helpful for general didactic purposes and for the training of new therapists. Most therapists seemingly agree on the traditional division of the treatment process into three stages: initial evaluation and creation of the therapeutic relationship or alliance, therapeutic work and working through, and termination (see table 3 for a summary).

In terms of the first stage, most authors agree that creating a good therapeutic relationship, therapeutic alliance, is very important. For self psychologists like Baker (chapter 11) this stage is crucial for any further work. Although Baker does not emphasize the development of the therapeutic alliance, he does stress the importance of the therapist's empathic understanding of the patient's problems. There is little doubt that these two concepts are closely related. Theorists diverge, however, on the techniques to be used to establish the therapeutic alliance. Some use the more supportive techniques of listening to the patient (Baker, chapter 11; Luborsky, 1984), while others emphasize the interpretation of resistance (Laikin, Winston, & McCullough, chapter 4; McCullough, in press).

TABLE 2

Recommended Length of Treatment

Theorist/Therapy	Length of Treatment
Malan	Trainees: limit of thirty sessions Difficult cases: limit of one year
Nielsen & Barth/STAPP	Usually twelve to fifteen sessions
Mann/TLP	Twelve sessions
Laikin, Winston, & McCullough/ISTDP	Five to thirty sessions Up to forty sessions for severe personality disorders
Pollack, Flegenheimer, & Winston/BAP	Up to forty sessions
Pinsker, Rosenthal, & McCullough/Dynamic supportive	Up to forty sessions
Luborsky & Mark/ Supportive-Expressive	Sixteen for major depression, time-limited version
Binder & Strupp/Vanderbilt TLDP	Twenty-five to thirty sessions
Benjamin/SASB-RCL	Relatively long term (one year on research setting)
Baker/Self psychology	Twenty to thirty sessions, not rigidly adhered to
Horowitz/STDP-SRS	Twelve sessions Time unlimited for more complex cases

The second stage of treatment, the therapy itself, has received less attention. Therapists of all kinds might have followed Freud's intuition about the game of chess: one can readily learn how to begin and finish, but the intermediate steps are more of a craft (see also Luborsky, 1984). We will discuss the processes that occur during this stage in the sections on mechanisms of change and techniques.

The last stage of treatment is often viewed as a stage of review and consolidation of gains. For most therapists it is the occasion to deal with the issue of termination. Termination often reactivates many of the issues and symptoms dealt with during treatment (see Mann, chapter 2, for an extended discussion of this issue). Although not all theorists mention it, important aspects of termination are the patient's internalization of gains

TABLE 3

Stages in Treatment

Theorist/Therapy	Stages
Benjamin/SASB-RCL	Collaborative relation Identification of maladaptive pattern Decision whether wishes are worth continuing Grief about losing old ways
Horowitz/STDP-SRS	(See chapter 7, table 3)
Baker/Self Psychology	Development of sympathetic understanding Therapist becomes a selfobject for the patient Interpretations of the patient's needs for selfobjects and disruptions in selfobjects Return to self-cohesion
Pinsker, Rosenthal, & McCullough/Dynamic Supportive	(None specified; the following have been inferred.) Creation of a supportive therapeutic relationship—the real relationship Therapist formulates core conflicts and defense structures Patient makes effort to change Increase in self-esteem follows
Mann/TLP	Formulation of the central issue Announcement of the twelve-session limit Connection between the central issue and patient's history Midtreatment deterioration and return of symptoms Dealing with separation issues and their relation to the central issue
Pollack, Flegenheimer, & Winston/BAP	Evaluation and contract agreement Formulation of the pattern and presentation to the patient Working through of the pattern Termination

TABLE 3 *(Continued)*

Theorist/Therapy	Stages

Laikin, Winston, & McCullough/ISTDP	Trial therapy
	    Survey
	    Challenge: clarification and then exhaustion of defenses
	    Transference interpretations
	Therapeutic contract
	Challenge of defenses
	Intense affective/cognitive involvement
	Transference interpretations
	Working through of the issues for each person of the triangle of person
	Termination and discussion of losses

Luborsky & Mark/ Supportive-Expressive	Goal setting Creating a helping relationship Increased self-understanding of the CCRT Internalization of therapeutic gains
Nielsen & Barth/STAPP	Selecting appropriate focus Formulating therapeutic contract Establishing therapeutic alliance Analysis of the transference and underlying wishes Resolution of the focal problem Termination
Binder & Strupp/Vanderbilt TLDP	Creating an accepting atmosphere Formulating the Cyclical Maladaptive Pattern Understanding the patient's interpersonal behavior, especially the transference, and conveying it to the patient Providing the patient with a model for identification Changing the Cyclical Maladaptive Pattern

made during treatment and the patient's becoming able to continue applying and generalizing what was learned during treatment. Interestingly, as Luborsky, Barber, and Crits-Christoph (1990) point out, this crucial aspect of treatment has received relatively little theoretical and research attention.

THEORIES OF CHANGE AND FOCUS OF TREATMENT

In comparing theories of change, we distinguish between the hypothetical psychological processes and constructs and the therapeutic techniques employed to effect changes. The former constructs were posited to answer the question: What changes during treatment? while the latter addressed the question: How is change achieved? In parallel, we attempt to integrate and explain the diverse processes hypothesized to be at work during psychotherapy.

Although what constitutes the focus of treatment is not necessarily what will change during therapy, for our present purposes these two issues are close enough to be addressed together. Focus is summarized in table 4.

One of the characteristics of short-term treatments is their specific and deliberate focus (Balint, Ornstein, & Balint, 1972) on one or few problems; in contrast, in psychoanalysis, the goal is to restructure the entire personality. It is worth mentioning that with the accumulation of experience, some brief therapists (such as Davanloo) have claimed that patients who suffer from more than one problem (multifocus) can be helped within the parameters of brief dynamic therapy.

Maintaining therapeutic focus has two important correlates. First, if therapists are to maintain focus, they have to become more active not only in adhering to the agreed-upon goals of treatment but also in preventing digressions into side issues. Second, maintaining focus decreases the likelihood of patients' regression. The maintenance of focus is in clear contrast to the psychoanalytic rule of free association. That does not mean that on occasion short-term dynamic therapists will not ask their patients to free associate about a specific or core issue, but they do not require their patients to do that constantly.

We have already suggested that the focus of short-term psychodynamic therapy, at least in theory, is partially related to the problems addressed by the particular therapy. Supportive dynamic therapy and BAP, for example, emphasize the relief of current symptoms more than most other therapies do; other therapies stress the modification of underlying structures or patterns of behavior. Nevertheless, a consensus seemingly exists regarding the importance of relieving patients' distressing symptoms. More ambitious therapists also try to uncover and bring the underlying conflicts toward resolution. It remains to be seen empirically whether changes subsequent to the different brief dynamic psychotherapies are related to the focus of treatment and to the use of their specific techniques.

TABLE 4

Focus of Treatment

Theorist/Therapy	Focus
Malan	Wish (impulse)-threat-defense triangle (triangle of conflict) Therapist-current-past (parent) relationships (triangle of insight)
Nielsen & Barth/STAPP	Unresolved conflict defined during the evaluation
Mann/TLP	Central issue related to conflict about loss (lifelong source of pain, attempts to master it, and conclusions drawn from it regarding the patient's self-image)
Laikin, Winston, & McCullough/ISTDP	Triangle of conflict Triangle of insight
Pollack, Flegenheimer, & Winston/BAP	Maladaptive and inflexible personality traits, and emotions and cognitive functioning, especially in the interpersonal domain Recognize, understand the origins, and understand how they prevent achievement of life goals
Pinsker, Rosenthal, & McCullough/Dynamic supportive	Increase self-esteem, adaptive skills, and ego functions
Luborsky & Mark/ Supportive-Expressive	Focus on the CCRT
Binder & Strupp/Vanderbilt TLDP	Change in interpersonal functioning, especially change in the Cyclical Maladaptive Patterns
Benjamin/SASB-RCL	Change in maladaptive interpersonal pattern or SASB through learning about ramifications, origins, and goals
Baker/Self psychology	Change in intrapsychic patterns Incorporate more diverse representations of others Make changes in information processing

TABLE 4 *(Continued)*

Theorist/Therapy	Focus
Horowitz/STDP-SRS	Patients' states of mind
	Working through the trauma and the accompanying reactions
	Integration of the traumatic event with existing schemata or development of new schemata (refer to his Table 2.)

One of the important tasks for any dynamic therapist, but especially important for therapists involved in brief treatment, is to infer the link between the patient's presenting symptoms and the core conflicts. Not much has been written about this creative process, and few guidelines are offered by the experts. The skills required seem to be transmitted through case reports rather than through articulated heuristics that can be easily taught to clinicians. One avenue that is often used is to frame the patient's problems in interpersonal terms and to translate simultaneously the problems into Malan's triangle of impulse, defense, and anxiety. It seems especially important for training purposes to ask therapists to frame the presenting complaints in these terms and then to accumulate information on how these three components can be observed in the transference, in the patient–parent link, and in the realm of patient–significant other relationships. Therapists who use Luborsky's CCRT method tend to view symptoms as responses from self. This method is very helpful in cases in which the presenting symptoms are in the form of depression or anxiety, but less so for characterological issues such as procrastination.

Most writers agree that a focal problem in interpersonal relationships exists and that its resolution or partial modification is required. Thus, these dynamic therapies have in common the view that the patient's symptoms are the results of conflicts or problems in interpersonal relationships. (Some writers explain the origins of the problems in intrapsychic terms while others stress the interpersonal arena.) All seem to agree that the achievement of better awareness of interpersonal issues is crucial. Different names have been given to the central issue (CCRT, CMP, dynamic focus, basic conflict, and so on) that has to be addressed during treatment. Moreover, differences exist with regard to how maladaptive behavior is perpetuated and how best to conceptualize it. Most writers view the pattern as a repetition or persistence of an underlying mental structure (schemalike) originating in childhood. Strupp and Binder (1984; Binder and Strupp, chapter 6), on the other hand, consider the dynamic focus a kind of script narrated by the patient, which despite its having originated in childhood, is repeatedly used because the individual has not developed better skills (Wachtel, 1977). The advantage of the conceptualization advanced by Strupp and Binder over more traditional ones is that it eliminates the need for positing very hypothetical concepts such as repetition compulsion or persisting schemata. Others (like Luborsky & Mark, chapter 5) do not specifically explain the pathogenesis of the patients' problems, relying instead on traditional psychoanalytic theory.

Mann (chapter 2) takes the concept of a focal problem further than other theorists by describing three important aspects of his central issue: first, the central issue revolves around a long-term source of patient's pain; second, it includes also how the patient has attempted to master the pain (the coping dimension); and third, it includes a generalized response from self about how the patient views himself or herself. To date, no researchers have tried to study systematically Mann's central issue or to integrate some of its aspects with their own measures of central conflicts.

Most theorists agree that the basic conflict has ramifications on how individuals create, maintain, and end their interpersonal relationships. Some (for example, Laikin, Winston, & McCullough, chapter 4) view this repeated behavior as influenced more by the intrapsychic pole of the phenomenon; that is, the interpersonal behavior reflects the balance of forces associated with the triangle of impulse, anxiety, and defense. ISTDP therapists like Davanloo adhere to traditional psychoanalytic theory and tend to formulate problems in oedipal terms. In contrast, other theorists view the repeated behavior from an interpersonal point of view; that is, the rigid interpersonal relationships are the perpetuation of earlier relationships and not necessarily the results of the projection of intrapsychic contents on another person (Binder & Strupp, chapter 6). In those last two statements, we have summarized our understanding of what is meant by the intrapsychic versus the interpersonal schools of psychodynamic therapy. We are not certain that observable differences exist in patients' behavior, although these two approaches might predict different outcomes when various techniques are used.

The possible existence of relatively persistent and rigid patterns of interpersonal relationships has just begun to receive empirical attention. This lack of research is intriguing in view of the central importance of the patterns for these theories. We especially refer to the fact that to the best of our knowledge, the principle has never been tested on normal subjects. If a survey were made with nonpatients, one would have a better sense of the base rate of the phenomenon. Moreover, assuming that these patterns are also found in nonpatients, one might perhaps better understand how their patterns differ from those of patients. More specifically, one could examine what is often meant by the rigidity, broadness, and maladaptiveness of the patterns in patients. We will review some of the findings relevant to this issue when discussing the mechanisms of change, especially when we refer to the transference.

So far we have focused on the mechanisms of change described in the more expressive kinds of dynamic therapies. Henry Pinsker, Richard Rosenthal, and Leigh McCullough (chapter 9) posit a challenging and different theory of change underlying supportive dynamic psychotherapy. They propose that in this form of dynamic therapy patients change as a result of learning from and identifying with the therapist and as a result of increased self-esteem and better coping skills developed during treatment rather than because of the resolution of deep buried conflicts.

Before turning to the question of how these changes occur, it seems worth mentioning that some theorists (Laikin, Winston, & McCullough, chapter 4) emphasize the importance of releasing buried feelings. Such cathartic release brings relief to the patients. Moreover, they also learn better ways to handle intense feelings. In most of the cases, such feelings arise following interpretations or clarifications, topics we turn to next.

TECHNIQUES

In table 5 we summarize some of the specific techniques described by the different theorists. In general, brief dynamic therapists use most of the techniques of open-ended (traditional) dynamic psychotherapy. Therefore, the authors' lack of mention of commonly used techniques, such as clarification, does not mean that they do not use them; they do. The table refers only to the techniques of brief therapy emphasized in the authors' writings.

Like those who describe other forms of treatment, many brief dynamic theorists arrive at a dynamic formulation; but unlike psychoanalysts, they may present the formulation to the patient; furthermore, the formulation always directs the therapist's work. Brief therapists are more likely to tell their patients not only what their main problems, besides the presenting symptoms, are but also to be more explicit about how treatment will proceed—that is, by examining the relation between the pattern and other aspects of the patient's life. It is also our impression that brief dynamic therapists give a focal and limited formulation of the patient's problems, while analysts try to incorporate all the materials. Unfortunately, no study has examined this question empirically.

Early brief therapists, including Ferenczi, limited the depth of interpretations given during brief therapy. In their view, genetic interpretations were the province of psychoanalysis and not dynamic therapy. Unlike the earlier theorists, Malan and his followers stressed that deep interpretations should be made, when relevant, even in brief dynamic psychotherapy. That is, interpretations not only deal with current life problems but also focus on the origins of these problems early in the patient's life.

Maintaining Focus

Although many of the authors in this book recommend selecting and maintaining one focus, they present few recommendations on how to maintain it. Malan (1963) suggested that once therapists have developed a focus they should adhere to it in a forceful way and not be distracted by side issues. Interpretations are chosen according to their consistency with the focus of treatment. Interpretations unrelated to the focus of treatment, even if accurate, are discarded. Patients' discussion of irrelevant issues is strongly discouraged, or patients are asked to relate new issues to the core issue. Davanloo (1980) strongly confronts any digression from the focus of treatment. A helpful heuristic is for therapists to consider whether an event or a thought can be related convincingly to the central issues (for more adjuncts, see Bauer & Kobos, 1987). If it can be, then interpretations related to the central issue may be proposed to the patient. If the current issue is unrelated to the central issue, then the therapist might be better off not saying anything.

Confronting Defenses and Resistance

One could draw a line to represent a continuum from not dealing with defenses and resistances to relentlessly confronting them and place all the theorists along the line. Supportive (Pinsker, Rosenthal, & McCullough, chapter 9), supportive-expressive (Luborsky & Mark, chapter 5), and self psychologists (Baker, chapter 11) do not generally confront defenses and resistance, whereas ISTDP therapists (Laikin, Winston, & McCullough, chapter 4) tend to confront strongly any resistance to the uncovering goal of treatment. Still, it is very likely that most therapists will address resistances when they seriously impede treatment progress. Therapists adhering

TABLE 5

Major Techniques

Malan	Transference–parent interpretive links Interpretation of 　wish-defense-anxiety triangle Wait until transference develops Trial interpretations
Nielsen & Barth/STAPP	Early transference interpretation Confrontation/clarifications/interpret- 　ations Anxiety-provoking questions Adherence to the therapeutic focus, 　avoidance of pregenital issues
Mann/TLP	Formulation of the central issue Presentation of the central issue Interpretations of the central issue Interpret connections between therapy 　and earlier losses Termination
Laikin, Winston, & 　McCullough/ISTDP	Relentless confrontation of defenses Early transference interpretation Analysis of character defenses Extensive referral to and connections 　between therapist–patient and 　patient–others Maintenance of focus Trial therapy/interpretations Gestalt focus on nonverbal cues
Pollack, Flegenheimer, & 　Winston/BAP	Maintain focus Focus on the transference Recognition, challenge, 　interpretations, and resolution of 　early resistance High level of therapist activity Focus on the triangle of insight Maintain therapeutic neutrality, no 　advice Trial interpretations

TABLE 5 *(Continued)*

Pinsker, Rosenthal, & McCullough/Dynamic supportive	Self-esteem boosters: reassurance, praise, encouragement Reduction of anxiety: no challenge, no silence Respect adaptive defenses, challenge maladaptive ones Clarifications, reflections, interpretations Rationalizations and reframing Advice Modeling, anticipation, and rehearsal Setting agenda
Luborsky & Mark/ Supportive-Expressive	Setting goals for treatment Supportive: creating therapeutic alliance through sympathetic listening Expressive: formulating the CCRT; interpreting the CCRT; relating symptoms to the CCRT and explaining them as coping attempts
Binder & Strupp/Vanderbilt TLDP	Examination of therapist–patient transactions Transference analysis within an interpersonal framework Recognition, interpretation of the Cyclical Maladaptive Pattern and fantasies associated with it Therapist as a new model for identification
Benjamin/SASB-RCL	Rogerian's empathic understanding, positive regard, and personal congruence Traditional psychoanalytic techniques (association, dream analysis) Gestalt techniques such as two-chair techniques Family interview
Horowitz/STDP-SRS	Interpret defenses and attitudes Suggest recollection Encourage abreaction and catharsis Encourage description and recollection Supply support and encourage emotional relationships

to the more supportive pole will address defenses in a gentle and nonconfrontational way.

BAP therapists (Pollack, Flegenheimer, & Winston, chapter 8) make use of less confrontational techniques; they do not especially seek affect. BAP is more cognitive in its emphasis, that is, therapists interpret resistances and relate them to maladaptive patterns. STAPP therapists emphasize less the patient's resistances than either BAP or ISTDP, although therapists from these three kinds of brief dynamic therapy are fairly active. The therapists on the other end of the continuum, SE therapists and self psychologists, are not only less confrontational but also less active, suggesting that degree of confrontation and activity level may go hand in hand.

Emphasizing Cognitive or Affective Experience

Similarly, one could align therapists according to their emphasis on the cognitive versus the affective pole of the patient's experience. We do not wish to view this distinction as a none-or-all dichotomy, but rather as a matter of relative emphasis. The cognitive aspect of dynamic therapy is captured, for example, in the therapist's insistence that the patients realize that their expectations from different people have explicit and potent similarities. The affective aspect of dynamic therapy reveals itself more in the experiential aspects of treatment, that is, in the recreation of feelings within the therapy session.

Some therapists (ISTDP, chapter 4) search for the hidden affect. Davanloo especially focuses on the anger, while Mann targets the pain. BAP therapists, on the other hand (chapter 8), emphasize more the cognitive part of treatment. Others (Luborsky & Mark, chapter 5) are not as explicit about their emphasis; it is our impression that supportive-expressive therapists tend to stress the cognitive aspects of treatment. McCullough (in press) recently described how Davanloo moves smoothly from the cognitive to the affective.

How Change Occurs

Although all therapists included in this book are psychodynamically oriented, the theories of change underlying their approaches are disparate. Most of the psychodynamic schools are represented in the brief therapy movement.

The interpersonal school of psychodynamic thought might be best represented by Jeffrey Binder and Hans Strupp (chapter 6). In their view the patient experiences the therapist as any other significant other and will "enact with him or her maladaptive patterns of behavior rooted in unconscious conflicts" (p. 142). Because the therapist is both a model and a source of feedback for the patient's interpersonal behavior, the patient becomes more conscious of the maladaptive patterns that reinforce negative feelings about himself or herself and about others. Concurrently, the therapist begins to be viewed as an ally, and that helps the patient's examination of the maladaptive patterns and of their related, often painful, emotions and fantasies.

The traditional school of psychoanalysis, in terms of theory of change, is best represented by Laikin, Winston, and McCullough (chapter 4) and Malan (1976a, b). For them the goal of treatment is to provide the patient with insight into his or her intrapsychic dynamics. But like Luborsky and Mark (chapter 5), most of the brief dynamic therapists more clearly associated with the drive (intrapsychic) and ego theories emphasize the role of the interpretation of transference in term of Menninger's (1958) triangle of insight (tranference, significant others, parents). In contrast, classical analysts, such as Bibring (1954), did not consider these therapeutic interventions as interpretations since they do not connect directly between the unconscious Oedipus complex and the latent material. According to Bibring, these are clarifications.

The Kohutian theory of change as summarized and interpreted by Baker (chapter 11) puts the emphasis first on understanding and then on interpretation. Providing the patient with a feeling of being understood has always been seen as a very important aspect of psychotherapy by most therapists and is viewed as crucial to self psychology. For Baker, as well as for Carl Rogers (1925), feeling understood provides the patient with self-functions that the patient did not receive during his or her development, as well as with the opportunity to reinstitute growth, to restore self-cohesion, and to experience a new relationship. In that sense, the patient is provided with a corrective emotional experience.

Another important aspect of treatment is to increase patients' awareness of the way they construe the world, in general, and interpersonal situations, in particular. In that sense, Baker, the "constructivist" self psychologist, is close to Aaron Beck (Beck, Rush, Shaw, & Emery, 1979), the cognitive psychologist. This is done through interpretations of how patients construe and respond to various situations. In contrast to traditional analysts, self psychologists do not emphasize drives or basic impulses. Through interpretations of the way the patient construes situations within an accepting atmosphere, it is assumed that the patient can continue to grow and therefore begin to construe the world in a more mature way.

Using a different language, self psychology differs from drive theory and ego psychology in the content of what needs to be understood and especially what needs to be interpreted. Self psychologists focus on the patient's *deficit,* which leads to a "diminution in self-cohesion," often experienced as low self-esteem. The therapist's understanding of the patient's difficulties restores a natural growth pattern as well as provides the patient with a mirroring experience. Following this mirroring experience, the patient's self-cohesion, as well as self-esteem, increases.

All the therapeutic schools represented in this book agree that therapeutic changes may occur because the accepting attitude of the therapist and the demand-free situation set the conditions for self-examination and self-understanding. The therapist helps and reinforces these processes by interpreting and clarifying the patient's narration. The patient becomes increasingly aware of the reasons for his or her behavior. Both long- and short-term dynamic psychotherapists view insight into and understanding of the basic conflicts as essential to the change process. However, no one seems to have explained why insight and understanding are so important and why they sometimes work and sometimes do not work. Moreover, the mechanism through which insight produces behavioral change has not been clearly specified. Most of the writers do not even try to answer the questions Why does insight help? and How does it help? perhaps because they accept the basic psychoanalytic view on this issue.*

The same questions can be asked about transference and the various interpretations relating current behavior to past behavior. More specifically, why is the analysis of the transference so helpful? Why is it helpful only sometimes? Most brief dynamic theorists assume that in order to achieve meaningful changes in behavior, the patient needs to become aware of how the past influences the present. On the other hand, some theorists propose that genetic (past–present or therapist–parent) interpretations, although helpful, are not necessary; these theorists suggest that it may be more important to identify the similarities between the patient's behavior in the therapy and his or her behavior in relation to other meaningful persons. Intrapsychically oriented theorists might propose that in order for these interpretations to help, the patient needs to understand how his or her interpersonal behavior is related to the underlying forces

---

*The traditional psychoanalytic view comes from Freud's economic model—repressed conflicts are cathected with energy. Insight into these ideas "lifts the repression" and releases or frees buried energies. These energies can then be channeled into more adaptive activities.

(wishes, threats, and defenses) (Davanloo, 1980; Malan, 1976a, b; Luborsky, 1984).

Addressing Understanding and Insight

There is little doubt that most dynamic therapists try to increase patients' insight or self-understanding. The question we wish to raise is, How is understanding helpful?

By *understanding,* we refer as a first approximation to the traditional view, that is, how a specific instance fits a more general law. Patients begin to understand how their particular behaviors with a specific person do not differ from their other relationships and how these are related to the general psychological principles favored by their therapists. But there seem to be additional aspects to understanding in therapy. First, understanding the causes of a particular behavior defines for the patient what the problem is. Once the problem is defined, the patient is somewhat reassured that his or her problem is not completely crazy. Now that the patient faces and defines his or her problems, the patient has a better chance to find a solution to them. Moreover, the pervasiveness of the problems across different situations gives him or her a feeling of understanding. Second, understanding the purpose of a symptom or any maladaptive behavior may help the patient find and use different strategies to achieve goals.

Behavioral change does not follow this increased understanding in some patients or on some occasions during the course of therapy. Traditionally, theorists have proposed two main explanations for this lack of result: either the interpretation is not correct or the patient has achieved only intellectual understanding or insight. In either case, more treatment and more interpretations are offered.* An additional concept that is often related to the role of interpretations is working through. *Working through* means that the problematic issue has to be repeatedly addressed in a variety of situations. In cases where working through gets into an impasse, analyses of the transference and of the resistance are recommended, since the lack of improvement is often viewed as an attempt at sabotaging the treatment—resistance.

It is our position, however, that these ideas do not go far enough to explain the instances in which understanding does not lead to behavioral change. Thus, there may be additional components to understanding or to

---

*This is a major reason why global correlations between the number of interpretations and any outcome measures are doomed to failure (Marzialli, 1984). The number of interpretations may reflect the therapist's frustrations, the patient's severity, or other circumstances.

working through. One such possibility, rarely discussed in the literature (a notable exception being Wachtel, 1977), assumes the functional autonomy of symptoms. Let us explain. Although symptoms might developmentally be best understood as faulty attempts at self-treatment or "compromise formation," it is possible that they slowly become independent of their cause. This might apply in traditional accounts of symptom formation as well as for Strupp and Binder's (1984) descriptions of dynamic vicious circles. When the symptoms become functionally autonomous, they may be viewed as bad habits that the patient wishes to get rid off. If so, behavioral techniques might be best for the patient.* One could, therefore, hypothesize that part of what analysts mean by working through may be similar to processes such as systematic desensitization. To a large extent, this is Barth and Nielsen's (chapter 3) position when they argue that during STAPP the patient's feared wishes or fantasies are exposed and confronted instead of being avoided. Similarly, McCullough (in press) argued that one of the reasons ISTDP might be effective is because patients' threatening feelings are extinguished through a process like the behavioral procedure of flooding. We would like to add that some of the techniques used by ISTDP are reminiscent not only of implosive therapies but also of Perls's Gestalt Therapy.

Dealing with Transference

The transference is deemed central to the change process of dynamic psychotherapy. Why is it so important in light of the claim that the transference represents just one instance of the patient's dysfunctional interpersonal relationships? Indeed, some therapists have argued that it is sufficient for the therapist to address the patient's relationships outside of the therapeutic relation, outside the transference. The therapist–patient relationship, however, is important since the therapist both refutes the patient's expectations of others and monitors the situation in a particular way. This monitoring enables the therapist to participate in the reenactment of the patient's conflicts (or in his or her "interpersonal evoking style") while simultaneously being able to reflect upon it. It makes sense for the patient to accept the therapist's interpretation that the client himself or herself creates particular forms of relationships since the therapist maintains a partial neutrality. The transference might be a more effective means to induce change than the discussion of other recent relationships

*Freud himself made the remark that some patients who have achieved insight might still need to actively and actually confront their fears, for example, in the real world.

since the more experientially something is learned, the better it is learned.

One might conclude that analyzing the transference is not always necessary for achieving the treatment goals. It remains an interesting question in which cases it makes more sense to use the transference and when it is most effective. Does it depend on the patient's diagnosis, or is it related to the severity of the disorder? Is it related to the specific problems encountered with the patients during treatment or to the particular complaint brought to therapy?

Another advantage of analyzing the transference is that the patient can observe how the therapist handles emotional problems in vivo. One needs to remember that the emotions emerging in connection with the transference are sometimes quite strong and intense, and it is not always easy for the therapist to deal with them. By therapeutically confronting these emotions, the therapist not only provides a model for the patient but also sends the patient a message that one can deal effectively and positively with him or her and his or her emotions.

As already mentioned, an important assumption underlying all the theories reviewed in this paper is that similar elements exist across the patient's most meaningful relationships. These elements should be observed in the transference, in actual relationships, and in past real or imagined relationships. Little research on this central facet of transference has been conducted (see review by Luborsky, Crits-Christoph, & Mellon, 1986). The closest examination has been done with the CCRT (Fried, Crits-Christoph, & Luborsky, 1990). This study has shown that the CCRT formulations for the therapist and for others were similar. Unfortunately, such findings, although consistent with the idea to be tested, might reflect the demand characteristics of the therapy since the therapist asks for such parallels. Similarly, Luborsky, Crits-Christoph, and Mellon (1986) used the Relationship Anecdotes Paradigm, or RAP (an interview that elicits the description of various relationships from the subject), and they showed similarities between the CCRT from within the treatment and the CCRT from outside of it. Similar patterns have been found between early relationships and the transference patterns. Such findings need to be replicated with patients interviewed before therapy to increase our confidence in them.

RECOMMENDATIONS FOR THERAPISTS

There is little doubt that brief forms of treatment will be used more and more with a variety of presenting problems. In this section we review some of our recommendations for therapists who intend to use these techniques.

As previously mentioned, the techniques presented in this book have been developed by practitioners with a wide range of personality characteristics. It is very likely that the various forms of treatment were reflective of some cognitive and personality characteristics of their originators. We have, however, chosen authors who have demonstrated that their techniques can be mastered with some level of success by other therapists. Therefore, one does not need to be a Davanloo to do ISTDP, for example. On the other hand, not all of us feel comfortable doing the kind of challenging, confrontational therapy that ISTDP therapists tend to do. Some of us might feel that not being comfortable using some of the techniques that have been shown to be effective reflects on the therapist's problems. Our view is that in order to to be effective in a role a person needs to feel quite comfortable performing it. Thus, therapists need to choose techniques that not only have been shown to be effective but that they will feel comfortable with within a reasonable amount of training time.

It is also quite possible that different versions of brief dynamic psychotherapy may be differentially effective with patients with different problems or personality traits. Gustafson's (1986) impression is that the therapies developed by Malan, Mann, Sifneos, and Davanloo each addressed what he calls different "stories" that can be told by patients and therapists. That is, each of these four therapists have developed a treatment for patients (and maybe therapists) who deal with one main theme. According to Gustafson, Malan's patients struggle between a strong sense of duty and some opposite feeling while Mann's patients struggle with a long and difficult attempt to be something and the pain involved in lack of success (1986, p. 133). Unfortunately, no study has attempted to examine this general thesis. We hope that one day enough data are accumulated to examine whether there is a clear advantage for one of these versions of brief dynamic therapy to help patients confronting a specific issue or theme.

It is possible to tailor the various forms of brief dynamic therapy to the patient's assets and life circumstances. Relatively psychologically healthy and psychological minded patients might be best suited for the more ambitious forms of treatment, while poorly functioning patients might be helped with a more supportive approach (Luborsky, 1984). The section on the selection of patients in this chapter gives therapists clues about the kinds of variables to which apprentice therapists should be sensitive when recommending short-term dynamic psychotherapy.

Some conditions, such as a moderate level of major depression, can be treated with a variety of techniques, including cognitive therapy (Beck,

Rush, Shaw, & Emery, 1979), interpersonal psychotherapy (Klerman, Weissman, Rounsaville, & Chevron, 1984), and various forms of dynamic psychotherapy.

CONCLUSION

In terms of therapeutic techniques, the reviewed theorists are close to Freud. One can still clearly identify in their writings Freud's major psychoanalytic techniques as well as his insights into the pervasiveness of neurotic and characterological problems. Interpretations, analysis of the transference, and analysis of resistance remain the essential techniques. The brief dynamic therapy approaches nevertheless represent a major development away from orthodox analysis in their active stance, their limited goals, and their time limits. Genetic reconstructions are less salient and regression is strongly discouraged. Moreover, the modern theorists heavily emphasize the commonality of the patient's various interpersonal relationships rather than the vicissitudes of the basic drives. By becoming active, psychodynamic therapists no longer allow nature do its work at its own pace; they catalyze it.

The basic ideas used by most of the theorists reviewed here represent the modern development of Freud's ideas or their contemporary translations. The personality and psychopathology theories underlying the modern approaches do not differ much from Freud's (with the exception of that of Strupp & Binder, 1984; Binder & Strupp, chapter 6; Benjamin, chapter 10; Baker, chapter 11). Nevertheless, the brief dynamic theorists also try to remedy some of the conceptual problems encountered by psychoanalysis and to clarify some of its concepts.

In most cases, it seems likely that different approaches result more from the therapists' idiosyncracies in treating patients and from the therapists' personalities than solely from attention to the patients' issues. Likewise, patients may approach and especially remain in treatment with therapists using techniques that fit their needs and personalities. It seems very likely that in the future therapists who are able to use a variety of techniques will use different techniques with different kinds of patients. For example, obsessive-compulsives with high resistance may be helped most with highly confrontational techniques, while hysterics may benefit from a more cognitive emphasis. There is little doubt that the study of patient–technique interactions will become a promising focus of research.

Finally, the "manual therapies" presented in this book allow more uniformity in the training of therapists and increase opportunities for investigating processes of change (Luborsky & DeRubeis, 1985). Furthermore, therapy manuals may contribute to future refinements in these theories in particular and in the processes of change in general. The disadvantages of such manuals are that they do not pass to the trainees the understanding the theorists have acquired as therapists or analysts and that they cannot cover every aspect of less structured therapies. Moreover, trainees can apply too rigidly the suggestions included in the manual. However, used properly, in the context of supervision by a very experienced practitioner of the modality, these treatment manuals or guides are, in our view, a significant step forward for the theory, research, and practice of short-term dynamic therapy.

References

Balint, M., Ornstein, P. H., & Balint, E. (1972). *Focal psychotherapy: An example of applied psychoanalysis.* London: Tavistock.

Bauer, G. P., & Kobos, J. C. (1987). *Brief therapy: Short-term psychodynamic intervention.* Northvale, NJ: Jason Aronson.

Beck, A. T., Rush, A. J., Shaw, B. I., & Emery, G. (1979). *Cognitive therapy of depression.* New York: Guilford Press.

Benjamin, L. S. (in press). *Structural analysis of interaction patterns in personality disorders.* New York: Guilford Press.

Bibring, E. (1954). Psychoanalysis and the dynamic psychotherapies. *Journal of the American Psychoanalytic Association, 2,* 745–770.

Budman, S. H., & Gurman, A. S. (1988). *Theory and practice of brief therapy.* New York: Guilford Press.

Crits-Christoph, P., & Luborsky, L. (1990). The measurement of self-understanding. In L. Luborsky & P. Crits-Christoph, *Understanding transference: The Core Conflictual Relationship Theme method* (pp. 189–196). New York: Basic Books.

Davanloo, H. (Ed.). (1980). *Short-term dynamic psychotherapy.* New York: Jason Aronson.

Davanloo, H. (1985, November). Short term dynamic psychotherapy. A two-day comprehensive audiovisual symposium and workshop on short term dynamic psychotherapy. With D. Malan and J. Marmor. New York, November 23–24.

Fried, D., Crits-Christoph, P., & Luborsky, L. (1990). The parallel of the CCRT for the therapist with the CCRT for other people. In L. Luborsky & P. Crits-

Christoph, *Understanding transference: The Core Conflictual Relationship Theme method* (pp. 147–157). New York, Basic Books.

Gustafson, J. P. (1986). *The complex secret of brief psychotherapy.* New York: Norton.

Kendell, R. E. (1975). *The role of diagnosis in psychiatry.* London: Blackwell.

Klerman, G. L., Weissman, M. M., Rounsaville, B. J., & Chevron, E. S. (1984). *Interpersonal psychotherapy of depression.* New York: Basic Books.

Luborsky, L. (1984). *Principles of psychoanalytic psychotherapy: A manual for supportive-expressive treatment.* New York: Basic Books.

Luborsky, L., Barber, J. P., & Crits-Christoph, P. (1990). Theory-based research for understanding the process of psychotherapy. *Journal of Consulting and Clinical Psychology, 58,* 281–287.

Luborsky, L., Crits-Christoph, P., & Mellon, J. (1986). Advent of objective measures of the transference concept. *Journal of Consulting and Clinical Psychology, 54,* 39–47.

Luborsky, L., Crits-Christoph, P., Mintz, J., & Auerbach, A. (1988). *Who will benefit from psychotherapy? Predicting therapeutic outcomes.* New York: Basic Books.

Luborsky, L., & DeRubeis, R. (1984). The use of psychotherapy treatment manuals: A small revolution in psychotherapy research style. *Clinical Psychology Review, 4,* 5–14.

Malan, D. H. (1963). *A study of brief psychotherapy.* New York: Plenum.

Malan, D. H. (1976a). *The frontier of brief psychotherapy.* New York: Plenum.

Malan, D. H. (1976b). *Toward the validation of dynamic psychotherapy: A replication.* New York: Plenum.

Malan, D. H. (1980). The most important development in psychotherapy since the discovery of the unconscious. In H. Davanloo (Ed.), *Short-term dynamic psychotherapy.* New York: Jason Aronson.

Mann, J. (1973). *Time limited psychotherapy.* Cambridge, MA: Harvard University Press.

Mann, J., & Goldman, R. (1982). *A casebook in time-limited psychotherapy.* New York: McGraw-Hill.

Marzialli, E. A. (1984). Prediction of outcome of brief psychotherapy from therapist interpretive interventions. *Archives of General Psychiatry, 41,* 301–304.

McCullough, L. (in press). Davanloo's short-term dynamic psychotherapy: A cross-theoretical analysis of change mechanisms. In R. Curtis & G. Stricker (Eds.), *How people change: Inside and outside therapy.* New York: Plenum.

Menninger, C. (1958). *Theory of psychoanalytic technique.* New York: Harper.

Rogers, C. R. (1925). The necessary and sufficient conditions of therapeutic personality change. *Journal of Consulting Psychology, 21,* 95–103.

Sifneos, P. E. (1972). *Short-term psychotherapy and emotional crisis.* Cambridge, MA: Harvard University Press.

Sifneos, P. E. (1979). *Short-term dynamic psychotherapy: Evaluation and technique.* New York: Plenum.

Strupp, H. H., & Binder, J. L. (1984). *Psychotherapy in a new key: A guide to time-limited dynamic psychotherapy.* New York: Basic Books.

Wachtel, P. (1977). *Psychoanalysis and behavior therapy: Toward an integration.* New York: Basic Books.

Woody, G., Luborsky, L., McLellan, A. T., O'Brien, C., Beck, A. T., Blaine, J., Herman, I., & Hole, A. V. (1983). Psychotherapy for opiate addicts: Does it help? *Archives of General Psychiatry, 40,* 639–645.

Index